Anti-Refugee Violence and African Politics

Using comparative cases from Guinea, Uganda, and the Democratic Republic of Congo, this study explains why some refugee-hosting communities launch large-scale attacks on civilian refugees whereas others refrain from such attacks even when state officials encourage them. Ato Kwamena Onoma argues that such outbreaks happen only when states instigate them because of links between a few refugees and opposition groups. Locals embrace these attacks when refugees are settled in areas that privilege residence over indigeneity in the distribution of rights, ensuring that they live autonomously of local elites. The resulting opacity of their lives leads locals to buy into their demonization by the state. Locals do not buy into state denunciation of refugees in areas that privilege indigeneity over residence in the distribution of rights because refugees in such areas are subjugated to locals who come to know them very well. Onoma reorients the study of refugees back to a focus on the disempowered civilian refugees that constitute the majority of refugees even in cases of severe refugee militarization.

Ato Kwamena Onoma is currently a Program Head at the Institute for Security Studies in Addis Ababa, Ethiopia. He was previously an Assistant Professor of Political Science at Yale University (2007–2011). He is the author of *The Politics of Property Rights Institutions in Africa* (Cambridge University Press, 2009).

To my mother, Ewurama Ofei-Addo,
and my father, Kwesi Neeyi

Anti-Refugee Violence and African Politics

ATO KWAMENA ONOMA

Institute for Security Studies, Addis Ababa, Ethiopia

CAMBRIDGE UNIVERSITY PRESS
Cambridge, New York, Melbourne, Madrid, Cape Town,
Singapore, São Paulo, Delhi, Mexico City

Cambridge University Press
32 Avenue of the Americas, New York, NY 10013-2473, USA

www.cambridge.org
Information on this title: www.cambridge.org/9781107036697

First published 2013

Printed in the United States of America

A catalog record for this publication is available from the British Library.

Library of Congress Cataloging in Publication Data
Onoma, Ato Kwamena, 1975–
Anti-Refugee violence and African politics / Ato Kwamena Onoma.
p.   cm.
Includes bibliographical references and index.
ISBN 978-1-107-03669-7 (hardback)
1. Refugees – Violence against.   2. Refugees – Public opinion.   3. Refugees – Government
policy.   4. Refugees – Guinea.   5. Refugees – Uganda.   6. Refugees – Congo (Democratic
Republic)   7. Guinea – Politics and government – 1984–   8. Uganda – Politics and
government – 20th century.   9. Congo (Democratic Republic) – Politics and government –
20th century.   I. Title.
HV640.4.A35O53   2013
325.21096652–dc23   2013004252

ISBN 978-1-107-03669-7 Hardback

Contents

List of Tables

List of Figures

Acknowledgments

The broad questions and issues concerning refugee–host relations that are at the heart of this book first began to occupy my mind in August 1997. I was one of thousands of refugees fleeing the war in Sierra Leone who had settled in the Guinean capital, Conakry. Relations between Guineans and refugees were not particularly cordial, but they were peaceful all the same. The two groups mostly lived parallel lives. My stay in Guinea ended up lasting for only a month as I made my way first to N'Zérékoré in the country's Forest Region, Abidjan in Cote d'Ivoire, and then Accra, where I enrolled at the University of Ghana, with the support of relatives. I had just commenced my first semester of graduate work at Northwestern University in Evanston, IL, when I began to hear of widespread attacks on refugees in Conakry in early September 2000. Reports from Human Rights Watch were confirmed by phone conversations with friends in Guinea and Sierra Leone. It was painful news that immediately suggested a dissertation topic to an eager graduate student. When I made an effort to actually begin to read about the wars in Sierra Leone and Liberia and the refugee situation in Guinea, I realized it was a rather traumatic exercise, so I shelved those issues and instead wrote my dissertation on a no-less-interesting subject – the politics of land rights in Africa.

When I arrived at Yale University in 2007, I decided to revisit the subject of refugee–host relations and received tremendous support from many colleagues with whom I discussed this. Yale University had a lot of faculty members with interests in violence and conflict. Elisabeth Wood, Peter Swenson, Stathis Kalyvas, Ellen Lust, Mike McGovern, Kiarie Wa'Njogu, Kamari Clarke, and James Scott contributed a lot to the formative stages of this work by reading proposals and/or providing feedback during presentations of the project. My work also benefited greatly from the general support that I received from the likes of Ian Shapiro, John Roemer, and Frances Rosenbluth. Very generous financial support from the Whitney and Betty MacMillan Center for International and Area Studies at Yale University allowed me to begin effective work on the project in late 2007.

Many institutions provided me with support in the form of affiliation that made possible my acquisition of research permits and generally facilitated my work. The Department of History and Development Studies at Makerere University in Uganda headed by Prof. Godfrey Asiimwe, the Institute for African Economies at the Gamal Abdel Nasser University in Conakry headed by Dr. Sekou Sangare in Guinea, and Statistics Sierra Leone granted me affiliation and provided me with other forms of support. I am very grateful for their help.

I worked with many research assistants in Uganda, Rwanda, Sierra Leone, Guinea, and Liberia on this project. Three stand out because of the extent of their contributions to my work. In Uganda, Elijah Kisembo conducted extensive archival research for this study and helped me secure a research permit. When I finally arrived in Uganda, we worked together on the project in Kampala and in the southwestern districts of Ntungamo and Isingiro. He then moved on to Masindi District to conduct interviews with more former refugees still based in Uganda while I went south to Rwanda's Nyagatare District in search of former refugees who had already repatriated.

In the Mano River Basin, I worked with two excellent research assistants – Alfred Borbor and Koya Toupou. Alfred provided tremendous assistance in my work in Guéckédou Prefecture (Guinea), Kono and Kailahun Districts (Sierra Leone), and Salayea District (Liberia). Koya Toupou, who grew into a researcher in his own right during this project, was invaluable during my work in what turned out to be the very heart of my research in the region – Yomou Prefecture, Guinea.

Most of my field research was conducted in Guinea. During my first trip there, the family of Haja Jeneba Barry in Conakry very warmly welcomed me into their home. Umu Dukuray, Fatu Dukuray, Bilol Barry, Muhammad Dukuray, Haja Jeneba Barry (II), Aruna Daramy, Haja Tigidanke Dukuray, Momodu Dukuray, Ali Kakay, Fanta Kakay, and the rest of the household contributed greatly to making Guinea a pleasant place in which to live and work. I will forever be grateful for their help and affection.

I have at various stages had the privilege of presenting and getting feedback on this work. Audiences at Yale University's Comparative Politics Workshop, the African and Afro-American Studies Colloquium at the University of Michigan, seminars at the Department of Political Science and School of Advanced International Studies at Johns Hopkins University, and the African Leadership Center in Nairobi provided very useful and lively feedback on this work. I thank participants for their contributions, which informed the multiple revisions that have, without doubt, improved this work.

I was about to send the manuscript out to publishers when Elisabeth Wood encouraged me to seek funding from the Whitney and Betty MacMillan Center at Yale for an author's workshop on the manuscript. The MacMillan Center responded favorably with a Kempf Family Fund award, and on the 2nd of May 2011, seven scholars who had read various parts of the manuscript met to give presentations on and discuss it. At the conference were Paul Richards, Jason Stearns, Mike McGovern, Stephen Wilkinson, James Scott, Adrienne Lebas, and Siba Grovogui. Kamari Clarke, Esther Mokuwa Richards, and Torjia Karimu also joined the discussions. Unsurprisingly, given the cast of characters present, the discussions were animated and rather heated. The workshop produced a wealth of feedback that I used to revise the manuscript extensively before submission to publishers.

The manuscript has since then also benefited from the comments of anonymous reviewers and the thoughts of Celine Bankumuhari and Grace Atim, who both agreed to read and discussed various parts of this work. Rita Effah, who was then at the Yale School of Forestry, provided the maps for this work.

I wish to express my heartfelt thanks to all of the persons and institutions listed for their contribution to this manuscript. To the many others whom I have not named here due to forgetfulness and a need to protect their identities, I am no less thankful. While taking responsibility for the defects in the manuscript, I hope I have been able to use your tremendous contributions to make the manuscript worthy of association with your names.

My daughters Ewuraba Khemes and Adjoa N'guide have been integral parts of the process of writing this book. They very effectively ensured that I did not take research and writing too seriously and that I maintained a healthy balance in life. My partner, Yaba Ndiaye, put up with my frequent research trips, tolerated my efforts at bringing up this work at every opportunity, and provided constructive feedback on various parts of the manuscript. To these three very dear companions of mine are due my greatest thanks.

While in Guinea I discovered *la musique Mandeng*. Very few words in this book were born without the enchanting midwifery of Mandeng music. I extend thanks to its chroniclers of our times and of epochs long gone.

List of Abbreviations

APL	People's Liberation Army
CFAO	*Compagnie Française de l'Afrique Occidentale*
CODESRIA	Council for the Development of Social Research in Africa
DP	Democratic Party
DRC	Democratic Republic of Congo
EAC	East African Community
ECOMOG	ECOWAS Monitoring Group
ECOWAS	Economic Community of West African States
Ex-FAR	Ex–Armed Forces of Rwanda
GLR	Great Lakes Region
LURD	Liberians United for Reconciliation and Democracy
MIB	Mission d'Immigration des Banyarwanda
MIP	Mission d'Immigration des Populations
MNC-L	Congolese National Movement–Lumumba
MRB	Mano River Basin
NGO	nongovernmental organization
NPFL	National Patriotic Front of Liberia
NRM	National Resistance Movement
OAU	Organization of African Unity
PARMEHUTU	Party of the Hutu Emancipation Movement
RPA	Rwandan Patriotic Army
RUF	Revolutionary United Front
ULIMO	United Liberation Movement for Democracy in Liberia

UN	United Nations
UNAR	Rwanda National Union
UNHCR	United Nations High Commission for Refugees
UNLA	Uganda National Liberation Army
UPC	Uganda Peoples Congress

Notes on Ethnic and Linguistic Nomenclature

- The Kpelle are also called Guerzé in Guinea.
- The Lorma are called Toma in Guinea.
- The Maninka are also known as Malinké and Mandingo in the Mano River Basin countries.
- Konianké and Maniang are Maninka-speaking people who are found in the Forest Region of Guinea.
- The prefixes "Ba" and "Mu," when placed before the names of ethnic groups, refer to more than one and one member of that group, respectively. The prefixes "Lu," "Ru," or "Ki," when placed before the name of an ethnic group, denote the language spoken by that group. Hence we have Muganda/Baganda who speak Luganda, Mutoro/Batoro who speak Rutoro, Munyankore/Banyankore who speak Runyankore, and so forth.
- Banyarwanda/Munyarwanda is used to refer both to citizens of the country of Rwanda and to an ethnic group – people who speak Kinyarwanda as their first language. These people are found in large numbers in Uganda and the Democratic Republic of Congo among other places, in addition to being in Rwanda. Munyarwanda refers to one person and Banyarwanda to two or more people.

Introduction

Generalized Anti-Refugee Violence

We never thought of just keeping them and not exposing them. You don't know a stranger. She just came and rented your place. If you hide her and there is a problem as the landlord what will you do?[1]

The Kamara siblings included three boys and two girls with ages ranging from eighteen to thirty. After the 1997 takeover of power by the Armed Forces Revolutionary Council (AFRC) junta in Sierra Leone, their parents sent them to Guinea as refugees. They spent a few days in the Sierra Leone Embassy in Conakry before their aunt in the United States rented them a house from a Guinean. The intermediary in this transaction was a Sierra Leonean who had lived in Guinea for a long time. The house was located in the Hamdalaye neighborhood of the capital. Their aunt paid the biannual rent to the intermediary, who passed it on to the landlord. The landlord lived in another house in the compound, but the siblings did not see him often. He was a businessman who spent most of his day out of the house. When the siblings met him or other members of his family, they greeted them, but that was mostly the extent of their relations. The landlord did not introduce the siblings to the *chef de quartier* or anyone else in the area.

Apart from paying the rent of the siblings, their aunt also sent them money to cover their expenses. None of the siblings worked. They spent most of their day at the Sierra Leone Embassy. When they were not at the Embassy, they often visited refugee friends. Some of the less-fortunate friends moved in part-time with the siblings. They would come to the

[1] Interview with a Guinean in Conakry, Guinea (MRB 387), July 18, 2011.

house at night to eat and sleep. They usually left early in the morning to go look for odd jobs to do, visit friends who were mostly refugees, or hang out at the Sierra Leone Embassy. Others came just to eat and left. The siblings did not introduce any of these friends and housemates to the landlord or his family members.

In September 2000, the president of Guinea, Lansana Conte, delivered a speech in which he accused refugees of collaborating with rebels invading Guinea. He ordered Guineans to round up, interrogate, and expel the refugees from the country. A group of local youth and a few gendarmes raided the home of the Kamara siblings. It was the landlord who called in the youths. The siblings were badly beaten and the girls were repeatedly raped. All of the valuable properties in the house were taken, and the siblings were dragged to Hamdalaye gendarmerie, where they were imprisoned for a few days. When they were eventually released, they went immediately to the seaport, where they boarded a boat for Freetown, the capital of their home country, Sierra Leone, which was still at war.[2]

Another refugee experienced life remarkably differently in Guinea. In the early 1990s, Nowai was just ten when she crossed with her family from Liberia into Guinea's Yomou Prefecture as a refugee. After a short stay in Melikpoma, she settled with her grandmother in nearby Gotoye village in Banie Sub Prefecture. One day she was walking around with her grandmother begging people for palm nuts to make palm kernel oil when they encountered a Guinean lady in a farmhouse. After they asked her for the nuts piled near her hut, she asked for Nowai's name. She then said, "I want this girl to be my friend here. I will be her host. You can take as much kernel nuts as you want. I will help her in any way I can."

The Guinean lady, who was a leader in the women's secret society in the village, became Nowai's host in Gotoye. She introduced her to people as her guest and supported her family with palm nuts as well as food. She also became Nowai's defender in the community. Once, a boy stole Nowai's slippers and spread rumors that they were lovers. He was forced to apologize to Nowai's host. When Nowai offended people, they most often complained to her host instead of her grandmother.

Nowai visited her host's home almost every day. She went to greet and perform domestic chores for her in the morning. Her host had only one child – a boy – and so Nowai came to play the role of her daughter. Nowai addressed her as "mother" and treated her with much respect.

---

[2] Interview with a former refugee in Freetown, Sierra Leone (MRB 335), October 2, 2009.

Nowai and her grandmother spent most days on the farm of her host breaking palm nuts to make kernel oil for sale. When they received their refugee rations from humanitarian agencies such as the United Nations High Commission for Refugees (UNHCR), Nowai always took some of it to her host, who most often refused to accept any of it. She would thank Nowai and gently remind her that as refugees, Nowai and her grandmother were more in need of those items. Nowai also helped her host with farm work. Her grandmother often tried to help, but the host always refused to allow her to do so, intoning, "Just break your nuts, I will do the work with my friend Nowai."[3]

Nowai was in Gotoye when soldiers from Yomou brought President Conte's orders calling for the gathering, investigation, and expulsion of refugees in early September 2000. Even after being briefed by the soldiers, local leaders in Gotoye did not respond in the way that the Kamara siblings' landlord and communities in Conakry did. There were no blanket attacks on refugees akin to what happened in Conakry. In the face of agitation by some youths to adopt a Conakry-like response, village leaders in Gotoye employed a more measured and discriminatory approach. They tried to detect rebels and rebel collaborators without victimizing all refugees, the vast majority of whom they rightly recognized as innocent of the charges raised by the president. Leaders organized a youth militia and imposed a curfew. They punished all those caught breaking the curfew regardless of whether they were refugees or Guineans. Curfew breakers whose identity could not be confirmed by anyone in the local or refugee community were sent to prefecture headquarters as rebel suspects. The refugees were told to only enter forests when accompanied by their local hosts to prevent rebel infiltration. Local leaders assembled all the refugees and forced them to individually take traditional oaths that were supposed to result in the deaths of all who had bad intentions for the town or knew of plots against the town but did not reveal them to local leaders. Many locals insulted the refugees, accusing them of belonging to an ungrateful nation whose members were willing to attack Guinea despite the country's hospitality to refugees.

Relations between refugees and host populations in Africa have on most occasions resembled the situation in Gotoye, with a lack of systematic generalized violence against refugees by local populations. Relations have been so good that it has led many a scholar to talk about the

---

[3] Interview with a former refugee in Salayea District, Liberia (MRB 327), September 28, 2009.

workings of a unique "traditional African hospitality" that protects African refugees from some of the hardships that refugees elsewhere suffer.[4] It is in this connection that Holdborn notes "the striking degree of hospitality shown by both the local population and the governments, to the incoming refugees. African hospitality is not simply an attitude: at the local level it is a matter of people with very little, sometimes pitifully little, sharing what they have with many others."[5]

Unfortunately, this widespread hospitality to refugees has occasionally been disrupted by violence involving refugees. Accounts of such violence and inhospitality toward refugees abound in the literature.[6] The task here is to delineate and explain one of these types of violence – generalized anti-refugee violence. Such violence, exemplified previously in the attacks in Conakry that affected the Kamara siblings, is conducted openly and systematically by the local population against refugees. It usually involves massacres, beatings, rape, seizure and destruction of property, violent evictions, and incarcerations.[7]

When considered within the broad universe of refugee–host relations on the African continent, such incidents of generalized anti-refugee violence are few and far between. However, these attacks have happened in the past with devastating humanitarian consequences and will probably happen again in the future. This book explains why such attacks by civilian nonstate local populations against civilian refugee populations happen. It equally explores why they do not happen in so many other situations. Given the disruptions that characterize many refugee situations, and the effort that some states and insurgent groups invest in

---

[4] Robert Chambers, "Hidden losers? The impact of rural refugees and refugee programs on poorer hosts," *International Migration Review* 20 (Summer 1986): 248; Robert Mathews, "Refugees and stability in Africa," *International Organization* 26 (Winter 1972), 83; and Barry Stein, "ICARA II: Burden sharing and durable solutions," in *Refugees: a third world dilemma*, ed. John Rogge (Rowman and Littlefield, 1987), 50.

[5] Louise Holborn, *Refugees: a problem of our time* (Metuchen, NJ: The Scarecrow Press, 1975), 843.

[6] Sarah Lischer, *Dangerous sanctuaries: refugee camps, civil war and the dilemmas of humanitarian aid* (Ithaca: Cornell University Press, 2005); Idean Salehyan and Kristin Gleditsch, "Refugees and the spread of civil war," *International Organization* 60 (Spring 2006); Idean Salehyan, "The externalities of civil strife: refugees as a source of international conflict," *American Journal of Political Science* 52 (October 2008); Mathews, "Refugees and stability"; and Robert Muggah ed., *No refuge: the crisis of refugee militarization in Africa* (London: Zed Books, 2006).

[7] Mike McGovern, "Conflit régional et rhétorique de la contre-insurrection: Guinéens et réfugiés en septembre 2000," *Politique Africaine* 88 (December 2002): 85.

fanning anti-refugee violence, the question of why these attacks do not happen in some situations is just as interesting as why they occur.

Based on investigations of refugee–host relations in Guinea, Uganda, and the Democratic Republic of Congo, I argue that whether civilian populations launch generalized attacks on refugees depends on the coincidence of two individually necessary but only jointly sufficient factors: whether some refugees get involved in major opposition movements against the host state and whether refugees settle in an area that privileges residence or indigeneity in the allocation of rights. Such outbreaks happen only when some refugees get linked to major opposition movements in the host country and refugees are settled in areas that privilege residence in the allocation of rights. Refugees escape such attacks in other situations.

The preceding stories of the two refugee families in certain respects typify two broad modes of refugee existence across the African continent. Many refugees such as Nowai settle in areas that privilege indigeneity and autochthony in the distribution of rights. In these areas, the rights one has depend on whether one is recognized as an indigene of the area. It is only the autochthones that have primary rights. Non-indigenes are denied original rights. Instead, whatever rights they have are seen as secondary and inferior to that of indigenes. Refugees that settle in such places, like Nowai, end up being subjugated to local elites in these communities.

When a few refugees link up with groups that pose a major threat to host governments, state leaders respond by authorizing and fomenting local violence against refugees. Even in such situations, local elites to whom these refugees are subjugated refuse to go along with the state's project and act to prevent other locals from joining in.

Other refugees like the Kamara siblings settle in areas that privilege residence in the allocation of rights. In these areas, ideas of origins play a far less important role in the apportioning of rights. Instead, whether one resides in an area or not plays a much greater role in what rights one can legitimately claim. Refugees who settle in such areas come to live autonomously of local elites. In situations in which states foment and authorize violence against refugees, local communities enthusiastically embrace such anti-refugee programs.

My argument in this book is that what we have here is not just a mere coincidence of facts that have no causal connections. The situations of Nowai and the Kamara siblings demonstrate the causal story behind generalized anti-refugee violence by certain local communities and the lack of such violence by others. The Kamara siblings settled in Conakry, the capital of Guinea, which, since its formative years under French colonial rule, was designed to privilege residence over indigeneity and autochthony in the allocation of land and political rights. In the 1990s, when the refugees settled there, it was thus a very open society defined as belonging to all residents regardless of their origins. Thus indigeneity did not play a big role in the allocation of rights, including those to land and leadership.

Because the distinction between indigenous and non-indigenous residents was not very salient in Conakry when the refugees arrived in the early 1990s, society did not have mechanisms for allocating rights to residents who were defined as non-indigenous and lacking in primary rights. Furthermore, society did not pressure non-indigenous residents to normalize their existence in society by attaching themselves to indigenous residents through whom they could access rights. So the Kamara siblings, like other refugees in Conakry, lived on their own, autonomously of local notables. The question of their lack of indigeneity played little role in their ability to access rights and standing in the community. The refugees did not demonstrate symbolic subjugation to locals or frequently exchange gifts with them, and locals did not share legal responsibility for the lives of the refugees.

The price of this autonomy from local elites was that local notables knew very little about the refugees. This made it more likely for local leaders to buy into the demonization of refugees by President Conte or be gripped by a fear of the unknown. It was this paucity of knowledge about the daily lives of refugees that made it possible for even landlords who were benefiting handsomely from the presence of the refugees to imagine the refugees, the vast majority of whom were innocent, as a mortal threat that had to be excised and tamed through violence.

Other refugees like Nowai settle in societies that privilege indigeneity in the distribution of rights. These societies are conceived of as belonging to certain indigenous communities who are the sole bearers of primary rights, including those to land and political power. Non-indigenous residents can live and operate in these societies only by subjugating themselves to indigenous residents. Refugees like Nowai who try to settle in such societies realize quickly that life on their own standing is almost impossible. They have to seek local hosts who will stand on their behalf and through whom they can access rights. Their subjugation to such hosts involves the performance of symbolic acts of subjugation and the frequent exchange of gifts with such hosts. Local hosts also come to share legal responsibility for the refugees.

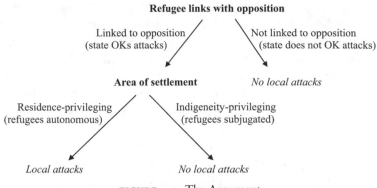

FIGURE 1.1. The Argument

A side effect of this relationship of subjugation is the accrual of significant information about the daily lives of refugees by local elites to whom
they are subjugated. Given the extent of knowledge about refugees in
these societies, it is unsurprising that local notables in Gotoye, in the
case of Nowai earlier, did not really buy into the virulent anti-refugee
fear mongering of President Conte. They were also not gripped by a fear
of the unknown. It is this pervasive knowledge about what the refugees
represented that allowed local elites in those communities to begin from
a position that not all the refugees were guilty of the crimes alleged
by the president. It is this knowledge that allowed Guineans in Gotoye
to proceed with a counterinsurgency strategy that sought to smoke out
the odd rebel collaborators among the refugees instead of victimizing
all of them. This is unlike their counterparts in Conakry, who were
unwilling to bet the future of their communities and country on the
innocence of refugees who mostly represented an unknown quantity to
them.

It is this impact of the structure of different societies on local knowledge and imaginaries about refugees that explains how local communities respond to state calls to anti-refugee violence. Explanations that focus
on political and economic competition, co-ethnicity, and refugee–host
numbers, among others, are more likely to lead us astray than help us
understand anti-refugee violence. Figure 1.1 presents the bare skeleton of
the argument in this book.

This book is unique in applying a sustained comparative lens in the task
of understanding large-scale attacks on noncombatant refugees by civilian
host populations. This dimension of refugee–host relations has received
little attention in a literature that is increasingly focusing on the role of

refugees as the propagators (instead of the victims) of violence.[8] One of the dividends of this comparative approach is the ability to assess key competing explanations that focus on co-ethnicity, refugee–host population numbers, and economic competition, and whether refugees self-settle or live in camps. I employ a mix of subnational comparative cases from the Forest Region of Guinea and evidence from elsewhere to show why these theories hold little explanatory promise when it comes to explaining generalized anti-refugee violence.

I make a counterintuitive contribution to the literature by teasing out the often-unrecognized potentials of residence and indigeneity-privileging societies. Scholars such as Mamdani, Mbembe, Nyamnjoh, Geschiere, Bauman, Meyer, Cueppens, Simone, and Jackson all portray indigeneity-privileging areas as more prone to violence against strangers. Residence-privileging societies are portrayed as more open and welcoming to strangers.[9] They are right in this assessment. However, I show that when it comes to generalized anti-refugee violence, indigeneity-privileging societies do have a redeeming quality. They hold the refugee in a subordinate

---

[8] Lischer, *Dangerous sanctuaries;* Mathews, "Refugees and stability"; Salehyan and Gleditsch, "Refugees and the spread"; and Salehyan, "The externalities."

[9] Mahmood Mamdani, *When victims become killers* (Princeton, NJ: Princeton University Press, 2001); Mahmood Mamdani, *Citizen and subject: contemporary Africa and the legacy of late colonialism* (Princeton, NJ: Princeton University Press, 1996); Mahmood Mamdani, "Political identity, citizenship and ethnicity in post-colonial Africa" (keynote address presented at New Frontiers of Social Policy Conference, Arusha, Tanzania, December 12–15, 2005); Achille Mbembe, "African modes of self-writing," *Public Culture* 14 (Winter 2002): 241; Achille Mbembe, "Ways of seeing: beyond the new nativism. Introduction," *African Studies Review* 44 (September 2004); Achille Mbembe, "On the power of the false," *Public Culture* 14 (Fall 2002); Francis Nyamnjoh, "Concluding reflections on beyond identities: rethinking power in Africa," *Identity and beyond: rethinking Africanity, Nordic Africa Institutite Discussion Paper* 12 (2001); Peter Geschiere, "Funerals and belonging: different patterns in South Cameroon," *African Studies Review* 48 (September 2005); Zygmunt Bauman, *Postmodernity and its discontents* (New York: New York University Press, 1997); Bambi Ceuppens and Peter Geschiere, "Autochthony: local or global? New modes in the struggle over citizenship and belonging in Africa and Europe," *Annual Review of Anthropology* 34 (2005); Peter Geschiere, *The perils of belonging: autochthony, citizenship, and exclusion in Africa and Europe* (Chicago: The University of Chicago Press, 2009); Birgit Meyer and Peter Geschiere, "Globalization and identity: dialectics of flow and closure. Introduction," in *Globalizagion and Identity: Dialects of flow and closure,* ed. B. Meyer and P. Geschiere (Oxford: Blackwell Publishers, 1999); Peter Geschiere and Francis Nyamnjoh, "Capitalism and autochthony: the seesaw of mobility and belonging," *Public Culture* 12 (Spring 2000): 430–432; Francis Nyamnjoh, *Insiders and outsiders: citizenship and xenophobia in contemporary Southern Africa* (Dakar: Codesria Books, 2006); and AbdouMaliq Simone, "On the worldling of African cities," *African Studies Review* 44, No. 2 (Sep 2001).

position and prevent her from enjoying full citizenship rights on a daily basis. However, it is this subjugation that facilitates the flow of information that saves the refugee from large-scale attacks by the local population. I also show that the residence-privileging society is not an unmitigated good when it comes to generalized anti-refugee violence. They are rightly portrayed as more open and welcoming. They accord refugees everyday rights and free them from the sort of subjugation to local elites that refugees in indigeneity-privileging societies are forced to endure. However, this autonomy also dooms refugees to generalized attacks at the hands of locals when the state urges such attacks by limiting the flow of information about refugees to local notables.

DELIMITING THE TERRAIN

The subject of this work is the incidence or lack thereof of generalized anti-refugee violence by local communities. There is a need to further clarify the sort of anti-refugee violence that is the focus of this work because there are multiple ways in which refugees are implicated in violence. In her work, Lischer argued that "political violence involving refugees manifests itself in five possible types."[10] These include "attacks between the sending state and the refugees; attacks between the receiving state and the refugees, ethnic or factional violence among the refugees, internal violence within the receiving state, inter-state war or unilateral intervention."[11] Lischer's typology is commendable in trying to distinguish between types of violence involving refugees. However, it is a bit limited for our purposes here in not listing violent attacks by the local population on refugees.

The typology I offer does two things. First, it focuses on refugees predominantly as the victims instead of perpetrators of violence. This involves a reorientation of the study of refugees and violence toward the civilian refugees who always constitute the vast majority of refugee populations. Even in situations of refugee militarization, as was the case with the Banyarwanda refugees in Eastern Congo in the early 1960s and mid-1990s and South African refugees in the frontline states during the era of Apartheid, the vast majority of refugees were civilians uninvolved in combat operations. When they contribute to the activities of their militarized colleagues, this often, more likely than not, is due to their being coerced than any interest in military activities.

[10] Lischer, *Dangerous sanctuaries*, 11.
[11] Ibid., 12.

Unfortunately, since the work of Zolberg, Suhrke, and Aguayo,[12] the militarized refugee has captured the imagination of those interested in refugees, politics, and security. Recent literature tends to overemphasize the role of refugees as propagators of insecurity and violence.[13] Metcalfe decried this "sustained tendency to regard the refugee solely in terms of his threat to political and economic stability."[14] Lischer and Whitaker[15] have laudably worked to question this orientation. Unfortunately, their work has sometimes fallen into the trap of not emphasizing the fact that civilian noncombatant refugees constitute the vast majority, even in highly militarized refugee situations. This book and the typology that follows attempt to redirect attention to the civilian refugees who are increasingly overlooked by the literature that focuses on refugees and security issues.

Second, the typology distinguishes between different types of perpetrators of violence against civilian refugees. One can raise the question of whether this atomizes perpetrators of anti-refugee violence that cannot and should not be atomized. Violence against refugees might be said to always involve a combination of perpetrators (state agents, local civilians, insurgent groups, etc.) contrary to the neatly compartmentalized picture painted here. One of the insights of Kalyvas's[16] work is the focus on the messy mix of perpetrators, victims, and motivations that characterizes situations of violent conflict. Anti-refugee violence by state agents and insurgent groups might be based on information provided by local civilian informants. The actions of local state agents in state-led attacks on refugees might be motivated more by local disputes than by the grand political considerations of senior state officials.

---

[12] Aristide Zolberg, Astri Suhrke, and Sergio Aguayo, *Escape from violence: conflict and the refugee crisis in the developing world* (New York: Oxford University Press, 1989).

[13] Salehyan and Gleditsch, "Refugees and the spread"; Salehyan, "The externalities"; Mathews, "Refugees and stability"; Robert Muggah ed., *No refuge*; Michael Brown, "The causes and regional dimensions of internal conflict," in *The international dimensions of internal conflict*, ed. Michael Brown (London: MIT Press, 1996); and Stephen Stedman, "Conflict and conciliation in sub-Saharan Africa," in *The international dimensions of internal conflict*, ed. Michael Brown (London: MIT Press, 1996).

[14] George Metcalfe, "Effects of refugees on the national state," in *Refugees south of the Sahara: an African dilemma*, ed. Hugh Brooks and Yassin El-Ayouty (Westport, CT: Negro Universities Press, 1970), 73.

[15] Lischer, *Dangerous sanctuaries*; Beth Elise Whitaker, "Refugees and the spread of conflict: contrasting cases in Central Africa," *Journal of Asian and African Studies* 38 No. 2–3 (2003); and Sarah Kenyon Lischer, Refugee involvement in political violence: quantitative evidence from 1987–1998," *New Issues in Refugee Research* 26 (July 2000): 1.

[16] Stathis Kalyvas, *The logic of violence in civil war* (New York: Cambridge University Press, 2006).

The distinction between different types of perpetrators of violence against refugees is not meant to deny these insights. Indeed, the argument I make here explicitly makes room for some of these insights in pointing out that civilian attacks on refugees are possible only in situations in which state agents not only permit, but work to foment attacks on refugees. Furthermore, within an environment of local attacks on refugees, my argument does not rule out the possibility that which specific local person attacks which particular refugee, when, and where might be influenced just as much by the settling of very personal scores as by the grand task of getting rid of an imagined refugee fifth column.

If we are going to hold people responsible for the humanitarian disasters that such attacks on refugees represent, we have to find ways of distinguishing between different perpetrators of such violence. The typology is meant to capture and distinguish between the major perpetrators and orchestrators of anti-refugee violence without rejecting the possibility of various actors simultaneously engaging in such attacks. Because sometimes one or more of these parties can dominate such violence to the near total exclusion of others, we need a typology that allows us to parse scenarios like these out without denying the possibility of combinations of perpetrators. The typology I provide thus offers us five possible *principal* perpetrators of violence against refugees:

1. Civilian nonstate actors
2. Host states
3. Insurgent groups
4. Foreign states
5. Other refugees

This book explores the first type of anti-refugee violence – generalized anti-refugee violence by local populations – because the other types of attacks have received extensive attention in the literature.[17] It is important

---

[17] Lischer, *Dangerous sanctuaries*, 79–80; Chambers, "Hidden losers?" 255; Art Hansen, "Managing refugees: Zambia's response to Angolan refugees 1966–1977," *Disasters* 3 (4–1979): 377; McGovern, "Conflit régional"; Holborn, *Refugees*, 1087–1089 and 1233–1234; and Rene Lemarchand, *Rwanda and Burundi* (New York Praeger Publishers, 1970), 210–211; Mamdani, *When victims become killers*, 168–169; Mamdani, "Uganda and background of the RPF invasion," in *Conflict and ethnicity in Central Africa*, ed. Didier Goyvaerts (Tokyo, Institute for the study of the languages and culture of Asia and Africa, 2000), 315; Virginia Hamilton, "Human rights in Uganda: the reasons for refugees," *United States Committee for Refugees Issue Paper* (August 1985): 19–20; Catherine Watson, "Exile from Rwanda: Background to an invasion," *United States Committee for Refugees Issue Paper* (February 1991): 10–11; Aristide Zolberg,

to note that the victims of the attacks studied here are civilian refugees that should be properly distinguished from the so-called refugee warriors.[18] Refugee warriors are combatants and are defined here as refugees who are involved, even if only on a part-time basis, in combat operations. The victims of attacks that I study here are those that are not or no longer involved in combat activities, even on a part-time basis. The principle I want to uphold is that most refugees are not even part-timers. If this is accepted, then blanket anti-refugee violence cannot but target many noncombatants. The goal of the project then is to understand why local populations target this category of refugees with violence.

This book focuses on generalized violence against refugees. This type of violence targets whole refugee populations and should be distinguished from violence targeting particular refugees, which is quite common in refugee situations.[19] Furthermore, it examines unilateral outbreaks of violence against civilian refugee communities. These are instances in which refugees feature only as the victims of attacks. This has to be differentiated from clashes between civilian refugees and local populations and attacks against local populations by civilian refugees. Incidents of both of these other possibilities are so uncommon on the African continent as to render them unsuitable for explanation. Clashes and attacks on local communities by refugees usually involve militarized refugees.[20]

Finally, this book is interested in explaining both incidents of generalized anti-refugee violence and the absence of such violence. In doing

---

Conflict and the refugee crisis in the developing world (New York: Oxford University Press, 1989), 67; Aristide Zolberg, Astri Suhrke and Sergio Aguayo, *Escape from violence*, 67–68; and Edward Khiddu-Makubuya, "Voluntary repatriation by force: the case of Rwandan refugees in Uganda," in *African refugees: development aid and repatriation*, ed. Howard Adelman and John Sorenson (Boulder: Westview Press, 1994), 150.

[18] See the following works for more on refugee warriors: Stephen Stedman and Fred Tanner, "Refugees as resources in war," *Refugee manipulation: war, politics, and the abuse of human suffering*, ed. in Stephen Stedman and Fred Tanner (Washington, DC: Brookings Institution Press, 2003); Peter Nyers, *Rethinking refugees: beyond states of emergency* (New York: Routledge, 2006), xvii–xviii & 99; Mathews, "Refugees and stability," 72; and Howard Adelman, "The use and abuse of refugees," in *Refugee manipulation: war, politics, and the abuse of human suffering*, ed. Stephen Stedman and Fred Tanner (Washington, DC: Brookings Institution Press, 2003), 96–99.

[19] See, for example, Human Rights Watch, *Seeking protection: addressing sexual and domestic violence in Tanzania's refugee camps* (New York: Human Rights Watch, 2000); Barbara Harrell-Bond, *Imposing aid: emergency assistance to refugees* (New York: Oxford University Press, 1986), 157; and Chambers, "Hidden losers?" 388.

[20] Koen Vlassenroot, "Identity formation and conflict in South Kivu: the case of the Banyamulenge," *Review of African Political Economy* 29 (September–December 2002): 508; and Adelman, "The use and abuse of refugees," 96.

this, it avoids the Hobbesian trap, which snares studies that characterize societies as inherently prone to violence.[21] The task that is assumed by the scholar then is to explain why peace is maintained some of the time despite this propensity for violence. The ability of the state to impose order has been one of the main explanations deployed to unravel this puzzle.[22] The other snare is the tendency highlighted by Kalyvas, Shapiro, and Masoud[23] to understand social order as a default position that is taken for granted and undeserving of explanation. Effort is then put into explaining why violence occasionally disrupts the civil peace. However, as Bates et al. noted, "contemporary events remind us that stability in political communities cannot be assumed; it must be achieved."[24]

This work, then, contributes to what Kalyvas, Shapiro, and Masoud rightly described as the need for "integration between the study of order and the study of conflict and violence."[25] I regard the occurrence of violence and of peace as equally worthy of explanation. This is based on an acknowledgment of the multiple potentialities that define these encounters between refugees and local populations.[26]

I find generalized anti-refugee violence by local populations interesting and dedicate time to explaining why it happens. I equally find the absence of such anti-refugee violence intriguing and devote equal attention to the question: "How does order emerge and how is it sustained?"[27] Why do

[21] Jasna Capo Zmegac has demonstrated the problems that refugees can face in relations with their coethnic hosts. "Ethnically privileged migrants in their homeland," *Journal of Refugee Studies* 18, No. 2 (2005): 201.

[22] See James Tong, *Disorder under heaven: collective violence in the Ming Dynasty* (Stanford: Stanford University Press, 1991), 93; and Denise DiPasquale and Edward Glaeser, "The LA riot and the economics of urban unrest," *National Bureau of Economic Research Working Paper* 5456 (February 1996); Ashutosh Varshney, Rizal Panggabean and Mohammad Zulfan Tadjoeddin, "Patterns of Collective Violence in Indonesia (1990–2003)," *United Nations Support Facility for Indonesian Recovery – UNSFIR Working Paper – 04/03* (July 2004); and Davidson, *Violence and politics*, 15.

[23] Stathis Kalyvas, Ian Shapiro and Tarek Masoud, "Introduction: integrating the study of order, conflict and violence," in *Order, conflict and violence*, ed. Stathis Kalyvas, Ian Shapiro and Tarek Masoud (New York: Cambridge University Press, 2008), 1.

[24] Robert Bates et al, "Introduction," in *Analytic narratives*, ed. Robert Bates et al. Princeton: Princeton University Press, 1998), 3.

[25] Kalyvas, Shapiro, and Masoud, "Introduction," 1. Also see page 3 of this work, where they lay out some of the important questions that warrant attention.

[26] In taking this stance, I deviate from Zmegac, who sees these encounters as inherently conflictual. "Ethnically privileged," 201. I also deviate from scholars who tend to emphasize a situation of hospitality as the norm in these refugee host encounters. See Holborn, *Refugees*, 843; Chambers, "Hidden losers?" 248; Mathews, "Refugees and stability," p. 83; and Stein, "ICARA II," 50.

[27] Kalyvas, Shapiro, and Masoud, "Introduction," 3.

these communities peacefully coexist in the face of all the disruptions that the sudden and massive influx of refugees often causes?[28] Why do these peaceful relations often survive droughts, famines, and active efforts by parties such as states to foment violence between these groups?

STUDY DESIGN AND CASE SELECTION

This book is divided into seven chapters. Chapters 1 and 2 present many of the theoretical interventions in the work. In Chapter 2, I lay out in greater detail the central argument of this book. I then use the argument put forward to explain generalized anti-refugee violence and its absence in subnational settings in Guinea, Uganda, and what is now called the Democratic Republic of Congo.

Chapters 3, 4, and 5 focus on the Mano River Basin and explain variations in relations between refugees from Sierra Leone and Liberia and their Guinean hosts in two areas of Guinea. Chapter 3 focuses on the capital city, Conakry. Chapter 4 explores events in three sub-prefectures (Fangamandou, Kondou, and Banie) in the Forest Region of Guinea. These subnational units give us variation in outcomes. After approximately ten years of living peacefully with the refugees, Guinean residents of the capital Conakry subjected refugees to rape, robbery, beatings, and killings in early September 2000. Both Guineans and former refugees informed me that no such attacks happened in the towns and villages in Kondou, Fangamandou, and Banie sub-prefectures in the country's Forest Region.

The fact of variation is puzzling. People generally attribute the outbreak of the anti-refugee violence to an incendiary speech by Guinean President Lansana Conte that incited violence against the refugees while blaming them for incursions into the country by rebels from Sierra Leone and Liberia.[29] A big problem with this explanation is that it makes no

---

[28] Robert Bates sets out explicitly to explain order in "Probing the sources of political order," in *Order, conflict and violence*, ed. in Stathis Kalyvas, Ian Shapiro and Tarek Masoud. New York: Cambridge University Press, 2008, 17–42.

[29] Lacey Andrews Gale, "The invisible refugee camp: durable solutions for Boreah 'residuals' in Guinea," *Journal of Refugee Studies* 21 (4–2008): 539–541; Human Rights Watch, "The refugee crisis in Guinea: another Macedonia?" *Human Rights Watch*, October 3, 2000, accessed October 10, 2012, http://www.hrw.org/news/2000/10/03/refugee-crisis-guinea-another-macedonia; Afrol News, "President's speech provokes mass rape of refugees," *Afrol News*, September 14, 2000, accessed January 21, 2011, http://www.afrol.com/News/gui002_refugees_raped.htm; James Milner and Astrid; Christoffersen-Deb, "The militarization and demilitarization of refugee camps

effort to understand why Guineans obeyed the president's orders. Because we cannot automatically assume that Guineans will obey the orders of their president, it means it can at best be only half of the explanation. Many chiefs in the Forest Region reported getting the president's orders. Despite this, they did not mobilize their populations to attack the refugees. Instead, they often clamped down on those who tried to go along with the orders. A complete explanation of the situation in Guinea will thus have to account for why people responded to the president's orders the way they did.

More nuanced accounts like that of McGovern[30] have laudably set out to answer precisely this question of the willingness of the Guinean population to buy into the anti-refugee discourse of the president. The problem is that they often use national phenomena to explain responses that were very local and that varied from location to location across the country. McGovern, for instance, uses the history of nationalist and socialist rhetoric and practice under the first Guinean president, Sekou Toure, to explain people's response to President Lansana Conte.[31] Instead of answering the question, what this reference to the legacy of Toure-era rhetoric and practice does is to make events in Guinea even more puzzling. If we make the plausible assumption that such rhetoric and mobilization permeated more than Conakry, we are left to wonder why people affected by Toure rule in other areas of the country did not respond like their counterparts in Conakry.

The nature of the variation is also interesting. Conte dressed his command to crackdown on the refugees in the garb of counterinsurgency. He accused the Sierra Leonean and Liberian refugees of helping rebels from their home countries to destabilize Guinea.[32] However, Conakry, where Guineans responded most enthusiastically to these attacks, is about 100 km from the closest border with Sierra Leone and Liberia. Like many African capitals, it was home to many military bases and installations, which gave it a relatively high level of safety. However, the citizens there responded enthusiastically to the president's call. Meanwhile, many of the

---

and settlements in Guinea, 1999–2004," in *No refuge: the crisis of refugee militarization in Africa*, ed. Robert Muggah (London: Zed Books, 2006), 52; and Alexis Arieff, "Still standing: neighborhood wars and political stability in Guinea," *Journal of Modern African Studies* 47 (3–2009): 343.

[30] McGovern, "Conflit régional." Also see Arieff, "Still standing."

[31] Michael McGovern, "Unmasking the state: developing modern subjectivities in 20th century Guinea" (PhD diss., Emory University, 2004), 555–562.

[32] McGovern, "Conflit régional," 85.

towns in Yomou and Guéckédou prefectures where Guineans refrained from attacking refugees were only a few kilometers from the frontline. Some were just a stone's throw from the border. They witnessed intermittent incursions by rebels throughout the 1990s and lived in daily fear of the rebels crossing the rivers that formed the international boundary. Bullets fired in Sierra Leone and Liberia often landed in and injured people in some of these towns and villages.

These citizens who were the most menaced by the possibility of rebel incursions did not get drawn into indiscriminate attacks against the refugees. Instead they resorted to more measured responses. These included inspecting the bodies of refugees *and Guineans* for what they considered rebel tattoos,[33] forbidding refugees temporarily from going to forests and rivers close to the borders, requiring them to take oaths against collaborating with the rebels, forcing them to form or join counterinsurgency militias, and so forth. It is important to note that this refrainment from anti-refugee violence by Guineans in the Forest Region was not due to fear of the refugees or their rebel countrymen. Even Guineans attested to their brutal treatment of refugees who were suspected of rebel activities in these parts of the country.[34]

Chapters 3 and 4 urge a focus on the characteristics of the different places where the refugees settled and the lives they established there to understand outbreaks of generalized anti-refugee violence. A mix of Sierra Leoneans and Liberians who ended up as refugees in Conakry faced such attacks in September 2000. Their counterparts from the same two countries who went to communities in the Forest Region were not subjected to these attacks. The different national identities and origins of the refugees did not make a difference. Where they settled did.

Chapter 5 uses evidence from the Forest Region of Guinea to assess two important competing explanations of refugee–host relations – co-ethnicity and refugee–host numbers. Located between the empirical chapters, this chapter serves to answer objections that creep up in the minds of readers as they go through Chapters 3 and 4 on the Mano River Basin. They also help to pave the way for the explanations of refugee–host relations in the Great Lakes Region that follow.

The task of reflecting on competing arguments is not just a preoccupation of Chapter 5. These reflections are also present in some of the other chapters. In Chapter 2, I reflect briefly on the power of refugee

---

33 McGovern, "Conflit regional," 91.
34 Chat with a young man in Kelema, Guéckédou Prefecture (MRB 119B), June 20, 2009.

militarization to help us understand outbreaks of large-scale violence by local populations against refugees. In Chapter 7, I reflect on competing arguments that focus on settlement patterns and on scarcity and competition for economic resources.

Chapters 6 and 7 focus on the Great Lakes Region and explain the varying fortunes of the so-called 59ers- Rwandan refugees who fled to Kivu province in the Democratic Republic of Congo (1959–1968) and southwestern Uganda (1959–1983) beginning in 1959. In Chapter 6, I show why the refugees who settled in southwestern Uganda had peaceful relations with the local population up to 1994, when many of them returned to Rwanda. These peaceful relations with locals even survived efforts by the government of Milton Obote to encourage locals to attack refugees in 1982–1983. State officials and the ruling party youth wing that carried out the anti-refugee attacks also had to actively prevent locals from aiding the refugees.[35] Chapter 7 explains why the local population there almost immediately subjected the compatriots of these refugees who opted for refuge in the eastern Congo to generalized attacks. UNHCR had to airlift some of these refugees to Tanzania, whereas others fled on their own to Burundi, Uganda, and Tanzania.

This pair of chapters helps us drive home a point made with the chapters on the Mano River Basin. The origin of the refugees does not seem to have had much of an influence on their relations with the local populations. The Banyarwanda refugees who went to southwestern Uganda and those who went to Kivu were part of the same state-in-exile and persecuted refugee group.[36] These were predominantly Tutsi refugees. Some were former leaders overthrown by the Social Revolution who had opted to form a government-in-exile to plot their return to Rwanda. Many were fleeing clashes with militant Hutu that formed part of and followed the Social Revolution. Sections of both refugee populations in Congo and Uganda sought to militarize and attack Rwanda in hopes of unseating the government there. The place where the refugees settled seemed to have trumped this similarity in origins.

This pair of cases also helps us tease out the local processes that influence host community participation in such violence. The Ugandan state

---

[35] Elijah Mushemeza, "Politics and the refugee experience: the case of Banyarwanda refugees in Uganda (1959–1994)," (PhD diss., Makerere University, 2002). Also see Jason Clay, *The eviction of Banyarwanda: The story behind the refugee crisis in southwest Uganda* (Cambridge, MA: *Cultural Survival*, 1984), 35; and Hamilton, "Human rights in Uganda," 19.

[36] I am using Lischer's categories here. *Dangerous sanctuaries*, 19.

under President Milton Obote and the Congolese state under President Mobutu Sese Seko both ordered the expulsion of the refugees and actively sought to promote civilian attacks against them.[37] Although locals embraced the state's project in eastern Congo, they refused to join it in southwestern Uganda. This variation in local responses to similar scheming by state officials allows us to examine the local dynamics that condition the propensity of local populations to go along with the state's violent project.

The two cases in which generalized anti-refugee violence by local communities did not occur were chosen with the intention of providing particularly difficult tests of my argument. These cases from Southwestern Uganda and the Forest Region of Guinea were situations in which states initially offered active and highly vocal support for and protection to refugee communities. It was thus not surprising that local communities did not attack these refugees, even if there were always elements that were willing to carry out such attacks. After a while states withdrew support from and encouraged attacks against the refugees in both countries. This leaves us with the difficult task of explaining the persistence of peaceful relations between refugees and local populations despite the strenuous incitement by host states.

Beyond summarizing the key points in this work, Chapter 8 explores some of the general lessons that ought and ought not to be drawn from the book. It also explores the significance of gender in refugee experiences and locates the work within broader literature on stranger–host relations in Africa.

METHODS AND FIELD RESEARCH

This work is based predominantly on ethnographic field research that centered on semistructured in-depth interviews with individuals. My first research trip was a one-month visit in May 2008 to the settlement of Buduburam close to the Ghanaian capital, Accra, which hosted a large camp for Liberian refugees. This was followed by a month of research in Conakry and the Forest Region of Guinea in July 2008. I visited these areas again in November/December 2008 and June to August 2009.

---

[37] Holborn, *Refugees*, 1093; Zolberg, Suhrke and Aguayo, *Escape from violence*, 46; and Edouard Bustin, "The Congo," in *Refugees south of the Sahara: an African dilemma*, ed. Hugh Brooks and Yassin El-Ayouty (Westport, CT: Negro Universities Press, 1970), 187; and Mamdani, *When victims become killers*, 168.

I then spent September 2009 interviewing former refugees in Sierra Leone and Liberia. I undertook final follow-up trips to Liberia in December 2010 and to Guinea in July 2011. I conducted research in Uganda in March and April 2010. I then crossed the border into Rwanda in May to conduct interviews with former refugees.

I conducted approximately 106 interviews with former refugees and hosts in Uganda and Rwanda and 359 interviews with former refugees and hosts in Guinea, Liberia, and Sierra Leone. In the host countries of Uganda and Guinea, I mostly interviewed former hosts, even though I was also able to speak with a few former refugees. In Uganda my research was concentrated in Ntungamo and Isingiro Districts. My work in Guinea was based in Conakry, Fangamandu, Kondou (Guéckédou Prefecture) and Banie Sub-Prefectures (Yomou Prefecture), and the towns of Guéckédou, Macenta, and N'Zérékoré. I also made occasional trips to other areas such as Daro in Macenta Prefecture and Lainé, Kounkan, Boreah, and Kountaya refugee camps. Observation of the surviving evidence of refugee life in the former host communities was a key part of my work.

I did most of the interviews with former refugees in their home countries where they had repatriated. In Sierra Leone, my research was based in the capital city, Freetown, Penguia Chiefdom in Kailahun District, and Mafindor Chiefdom in Kono District. In Rwanda, I interviewed former refugees in Nyagatare District. Salayea District and neighboring areas of Zorzor District in Liberia's Lofa County provided me access to former refugees in Liberia.

Interviews and observations are supplemented by some archival research done in Conakry and in the Ugandan capital, Kampala. My analysis is also deeply informed by my personal experiences. I have drawn much insight from a month I spent as a self-settled refugee in the Guinean capital, Conakry, in September 1997, long before I began to contemplate writing about refugee life.

I did not conduct field research in Eastern Congo because continuing instability there will have made research difficult. Furthermore, multiple rounds of violence have happened since the expulsion of the refugees in 1964. Many of these have centered on the question of Kinyarwanda speakers in the area. This will have made it difficult to get people to reflect on their relations with the refugees up to the end of 1964 in ways that were free of later experiences of violent conflict in the area.

I was fortunate to locate some of the former refugees who were expelled from Congo in the early 1960s in Masindi District, Uganda, where they had settled. This gave me first-hand sources of information to complement the secondary materials that work on Congo is otherwise based on. It constitutes a problem because it gives voice to the former refugees without according space to their hosts. My hope is that secondary materials that reflect on things from the point of view of the Congolese will help bring some balance, but fundamentally this is a flaw of which readers must be aware.

I decided to conduct research in the refugee-sending countries even though they were not my sites of study for three reasons. First, it was much easier to find the former refugees there since many had repatriated. Second, I suspected that former refugees who had stayed on in the host country might feel more constrained to speak because they were still living with their former hosts, unlike those who had repatriated. Finally, there was the possibility of a systematic bias resulting from only talking to former refugees whom I found in the former host countries. These might be those refugees who had such a good experience that they refused to return to the countries they had fled.

In the end these concerns over a systematic bias seemed to have been unfounded. In both the former host and sending countries, people were willing to speak freely when they were interviewed in private settings after the process for guaranteeing their confidentiality had been carefully explained.

Whether the former refugees were still in the host country or had repatriated did not seem to significantly influence their views. Those who went back were not necessarily having a particularly harder time than those who stayed. People seemed to have made hard choices with their eyes wide open.[38] Some stayed despite the difficult conditions in the host country, whereas others repatriated despite the vagaries of life back "home." Others went back and forth between the two countries. Many were unwilling to tie themselves to any one country. For many of the former refugees, where I found them was partly a function of when I visited the area. If I had gone a month or two before or after, I might have found them in the other country.

The straddling lifestyle of these former refugees reflects the life story of the female character "Bintu" as retold by Mats Utas in his account

---

[38] Jacobson discusses reasons why refugees often stay in country of asylum even after peace returns to their home coutnries. See Karen Jacobson, *The Economic Life of Refugees* (Bloomfield, CT: Kumarian Press, 2005), 8–9.

of life and female agency during the wars in the Mano River Basin.[39] The straddling strategy is what Hovil writes of as a combination of the "durable solutions" of local integration and repatriation.[40] It is tempting to see such movement and straddling as the unique effects of conflict and postconflict dislocations. However, as Barret notes, migration during war is only part of movement that goes on even during times of peace.[41] Studies of the Great Lakes Region and the Mano River Basin before, during, and after colonialism all point to the ongoing movement of people in search of better lives.[42] This is true for many other areas of Africa as well.[43] It is on account of this that some scholars are critical of the conceptualization of refugee repatriation as some special return to a lost "home" that has to be recovered.[44]

The ability of many Africans to speak multiple languages and to comfortably participate in cultural processes and forms across national borders has facilitated such movement and straddling. This is in addition to the fact that long histories of migration usually mean that people can draw on kin and friendship relations across frontiers.[45] Even where they cannot do so, cultural processes that allow for the incorporation of strangers facilitate movement.

[39] Mats Utas, "West-African Warscapes: Victimcy, Girlfriending, Soldiering: Tactic Agency in a Young Woman's Social Navigation of the Liberian War Zone," *Anthropological Quarterly* 78 (Spring 2005): 413–426.

[40] Lucy Hovil, "Hoping for peace, afraid of war: the dilemmas of repatriation and belonging on the borders of Uganda and South Sudan," *New Issues in Refugee Research* No. 196 (November 2010): 1.

[41] Barret, "Social landscapes," 1.

[42] Jean-Pierre Chretien, *The great lakes of Africa: two thousand years of history* (New York: Zone Books, 2003), 45; P. G. Powesland, "History of the migration in Uganda," in *Economic development and tribal change: a study of immigrant labour in Buganda*, ed. Audrey Richards (Cambridge: W. Heffer and Sons Ltd., 1952), 19–51; and Jacques Germain, *Peuples de la Foret de Guinée* (Paris, Academie des Sciences d'outre-Mer, 1984), 19–69.

[43] Bakewell, "Returning refugees or migrating villagers? Voluntary repatriation programmes in Africa reconsidered," *New Issues in Refugee Research* No. 15 (December 1999): 1; and Michael Barret, "Social landscapes and moving people: the mysterious meaning of migration in western Zambia," *New Issues in Refugee Research* No. 78 (February 2003): 1.

[44] Bakewell, "Returning refugees," 1; Nicholas Van Hear, "From durable solutions to transational relations: home and exile among refugee diasporas," *New Issues in Refugee Research* 83 (March 2003): 1; Hovil, "Hoping for peace," 1; and Barret, "Social landscapes," 1.

[45] Art Hansen, "Once the running stops: assimilation of Angolan refugees in to Zambian border villages," *Disasters* 3 (4–1979): 370–71.

THE USE OF ETHNOGRAPHY

This work employs qualitative methods with a heavy reliance on semi-structured interviews. Observation, secondary literature, and archival research help me put interviews in perspective. I ensured the richness of interviews by engaging a diverse set of interviewees. These included locals of various stripes, refugees who did not repatriate as well as those who repatriated, men and women, young and old, rich and poor, those in authority and those lacking power. I achieved this diversity by supplementing snowballing and convenience sampling with the purposive selection of interviewees.

I have tried to give particular weight to critical interview evidence understood as evidence from interviews in which the respondent lacks an incentive to dissemble or has an incentive to dissemble in exactly the opposite direction from what she does say. This emphasis on critical interview evidence is important in the study of refugee issues. Many observers of refugees point at the tendency of these seekers of refuge to create innovative accounts of their lives that do not exactly mirror their lived realities.[46] International structures for dealing with refugees and the incentives that they give refugees to depend on their powers of innovative storytelling have been cited as explanations.[47] These institutions motivate even locals to engage in the same types of dissembling. In Guinea, many hosts posed as refugees to access humanitarian aid, gain spaces on third-party resettlement programs, and so forth.[48]

Ethnography has particular strengths in sorting through these types of situations in which dissembling is routine. For one, identifying what constitutes critical evidence requires the deep understanding of structures that ethnographic immersion allows for. Immersion by a researcher can also take away some of the incentives that people have to dissimulate. Much of such dissembling in refugee situations is aimed at humanitarian

---

[46] Kibreab, Gaim, "Pulling the wool over the eyes of the strangers: refugee deceit and trickery in institutionalized settings," *Journal of Refugee Studies* 17 (2004): 1–26; Lacey Andrews Gale, "Bulgur marriages and 'Big' women: navigating relatedness in Guinean refugee camps," *Anthropological Quarterly* 80 (Spring 2007): 355–378. Trycia Hynes discusses the pervasive mistrust that characterizes refugee situations. "The issue of 'trust' or 'mistrust' in research with refugees: choices, caveats and considerations for researchers," *New Issues in Refugee Research* No. 98 (November 2003).

[47] Kibreab, "Pulling the wool"; and Gale, "Bulgur marriages."

[48] My own work in Guinea and Ghana revealed evidence of many locals posing as refugees to accrue benefits that were otherwise reserved for refugees. Both refugees and locals admitted to this. Also see Kibreab, "Pulling the wool."

agencies and is done to accrue benefits. Ethnographic immersion can contribute to convincing research subjects that the researcher is not a humanitarian worker.

It is never certain that the researcher will be able to convince everyone no matter how long she spends in the field, and research subjects have good reasons to doubt researchers' efforts at distancing themselves from humanitarian workers. Many researchers will at some point work as consultants for such agencies, many associate with humanitarian workers while in the field, and humanitarian workers sometimes read work produced by researchers. The ethnographic researcher who immerses herself in a community gives community members more of an opportunity to discern the nature of links that might exist between her and these humanitarian agencies.

Self-Selection and Representativeness

A key question that is worth considering is the extent to which the sample I draw my evidence from is representative of other refugee situations on the African continent. The diversity of the settings I study assures me that they are representative of wider refugee situations on the continent. My work focused on many areas in Conakry, the Forest Region of Guinea, Eastern Congo, and Uganda, where refugees self-settled. Some lived in cities, whereas others were in smaller towns and villages. I also studied situations in which refugees lived in camps and settlements. Some of these settlements were very large, whereas others were small. Some of the refugees always lived in camps, whereas others were always self-settled. However, there were many who switched back and forth between the two modes of settlement.

Many of the refugees in the Mano River Basin were sedentary cultivators, whereas many Batutsi refugees in the Great Lakes Region were pastoralists. Most of the refugees in the Mano River Basin had escaped their countries because of general violence. Many of the Batutsi refugees in the Great Lakes Region fled because of the violent targeting of Batutsi in Rwanda during and after the Social Revolution. Some were former leaders in Rwanda who escaped to form a government-in-exile with the goal of returning to take over power in Rwanda. Given all of this diversity, it is hard to see why these cases will not be representative of wider refugee situations on the continent.[49]

---

[49] See Karen Jacobson and Loren Landau, "Researching refugees: some methodological and ethical considerations in social science and forced migration," *New Issues in Refugee*

Language

Language has had a very big impact on the conduct and results of this study. I carried out interviews with people who preferred to express themselves during interviews in a wide variety of languages. Because of this, I employed multilingual research assistants to do translation in most interviews. A lot of meaning got lost and added in the process, but on the whole, the broad comparative work that this use of translators allowed makes up for some of the problems of translation.

I did not use any voice or video recording instruments to better ensure the confidentiality of research subjects and to better encourage them to express themselves freely. It is important, then, to note that the quotations of interviewees in this book are all paraphrased approximations of what people said. I have tried to reproduce them as exactly as I can, but some meaning surely must have been lost and gained in the process.

CONCLUSION

I should emphasize that what I seek to explain is the presence or absence of generalized anti-refugee violence by local populations. Asserting that refugee–host interactions are free of such generalized violence is not to say that relations are free of all violence or that relations are good. As I demonstrate in various chapters later, refugees very often suffer from arbitrary and extrajudicial violence in their lives. State officials, local populations, and even humanitarian agency workers perpetrate such violence. The difference between such violence and that which is the main focus of this book is that it is not aimed at a refugee community as a whole.

During my research in Sierra Leone and Liberia with former refugees who had been in areas of Guinea where no generalized violent attacks happened, I got used to hearing of such particularized abuse. One refugee palm wine seller was given what he described as a "very heavy slap" across the face for protesting when a Guinean refused to pay after drinking palm wine.[50] An old refugee leader was undressed, doused with cold water in public, and then jailed because someone who went

---

Research No. 90 (June 2003) for some thoughts on ethical and methodological issues in refugee research.

[50] Interview with a former refugee in Nyandehun village, Penguia Chiefdom, Sierra Leone (MRB 282), September 14, 2009.

fishing in a river against local laws had said the old man knew of his activities.[51]

Even in the absence of physical violence, refugees' lives were often marked by the abuse of their rights on a routine basis. Prearranged wages often went unpaid after refugees had completed jobs given them by locals. Palm wine tappers sometimes had their wine seized and jugs destroyed. Fishermen sometimes had their fishes confiscated from them, ostensibly because they had fished in Guinean rivers. When they protested, those who were lucky to escape slaps were often asked, "Did you bring any river/palm tree with you from your country when you were coming?"

The difference I am trying to draw here is that between everyday structural violence and occasional outbursts of extreme violence. Although everyday structural violence lacks the attention-drawing characteristics of spectacular outbursts of generalized attacks, they are no less physically and emotionally damaging. In fact, their unspectacular nature might make them all the harder to detect and deal with.[52]

My work is not meant to explain such routine types of violence. However, I discuss them in great detail as I seek to make sense of occasional outbreaks of generalized anti-refugee violence because of their contributions to the occurrence or lack thereof of such outbursts.

---

[51] Interview with a former refugee in Kpayea, Salayea District, Liberia (MRB 329), September 28, 2009.

[52] Utas describes how the magnitude of such violence and hardship drove some refugees back to the warzones they had escaped. "West African warscapes," 421.

2

Explaining Generalized Anti-Refugee Violence

No matter how strong a cockroach may be, it will never take a stroll in the country of chickens.[1]

REFUGEEHOOD AND DISEMPOWERMENT

The argument developed here is uniquely suited to explaining violence against civilian refugees because the majority of these refugees, unlike many other migrants, are often disempowered people. These refugees do not usually pose significant political and economic threats to the *powerful* local actors that heavily influence the use of collective violence in the communities in which they settle.[2] As I demonstrate throughout the work, these refugees often inflate the influence of powerful local actors, further widening the power and wealth gap between rich and powerful local notables and poorer members of the refugee-hosting communities.[3] This is why influential explanations that focus on political and economic competition between groups offer little promise for understanding generalized violence against civilian refugees, even if they convincingly explain intergroup violence between less-disempowered populations.

---

[1] A former Sierra Leonean refugee in Sambaya, Mafindo Chiefdom, Kono District, Sierra Leone (MRB 226), September 4, 2009.

[2] Katharina Inhetveen notes that Angolan refugees in Zambia resorted to their powerlessness to explain many of the negative things that plagued their existence. "'Because we are refugees:' utilizing a label," *New Issues in Refugee Research* 130 (October 2006): 8.

[3] This is a point that others have also made. See Chambers, "Hidden losers?" and Beth Whitaker, "Refugees in Western Tanzania: the distribution of burdens and benefits among local hosts," *Journal of Refugee Studies* 15 (2002).

Part of the reason for the disempowerment of refugees lies in international laws governing refugees. These laws construct them as quintessential sojourners. They are people fleeing a country where they properly belong for another country where they do not belong for a certain period, after which they are supposed to return to their country.[4] At the heart of the concept of the refugee is this understanding of the relationship between space and rights. The globe is neatly divided into nation-states. People belong to and own rights in certain states. Their departure from their state thus spells a loss of certain key rights. This loss of rights is more pronounced for the refugee inasmuch as, unlike other migrants, he or she is constructed as a temporary seeker of refuge who will return in due course.

It is on account of this that repatriation continues to be conceived of as the main solution to refugee crises.[5] The other two solutions in the United Nations High Commission for Refugees (UNHCR) triumvirate of durable solutions require the undertaking of a special process to convert the refugee from a sojourner into an ordinary migrant on the path to shedding their claims to belonging in an old country to acquire citizenship rights in a new one. When such a process is undertaken in the country where refugees are already located, it is called *integration*.[6] When it is done in a third country, it is termed *third country resettlement*.

State practice has worked to subvert even those legal instruments that would free refugees of some of the burdens imposed on them by this understanding of their status. The 1951 Convention Relating to the Status of Refugees defined a refugee in Article 1.A.2 as a person who

As a result of events occurring before 1 January 1951 and owing to well founded fear of being persecuted for reasons of race, religion, nationality, membership of a particular social group or political opinion, is outside the country of his nationality and is unable or, owing to such fear, is unwilling to avail himself of

---

4 Bakewell, "Returning refugees," 1; Nyers, *Rethinking refugees*; I. William Zartman, "Portuguese Guinean refugees in Senegal," in *The internationalization of communal strife*, ed. Manus Midlarsky (London: Routledge, 1992); Bond, "Are refugee camps good for children," 4–5; and Alexandra Fielden, "Local integration: an under reported solution to protracted refugee situations," *New Issues in Refugee Research* 158 (June 2008): 1.

5 Jeff Crisp, "Local integration and local settlement of refugees: a conceptual and historical analysis," *New Issues in Refugee Research* 102 (April 2004): 6; and Naohiko Omata, "Repatriation is not for everyone: the life and livelihoods of former refugees in Liberia," *New Issues in Refugee Research* 213 (June 2011): 1.

6 Many host countries resist local integration, as noted by Samuel Agblorti, "Refugee integration in Ghana: the host community's perspective," *New Issues in Refugee Research* 203 (March 2011): 2.

the protection of that country; or who, not having a nationality and being outside the country of his former habitual residence as a result of such events, is unable or, owing to such fear, is unwilling to return to it.

The 1967 Protocol Relating to the Status of Refugees removed the restriction imposed by the 1951 date in Article 1.2 by extending the definition to all who fit the preceding characteristics. The 1969 Organization of African Unity (OAU) Convention Governing the Specific Aspects of Refugee Problems in Africa, Article 1, further expanded the definition of refugees[7] to include persons fleeing from "external aggression, occupation, foreign domination or events seriously disturbing public order."

The provisions of the Economic Community of West African States (ECOWAS) and the East African Community (EAC) should ordinarily free West and East Africans seeking refuge in countries in their subregions from the debilitating impact of the refugee tag. Unfortunately, many of the rules on free movement and establishment provided for in the rules of these organizations have not been implemented to the point where they can make a difference in the lives of refugees. The May 1979 ECOWAS Protocol on the Free Movement of Persons, Residence, and Establishment was meant to move the subregion toward a situation in which citizens of member states could travel to, reside in, undertake business in, and be employed in other states.[8] By 2007, "only visa free entry for up to 90 days ha[d] been completely implemented in all ECOWAS countries."[9] Sometimes movement requires payment of fees.[10] Despite being ECOWAS citizens, refugees often depended on their status as refugees to enjoy rights of residence in West African host countries.[11]

---

[7] Micah Rankin, "Extending the limits or narrowing the scope: deconstructing the OAU refugee definition thirty years on," *New Issues in Refugee Research* 113 (April 2005): 1; and Marina Sharpe, "Engaging with refugee protection: the Organization of African Unity and African Union since 1963," *New Issues in Refugee Research* 226 (December 2011): 6.

[8] Aderanti Adepoju, Alistair Boulton, and Mariah Levin, "Promoting integration through mobility: free movement and the ECOWAS protocol," *New Issues in Refugee Research* 150 (December 2007): 1. This protocol was buttressed by 1985 Supplementary Protocol A/SP.1/7/85 on the Code of Conduct for the implementation of the Protocol on Free Movement of Persons, the Right of Residence and Establishment; 1989 Supplementary Protocol A/SP.1/6/89 amending and complementing the provisions of Article 7 of the Protocol on Free Movement, Right of Residence and Establishment; and 1990 Supplementary Protocol A/SP.2/5/90 on the Implementation of the Third Phase (Right to Establishment).

[9] Adepoju, Boulton, and Levin, "Promoting integration," 4.

[10] Ibid., 6–7.

[11] Ibid., 15.

Refugees in East Africa do not fare much better than their counterparts in West Africa even today. The Treaty for the Establishment of the East African Community in Article 104 makes provision for progress toward the "free movement of persons, labor and services" and enjoyment of "rights of establishment" by citizens of the community in all member countries. The EAC Common Market Protocol that allows citizens rights to free movement, residence, and establishment was adopted in 2009 and went into effect only in July 2010. However, by the end of that year, "the modalities of [its] implementation remain[ed] unelaborated."[12]

It is within this broad construction of the refugee as someone temporarily seeking refuge who will ultimately return to his or her "own" country that much of the measures that serve to radically disempower refugees are couched. First, the movement of refugees is restricted in many countries. Many countries force refugees to settle in particular areas and require them to have permits to leave camps and settlements.[13] This confinement limits the opportunities refugees can take advantage of, thus stunting their social mobility and power. When refugees move in defiance of these rules, they become vulnerable to police officers and local authorities who can exchange toleration of unapproved refugee movement and settlement for favors and quiescence. Utas writes of female refugees in Guinea having "to provide sexual favors just to pass checkpoints."[14]

Some countries also prevent refugees from working or acquiring real estate. These rules make it hard for refugees to get jobs or buy real estate. They also render those who find jobs or acquire property vulnerable to powerful locals who know their status as refugees and can use threats of its revelation to keep them pliable. Refugees often have to pass as locals to

---

[12] Refugee Studies Center, Oxford University, "Refugee status determination and rights in southern and east Africa," International Workshop Report, Kampala, Uganda, November 16–17, 2010 (December 2010), accessed October 13, 2012, http://www.rsc.ox.ac.uk/events/refugee-status-determination-and-rights/RSDinAfricaWorkshopReport.pdf.

[13] Jacobson, *The economic life of refugees*, p. 7; and Saskia Hoyweghen, "Mobility, territoriality and sovereignty in postcolonial Tanzania," *New Issues in Refugee Research* 49 (October 2001): 1–2; Bakewell, "Refugee aid and protection in rural Africa: working in parallel or cross-purposes," *New Issues in Refugee Research* 35 (March 2001): 3–7; and Susan Banki, "Refugee integration in the intermediate term: a case stud of Nepal, Pakistan and Kenya," *New Issues in Refugee Research* 108 (October 2004): 12 & 16; Refugee Studies Center, Oxford University, "Refugee status determination," 5; Inhetveen, "'Because we are refugees,'" 8; Sarah Dryden-Petersen and Lucy Hovil, "Local integration as a durable solution: refugees, host populations and education in Uganda," *New Issues in Refugee Research* 93 (September 2003): 7; Jacobson, *The economic life of refugees*, 6.

[14] Utas, "West African warscapes," 421.

buy real estate, get jobs, get positions in educational institutions, and so forth. Their passing depends on their prostration at the feet of powerful people who can grant them identity papers or denounce and unmask them as refugees. Laws barring refugees from business activities often tend to force many into the informal sector. Their concentration in this sector, which has been noted by Jacobson,[15] means that they lack the protections and benefits that participation in formal sectors brings.

Similarly, the injunction against refugee participation in the politics of host communities makes it hard for them to organize in pursuit of their interests. Instead, on those occasions when they get involved in local politics, they most often become the instruments of powerful local actors who manipulate them in exchange for paltry favors.

These disempowering effects of the international refugee system would not have meant much in Africa if the much-vaunted weakness of African states and their boundaries were actually true. If the distinction between states and Africans' sense of nationalism were as weak as authors such as Zartman[16] suggest, then crossing international boundaries would have been of little consequence in Africa. However, the often-calumniated African state and its boundaries turn out to be much stronger than is generally suggested. Herbst[17] has made this point, and when one studies refugee situations on the continent, one realizes how strong national identities and borders are. In many of these refugee situations, the "refugee" concept and its various implications are widely deployed by both locals and refugees.[18] African states have deployed many of the mechanisms listed previously, such as those restricting movement, work opportunities, and property ownership against refugees. In addition, they have not automatically granted refugees citizenship rights. People often cite Tanzania's grant of citizenship rights to refugees precisely because it is exceptional.[19]

Civilian refugees are frequently disempowered in Africa as elsewhere, and this disempowerment is a key premise on which this argument is based. Given that they often reinforce the power of the rich and influential, how do we understand the fact that these elites not only occasionally

---

[15] Jacobson, *The economic life of refugees*, 11.

[16] Zartman, "Portuguese Guinean refugees," 144.

[17] Jeffrey Herbst, *States and power in Africa: comparative lessons in authority and control* (Princeton: Princeton University Press, 2000).

[18] I witnessed this during my research in Ghana, Guinea, Sierra Leone, Liberia, Uganda, and Rwanda for this work. Also see Inhetveen, "'Because we are refugees,'" 7.

[19] Harrell-Bond, *Imposing aid*, p. 1. Also see Gaim Kibreab, "Local settlements in Africa: a misconceived option," *Journal of Refugee Studies* 2, No. 4 (1989): 471.

permit the masses in society to attack these refugees but sometimes even lead these attacks? I argue here that we need to respond to this question by focusing on the level of the imaginary, on how people come to conceive of others, and on the roles that knowledge, uncertainty, and doubt play in this process of imagination.

THE STATE'S CHANGING ATTITUDE

The host state's permission and promotion of violence against refugees are a necessary although not sufficient condition for generalized anti-refugee violence by the host population. Refugees do not suffer such generalized violence when the host state offers them protection. It is only when the host state withdraws protection from refugees and promotes attacks against them by painting them as serious threats to the state and host communities that locals launch such anti-refugee assaults.

To protect and administer refugees, states deploy a mix of civilian officials usually under ministries of interior, home affairs, and defense, such as police and gendarmes, officials of national refugee agencies, and the armed forces. Their work often includes running refugee camps, patrolling and setting up bases in refugee-populated areas, and offering humanitarian aid and legal services to refugees.[20] National refugee agencies often work closely with international agencies such as the UNHCR to deal with refugee populations.

It is one thing to claim that states often extend protection to refugees and another to assert, as this book does, that such protection is enough to prevent local populations from undertaking generalized anti-refugee violence. Asserting the second claim needs justification, especially because we are dealing with African countries that are thought to be particularly weak. There is a growing literature that has focused on exploring the weakness of African states.[21] The general impression one gets from this

[20] Margaret Legum, "Problems of asylum for Southern African refugees," in *Refugee problems in Africa*, ed. Sven Hamrell (Uppsala: The Scandinavian Institute of African Studies, 1967), 60; Milner and Christoffersen-Deb, "The militarization," 64; Agblorti, "Refugee integration," 4; Gaim Kibreab, *Ready and willing... but still waiting* (Upsalla: Life and Peace Institute, 1996), 48 & 203; and Robert Muggah and Edward Mogire, "Arms availability and refugee militarization in Africa-conceptualizing the issues," in *No refuge: the crisis of refugee militarization in Africa*, ed. Robert Muggah (London: Zed Books, 2006), 4.

[21] Atul Kohli, *State-directed development: political power and industrialization in the global periphery* (New York: Cambridge University Press, 2004), 9; Robert H. Jackson, *Quasi states: sovereignty international relations and the Third World* (New York:

literature is that many African states lack the capacity to do much beyond the occasional exercise of brute force in areas of their territory. How do we reconcile this idea of the weakness of some African states to the claim that the protection of the state is sufficient to prevent generalized anti-refugee attacks by locals?

I argue that even if African states were weak (and this is a contentious claim that deserves ongoing debate), their offer of protection to refugees would be sufficient to prevent generalized anti-refugee attacks by the local population. We can try to understand this first from the point of view of the state. Here we must distinguish between the state's ability to exercise brute force occasionally against segments of its population and its capacity to manage affairs through routine and sustained bureaucratic interventions in diverse sectors throughout its territory. The first might be equated with what Mann calls the autonomous power of the state and the second with what he calls the infrastructural power of the state.[22] The distinction also partially reflects that drawn by Evans between what he calls predatory and developmental state capacity.[23]

I agree with Evans that even weak African states can wreak serious occasional violence on various segments of the civilian population under their control,[24] and that is the basic level of power the state needs to deter local populations from launching generalized attacks on refugees. The state can use credible threats of violent reprisals to keep a local population from launching generalized attacks on refugees.[25] What this sort of state capacity cannot do is protect refugees from more particularistic attacks and routine abuses. Dealing with these requires what Mann calls infrastructural power.

Cambridge University Press, 1990); Robert H. Bates, *When things fell apart: state failure in late century Africa* (New York: Cambridge University Press, 2008); and Herbst, *States and power*; Merilee Grindle, *Challenging the state: crisis and innovation in Latin America and Africa* (Cambridge: Cambridge University Press, 1996); and William Reno, *Warlord politics and African states* (London: Lynne Reinner, 1998), 26

[22] Michael Mann, "The autonomous power of the state: its origins, mechanisms and results," *European Journal of Sociology* 25 (1984): 185–213.

[23] Peter Evans, *Embedded autonomy: states and industrial transformation* (Princeton: Princeton University Press, 1995), 12.

[24] Evans, *Embedded autonomy*, 45.

[25] This view finds some support in Wilkinson, who comes to a similar conclusion that "Abundant comparative evidence shows that large-scale ethnic rioting does not take place where a state's army or police force is ordered to stop it using all means necessary." Steven Wilkinson, *Votes and violence: electoral competition and ethnic riots in India* (New York: Cambridge University Press, 2004), 5.

We could also look at it from the point of view of social actors seeking to resist the impositions of the state. The works of Scott[26] and Hyden[27] are instructive here. The community is a relatively large entity lacking the ability for quick mobility and concealment. This is unlike the individual in such a community who is a smaller entity possessing a greater capacity for mobility and evasion.[28] Consequently, the individual has a lower capacity to engage in head-on confrontations with the state compared with the community as a whole but possesses a greater capacity for evasive resistance of state impositions. The state's capacity for brutal reprisals is more likely to have a deterrent effect on local communities seeking to launch generalized anti-refugee attacks than on opportunistic attacks by individuals on particular refugees.

Of importance here also is the help that states receive to develop their capacity for caring for and protecting refugees. Such help comes in the form of funds, the provision of logistical support, and personnel training. This support is provided by organizations such as UNHCR as well as foreign states. It often has the effect of creating islands of relative efficiency and capacity in the apparatus of states possessing only autonomous capacity. The help is used to train, pay, and arm police and soldiers involved in dealing with refugees, set up and sustain special bureaucracies involved in the protection and management of refugees, and so forth.[29] This means that even states that demonstrate only autonomous power in most sectors can approximate infrastructural capacity in those key sectors dealing with refugee protection. It is for these reasons that I argue that in areas that are not under the control of other actors such as insurgents, the protection of refugees by the state is enough to prevent large-scale anti-refugee attacks by host communities. It is only in those cases in which the state withdraws protection from refugees and promotes attacks against them that locals can undertake generalized attacks.

The withdrawal of protection and demonization can take verbal or written forms. State leaders often blame refugees for various wrongs

[26] James Scott, *Weapons of the weak* (New Haven: Yale University Press, 1985), xvi–xvii; and James Scott, *Domination and the arts of resistance: hidden transcripts* (New Haven: Yale University Press, 1990), Ch. 2.
[27] Goran Hyden, *Beyond Ujamaa in Tanzania* (London: Heinemann, 1980), 209–210.
[28] Hyden, *Beyond Ujamaa*, 231.
[29] Adelman, "The use and abuse of refugees," 102; Kibreab, *Ready and willing*, 207–208; Edward Mogire, "Preventing or abetting: refugee militarization in Tanzania," in *No refuge: the crisis of refugee militarization in Africa*, ed. Robert Muggah (London: Zed Books, 2006), 164; and Milner with Christoffersen-Deb, "The militarization," 63–74.

in society and instruct the civilian population to crack down on them. Milton Obote's Senior Minister Chris Rwakasisi verbally called for and led the forcible eviction of refugees in southwestern Uganda, painting them as dangerous threats to the country and the local community.[30] In the former Zaire, the government issued a formal order calling for the removal of all Rwandese refugees from the country in 1964 after painting them as representing a serious danger to both the government and local communities.[31] I have already made reference to President Lansana Conte's notorious speech instructing Guineans to gather, interrogate, and expel refugees, whom he accused of collaborating with rebels in early September 2000.[32]

Explaining the Changing Attitude of the State

Why do states extend protection to refugees in some instances but actively promote attacks on them in others? Lansana Conte's fulminations against refugees in 2000 were a marked departure from his earlier stance. In the early 1990s, when refugees from Liberia and Sierra Leone were pouring into Guinea, President Lansana Conte took the lead in advocating the humane treatment of refugees. As one Guinean village official in Yomou Prefecture told me, "The president came to Yomou-Centre and told us to take care of the refugees like our own people. He said we should give them half of whatever we put into our mouths because we are the same people."[33] Many Sierra Leoneans and Liberians, who were formerly refugees in Guéckédou and Yomou prefectures, praised what they saw as Lansana Conte's support for refugees in Guinea.[34]

---

[30] Hamilton, "Human rights in Uganda," 19.

[31] Holborn, *Refugees*, 1093.

[32] Lansana Gberie, "Destabilizing Guinea: diamonds, Charles Taylor and the potential for wider humanitarian catastrophy," *Partnership for Africa Canada Occasional Paper No. 1* (October 2001): 2; and Afol News, "Sierra Leone conflict spills over into Guinea," *Afrol News*, September 14, 2000, accessed August 26, 2010, http://www.afrol.com/News/gui003_conflict_spillover.htm.

[33] Interview with a village official in Dongueta, Yomou Prefecture, Guinea (MRB 212), July 30, 2009.

[34] Interviews with a former Liberian refugee in Gorlu, Salayea District, Liberia (MRB 310), September 25, 2009; a former Liberian refugee in Forofonye, Yomou Prefecture, Guinea (MRB 189), July 27, 2009; a former Sierra Leonean refugee in Kamiendor, Mafindor Chiefdom, Sierra Leone (MRB 220), September 3, 2009; and a former Liberian refugee in Gorlu, Salayea District, Liberia (MRB 319), September 27, 2009.

Drawing insight from Mamdani and Mushemeza,[35] I argue that whether states offer or withdraw protection from refugees is dependent on whether or not some of the refugees get linked to major opposition groups. State officials normally offer protection to refugees for various reasons that I discuss later. They only withdraw protection from and promote attacks on refugees when sections of refugee populations are associated with groups that pose a real threat to the host government. These opposition groups may be civilian groups or armed movements. Refugees' links to these groups may take the form of a few refugees joining an armed movement or of refugees participating in campaigns and voting for parties that pose a serious threat to the power of state leaders.

Whichever of these forms it takes, states seize on these links between a few refugees and major opposition movements to crack down on whole refugee populations partly because the violent expulsion and repression of refugees become punitive and reformative tools. Furthermore, the focus and crackdown on refugees become a way of delegitimizing national opposition forces by painting them as foreign invaders or the pawns of foreign refugees. Also, states can seize on links between refugees and opposition groups to expel citizens belonging to opposition groups under the guise of expelling refugees. Thus the expulsion of refugees should not always be seen as an effort by the state to get rid of foreigners of which it is genuinely scared. Sometimes it is more the use of these foreigners to target and get rid of nationals it is worried about.

Refugees must be involved in opposition politics, and the opposition groups with which they are involved must pose a significant threat to the state. States do not withdraw their protection from refugees just because they are involved in local politics in the host country. Refugees can and are sometimes involved in the politics of their host countries without incurring the wrath of the state as long as they do not go against the interests of state leaders. In fact, it is often the state that involves refugees in politics. In the 1990s, a few of the Sierra Leonean and Liberian refugees in cities such as Macenta, Guéckédou, and N'Zérékoré in the Forest Region of Guinea participated in political rallies during elections. Some even voted and participated in election riots. Many refugees and Guineans

[35] Mamdani, "The political diaspora," 315; and Mamdani, *When victims become killers*, 164; and Elijah Mushemeza, *Banyarwanda refugees in Uganda 1959–2001* (Kampala: Fountain Press, 2007), 90–97.

I interviewed attested to this.[36] Many also pointed out that they were brought into these activities by ruling party officials.[37] A *chef de quartier* in the town of Macenta confirmed all of this in an interview.[38]

Similarly, it is worth noting that the involvement of refugees in military activities on its own does not provoke the withdrawal of state protection. Militarization has been cited as an explanation of generalized anti-refugee violence by at least one scholar.[39] The argument here would be that when refugees militarize, they often draw hostile action against the area in which they have settled from the targets of their militarization, which could be the government of the host country, that of their home country or other rebel groups.[40] The damage inflicted on these areas by such attacks adversely affects the local population. At some point, one might expect the host state, which is fed up with these attacks, to violently crack down on refugees with the goal of either expelling them altogether or suppressing their military activities.

However, an examination of the literature shows that one thing the militarization of refugees certainly cannot do well is explain hostility toward refugees by the host state. The militarization of refugees is very often either encouraged and actively supported or tolerated by states. Frequently, militarized refugees are foreign policy instruments of host states.[41] Because of this, governments and local communities are often willing to pay the very high price that comes with military activities by

[36] Interviews with a former refugee in Diécké, Yomou Prefecture, Guinea (MRB 1) December 17, 2008; a Guinean in Diécké, Yomou Prefecture, Guinea (MRB 2), December 17, 2008; a Guinean in Guéckédou Centre, Guéckédou Prefecture, Guinea (MRB 22), December 11, 2008; a former refugee in Guéckédou Centre, Guinea (MRB 28), December 12, 2008; a former refugee in Guéckédou Centre, Guinea (MRB 30), December 12, 2008; a Guinean in Guéckédou Centre (MRB 52), December 10, 2008; a former refugee in Guéckédou Centre (MRB 54) December 11, 2008; a former refugee in Guéckédou Centre (MRB 55), December 11, 2008; and a former refugee in Guéckédou Centre (MRB 56), December 11, 2008.

[37] Interviews with a former refugee in Macenta Centre, Guinea (MRB 36), December 13, 2008; and a former refugee in Macenta Centre, Guinea (MRB 45), December 12, 2008.

[38] Interview with *chef de quartier* in Macenta Centre, Guinea (MRB 43), December 14, 2008.

[39] Frederic Grare, "The geopolitics of Afghan refugees," in *Refugee manipulation: war, politics, and the abuse of human suffering*, ed. Stephen Stedman and Fred Tanner (Washington, DC: Brookings Institution Press, 2003), 65.

[40] Chambers, "Hidden losers?" 255; and Holborn, *Refugees*, 1233–1234.

[41] McGovern, "Conflit regional," 87; Lischer, *Dangerous sanctuaries*, 54–56 & 84–87; Milner and Christofferssen-Deb, "The militarization," 59; Arieff, "Still standing," 340; Crawford Young and Thomas Turner, *The rise and decline of the Zairian state* (Madison: University of Wisconsin Press, 1985), 253–254; Mogire, "Preventing or abetting," 147; International Crisis Group, "Stopping Guinea's slide," *ICG Africa Report* No. 94 (June

refugees. Two such examples are Guinea's willingness to bear the high costs of supporting Liberian refugees militarized under the groups United Liberation Movement for Democracy in Liberia (ULIMO) and Liberians United for Reconciliation and Democracy (LURD)[42] and Zaire's stubborn insistence on supporting militarized Angolan refugees under the umbrella of the Union of Peoples of Angola and the National Liberation Front of Angola.[43]

The pursuit of military activities hostile to the interests of host government has indeed led to friction between refugees and their host governments and communities. As I explain in Chapter 6, the support of Rwandan Tutsi refugee elements for the Lumumbist rebellions in eastern Zaire was responsible for Mobutu's expulsion of Tutsi refugees from Zaire in 1964.[44] However, it is important to note that this was not the effect of militarization per se, but the goals of the militarization. This is then very much in line with my argument about how links between refugees and major opposition movements motivate governments to instigate violence against refugees.

State withdrawal of protection from and promotion of attacks on refugees is a rare phenomenon. This is a somewhat controversial claim to make given the literature on the political uses of disorder by African politicians. This literature portrays civil and international conflict across Africa as often the deliberate products of politicians who are interested in drawing political and economic gains from the resultant disorder. Because violent attacks on refugees have the potential for producing disorder, why do state leaders engage in them so rarely?

State interest in protecting refugees stems from a series of factors. The protection of refugees is a strong norm that is actively advocated by various national groups and organizations as well as international institutions such as UNHCR. Its violation usually comes at some cost to the national and international legitimacy of the violating government.

2005), 18, 21; Human Rights Watch, "Liberian refugees in Guinea: refoulement, militarization of camps, and other protection concerns," *Human Rights Watch Report* 14 (November 2002): 2, 10, 19–22; and Amos Sawyer, "Violent conflicts and governance challenges in West Africa: the case of the Mano River Basin area," *Journal of Modern African Studies* 42 (3–2004): 450.

[42] Human Rights Watch, "Liberian refugees in Guinea," 10; and McGovern, "Conflict régional," 92–94.

[43] Zolberg, Suhrke, and Aguayo, *Escape from violence*, 77; Bustin, "The Congo," 185; Holborn, *Refugees*, 969; and Rene Lemarchand, "Historical setting," in *Zaire: a country study*, ed. Sandra Meditz and Tim Merrill (Washington, DC: 1993), 247–266.

[44] Lemarchand, *Rwanda and Burundi*, 214.

However, of greater importance is the fact that hosting and protecting refugees come along with many political and economic benefits for host states and government officials.[45] Humanitarian aid for refugees usually pours in, enriching officials who are linked with the government.[46] State and humanitarian officials sometimes siphon off some of this aid. The delivery of such aid usually requires the construction and improvement of roads and bridges by humanitarian agencies. Such work on roads, wells, schools, and clinics increases the legitimacy of states by providing services accessible to local populations that states may not have ordinarily provided but for which they can take some credit.[47] More importantly, it aids the extension of state power and extractive capabilities by allowing the state to use these new roads to project its power into remote areas.[48] Aid agencies' funding and support for state security presence in refugee-populated areas for protection reasons also furthers along this projection of state power.[49] Fergusson makes a similar point in his interesting analysis of the workings and effects of development projects in Lesotho.[50]

State leaders also offer protection to refugees because they can use them in domestic and international struggles. Politicians occasionally try to mobilize refugees to vote. Earlier, I discussed such a scenario in Guinea under the reign of President Lansana Conte. Some have pointed out that President Siad Barre of Somalia was eager to welcome and protect ethnic Somali Ethiopian refugees fleeing conflict in the Ogaden because their clan – the Ogaden clan – is related to the Marehan clan of Siad Barre. They were, therefore, thought to be politically supportive of Siad Barre.[51] More commonly discussed is the role that state leaders put refugees to in domestic and international military confrontations. As pointed out previously, states often actively encourage and support the militarization of sections of a refugee community that they then deploy against domestic and international foes.

---

[45] Kibreab, *Ready and willing*, 205; and Arieff, "Still standing," 339; Fielden, "Local integration," 3.
[46] Jeff Crisp, "Africa's refugees: patterns, problems and policy changes," *New Issues in Refugee Research* 28 (August 2000): 5.
[47] Arieff, "Still standing," 339.
[48] Arieff, "Still standing," 339.
[49] Mogire, "Preventing or abetting," 164; and Milner with Christoffersen-Deb, "The militarization," 65–67.
[50] James Ferguson, *The anti-politics machine : 'development,' depoliticization, and bureaucratic power in Lesotho* (Minneapolis: University of Minnesota Press, 1994).
[51] Gaim Kibreab, "The myth of dependency among camp refugees in Somalia 1979–1989," *Journal of Refugee Studies* 6 (4–1993): 322.

The hosting and protection of refugees often also involve significant costs that include the potential lowering of some wages, inflation of prices for some goods, deforestation, subversion of local food economies through the massive importation of food aid, and so forth.[52] However, usually these costs are not borne by key state officials or their allies.[53] They fall disproportionately on the less powerful and less well-connected members of society who have little influence over national refugee policy.[54] Therefore, these costs do not have much of an influence on state policy.

THE RESPONSE OF LOCAL COMMUNITIES

The withdrawal of protection from and demonization of refugees by state authorities do not necessarily doom refugees to generalized attacks at the hands of the local civilian population. Although some communities respond to the state's campaign against refugees with attacks, others do not. Some even seek to protect refugees from attacks by state authorities and sections of the local population that might be tempted to join the state's violent project. What explains this variation in how locals respond to the withdrawal of state protection?

Knowledge, Uncertainty, and Anti-Refugee Violence

State leaders justify their promotion of attacks on refugees by charging them with serious crimes against the state and local population. The impact of these charges is only magnified by the fact that they are typically made in times of grave crises. Communities embrace the state's project where local elites know very little about the lives of the refugee population. In such a situation, some might believe in the state's demonization of the refugees. They join the state's project in a bid to keep refugees from perpetrating the evils of which the state accuses them. Some elites may not entirely believe the state's account but will still succumb to a fear of the unknown, resulting from uncertainty about the lives of the refugees. This will spur them into embracing the state's project.

These are usually times of crises when choices can have far-reaching consequences for the security of communities. Faced with uncertainty,

---

[52] Leah Berry, "The impact of environmental degradation on refugee-host relations: a case study from Tanzania," *New Issues in Refugee Research* 151 (January 2008): 1.

[53] Kibreab, *Ready and willing*, 205.

[54] Whitaker, "Refugees in Western Tanzania," 341.

local elites could reject the anti-refugee appeals of the state. This will put them at risk of suffering serious and sometimes fatal harm if the state happens to be right about the subversive activities of the refugees. Alternatively, local elites could go along with the state's violent anti-refugee project. It may well be that the refugees are innocent of the accusations, but attacking them ensures that if the state were right in its accusations, the threats posed by the refugees would not materialize.

One option maximizes the chance of elites' not harming the refugees and the other the chance of harm not befalling local communities. People usually go along with the state and attack the refugee just in case the state happens to be right. Furthermore, these elites, even when they happen to be exceptionally well-meaning, are very much unlikely to stake their reputations on protecting refugees about whom they know little because of possible repercussions in the event of state accusations turning out to be true.

When locals know a lot about the refugees, they are unlikely to buy into the state's propaganda. They will not be motivated to attack the refugees on account of uncertainty over what they represent. Furthermore, when they are very confident about the refugees, they might even act to protect the refugees if they can get away with it.

Some poor and powerless people in society are almost always disposed to buying into the state's violent project. Usually they are the ones whose economic and political interests are harmed the most by the presence of the refugees. These are often the people who suffer from the inflationary effect of the arrival of refugees and their accompanying humanitarian apparatus on the economy. They are the ones whose wages are undercut by the massive inflow of refugee labor. They are also the most likely to suffer from the pressure put on land by large numbers of refugees. State officials further motivate people to act on these grievances by promising them the properties abandoned by fleeing refugees. "Drive them away and you can take their property" is usually a refrain heard in these situations.

My contention is that the response of these sections of the masses to the proposition of the state depends on the signals sent by local notables. When the masses see local notables staying away from, frowning on, and denouncing anti-refugee violence, they will not join in the attacks because they fear local elites. Thus in the society in which local elites know a lot about refugees, the local population will not go along with the state's call for undiscriminating attacks on refugees. The local elites will be unwilling to attack the refugees and the sections of the masses tempted to do so will be unable to because of their fear of local elites.

In societies in which locals elites have little information about the daily lives of refugees, the masses will receive a different signal. They will see their local leaders embracing and participating in the attacks and doing nothing to discourage the violence or protect refugees. Encouraged by the state and unconstrained or even further encouraged by their local notables, the masses will go on the attack against refugees. Indeed, local elites might order, organize, and arm the masses to attack refugees.

This causal story is based on a view of society that privileges the ability of local elites to exercise significant control over local populations, even in situations in which the state seeks to break this control. It is tempting to see this as particularly suited to analyzing African states, whose ability to project their power and influence into local communities is under much doubt.[55] However, there is a more fundamental point here about how societies, understood as subaltern spaces under pressure from state officials, can shield themselves from state influence and enforce compliance with local rules.

Local elites can employ what Scott called "social control and surveillance from below"[56] to exert significant influence on the masses in their community. This is particularly so when it only involves dissuading action by locals and does not require face-to-face armed confrontation with the state. Having less in the way of coercive force and economic power compared with the state, the weapons through which this policing is done includes "slander, character assassination, gossip, rumor, public gestures of contempt, shunning, curses, backbiting, outcasting."[57] All of these work by denting the reputation, on which well-being is heavily dependent in many of these communities. As Scott noted, "A peasant household held in contempt by their fellow villagers will find it impossible to exchange harvest labor, to borrow a draft animal, to raise a small loan, to marry their children off, to prevent petty thefts of their grain or livestock, or even to bury their dead with any dignity."[58]

The heavy emphasis on the damaging of reputations should not lead us to underplay the deployment of more coercive measures. Policing techniques can include physical attacks. The leaders in these communities can

---

[55] Joel Migdal, *Strong societies and weak state: state-society relations and state capabilities in the Third World* (Princeton, NJ: Princeton University Press, 1988); Hyden, *Beyond Ujamaa*; Jackson, *Quasi states*; Bates, *When things fell apart*; and Herbst, *States and power*; and Grindle, *Challenging the state*.

[56] Scott, *Domination and the arts*, 129.

[57] Ibid., 131.

[58] Ibid., 131.

withhold justice from those seen as deviating from social norms. I have cited elsewhere how chiefs in colonial southern Ghana coerced potential defectors from a cocoa hold-up against European buyers. They refrained from punishing those accused of committing adultery with the spouses of the defectors. Chiefs also used traditional oaths to enforce compliance in that case.[59]

Also, elites in these societies often have privileged access to resources on which the masses depend. They can use this control to influence the behavior of the masses. Peasants, for example, might be wary of offending notables on whose land they sharecrop. It is for all of these reasons that I hold that the masses in these societies pay a lot of attention to signals sent by their local notables, even when these deviate from the orders of the state.

This argument draws significantly from the works of Appadurai, Hoffman, and Bauman,[60] who have all reflected on the possible contributions of uncertainty and doubt to violence. Appadurai's reflection on the links between uncertainty and "violence involving neighbors, friends, and kinsmen"[61] is particularly relevant here. He noted how globalization creates "a new order of uncertainty in social life" impinging on the meaning of certain "identity monikers," the size and activities of certain groups, and general suspicion over whether people are "what they really claim or appear to be or have historically been."[62] It is within this context that certain forms of violence become a form of "folk discovery-procedure"[63] aimed at detecting, unmasking, and getting to know in the most intimate manner the other.[64]

Next I provide an account of how the structures of some societies deal with refugees in ways that tend to facilitate the flow of information about their daily lives to locals and so work to reduce uncertainty about refugees. I also show how the structures of other societies stymie the flow of information about them to local elites and work to further increase local uncertainty over what refugees represent. It is these local structures

[59] Ato Onoma, *The politics of property rights institutions in Africa* (Cambridge University Press, 2009), 133.

[60] Arjun Appadurai, "Dead certainty: ethnic violence in the era of globalization," *Public Culture* 10 (2–1998); Piotr Hoffman, *Doubt, time, violence* (Chicago: The University of Chicago Press, 1986); and Bauman, *Postmodernity.*

[61] Appadurai, "Dead certainty," 227.

[62] Ibid., 229.

[63] Ibid., 229.

[64] Ibid., 231.

and their impact on uncertainty about refugees that explain the attitudes of local elites toward refugees.

The Subjugation and Autonomy of Refugees

Everyone's stranger is his first son.[65]

They were like our sons.[66]

I want to argue here that in communities where refugees are subjugated to local elites, these notables acquire a lot of knowledge about the daily lives of refugees. It is in those communities where they live autonomously of local notables that they come to represent black boxes and unknown quantities to locals. To understand the distinction between autonomous and subjugated refugees, we can revert to the stories of the Kamara siblings in Conakry and of the Nowai in the Forest Region of Guinea in the initial pages of Chapter 1. Nowai was a subjugated refugee. The Kamara siblings were autonomous ones.

The distinction I draw here between subjugated and autonomous refugees hinges on three important components: (1) the performance of symbolic acts of submission by the refugee to a local notable; (2) the assumption by the local of some legal responsibility for the acts of the refugee, and (3) the frequent exchange of gifts between the refugee and the host. The situation of subjugated refugees is marked by these components. The situation of autonomous refugees is characterized by the absence of these components. I deal with these next.

Symbolic submission: The performance of symbolic acts of subjugation to their host is one of the main defining characteristics of subjugated refugees. This starts with the seeking of a relationship with the host. This can take various forms. Sometimes refugees verbally ask for a relationship with a local: "Please can you be my friend so that I can live with you here?" At other times refugees approach the task through nonverbal means. They may visit the local person frequently and hang around her place, bring her gifts, and help her do farm and domestic work. After a while, a relationship begins. Sometimes, the local person, after noting the overtures of the refugee, will make a verbal request for a

---

[65] Interview with a farmer in Gotoye, Yomou Prefecture, Guinea (MRB 160), July 22, 2009.
[66] Interview with a Guinean in Gotoye, Yomou Prefecture, Guinea (MRB 378), July 12, 2011.

relationship: "You are a very nice person. I want you to be my son/daughter/friend."

The refugee also performs submission by consulting the local person on a regular basis on things going on in her life. When the refugee wants to move to another part of the host country or return to his home country, he informs the host and symbolically seeks her approval. For example, "Madam, you are the one who kept us here as your children. Now we hear the war in our country is over so we would like to go home." When refugees have children, they may name the children after the host or a relative of the host. Refugees may also send their kids to live with the locals for a while. This is not because the refugee cannot care for her kids. It is meant to be a sign of trust and friendship. When distance allows, the refugee will make sure to go to the host's house every morning to greet the host and ask if there is anything she can do for the host.

Autonomous refugees do not symbolically submit themselves to locals. Sometimes they have few relations with locals. Where they develop relationships, it is usually devoid of symbolic submission by the refugees.

The sharing of legal responsibility: One of the key characteristics of the relationship between refugees and the elites to whom they are subjugated is the phenomenon of shared legal responsibility for the actions of the refugee. The refugee does not bear full legal responsibility for his actions. Once the refugee subjugates himself to the local person, that person is supposed to introduce him to the leaders in the community. The local person then becomes, in the eyes of the community, the "owner" of the refugee. She assumes ultimate responsibility for the actions of the refugee. When the refugee offends someone, that person can go straight to the host to complain. More importantly, he or she can seek compensation and apologies from the host for the actions of the refugee. The authorities can even punish the host for the actions of the refugee. The refugee in a sense becomes like an extension of the host. Just as one must pay compensation when one's child destroys part of someone's farm, one is also held responsible when one's "refugee/stranger" tramples someone's rice or steals someone's property. This does not mean that the refugee escapes punishment for all his activities, but where aggrieved parties sense that refugees cannot make recompense for wrongs, they can legally hold the hosts of the refugees accountable.

Local elites do not bear legal responsibility for the activities of autonomous refugees. These refugees are often fully responsible for their activities.

The exchange of gifts: The frequent exchange of gifts is another important component of the relationship between a subjugated refugee and local.

The sorts of gifts exchanged vary and depend on the specific endowments of the parties involved. Very often, locals offer refugees accommodation and land parcels to temporarily cultivate or graze cattle on. These parcels are usually free of charge. Others enter into sharecropping arrangements with "their" refugees. Some locals grant refugees the rights to gather sticks, medicinal plants, palm fronds, wood and wild foods on their lands. Locals also give food free of charge to refugees or give them plantations that they can work and survive on for the duration of their stay in an area. Furthermore, hosts may help the refugees to find employment. When refugees have social events such as funerals and naming and marriage ceremonies, they can depend on their hosts for some support.

This giving of gifts is not a one-way affair, and some refugees give just as much as they receive from their hosts. One of the most common things that refugees offer to locals is labor. Usually after losing a lot of their properties as a result of their flight, labor is one of the few things refugees have to offer. This labor is often totally free or highly subsidized. Sometimes the refugee goes to the local person and offers free labor. After the day's work, the local usually gives the refugee food anyway. At other times an informal arrangement comes into existence in which the refugee works for a local who then decides what to give the refugee at the end of the day. This usually guarantees the local highly subsidized labor.

Even when there are labor arrangements, locals end up taking care of refugee guests like their children or clients instead of just giving them the agreed-on payment. Refugees help with cultivation, herding cattle, doing domestic chores, building houses, and so forth. Skilled refugees also provide other services such as sharpening the knives and machetes of their hosts, setting traps, cutting palm kernel, and building houses for their hosts. More endowed refugees offer other things including milk, butter, goats, and even cows.

These sorts of routine exchanges of gifts do not exist between autonomous refugees and local elites. Relations of exchange, where they exist, are market ones involving the selling and buying of labor, goods, and services.

The relations between subjugated refugees and their hosts constitute only part of long-standing modes of dealing with strangers in many African communities. Scholars such as Dorjahn and Fyfe, Brooks, McGovern, Shack, and Bledsoe,[67] who study West Africa seem to have done the most in analyzing these relations. However, there is evidence

---

[67] I list only a few of these works here because of space constraints. V.R. Dorjahn and Christopher Fyfe, "Landlord and stranger: change in tenancy relations in Sierra Leone," *Journal of African History* 3 (3–1962): 391–397; George Brooks, *Landlords*

that they existed in other areas of the continent. Colson's[68] analysis of relations between locals and strangers among the Tonga of Zambia bears an uncanny resemblance to accounts of stranger–host relations by some of the West Africanist scholars just listed.

Historically, these stranger–host relations went beyond the three elements listed earlier to include the establishment of fictive kinship relations, intermarriages, and other rites of incorporation. Through these mechanisms, many of these strangers and their descendants eventually became rights-bearing indigenes. This is a very rich literature that is worth exploring on its own account. Because of its wealth, I have desisted from going into much detail on it. I limit myself to the three elements highlighted earlier because these are the elements that are significant to the causal story that I tell here.

Because of the international refugee regime's tendency to transform refugees into sojourners that I comment on previously, many of the elements that worked earlier to transform migrants into indigenes do not seem to have characterized the refugee–host relations that I studied. Colson pointed to the ability of Tonga communities to transform a settler into a native with "the same right as the native-born to die and be buried in its soil without pollution to the earth" in as little as a year.[69] However, many Banyarwanda refugees stayed in Uganda for more than thirty years without shedding their refugee status and promptly repatriated as the Rwandan Patriotic Front conquered Rwanda in the early 1990s.

Refugees interact with the local elite to whom they are subjugated in ways that maximize the amount of knowledge these notables have about them. The performance of symbolic subjugation and the frequent exchange of gifts serve the important function of laying bare the lives of the refugees to their local hosts. Daily visits, living and working in close proximity, frequent consultation of hosts, and deep involvement of local elite in the lives of the refugees give notables extensive insight into the

---

and strangers: ecology, society, and trade in Western Africa, 1000–1630 (Boulder: Westview Press, 1993); McGovern, "Unmasking the state"; William Shack, "Introduction," in William Shack and Elliott Skinner eds. *Strangers in African societies* (Berkeley: University of California Press, 1979); and Michael McGovern, "Negotiation of displacement in southeastern Guinea, West Africa," *Africa Today* 45 (July–December 1998): 307–321; and Caroline Bledsoe, *Women and marriage in Kpelle society* (Stanford: Stanford University Press, 1980).

[68] Elizabeth Colson, "The assimilation of aliens among Zambian Tonga," in *From tribe to nation: studies in incorporation processes*, ed. Ronald Cohen and John Middleton (Scranton, PA: Chandler Publishing Company, 1970).

[69] Colson, "The assimilation of aliens," 36.

lives and activities of refugees. It radically reduces the level of uncertainty that local notables might have about the refugees.

The phenomenon of shared legal responsibility has an even more critical effect on the strikingly different extents to which locals know refugees. The refugee's constant process of unmasking himself or herself before the host is critical to the working of the system of shared legal responsibility, which is absent when refugees are autonomous of local elites. Refugees know they need to open their lives to locals to increase their chances of being accepted as guests. Locals often will not agree to host refugees who are reputed to be thieves or constant lawbreakers. When they know little about refugees, some locals will ask for a probationary period to observe refugees before agreeing to a proposition to become a host. Locals know they need to keep close tabs on refugees to avoid the significant costs of having a bad stranger. Locals have been known to formally cut ties with refugees who are constant troublemakers. Convincing a local that one is not a troublemaker requires the refugee to show his or her good character to the host.

Autonomous refugees often have relations with some locals, but these horizontal relations do not facilitate the systematic and highly invasive scrutiny by local notables that partly defines the relationship of subjugation. Subjugated refugees are called on day in and day out to bare themselves in front of their local patrons in ways that autonomous refugees are not.

Residence and Indigeneity-Privileging Societies

So why are some refugee populations subjugated to local elites whereas others live autonomous of these notables? I argue that this is the effect of the institutional structure of the society in which refugee populations settle. Refugees tend to be subjugated to local elites when they settle in indigeneity-privileging societies. However, when they settle in residence-privileging areas, they tend to live autonomous of local elites. Next I define and demonstrate the effects of these two types of societies on how refugees relate to local elites.

Rights-Based Institutional Definitions
Scholars who work on citizenship and identity often draw a distinction between two types of societies. In a piece he did for the Council for the Development of Social Science Research in Africa (CODESRIA) on the crisis in Kivu, Mamdani dwells in very clear terms on this dichotomy

when he reflects on "two radically different" ways of defining belonging: "a more inclusive basis of rights" based on residence in a territory and a more restrictive one based on "origins."[70] This is a distinction that informs his other works such as *Citizen and Subject* and *When Victims Become Killers*. Geschiere and Nyamnjoh drew a similar distinction between two orientations to space and belonging in Cameroon where a 1972 constitution privileged residence in the definition of citizenship. It declared that "Everyone has the right to settle in any place and to move about freely. . . . No one shall be harassed because of his origins."[71] Opposed to this was a series of laws and state practices in the 1990s that made indigeneity paramount in the allocation of rights. They installed ethnic origins as the key determinant of the right to contest polls in an area[72] by requiring elected bodies to "reflect the sociological components" of an area.[73]

In his frequent denunciations of what he terms "nativism," Mbembe similarly distinguishes understandings of Africanity that privilege residence on the continent and those that privilege indigeneity and race.[74] This is a distinction that informs the work of many other authors, including Cueppens, Meyer, Geschiere, and Nyamnjoh.[75]

The residence-privileging society *does* distinguish between those who belong and those who do not. However, this differentiation is done on the basis of residence instead of indigeneity, ethnic origins, and ancestry. All residents belong, regardless of their origins. This is in stark contrast to the indigeneity-privileging one, which territorializes the individual. In such a society, tropes of indigeneity and ancestry displace residence as organizing principles for according rights. It is on account of this that Mbembe described the organizing principle behind such a society as an "ideology of difference par excellence."[76] This territorialization of the individual is nicely captured in the comment of a local of North Sulawesi, Indonesia, on internally displaced people who had settled in his community. "Everyone

70　Mahmood Mamdani, "Understanding the crisis in Kivu: Report of the Codesria Mission to the Democratic Republic of Congo September, 1997" (Text report to be submitted to the General Assembly of the Council for the development of Social research in Africa [CODESRIA] in Dakar, Senegal, December 14–18, 1998).

71　Cited in Geschiere and Nyamnjoh, "Capitalism and autochthony," 429.

72　Geschiere and Nyamnjoh, "Capitalism and autochthony," 429.

73　Ibid., 430.

74　Mbembe, "African modes of self-writing," 241.

75　Meyer and Geschiere, "Globalization and identity"; Geschiere, *The perils of belonging*; Nyamnjoh, "Concluding reflections"; and Nyamnjoh, *Insiders and outsiders*.

76　Mbembe, "Ways of seeing," 3.

in Indonesia has a homeland and they [the internally displaced people] must return there, they cannot live on someone else's land or eventually there will be conflict."[77]

The indigeneity-privileging society does not have to be conceptualized in the terms used by the nativist of North Sulawesi as one that should be devoid of "strangers." Non-natives can reside and exercise rights in such a society. However, these rights are seen as derivative in the sense that they are fragments hewn from the primary rights that only natives possess. For example, strangers might well be allowed to access land rights in such a society, but this will be on the understanding that they are secondary to and derived from the primary land rights of natives who play the role of landlords.

The distinction between native and stranger in the indigeneity-privileging society has to be understood in all its senses. The fact that one can reside in such a society all one's life and still not belong is one implication of boundary making in the indigeneity-privileging society. Another is the fact that even birth in an area or the birth of someone's grandparents in an area does not confer rights to belonging.[78] This relies on deeper notions of origins and ancestry. Also, one can belong to a place without being born in or having ever lived or visited there as long as one is defined as a member of the indigenous group that "owns" the place.

I use the word *trope* deliberately earlier to describe indigeneity, autochthony, and ancestry as the organizing principles in the indigeneity-privileging society. They are tropes in the sense of being metaphorical devices used to create and divide communities through the embellishment and invention of boundaries. The "indigenous" and "stranger" communities in these indigeneity-privileging societies are by no means pure and completely bounded ones or "uncontaminated survivals," to use Glissant's terminology.[79] Much has been done to unmask the mythical nature of claims of pure and bounded cultures and the hybrid nature of all cultures.[80] Glissant is pioneering in going beyond this to note the need to even move beyond the view of cultures as the end product of

[77] Quoted in Christopher Duncan, "Unwelcome guests: relations between internally displaces persons and their hosts in North Sulawesi, Indonesia," *Journal of Refugee Studies* 18, No. 1 (2005): 40.

[78] Geschiere and Nyamnjoh, "Capitalism and autochthony," 437.

[79] Edouard Glissant, *Caribbean discourse: selected essays* (Charlottesville: University Press of Virginia, 1989), 14.

[80] McGovern, "Unmasking the state"; Lionel Caplan, "Creole world, purist rhetoric: Anglo-Indian cultural debates in colonial and contemporary Madras," *Journal of the Royal Anthropological Institute* 1 (December 1995): 744; Charles Steward, "Syncretism

mixture; as "being fixed."[81] He advocates seeing cultures more in terms of the *process* of mixture itself. As he rightly observed, asserting the hybrid character of identities is not to "define a category that will by its very nature be opposed to other categories ('pure' cultures)." It is to "deconstruct in this way the category of the 'creolized' that is considered as halfway between two 'pure' extremes."[82] This is what Diagne called a "desubstantiation" of cultural identity and difference.[83]

There are always ongoing flows and interactions between strangers and natives in the indigeneity-privileging society. This means that invoked clear-cut distinctions are social fabrications. The pure and completely bounded indigenous or stranger community is, to borrow the words of Jeyifo, a "discursive construct without a real-world referent."[84] We need to understand such differentiations as exercises in *building* instead of describing communities.[85]

The process of differentiating between natives and strangers in the indigeneity-privileging society is a very political exercise. It creates and draws lines between communities using instruments that are far less obvious and "natural" than the rhetorical emphasis on origins and ancestry suggests. As demonstrated by Jackson in his analysis of discourses of autochthony in Kivu, the Democratic Republic of Congo, the language in which these claims are couched is permeated with "ambiguities." It is "slippery, nervous and paranoid,"[86] with many "autochthonous" groups readily recognizing the pygmy population as original residents.[87] The paranoia associated with this discourse of indigeneity is partly the result of the multiple uses to which the instrument lends itself. The "indigene" who uses autochthony to exclude others today might find himself or herself the victim of this weapon wielded by "more native" people, who

---

and its synonyms: reflections on cultural mixture," *Diacritics* 9 (Autumn 1999): 41; and Nyamnjoh, "Concluding reflections," 29–30.

[81] Glissant, *Caribbean discourse*, 14.

[82] Ibid., 140.

[83] Souleymane Bachir Diagne, "Keeping Africanity open," *Public Culture* 14 (Fall 2002): 621.

[84] Biodun Jeyifo, "Whose theatre, whose Africa? Wole Soyinka's *The Road* on the road," *Modern Drama* 45 (Fall 2002): 450.

[85] Caplan, "Creole world," 754–55.

[86] Stephen Jackson, "Sons of which soil? Language and politics of autochthony in eastern DR Congo," *African Studies Review* 49 (September 2006): 111.

[87] Jackson, "Sons of which soil?" 112–112.

upon further research "uncover" that the original bearer is a "fake."[88] And as Geschiere documented, such differentiations can happen even among members of very minute communities lacking discernible difference in origins.[89]

The nudge toward a residence-privileging society is usually the effect of a combination of two factors. One is a history of extensive migration to an area. However, this flow of migrants is not sufficient. Such migrants can be held as "strangers" with temporary and conditional rights by groups claiming indigeneity and autochthony for a long period of time. The mere fact of coexistence and even mixture of groups of diverse origins in an area does not confer equal rights on them. This is because such a focus on mixture does not really tackle the question of rights. It does not reflect on the issue of power and its exercise in the ongoing production and performance of cultures.[90]

State efforts at granting and/or enforcing the rights of migrants serve as the decisive factor in transitions from indigeneity to residence-privileging societies. This reinforcement of the rights of new arrivals in a community covers two primary areas. These are the ability to hold political office in an area and access to land rights. The state can move society in a residency-privileging direction by divorcing access to land rights and the ability to hold political office from questions of indigeneity.

The state also can and has often played a major role in pushing society in the opposite direction. In much of Africa, the advent of colonial rule coincided with the dissection of territories into ethnic homelands to which groups were tied. Each homeland belonged to an autochthonous group that had customary rights in the area. People were considered strangers in all other ethnic homelands outside of theirs.[91] The British system of indirect rule has thus been termed an "ethnic federation" by Mamdani.[92] Even the French were later to shift in the 1920s and 1930s from the universalist (and ethnocentric, as "The French" was set up as the universal "good") system of assimilating all in their realm to what they termed an

---

[88] Geschiere, *The perils of belonging*, 90.

[89] Ibid., 89.

[90] Paul Tiyambe Zeleza, *Rethinking Africa's 'globalization': Volume 1* (Trenton: Africa World Press, 2003), 392; and Caplan, "Creole world," 744.

[91] Mamdani, *When victims become killers*, 24–31; Mamdani, "Understanding the crisis"; Mahmood Mamdani, "Political identity," 6–11; and Jackson, "Sons of which soil?" 98.

[92] Mamdani, "Political identity," 6.

acceptance of cultural difference under the system of association. This system parceled groups and territories on the basis of ethnicity.[93] The Belgians made a similar move.[94]

A few warnings are in order here. It should be obvious from the preceding comments that the privileging of indigeneity or residence is not an eternal characteristic of a society. Societies move from one system to another with time. In exploring such movement, it is important to avoid a teleological reading in which we portray societies as moving gradually from an ancient period when they all privileged indigeneity to a situation in which they privilege residence. There are movements in both directions. As Geschiere and Nyamnjoh, Geschiere, Simone, and Jackson[95] all point out, there has been a recent rise in exclusionary politics pitting "natives" against "strangers" in many African societies. This is so despite the fact that people had previously coexisted peacefully and shared rights in ways that did not emphasize ethnic origins.[96]

What is important in this work is not the eternal organizing principle of each of the societies studied here. There never was such a thing. Instead there is, to use the term of Geschiere and Nyamnjoh, a "seesaw" of the two principles. What is of causal significance here is the dominant organizing principle during the time when refugees resided in the society, with particular significance going to the initial period of their arrival. I spend some time going through the history of each society to reflect on such evolutions and how they got to be the way they were when the refugees arrived.

I speak of the dominant organizing principle because the two principles are often at work simultaneously in each society. Because they divide costs and benefits in society in different ways, each has its supporters and advocates in society. However, one of these tendencies usually happens to be dominant in a society at any one period. What interests me is what that dominant organizing principle is during the epoch of the refugee crisis I examine. My argument is that refugees in societies that privilege residence are more likely to live autonomously of local notables in the

---

[93] Mamdani, "Understanding the crisis"; Gwendolyn Wright, *The politics of design in French colonial urbanism* (Chicago: University of Chicago Press, 1991), 73–75.

[94] Mamdani, "Understanding the crisis."

[95] Jackson, "Sons of which soil?" 97; Geschiere, "Funerals and belonging," 47; Simone, "On the worldling," 25; Ceuppens and Geschiere, "Autochthony," 386; and Geschiere and Nyamnjoh, "Capitalism and autochthony."

[96] Ceuppens and Geschiere, "Autochthony," 387; Simone, "On the worldling," 25; and Geschiere and Nyamnjoh, "Capitalism and autochthony," 423.

societies in which they seek refuge. People who seek refuge in societies that tend to privilege indigeneity are more likely to be subjugated to local elites in these communities.

The Relevant Effects of the Two Societies

First, because the indigeneity-privileging society is seen primarily as the home of natives to which only they belong, these societies usually develop mechanisms for incorporating non-indigenous strangers who lack primary rights in such societies. These mechanisms can include institutions for enabling strangers to access land rights, mechanisms for dealing with the infractions of strangers, and structures for caring for strangers. These are institutions for dealing with an aberration or abnormality. This abnormality can be thought of as the stranger in a place that only belongs to indigenes. Murphy and Bledsoe, McGovern, Colson, Brooks, Dorjahn, and Fyfe[97] all reflect on these mechanisms. They explore the institutions that such societies have developed and deployed to harness the potential resources that newcomers represent without undercutting autochthony as the dominant organizing principle of their societies. In many societies, the processes governed by such institutions ultimately resulted in the transformation of these newcomers into indigenous holders of primary rights.

Second, such societies exert pressure on strangers to seek to normalize their existence. Strangers in such a society are aberrations, and society has ways of making them realize that. New arrivals notice through subtle and not so subtle means that people may not be willing to accommodate, associate with, or even enter into market transactions with them on their own standing. Many of these societies have strict rules forbidding hosting or interacting with strangers on their own standing alone as strangers. They have to first be normalized through the local institutions for dealing with non-indigenes, as discussed earlier. It is in this context that seeking relations with notable locals who can guide one through the process and act as one's patron and protector becomes attractive to the non-indigene. Local notables who strangers seek out usually have various levels of

---

[97] William Murphy and Caroline Bledsoe, "Kinship and territory in the history of a Kpelle Chiefdom (Liberia)," in *The African frontier: the reproduction of traditional African societies*, ed. Igor Kopytoff (Bloomington: Indiana University Press, 1987); Dorjahn and Fyfe, "Landlord and stranger"; Brooks, *Landlords and strangers*; McGovern, "Unmasking the state"; Shack, "Introduction"; McGovern, "Negotiation of displacement"; Bledsoe, *Women and marriage*; and Colson, "The assimilation of aliens."

obligation to take in these strangers as part of local mechanisms for incorporating non-natives.

It is this combination of the pressure on non-indigenes to seek incorporation through local institutions and the existence of institutions for dealing with strangers that ensures that refugees who settle in indigeneity-privileging areas end up being subjugated to local notables.

In residence-privileging societies, the distinction between native and stranger residents does not exist. There are only residents and non-residents. Such societies thus have no mechanisms for dealing with resident strangers or non-natives, conceived of as non-indigenes who do not belong. Also, instead of feeling pressure to seek links with and subjugate themselves to local elites as a way of normalizing their existence, new arrivals in such societies feel a nudge to go about their lives like everyone else. People are willing to deal with them on their own standing just like other residents. They are pressured to just go about negotiating life through the various means that others adopt to give meaning to life and make ends meet. These two characteristics of the residence-privileging society ensure that people who seek refuge in such environments live autonomously of and are not subjugated to local elites.

Whether refugees are subjugated to or autonomous from local elites is thus not a question of the character of individual refugees. Because of this, we do not see significant variation in refugee–host relations within the same community. Instead, the relations are broader patterns that vary across societies. In indigeneity-privileging societies, refugees are overwhelmingly subjugated to local elites. In residence-privileging ones, they are not. Whether the host society privileges residence or indigeneity in the apportionment of rights explains this.

The Pacifying Effects of Closed Societies

It is the indigeneity-privileging society that tends to exert a pacifying influence on local communities when it comes to outbreaks of generalized anti-refugee violence. It ensures the subjugation of refugees to local elites. This in turn facilitates the flow of information about the daily lives of refugees to notables in host communities, making it easy for them to discount efforts by state officials to demonize and foment violence against refugees. The residence-privileging society works to facilitate such violence. By ensuring that refugees live autonomously of local elites, it minimizes the flow of information about refugee populations to these notables. This lack of knowledge about the lives of refugees makes it easy for locals to buy into state denunciations of refugees. Even those who do not buy into the denunciations may resort to anti-refugee violence due to a fear of the unfamiliar in the face of such state campaigns.

Liberians and Sierra Leoneans fleeing wars in their countries in the 1990s sought refuge in Guinea. I study the plight of some who settled in Conakry, where residence towered over indigeneity as the standard for determining rights of belonging, and others who settle in three areas in the Forest Region, where indigeneity was more dominant as an organizing principle in the distribution of rights. For almost ten years, the refugees across these two spaces in Guinea lived peacefully with local populations, and the Guinean state received international plaudits for its hospitality to the refugees.[98] However, in September 2000, when groups to whom some refugees were linked attacked Guinean towns and villages, the president called for the gathering and expulsion of the refugees from Guinea, accusing them of collaborating with the invaders.[99]

In residence-privileging Conakry, civilians joined the security forces in large numbers to beat, rape, evict, rob, imprison, and kill refugees in large-scale coordinated and very open attacks.[100] This is because refugees who had settled in Conakry were not subjugated to local elites. Local notables knew little about the refugees and either bought into the president's narrative or were gripped by a fear of the unfamiliar. In the tense situation in which the country was under attack from rebels with a fearsome reputation, even landlords who were reaping significant gains from refugee tenants invited marauding mobs into their houses to attack the refugees.

In Banie, Fangamandou, and Kondou, sub-prefectures in the Forest Region, community elders blatantly refused to heed the president's orders and even clamped down on some local youth who tried to attack refugees.[101] This is because refugees in these areas that privileged

---

[98] McGovern, "Conflit régional," 85.

[99] Ibid., 84–86.

[100] McGovern, "Conflit régional," 85; Human Rights Watch, "Refugee women in Guinea raped," *Human Rights Watch*, September 13, 2000, accessed August 11, 2012, http://www.hrw.org/en/news/2000/09/13/refugee-women-guinea-raped#_Fuller_Testimonies_from; "Sierra Leone conflict spills"; and interview (MRB 335).

[101] Interviews with former a Sierra Leonean refugee in Kamiendor, Mafindor Chiefdom, Sierra Leone (MRB 222), September 3, 2009; a former Sierra Leonean refugee in Sambaya, Mafindor Chiefdom, Sierra Leone (MRB 226), September 4, 2009; a former Sierra Leonean refugee in Tintor, Mafindor Chiefdom, Sierra Leone (MRB 228), September 4, 2009; a guide in Mafindor Chiefdom, Sierra Leone (MRB 231), September 4, 2009; a former refugee in Penguia Chiefdom, Sierra Leone (MRB 257), September 11, 2009; a former Sierra Leonean refugee in Simabu, Penguia Chiefdom, Sierra Leone (MRB 258), September 12, 2009; a former Liberian refugee in Gorlu, Salayea District, Liberia (MRB 306), September 25, 2009; a former Liberian refugee in Gorlu, Salayea District, Liberia

indigeneity were thoroughly subjugated to local elites there. These elites knew a lot about them and so saw through the fabrications of the president.

From 1959, tens of thousands of predominantly Batutsi Rwandese fled their country to seek refuge in Kivu in eastern Congo and southwestern Uganda, among other places.[102] In Congo these refugees lived in relative peace with the protection of the state for a short while. This was until a few of them joined the Lumumbist rebellion in the east of the country that captured a third of Congolese territory and threatened to overthrow the government in the early 1960s.[103] The Congolese government responded by ordering the expulsion of all the refugees, accusing them not only of fighting with the rebels, but also of seeking to dominate Congolese communities in the areas where they settled.[104] Local communities, who knew very little about the refugees, embraced the views of the state and joined the security forces with much zeal in attacking the refugees.[105] This was because the refugees were not subjugated to local elites, having settled in Kivu, where Belgian colonizers had done a great deal over three decades to undermine indigeneity as an organizing principle.

The counterparts of these Rwandese refugees who went to south-western Uganda had a similar story but with a significant twist in the end. They also enjoyed the protection of the state and lived in peace until the early 1980s. In 1982, the state ordered their eviction from all areas in southwestern Uganda outside of the official UNHCR settlements. The Uganda Peoples Congress (UPC) government accused them, among

(MRB 307), September 25, 2009; a former Liberian refugee in Gorlu, Salayea District, Liberia (MRB 309), September 25, 2009; a Guinean in Kolomba, Guéckédou Prefecture, Guinea (MRB 104), June 19, 2006; a Guinean in Kelema, Guéckédou Prefecture, Guinea (MRB 110), June 20, 2009; a Guinean in Kondou Lengo Bengou, Guéckédou Prefecture, Guinea (MRB 134), June 27, 2009; a Guinean in Gotoye, Yomou Prefecture, Guinea (MRB 158), July 22, 2009; and a Guinean in Dongueta, Yomou Prefecture, Guinea (MRB 198), July 28, 2009.

[102] Holborn, *Refugees*, 980; Lemarchand, *Rwanda and Burundi*, 173.

[103] Lemarchand, *Rwanda and Burundi*, 214; and William Galvez, *Che in Africa: Che Guevara's Congo Diary* (Melbourne: Ocean Press, 1999).

[104] Holborn, *Refugees*, 1093.

[105] Interviews with a former Rwandese refugee in Nyabitekeri, Rwanda (GLR 86), May 22, 2010; a former Rwandese refugee in Kibanda County, Masindi District, Uganda (GLR 96), May 14, 2010; a former Rwandese refugee in Kibanda County, Masindi District, Uganda (GLR 97), May 14, 2010; and a former Rwandese refugee in Bujenje County, Masindi District, Uganda (GLR 99), May 19, 2010; Holborn, *Refugees*, 1087–89; and Lemarchand, *Rwanda and Burundi*, 210–211.

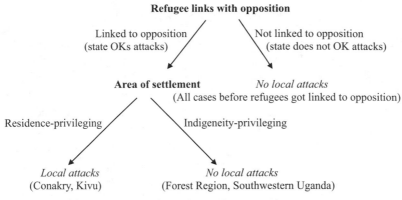

FIGURE 2.1. The Argument and Cases

other things, of participating in former president, Idi Amin's notoriously abusive security forces. They also accused the refugees of cattle theft and of supporting the ongoing National Resistance Movement (NRM) insurgency in the Luweero Triangle.[106] Significantly, unlike in Kivu, the local population did not join the attacks on these refugees by state security forces and the paramilitary ruling party militia. They mostly stood by and watched or tried to protect the refugees. This drew the ire of state agents, who threatened those seeking to protect refugees with similar expulsion.[107] Indigeneity was the dominant organizing principle in southwestern Uganda, and the refugees who settled there were subjugated to local elites. These elites knew enough about the refugees to see through the blanket accusations of refugees levied by state authorities.

---

[106] Watson, "Exile from Rwanda," 149–150; Mamdani, "The political diaspora," 315; and Mamdani, *When victims become killers*, 172.

[107] Interview (GLR 86); interviews with a former Rwandese refugee in Nyabitekeri, Nyagatare District, Rwanda (GLR 87), May 22, 2010; a former Rwandese refugee in Nyabitekeri, Nyagatare District, Rwanda (GLR 88), May 22, 2010; a Ugandan of Rwandese origin in Ntungamo District, Uganda (GLR 6), March 27, 2010; a former Rwandese refugee in Ruhaama County, Ntungamo District, Uganda (GLR 16), March 30, 2010; a Ugandan in Ruhaama Town, Ruhaama County, Uganda (GLR 17), March 31, 2010; and a Ugandan in Ntungamo Town Council, Ntungamo District, Uganda (GLR 8), March 27, 2010; Mamdani, *When victims become killers*, 168–169; The political diaspora, 315; Hamilton, "Human rights in Uganda," 19–20; Watson, "Exile from Rwanda," 10–11; Zolberg, *Conflict and the refugee crisis*, 67; Zolberg, Suhrke and Aguayo, *Escape from violence*, 67–68; and Khiddu-Makubuya, "Voluntary repatriation," 150.

CONCLUSION: SUBJUGATION AND INTEGRATION

One might object to this argument on the grounds that a key component of it is tautological. We can lay out this objection thus. Refugees who are subjugated to local elites are well integrated into their host communities. Freedom from the sort of violence that is the outcome under study here is a key part of the definition of refugee integration. The argument in this book is then reduced to the tautological form: refugees who are well integrated, which by definition means they are free from generalized violence, are the ones who escape generalized violent campaigns by local communities. Rendered thus, the argument is clearly tautological.

An objection like this will be flawed because its key premise is faulty. Subjugated refugees are not necessarily well integrated, just as autonomous refugees are not necessarily badly integrated. The subjugation/autonomy dichotomy and the integration/non-integration one are two very different things. Some subjugated refugees are rather well integrated. Others are not. Although some autonomous refugees are well integrated, others are not. A look at the definition of refugee integration makes the difference between the two dichotomies clear.[108]

Mushemeza, paraphrasing Harrell-Bond, defined integration as "a situation in which host and refugee communities are able to exist, sharing the same resources both economic and social – with no greater mutual conflict than that which exists within the host community."[109]

In a note on the integration of refugees in Central Europe, the UNHCR defines the integration of refugees as involving the granting of "full economic, social, cultural and political participation" rights to refugees by the receiving state.[110] Integration is also widely acknowledged to include the granting of "a wide range of civil, political, economic, social and cultural rights and entitlements that are commensurate to those enjoyed by citizens."[111]

With this definition in mind, it is easy to see that the integration of refugees and their subjugation to local elites are two very different things.

---

[108] Mushemeza, "Politics and the refugee experience," 123.
[109] Mushemeza, *Banyarwanda refugees*, 73. See Dryden-Petersen and Hovil, "Local integration as a durable solution," 2–4 for a similar definition.
[110] UNHCR, "UNHCR note on refugee integration in Central Europe," *UNHCR*, April 2009, accessed, October 13, 2012, http://unhcr.org.ua/img/uploads/docs/11%20UNHCR-Integration_note-screen.pdf.
[111] UNHCR, "UNHCR note," 10. Also see the definition of integration by Jacobson. Jacobsen, "The forgotten solution," 9.

The subjugation of refugees to local elites in an area does not necessarily mean that they enjoy all the legal rights and protections and socioeconomic rights that are held by well-integrated refugees. As is clear from the more detailed exploration of the lives of subjugated refugees in the Forest Region of Guinea and southwestern Uganda, many of the refugees did not enjoy anything close to the rights enumerated previously. Many complained of living in extremely difficult conditions. Autonomous refugees are similarly not necessarily deprived of all these rights and protections. Some autonomous refugees might even enjoy these rights and protections more than subjugated refugees. In short, the issue of refugee integration and the subjugation of refugees to local elites are two very different things.

FIGURE 2.2. Map of the Mano River Basin[112]

[112] This map was created by Rita Effah, using the following resources: FAO-Africover, 2002, "Multipurpose Africover Database for the Environmental Resources (MADE)." Accessed July 1, 2012, http://www.fao.org/geonetwork/srv/en/main.search? title=africover; GADM, 2011, "Database of Global Administrative Areas." Accessed July 1, 2012, http://www.gadm.org/country; and WRI, 2009, "Waterbodies in Uganda." Accessed July 1, 2012, http://www.wri.org/publication/uganda-gis-data# base.

3

An Outburst of Anti-Refugee Violence in Conakry, Guinea

The Guineans did a lot of bad things to those Sierra Leonean refugees. It was five brothers and sisters in their teens to 30s. They raped the two girls and stole all they had. They jailed and beat the boys. After they returned from jail they came back to Sierra Leone. I did not see them again. The landlord was in the compound when this happened and did nothing to help them. The landlords were very wicked.[1]

Early September 2000 witnessed an outbreak of anti-refugee violence in the Guinean capital, Conakry.[2] Attacks in broad daylight by groups of Guinean civilians, sometimes accompanied by state security agents, on refugees from Sierra Leone and Liberia went on for about a week.[3] Many landlords who were earning significant money by renting houses to refugees forcibly evicted their refugee tenants, telling them to go back to their country. The more malevolent landlords invited state security agents or people from the neighborhood to attack their refugee tenants. Once the crowds got into these homes, they looted properties and subjected occupants to rape and other forms of sexual and nonsexual violence. Some refugees died in the process. Most were then taken to gendarmeries where they were imprisoned for days. Women were further sexually assaulted in the gendarmeries.[4] One of many testimonies gathered by Human Rights Watch from refugees concerning the attacks follows.

---

[1] Interview (MRB 335).
[2] Human Rights Watch, "Refugee women in Guinea raped."
[3] Interview with two UNHCR officials in Conakry, Guinea (MRB 13), December 22, 2008.
[4] Interview with a former refugee in Freetown, Sierra Leone (MRB 342), October 7, 2009; and interview (MRB 335).

On Saturday at 5:00 am five soldiers and many civilians knocked at the door saying, "police, police . . . if you don't open we'll shoot you all." When we heard them cock their guns we felt we had to open. . . . The civilians were with iron bars, knives, sticks . . . they started looting . . . Then one of those civilians who knew my daughter from the neighborhood grabbed her saying "you're the rebels, you're bringing the fight to our country. We'll kill you." Then they pulled my daughter away and started raping. . . . After they left our landlord came and said we had to leave . . . then we fled to the Sierra Leonean Embassy. (Testimony taken Monday, September 11, Conakry)[5]

Fearing attacks, many refugees fled to the embassies of Sierra Leone and Liberia, which quickly became packed de facto refugee camps where people slept, bathed, cooked, and ate.[6] Some refugees were able to make it on board boats bound for Sierra Leone. However, the trip to the port and the embassies was a dangerous one. Many taxi drivers who sensed that their passengers were refugees took them to gendarmeries or handed them over to groups of youth out hunting refugees.[7] Rampaging groups of neighborhood youth, policemen, and gendarmes roamed the neighborhoods looking for and attacking refugees.

Although state security agents such as soldiers, police, and gendarmes sometimes led attacks on refugees, of particular significance here is the fact that there was widespread participation by the civilian population of Conakry in these attacks. Large groups of civilians, sometimes working with state agents, rose up in search of refugees in their neighborhoods. The participation of civilians severely dwarfed that of state security agents in these attacks. Civilians were often the ones that led state security agents in search of refugees. This chapter's main goal is to explain why Guinean civilians in Conakry undertook a week of widespread generalized violence against refugees in September 2000.

WITHDRAWING VOCIFEROUS SUPPORT

On September 9, 2000, President Lansana Conte gave a speech broadcast nationwide after a series of rebel attacks on Guinean towns and villages. He condemned the attacks and blamed them on Sierra Leonean and Liberian fighters. He singled out refugees from those two countries for castigation. He ordered pointedly: "I am giving orders that we bring

---

[5] Human Rights Watch, "Refugee women in Guinea raped."
[6] Interview (MRB 13); interview with an official of the Sierra Leone Embassy in Conakry, Guinea (MRB 14), December 3 and 4, 2008.
[7] Interview (MRB 342).

together all foreigners . . . and that we search and arrest suspects. . . . They should go home. We know that there are rebels among the refugees. Civilians and soldiers, let's defend our country together. Crush the invaders."[8]

This was a marked departure from the state's support for and protection of refugees from Sierra Leone and Liberia earlier. It is best explained not by the economic strain the refugees put on the country and the mere involvement of refugees in the politics of Guinea. It was due to links between certain refugees and a dangerous insurgency that threatened to wreak havoc on the country and seriously undermine the power of state leaders.

Before this speech, the government of Guinea, along with its leader Lansana Conte, had "been praised by the international community for its generous policy of sheltering refugees."[9] Support for refugees and speeches urging the civilian population to accept and show hospitality to refugees came from as high as the seat of the presidency. During my research, I discovered that many former refugees remember President Conte for his vocal support for refugees and encouragement of Guineans to show compassion to and share resources with them. Many people who were formerly refugees in the Forest Region recall a trip by Lansana Conte to Yomou Prefecture where he made one such speech. As one refugee put it: "I heard Lansana Conte was coming to Yomou and went there to see him but he was gone by the time I got there. People were saying he had said the citizens should not ill-treat the refugees because they are like orphans. He told the citizens to take care of the refugees. This was when we first got to Guinea in the early 1990s."[10] A refugee who witnessed another visit by Lansana Conte to Yomou recalled him saying: "Citizens and refugees should be one. Don't disturb the refugees. You are all my children and you should live together."[11]

Below the president, prefects, sub-prefects, and many administration officials campaigned very heavily on behalf of the refugees, convincing local communities to accept proposed camps and to share their resources with the refugees. They sought to encourage methods of dealing with conflicts between refugees and locals that prevented violence. They also instructed refugee leaders on how to coexist with local communities in

[8] "Sierra Leone conflict spills."
[9] Human Rights Watch, "Refugee women in Guinea raped."
[10] Interview (MRB 310).
[11] Interview with a former Liberian refugee in Mementa, Salayea District, Liberia (MRB 345), December 7, 2010.

ways that reduced the possibility of conflicts. This advocacy was so intense that some members of those communities began to blame state leaders for what they saw as the high costs of hosting refugees. These costs ranged from rapid deforestation and rampant theft to what they characterized as the corruption of local youth. One exasperated leader told me: "They [state leaders] are the... ones who used to come here earlier and say: 'You should take the refugees like yours. Give them half of what you eat.' So they [the refugees] destroyed our forests and we did nothing."[12] Another noted:

When the refugees arrived the government was very supportive of them. The officials in Yomou sent a paper here saying we should host them, give them places to farm and put them in our houses. If someone in Liberia owed you while he was in Liberia and you arrested that person when you saw him here as a refugee and took him to Yomou the officials told you: "Leave him alone. He is now a refugee. When he goes back to Liberia you can go and catch him there."[13]

This fierce advocacy of hospitality toward refugees by various cadres of state officials was due to the fact that those officials were often beneficiaries of a situation that sometimes heaped heavy costs on less powerful and influential members of society.[14] The Guinean government was able to use the presence of the refugees and the problems that it supposedly caused to access humanitarian aid that it exercised considerable control over and could deploy to reinforce its power.[15] State officials also received very personal economic benefits from operations that were meant to support the refugees. Officials acquired and sold off some of the supplies meant for refugees. Some of these materials were stolen in warehouses with the collaboration of relief agency officials before they even made it to the camps. Many officials got large numbers of refugee ration cards that they used to collect supplies for sale in towns. Some of the names on these cards were those of nonexistent refugees. Others had the names of real refugees whose cards had been given to these officials instead of the

---

[12] Interview (MRB 212).

[13] Interview with a Guinean in Gotoye, Yomou Prefecture, Guinea (MRB 373), July 11, 2011.

[14] The following authors have explored the ways in which such migratory flows heap varying levels of costs and benefits of different members of the host population and how the poorest often bear the heaviest cost. Tom Kuhlman, *Burden or boon: a study of Eritrean refugees in the Sudan* (Amsterdam: VU University Press), 63–70; and Whitaker, "Refugees in Western Tanzania," 341; and Robert Chambers, "Rural refugees in Africa: what the eye does not see." *Disasters* 3 (4–1978): 389.

[15] Arieff, "Still standing," 339.

actual owners. Some of these refugees were not present when cards were handed out. Others did not hear when their names were called out or were told that their names had not appeared on the list of card recipients.[16]

Beyond these personal benefits, refugee operations boosted state power. In Guinea, agencies dealing with refugees constructed or refurbished long stretches of roads and other infrastructure such as schools, clinics, latrines, and boreholes in remote areas of the country. This helped to legitimize the state in the eyes of locals who also benefited from these projects. It also made accessible to state agents sections of the country that had been previously very difficult to access. This allowed the state to extend its power to these remote areas and extract more resources from there.[17] While doing fieldwork, a former local official showed me the new prefecture headquarters that a United Nations (UN) agency had constructed for Guéckédou Prefecture.[18] This extension of state power also included the stationing of policemen, gendarmes, and soldiers close to some of the refugee camps, sometimes with funding and training from the UN High Commission for Refugees (UNHCR) and its partners.[19] These camps were often located in very remote areas where the state's coercive machinery was previously not present in a strong way on a consistent basis.

For some of the state politicians, the arrival of the refugees was also an opportunity to bolster their political base. They recruited some of the refugees to take part in political rallies and even got some to vote.[20]

It was for all of these reasons that the former President Lansana Conte, other central state officials, and local functionaries all advocated the acceptance of refugees by Guinean populations. This support was in the face of significant costs imposed by the arrival of the refugees. One widely recognized cost was the rapid deforestation that ensued in certain areas of the Forest Region. By the time the refugees left in the early 2000s many areas of the Forest Region that had large numbers of refugees had witnessed significant deforestation. To say the arrival of the refugees was

---

[16] Beyond the many conversations with ordinary refugees, my discussion with a former low-level security official in one of the camps in Albadariah Sub-Prefecture in Kissidougou Prefecture, Guinea, gave me a very good understanding of the workings of these fraudulent schemes. She became involved in some of them and so had a very good understanding of the system. Interview with a former refugee in Woroma, Penguia Chiefdom, Sierra Leone (MRB 276), September 13, 2009.

[17] Arieff, "Still standing," 339.

[18] Interview Guéckédou (MRB 87).

[19] Milner with Christoffersen-Deb, "The militarization," 63–67.

[20] Interview (MRB 43).

a big cause of this deforestation is not necessarily to blame the refugees for the deforestation. The deforestation was not always the work of the refugees. Refugees did clear land to farm. Similarly, they cut trees to make charcoal, sell as wood, and construct their houses. However, Guineans did a lot of the deforestation. Many Guineans cut timber and grass used for roofing to sell to refugees or to nongovernmental organizations involved in providing housing for refugees. The massive influx of cheap labor that the refugees represented allowed many Guineans to expand their farms and plantations at the expense of the forests. The deforestation that resulted had severe consequences for many of these communities that were heavily dependent on the forest. The arrival of the refugees also undercut wages and held them almost stagnant for long periods in the face of rising inflation. This harshly affected rural and some urban populations that were dependent on selling low-skilled labor.

The national and local state officials involved in advocating the acceptance and protection of refugees did not bear many of these costs. Because of this, the benefits they received were enough to motivate them to encourage local acceptance and tolerance of refugees.

The withdrawal of protection for the refugees and advocacy of attacks on them by President Conte and his allies were thus not due to the economic costs of hosting the refugees. They were due to what state leaders saw as links between some refugees and a string of rebel attacks that severely threatened the country in 2000. On September 1, 2000, a group attacked Massadou village in Macenta Prefecture, close to Guinea's border with Liberia. They killed tens, looted, burnt houses, and displaced many Guineans and refugees living in that village. Two days later on September 3, another attack was launched on Madina Woula in Kindia Prefecture on the border with Sierra Leone. This was followed by an attack on September 6 on the heavily populated town of Pamlap in Forecariah Prefecture also on the border with Sierra Leone. The attack on Pamlap went along with an attack on a nearby army garrison.[21]

These attacks caused panic among state officials, even though they were not the first attacks on Guinean soil by people believed to be fighters from Sierra Leone and Liberia. During the wars in those countries, fighters often crossed the border to steal and settle scores. They killed and injured people in the process. One of the worrying things about these attacks was that at least some of them seemed to be well-coordinated attacks with

---

[21] "Sierra Leone conflict spills."

fighters that were intent on more than just stealing things and slipping back across the border. They also involved large numbers of heavily armed fighters. Even more worrying was the spread of the attacks. Massadou is in the south of Guinea in Macenta Prefecture. Madina Woula is much further north in Kindia Prefecture, and Pamlap is close to Guinea's Atlantic Coast in Forecariah Prefecture. The rebels seemed intent on exploiting Guinea's very long and porous borders with Liberia and Sierra Leone. Furthermore, there was the sense that the Revolutionary United Front (RUF) in Sierra Leone and National Patriotic Front of Liberia (NPFL) were working together in the attacks. These attacks followed various complaints by Liberia's president, Charles Taylor, about Guinean support for anti-NPFL groups and their activities. In 1992, he had complained that Guinea was allowing the Economic Community of West African States Monitoring Group (ECOMOG) to use the N'Zérékoré airstrip to launch airstrikes on NPFL positions in Liberia.[22] He later accused Guinea of supporting United Liberation Movement for Democracy in Liberia (ULIMO), which was involved in heavy fighting against NPFL forces in Liberia. He threatened retaliatory action and attacked Diomandou in Macenta Prefecture in 1999.[23] The Guinean authorities were expecting attacks, which led them to close the border with Sierra Leone in August 2000.[24]

State leaders' attention turned to the refugees because of indications of refugee participation in some of the attacks. There were reports that the fighters who attacked Massadou included people who had lived there as refugees before and had disappeared before the attacks.[25] There are stories in various areas of the Forest Region of invading rebels looking for specific people to kill or protect from harm when they attacked Guinean towns and villages. This indicated that they knew those people or had learned of them from people who had lived in those areas. One *chef de quartier* in Macenta told me of how rebels who were entering the town at dusk asked a woman where the chief of that neighborhood lived, mentioning his name. He was holding ablutions next to the woman when the question was posed. He concluded that someone who had lived

---

[22] Dane Smith Jr., "US-Guinea relations during the rise and fall of Charles Taylor," *Journal of Modern African Studies* 44 (3–2006): 425.

[23] Smith, "US-Guinea relations," 431.

[24] "Sierra Leone conflict spills"; McGovern, "Conflit régional," 87; and Human Rights Watch, "Youth, poverty and blood: the lethal legacy of West Africa's regional warriors," *Human Rights Watch Report* 17 (April 2005): 31–32.

[25] "Sierra Leone conflict spills."

in the area must have told the rebels to look for him.[26] Those who could not escape fast enough and hid in their homes after rebels captured towns often spoke of rebels arguing over which houses to burn. They discussed how the owners of houses had been kind or wicked to refugees, indicating that they had lived in those communities before.[27] There was the widespread belief that people who had lived as refugees in some of those towns and villages were working with the attackers.

The RUF was known to have harbored designs of recruiting refugees in some of the camps in Guinea.[28] One of the commanders who led some of the attacks in Guéckédou Prefecture confessed to their widespread practice of capturing refugees to use as guides. "We captured many refugees from the camps because we wanted them to guide us. I personally abducted twelve refugees from a camp two miles from Guéckédou," he told a Human Rights Watch interviewer.[29] The RUF also routinely sent spies to places they intended to attack,[30] leading people to believe that some of the refugees were spies.

However, Lansana Conte's speech, which painted all the refugees as insurgents and collaborators who should be forcibly expelled, was not motivated by fear of all refugees. Like in Uganda, the government was cynically exploiting the links between a few refugees and the attackers to achieve wider political goals. One goal was to unite Guineans against rebels who actively sought to exploit known fault lines in Guinea. He was also seeking to transform a rebellion that contained many Guinean elements into a totally foreign invasion.

The government most certainly did not fear all refugees or suspect all of them of involvement in the attacks. This is because at the very time that the state was painting all refugees as enemies and calling for their expulsion, they were recruiting, training, and arming refugees from Sierra Leone and Liberia to defend Guinea and attack various armed groups in Liberia and Sierra Leone. Many have written of the state's links with ULIMO/Liberians United for Reconciliation and Democracy (LURD), which included a lot of Liberian refugees. The government permitted the group to operate in Guinea, helped to train their fighters, and provided

[26] Interview (MRB 43).
[27] Interview (MRB 22).
[28] McGovern, "Conflit régional," 86–87.
[29] Human Rights Watch, "Youth, poverty and blood," 32.
[30] Paul Richards, "West African warscapes: War as smoke and mirrors: Sierra Leone 1991–92, 1994–95, 1995–96," *Anthropological Quarterly* 78 (Spring 2005): 382; and Utas, "West African warscapes," 418.

them with weapons and logistical support.[31] It turned a blind eye to ULIMO's transformation of the Kouankan Refugee Camp in Macenta Prefecture into a rear base.[32] Refugees were also recruited to fight with Sierra Leonean *Kamajor* civil defense forces in Guinea and Sierra Leone.[33]

The government was intent on painting the incursions as a straight-forward invasion of Guinea by foreign elements from Sierra Leone and Liberia that was a threat to all Guineans and that all Guineans should rise up against in a united manner. In fact, the picture was more complex, and this was a deliberate misrepresentation of the conflict by state leaders to gain an upper hand. First, although most of the fighters were Liberian and Sierra Leonean, many reports indicate that the insurgents included Guineans who were opposed to the government of Lansana Conte. Mohamed Lamine Fofanah who claimed the attacks as the work of the *Rassemblement des forces démocratiques de Guinée* made up of Guineans confirmed the participation of some Guineans in the attacks.[34]

Furthermore, the attackers did not pose the same threats to all Guineans. Fault lines in Liberia that pitted the heavily Mandingo (Malinké) ULIMO/LURD against Charles Taylor's NPFL, which drew a lot of fighters and support from the Gio, Mano and Kpelle groups, were somewhat similar to fault lines in the Forest Region of Guinea. There is a history of tensions between various Maninka communities such as the Konianké and Maniang and Forest groups such as the Toma [called *Lorma* in Liberia] and Guerzé [called *Kpelle* in Liberia]. This had some-times resulted in violent clashes in which up to hundreds had sometimes been killed in places such as N'Zérékoré and Macenta.[35] The NPFL rebels knew of this and sometimes deliberately sought to exploit it by approach-ing and selling to members of the Forest groups their project of attacking and driving the Maniang and Konianké out of the Forest Region.

A Guinean told me, "I was in a village near Koyama when the rebels started infiltrating the place. They approached the Toma elders and told them they were going to come and kill and drive the Maniang away

---

[31] McGovern, "Conflit régional," 87; Arieff, "Still standing," 340–341; Human Rights Watch, "Liberian refugees in Guinea: refoulement, militarization of camps and other protection concerns," 10; and International Crisis Group, "Stopping Guinea's slide," 21.

[32] Human Rights Watch, "Liberian refugees in Guinea," 10.

[33] International Crisis Group, "Stopping Guinea's slide," 18.

[34] Arieff, "Still standing," 343; and Smith, "US-Guinea relations," 431.

[35] Wim Van Damme, "How Liberian and Sierra Leonean refugees settled in the forest region of Guinea (1990–1996)," *Journal of Refugee Studies* 12 (1 1999): 49.

but will not harm the Toma so we should not fear."[36] There is evidence that during the attacks, rebels sometimes selectively targeted members of certain communities. A young man in Macenta told me, "When the rebels attacked, they met me here. I could not run. One of them pointed a gun at me and asked me what group I belonged to. I told him I was Kpelle and they just left me here and went away."[37] Had the strategy of mapping itself onto existing fault lines worked, the invasion would have been far more catastrophic for Guinea.

Lansana Conte's speech invoked Guinean nationalism, national pride, and the protection of the homeland, papering over divisions in Guinean society in an attempt to forge a united front against the invasions. It demonized all foreigners and blamed them not only for the invasions, but also for other ills in Guinean society. It elided the fact that the state was itself in league with and heavily supporting foreign elements whose activities might have instigated the attacks in the first place.[38]

This strategy seemed to have worked. There was a pervasive uprising by Guineans against the invasions *that manifested itself in different forms across the country*. Many Guineans came to buy into the idea that the attacks constituted a foreign invasion and nothing more. This was so even in cases in which they knew Guineans who had been killed or captured while fighting alongside the foreign invaders. This rather bizarre thinking was evidence of how successful Lansana Conte's speech was. The response of a resident of Daro in Macenta Prefecture who I interviewed exemplifies this:

When the rebels attacked Guinea I was here. This prefecture [Macenta] suffered fifty-two attacks. I was a volunteer against the foreign invasion. The invaders did not succeed in Guinea because even if we have problems with each other as Guineans when someone from outside attacks us we get together and defend ourselves against the outsiders. Then there are no Kissi, Malinké, or Toma. We are all just one. It was a foreign invasion. It is true there were many Guineans among the rebels. I had a friend who I sat on the same bench with in school. He was a Guinean and a rebel and was killed in the military camp in Macenta. But for us even though there were Guineans among the rebels, we saw it as foreign aggression because the fighters came from the direction of other countries, even if some of them were our relatives.[39]

[36] Interview with a Guinea in Macenta Centre, Guinea (MRB 35), December 13, 2008.
[37] Interview (MRB 45).
[38] McGovern, "Conflit régional," 85–86; and Arieff, "Still standing," 344.
[39] Interview with a man in Daro, Macenta Prefecture, Guinea (MRB 41), December 14, 2008.

McGovern[40] has noted that the speech tied the then-opposition leader and now president, Alpha Conde, the refugee rebel collaborators, and other national and international actors together as threats to national security. McGovern portrayed it as, at least in part, a deliberate attempt at quieting the opposition and has reflected on how Lansana Conte tapped into earlier rhetorical devices deployed by Guinea's first president, Sekou Toure. These emphasized national unity and betrayal by foreigners and domestic traitors. This strategy was akin to how Obote's Uganda People's Congress used the cover of attacking refugees in south-western Uganda to target even citizen opponents in that part of the country.[41]

RESPONDING TO THE CALL

Why did Guineans in Conakry, among whom refugees had lived for a decade, respond to the president's speech by beating, killing, raping, robbing, evicting, and imprisoning refugees? I argue that once the president incited the population to take up arms against the refugees, the response of the population of Conakry was conditioned by the fact that refugees there had settled in a city where residence was privileged over indigeneity in the apportioning of rights of belonging. Because of this, when the refugees arrived, there was no pressure on them to normalize their presence as non-indigenous residents of the city through subjugation to indigenous local notables. Also, the fact that residence was privileged over indigeneity in the distribution of rights meant that neighborhoods lacked well-functioning institutions for incorporating non-natives who are seen as residents who do not belong. Because the refugees were not subjugated to local notables, these elites who had a lot of control over the exercise of violence by the civilian population in their neighborhoods did not really know what the refugees represented. When the state urged locals to attack the refugees, accusing them of collaborating with rebels at a time when the country was facing serious security threats, local notables did nothing to protect the refugees. Some bought into the narrative of the president. Others just lacked enough information about the refugees to conclude otherwise, even if they did not necessarily accept the president's allegations. They joined in the attacks and encouraged the youth who had

---

[40] McGovern, "Conflit régional," 87–88.
[41] Mamdani, *When victims become killers,* 168.

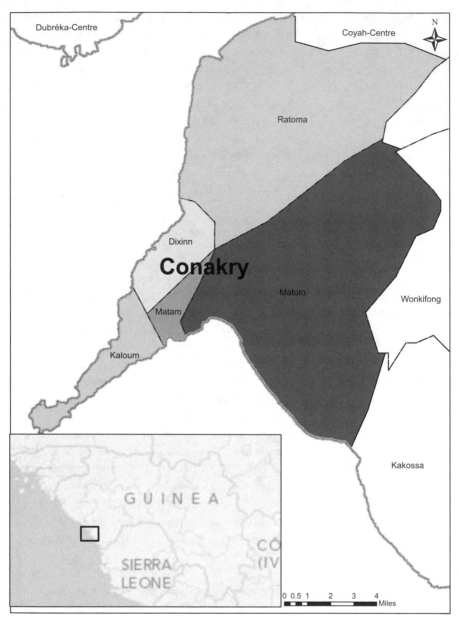

FIGURE 3.1. Map of Conakry[42]

[42] This map was created by Rita Effah, using the following resources: FAO-Africover, "Multipurpose Africover"; GADM, "Database of Global"; and WRI, "Waterbodies in Uganda."

come to blame refugees for all sorts of ills to attack the refugees. Even the well-meaning locals who felt compunction for the refugees were very often not willing to protect them. This is because they were not sure that the refugees were innocent and were afraid of the terrible consequences of their actions if the charges against them turned out to be true.

Configuring a Residence-Privileging Society

A visit to Conakry in the 1990s when the refugees resided there will have revealed a city that privileged residence over indigeneity in the determination of belonging. It was not only one in which there were people from different groups interacting in daily life, but also one that was not seen and treated as the privileged property of any particular group(s). To understand this character of the city, we need to explore the colonial origins of Conakry as the capital of Guinea. It was during these formative moments that the first and most telling deathblows were dealt to the dream and designs of those who wished to privilege indigeneity in the distribution of rights in the area.

In 1885,[43] when the French finally picked the area that is now Conakry as the site of the capital of French Guinea, the low population of the area, standing at a modest 300, and lack of a strong political authority were influential in the choice.[44] Both of these factors promised the French a free hand in ordering and developing the capital. The area had the three villages of Boulbinet, Tombo, and Conakry. The population consisted mostly of indigenous Baga people, as well as Susu, who had arrived in the area later but were in the process of gradually assimilating the Baga.[45] After a long series of pact making with local rulers laced with threats and military action, the French were able to imprint their dominance on the area and see off competition from the British and Germans.[46]

The French were intent on taking full advantage of the characteristics of the area in the creation of a capital that Governor Ballay hoped would

---

[43] Odile Goerg, "Chieftainships between past and present: from city to suburb and back in colonial Conakry, 1890s–1950s," *Africa Today* 52 (Summer 2006): 6.

[44] Odile Goerg, "La Guinée Conakry," in *Rives colonial: architectures de Saint-Louis a Doula*, ed. Jacques Soulillou (Marseiles: Editions Parenthèses, 1993), 84; and Odile Goerg, *Commerce et colonisation en Guinée 1850–1913* (Paris: Editions L'Harmattan, 1986), 254 & 300.

[45] Odile Goerg, "La genèse du peuplement de Conakry," *Cahiers d'études Africaines* Vol 30, No 117 (1990): 75 ; Goerg, "La Guinée Conakry," 84.

[46] Goerg, *Commerce et colonisation*, 121.

become the "jewel of the West African coast."[47] One of the key goals of the French in the creation and operation of the new city was the reinforcement and display of their authority over all others in the area. This included rival colonial powers, local leaders, and populations as well as European business houses. Promoting commerce and ensuring the economic success of the city was also a big goal. Beyond these, there were the concerns over sanitation and health issues that figured in city planning and management in many colonies at the time. Aesthetic concerns also repeatedly came to the fore.[48] There was a constant obsession with laying out the city in a neat and well-planned grid that differed from what they saw as the torturous streets of Dakar, Senegal.[49] Ultimately, the actions they took in pursuit of these goals came to constitute what one can describe as a model of how to create the city as a space not only with a heterogeneous population but as one that gives little credence to indigeneity in the distribution of rights. This approach was not unique to Conakry, because the French tended to see their cities as "detribalized" spaces.[50]

Bringing People to Conakry

The colonial goals just described led to the assemblage of a radically diverse population in the city. Aggressive efforts by colonial officers to make it the seat of government and unrivaled commercial center in the country predictably attracted hordes of people from outside of the colony as well as more rural areas of the colony to the burgeoning city.[51] The dynamic interaction of urban bias and rural–urban migration is seen in many other African contexts, making it unsurprising that Africa is still one of the fastest urbanizing areas of the world.[52]

---

[47] Goerg, "La Guinée Conakry," 85.
[48] Wright, *The politics of design*, 54; Odile Goerg, "From Hill Station (Freetown) to Downtown Conakry (First Ward): comparing French and British approaches to segregation in colonial cities at the beginning of the twentieth century," *Canadian Journal of African Studies* 32 No. 1 (1998): 22; and Goerg, *Commerce et colonization*, 131.
[49] Goerg, *Commerce et colonisation*, 263.
[50] Wright, *The politics of design*, 303.
[51] Claude Riviere, *Mutations sociales en Guinée* (Paris: Editions Marcel Riviere et Cie, 1971), 44.
[52] Rodney White, "The influence of environmental and economic factors on the urban crisis," in *African cities in crisis: managing rapid urban growth*, ed. Richard E. Stren and Rodney R. White (Boulder: Westview Press, 1989), 2; and Francesca Locatelli and Paul Nugent, *African cities: competing claims on urban spaces* (Lieden: Brill, 2009), 2. On urban bias in Africa, see Robert Bates, *Markets and states in tropical Africa: the political basis of agricultural policies* (Berkeley: University of California Press, 1981).

Many of the migrants were intimately connected to the colonial administration and the project of creating a new city "practically ex nihilo," as Georg[53] described it. Many Senegalese from the Four Communes, Dahomeans (Beninois), and Togolese familiar with French colonial administration arrived to work for the government.[54] After coercing business houses to locate their operations in Conakry through a combination of tax and custom policies,[55] there was a critical need for skilled workers in these firms. Many from Senegal and Sierra Leone came to take up these positions.[56] Europeans, Lebanese, Syrians, Hausa businessmen, fishermen from Ghana, and Gabonese carpenters also joined the flow into the new city.[57] This mixture of people with diverse identities in the city was typical of other new colonial cities.[58]

The need for skilled workers in the vibrant construction sector was probably one of the big drivers of immigration into Conakry. Work on the port of Conakry was begun in May 1889.[59] The building of a system of roads, government offices, hospitals, and official residences all created a constant need for skilled workmen and laborers that was not readily met by the local population of the area. On the whole, the French authorities thought very lowly of the local Baga, whom they described as both lazy and unskilled. Only the lowest sort of work was reserved for them. When they were not being compelled through forced labor regimes to undertake such work, they were offered wages even lower than those of migrants. The French looked to two main sources for laborers and skilled workers: Senegal and Sierra Leone. Many in these two colonies were familiar with European architecture and technology.[60] Large numbers of

---

[53] Goerg, "La Guinée Conakry," 84.

[54] Riviere, *Mutations sociales*, 44; and Laurent Fourchard, "Dealing with 'strangers': allocating urban space to migrants in Nigeria and French West Africa, end of the nineteenth century to 1960," in *African cities: competing claims on urban spaces*, ed. Francesca Locatelli and Paul Nugent (Lieden: Brill, 2009), 196.

[55] Goerg, *Commerce et colonisation* 256–258.

[56] Riviere, *Mutations sociales*, 44.

[57] Riviere, *Mutations sociales*, 44; and Odile Goerg, "Chefs de quartier et 'tribal headman:' deux vision des colonisés en ville," in *Les ethnies ont une histoire*, ed. Jean-Pierre Chrétien and Gérard Prunier (Paris: Editions Karthala, 1989), 270.

[58] Valdo Pons, *An African urban community under Belgian administration* (London: Oxford University Press, 1969), 6; J.S. La Fontaine, *City politics: a study of Leopoldville, 1962–63* (Cambridge: Cambridge University Press, 1970), 45–46; and J.R. Rayfield, "Theories of urbanization and the colonial city in West Africa," *Africa: Journal of the International African Institute* 44 (April 1974): 173.

[59] Goerg, "La Guinée Conakry," 90.

[60] Goerg, "La genese," 82.

Temne, Limba, and Mende from Sierra Leone and citizens of the Four Communes of Senegal came to take up positions in Conakry. A few Liberians were also recruited for such work.[61]

Like in Kivu, Congo, which I write about later in this book, many of these workers were brought in directly by the colonial authorities or its contracted agents. The former indigenous rulers and communities in the area played almost no role in their settlement, unlike in indigeneity-privileging areas, where the indigenous owners of communities set the terms on which strangers are let in. When the authorities wanted to begin work on the Government Hotel, the French contacted their consul in Freetown and colonial counterparts in Senegal for labor. In Sierra Leone, the French firm *Compagnie Française de l'Afrique Occidentale* (CFAO) also acted as an agent of the French authorities to recruit and transport workers to Conakry.[62] The state also contracted local notables in these neighboring countries to deliver workers.[63]

Like in Kivu, the colonial authorities were initially not intent on the permanent settlement of these people in Conakry. Although some of these migrant workers stayed on in the capital, many of them voluntarily returned to their places of origin on the completion of their work. However, the scale of infrastructural work meant there was a ceaseless flow of workers coming to and going out of Conakry. As the Belgians in Kivu did, the French in Conakry quickly adopted the more drastic step of seeking to settle these workers permanently in Conakry for a few reasons. The constant coming and going of workers was an expense the authorities did not want to bear. Settled workers would have made skills and labor readily and predictably available on demand, eliminating the uncertainties that came with contracting people from abroad repeatedly. Also, settling the workers permanently would encourage them to spend more of their wages in the city, thus boosting the economy.[64] It was in line with this policy that one Samawa was officially conferred the title "Chief of the Mende" to get him to dissuade the Mende workers under his leadership who had worked on the *Route de Niger* from returning to Sierra Leone.[65]

[61] Goerg, "La genese," 82; Goerg, *Commerce et colonisation*, 264; and Riviere, *Mutations sociales*, 44.
[62] Goerg, "La genese," 82–83.
[63] Ibid., 85.
[64] Ibid., 83–84.
[65] Goerg, "Chefs de quartier," 271–272.

The inflow of people into the capital was boosted by the colonial policy of severing connections between the former great chieftains that the French saw as rivals and their populations. Although many chiefs were sent into exile away from Guinea, others were settled in areas of Conakry away from their traditional bases. This undercut their links to their people and enhanced French ability to keep an eye on them. The King of Dubreka, who previously had Conakry under his control, was "forced to move to Conakry in 1888 as a sign of submission."[66] Similarly, the defeated rulers of Fouta-Djalon were coerced into settling in Conakry.[67]

The French did not enunciate a policy of racial or ethnic segregation in the city, and neighborhoods were mixed. However, members of each group occasionally created their own settlement that sometimes came to be named after them. The subjugated royals from Fouta-Djalon (Peul/Foula) and their followers were to form the settlement of Dixinn-Foula. There was also a Dixinn-Soussou (Susu) and a Teminetaye (Temne), Limbanta (Limba), and Krowtown (Kru). The Mende also created their own neighborhood, and religious followers like the Tidjaniya and Quadiriya also settled heavily around their mosques.[68]

Land Policy

Land policy in Conakry became a key instrument for furthering the colonial goals highlighted previously. The French were intent on exercising unchallenged power over the allocation, management, and use of land in the area. They began to demonstrate this intent even before they acquired full control of the area. Even while the first colonial resident was staying in lodgings provided by CFAO, he was already accusing the firm of wanting to monopolize access to the sea.[69] After overseeing the installment of Bale Siahka as the new King of Dubreka, the French signed a treaty with him in 1889 that gave them full proprietary rights to the area that was to become the city.[70] They began to effectively exercise these rights by taking over the management and administration of land in the area. Once this was done, people seeking land had no business with the indigenous traditional authorities in the area. They had to go through

---

[66] Goerg, "Chieftainships," 6.
[67] Goerg, "La genese," 77.
[68] Goerg, "La genèse," 76; Goerg, "Chefs de quartier," 270; and Riviere, "La Toponymie."
[69] Goerg, *Commerce et colonisation*, 130.
[70] Goerg, "Chefs de quartier," 269.

the French authorities,[71] who undertook a cadastral survey, planned the area into three zones, established development rules, and proceeded to allocate plots.[72] This colonial monopoly over the administration of land in Conakry was only reinforced by the decree of October 1904, which stated that "The empty ownerless lands in the colonies and territories of French West Africa shall belong to the [French] state."[73]

The treaty of 1889 marked the effective end of any privileged rights that the Baga as indigenes of Conakry had to land in two senses. First, they had no privileged authority to grant land rights to others seen as strangers in the city. All, including the Baga, who wanted new plots, had to apply to the French. Second, the land rights acquired by migrants to the city were just as good as those of Baga who acquired rights in the area. On receipt of a plot, the rights of all depended on the fulfillment of development covenants that had nothing to do with origins and did not favor the Baga in anyway. A 1905 law confirmed earlier rules that required plot owners to spend 7.5 francs per square meter on plots they were allocated in the city's first zone, 2 francs per square meter in the second zone, and 1.5 francs in the third zone. The authorities did not always stridently enforce these covenants in the interest of attracting and keeping people in the city, but this had nothing to do with whether or not those acquiring land were Baga.[74]

The French jealously guarded this unrivaled control over land in the area and exercised it in ways that left all with no doubts about the source and guarantor of land rights. They even interpreted the treaty that gave them this right in retroactive ways. They did not even hesitate to expropriate the rights of the few European business houses like CFAO and Colin who had acquired large and strategic parcels in the area before the King of Dubreka signed it over to the French. The colonial authorities relocated these business concerns, just as they did people whose properties were in the way of colonial plans in the area.[75] They routinely used the breach of development covenants to take back land they needed for other purposes.[76]

[71] Jean Suret-Canale, *French colonialism in tropical Africa 1900–1945* (New York: Pica Press, 1971), 75.
[72] Goerg, "La Guinée Conakry," 85–86.
[73] Suret-Canale, *French colonialism*, 75. Also see his footnote 11 on page 90.
[74] Goerg, "La Guinée Conakry," 86; and Goerg, "From Hill Station," 13.
[75] Goerg, *Commerce et colonisation*, 130.
[76] Ibid., 20.

In Conakry, there was one authority that governed land rights. The French made it clear that this authority was not the traditional Baga chief or family head. It was the French colonial authority. Furthermore, there were rules that governed access to and continued enjoyment of land rights. These had nothing to do with whether one was Baga or not. It had all to do with rules imposed by the French that did not give any privileged access or protection to the indigenes of the area. Migrants to the area got a clear picture of an area where one's access to land rights had nothing to do with one's ethnicity and indigeneity and where the indigenous had no better right to land than migrants. This was one giant step toward privileging residence over indigeneity in the apportioning of rights in the city.

Chieftaincy Policy

French colonial policy on chieftaincy in the area represented the other step toward elevating residence over indigeneiety in the city. In those import-ant formative years, the French cracked down on traditional chiefs in the area and also paid little attention to indigeneity in the making and unmaking of chiefs in the zone. As Suret-Canale[77] has noted, French assimilation policies were in no way intended to reproduce French met-ropolitan conditions in the colonies, but they did serve the valuable end of subverting the authority of traditional chiefs, which the French saw as rival claimants to control over local populations. Many of the traditional leaders who had resisted militarily and had finally been defeated by the French were exiled.[78] To obviate the rise of new competitors to French rule in these areas, the colonial authorities often undertook the radical reorganization of societies.[79]

Alarmingly for local chiefs, even those who had given in to French rule and aided it militarily were not spared. Bale Siakha, who had signed off the island of Kaloum to the French in 1889, was not spared the ignominy of forcible resettlement in Conakry as a sign of submission.[80] Benti Sori, the chief of Conakry who had allied himself with the French, was exiled to Senegal in 1887.[81] In 1889, another chief of Conakry, Fode

---

[77] Suret-Canale, *French colonialism*, 83.
[78] Suret-Canale, *French colonialism*, 75; and Goerg, "Chefs de quartier," 269.
[79] Suret-Canale, *French colonialism*, 75.
[80] Goerg, "Chieftainships," 6.
[81] Goerg, "Chefs de quartier," 269.

Bokary, was exiled to the Ile de Los.[82] Even the great chief of Labe, Alfa Yaya, who had aided the French in their military campaigns, was lured to Conakry, arrested, and exiled to Dahomey in 1904. When he returned from Dahomey, he was imprisoned again in Port Etienne in Mauritania till his death in 1911.[83]

Chiefs became mere instruments of mediation at the whims of the colonial authorities, and the French repeatedly stated their aspiration of ensuring that there was only one authority – the French – in the colony. Governor-General William Ponty thus instructed the Council of the Government of French West Africa to "fight the influence of the local aristocracies so as to make sure of the sympathies of the communities; suppress all great principalities which nearly always act as a barrier between us and the mass of people under our administration. The application of these principles in Senegal and Guinea has begun to bear fruit."[84] The French even harbored ambitions of replacing chiefs as intermediaries with local veterans of the World Wars.[85]

In Conakry, French policy on the appointment of these new administrative chiefs who were instruments of colonial rule was to further undermine indigeneity in the allocation of rights of belonging in the city. Up to the 1910s, the French enunciated and applied a radical policy that gave no privileged consideration to indigeneity in the appointment and retention of chiefs in Conakry. Instead, they seemed intent on *not* appointing chiefs who were indigenous to the area. They partly justified this by pointing to the heterogeneous character of the population in the area, questioning the ability of Baga chiefs to govern the medley of people in the growing city.[86] Like in the recruitment of labor, they seemed to think little of the abilities of the Baga. They argued that the "Baga and Soussou chiefs are all, in fact, more or less drunkards and not to be taken seriously, apart from the chief of Kaporo, who is too far away and who has just fallen victim to attempted poisoning."[87] In line with colonial fascination with

---

[82] Ibid., 269.
[83] Suret-Canale, *French colonialism*, 75–76.
[84] Suret-Canale, *French colonialism*, 78. Also see Anne Summers and R. W. Johnson, "World War I conscription and social change in Guinea," *Journal of African History* 19 (1–1978): 26.
[85] Summers and Johnson, "World War I conscription," 26.
[86] Goerg, "Chieftainships," 11.
[87] Ibid., 12.

the Hamitic Myth,[88] the Fulani tended to be favored in the appointment of chiefs.[89]

So it was that Mamadou Thiam, a Fulani from the family of the former rulers of Fouta-Djallon who had been humbled and forced to settle in Conakry, was made village chief of the neighborhood of Dixinn-Foulah, which had been created by his family. This was in accordance with the general colonial policy of appointing a member of each ethnic group to be the chief of that group and intermediary between them and the French.[90] This was similar to Belgian policy in Kivu, Congo, where migrant Banyarwanda were also appointed as chiefs of their villages. Like in Kivu, this move took a more radical turn later. Thiam was made "Chief of the Province of the Suburbs," a position that was later changed to "Canton Chief of Conakry." This placed him above all the chiefs in the area of the Guinean capital, including the indigenous Baga ones. He even now had under him the village of Kaporo, where the former family that ruled Kaloum resided.[91]

This subversion of the privileged position of indigeneity was a move that sparked resentment and protest from the autochthonous Baga. The French were to accuse them of complaining "that the land of Conakry and the coast belong to the Baga alone and that no foreigner has the right to govern there."[92] However, the French were not particularly interested in placating these calls to privilege indigeneity by appointing chiefs who were indigenous to the area they ruled. Kaly Salifou, the son of the former King of Nalou in the Rio Nunez, had sought for some time to be given the title of "Chief of the Province of the Nalous." The French were intent on not pandering to such privileging of indigeneity in the area. Instead, when Mery Sekou, Almany of Conakry, passed away, they saw an opportunity to deal two blows against indigeneity. They refused to appoint his brother Coni Cine to the vacant position, subverting indigenous claims to special chiefly privileges in the area as they had done by repeatedly refusing the requests of Kaly Salifou. They instead decided to install Kaly Salifou of the Rio Nunez, a traditional foe of Kaloum, as the new Almamy of

---

[88] For an explication of the Hamitic Hypothesis, see Edith R. Sanders, "The Hamitic Hypothesis: its origin and functions in time perspective," *The Journal of African History* 10, No. 4 (1969): 521–532.

[89] Goerg, "Chieftainships," 12.

[90] Goerg, "Chefs de quartier," 271.

[91] Goerg, "Chieftainships," 7.

[92] Ibid., 7.

Conakry in 1908. In the face of particularly fierce Baga opposition to this appointment, the French opted to do away with the position altogether instead of appointing a Baga of Tombo.[93]

The decade of the 1910s seemed to have brought along with it some respite for locals and colonial officials who wanted to reinforce the privileged rights of indigenes in the area. It was in 1909 that the colonial administrator, William Ponty, pronounced the "policy of the races" that called for the choice of chiefs from the ethnicity of the governed.[94] Félix Eboué, the French colonial administrator, was to argue that "In every society there is a ruling class, born to direct, without whom nothing is done. We must make it serve our interests."[95] This was all in line with the purported shift of French colonial policy from assimilation to one of association in which there was respect for the diverse cultures that made up the French empire. As Georg noted,[96] the move toward the privileging of indigeneity in the appointment of chiefs was only conveniently invoked after local chiefly lineages had been thoroughly subverted and French authority established as supreme. There was thus little possibility of chiefs challenging French authority.

The shift to a policy of association is said to have led to a privileging of indigeneity in the city. It is said that people explicitly drew on their lineage to assert their qualifications for chiefly positions they sought, and the colonial authorities used lineages to justify their appointment of people to chieftaincies.[97] The long-suffering Soumah Family, former rulers of Kaloum who had been sidelined in favor of strangers to the area, were to issue a communiqué urging the colonial authorities to privilege indigeneity that read like a nativist's manifesto:

In fact, both before and after French penetration of the French Guinea, as indeed throughout all black Africa, each people had its ruling family, its local dignitaries, who were well established and respected by their neighbors. No one had the right to participate in the discussion of the serious issues, such as chieftainship, proprietorial or social issues, or even political matters, if he did not belong to the very same region or caste of the local dignitaries as that of the existing ruling family. They alone were able to succeed each other to positions of authority, it goes without saying that strangers were strictly excluded from such questions . . . Since

---

[93] Goerg, "Chefs de quartier," 272–273.
[94] Suret-Canale, *French colonialism*, 82.
[95] Cited in Suret-Canale, *French colonialism*, 323.
[96] Goerg, "Chieftainships," 13.
[97] Ibid., 13–20.

we are dealing here with the Peninsular of Kaloum, why should one allow dignitaries from other regions in Lower Guinea to have their say, when the Baga of Kaloum, who own the land, never have and never will dare to do the same to others?[98]

In line with this new shift in policy, when Mamadou Thiam, the canton chief of Conakry, died in 1926, the French, after much deliberation and hand wringing, declined to hand the position to his highly qualified brother, Alpha Ibrahima Sy. They instead gave it to Kerfalla Soumah from the old ruling family of Kaloum, whom they thought was unqualified but was a "native of the land" and from a ruling family.[99]

It is important to note that amidst all this flowering of indigeneity, the colonial authorities' suspicion of autochthony still ran deep. They were never unambiguously committed to this new privileging of indigeneity. Suspicion of the disloyalty and scheming of the ruling families was rife. Many French officials saw the use of chiefs as a necessary evil that could only be countenanced through the selection of chiefs that were strangers to the area they ruled. This would make clear their existence as mere administrative instruments of the French.

The French were never unambiguously committed to privileging indigeneity. In 1930, Governor Reste was to note that the choice of chiefs depended on circumstances even if there was a preference for old ruling families. The French still rated loyalty, education, and general competence highly as criteria and used them often in the appointment and retention of chiefs.[100] Governor General Carde noted in 1929 that "We cannot indefinitely tolerate the hegemony of certain incapable or undesirable families." He recommended the employment of "educated native officials" when suitable ones could not be found from among the ruling lineages.[101] Thus new chiefs were often drawn from "the traditional hierarchies, but they were quickly replaced when they proved insufficiently docile or otherwise according to the whims of the administrators."[102] George Hardy wrote that colonial authorities dissatisfied with the incapacity and disloyalty of rulers had begun to "break up the traditional forms, which they found more cumbersome than useful, and to replace the representatives of ancient families as chiefs by small men without prestige, and

---

[98] Cited in Goerg, "Chieftainships," 16–17.
[99] Goerg, "Chieftainships," 18–21.
[100] Suret-Canale, *French colonialism*, 323–324.
[101] Suret-Canale, *French colonialism*, 323–324.
[102] Ibid., 80.

too often without scruples."[103] And so it was that late into the colonial period "Chiefs without traditional authority, or else strangers to the country, continued to be haphazardly nominated...."[104] It is important to remember after all that the elevation of Mamadou Thiam, a Fulani, to the position of canton chief of Conakry' was in 1914,[105] five years after Governor General William Ponty enunciated his "policy of the races" and well into the era of what was supposed to be a new nativism.

The colonial privileging of non-natives in Conakry was seen partly in the extent to which non-Baga felt free to embrace their identities instead of assimilate into Baga communities. Many formed their own neighborhoods that were named after their ethnic groups instead of trying to dissolve themselves in old Baga neighborhoods. Some even went to the extent of forming ethnic and national associations. For instance, there were the *Alliance Senegalais*[106] and the *Union amicale de Teminetaye*.[107]

The Postcolonial Period

Any respite that Baga nationalists might have had in the late colonial era was effectively quashed with the advent of Sekou Toure as the first leader of postcolonial Guinea. In December 1957, he banned the institution of tribal chieftaincy in Guinea, putting a stop to "the days of chieftainship and of exalting the past."[108] This policy was only worsened by his general hostility to the claims of autochthony. His rule led to the dispossession of indigenes by people that they previously had regarded as their guests in many areas of the country.[109]

The aspiring Baga nationalists in Conakry had been done irreparable damage by 1984, when Sekou Toure passed away. Lansana Conte, who succeeded Toure and ruled Guinea until 2008 when he passed away, did little to undo the damage to Baga nationalism in Conakry. Sarro[110] noted that the death of Sekou Toure and ascension to power of Lansana Conte, a Susu who was married to a catholic Baga woman, gave many Baga

---

[103] Ibid., 78.

[104] Ibid., 324.

[105] Goerg, "Chieftainships," 7.

[106] Goerg, "La genese," 85.

[107] Goerg, "Chefs de quartier," 271.

[108] Goerg, "Chieftainships," 21. Also see Jean Suret-Canale, "La fin de la chefferie en Guinée," *The Journal of African History* 7 (3–1966), 488–492.

[109] Ramon Sarro, "Map and territory: the politics of place and autochthony among the Baga Sitem (and their neighbors)," in *Integration and conflict along the Upper Guinea Coast*, ed. J. Knorr and Trajano Filho (Leiden: Brill, 2010), 8.

[110] Sarro, "Map and territory."

nationalists a lot of hope for the restoration of their privileged position as the owners of what they saw as their homelands along the coast. They gave massive support to the president because of this. However, as time wore on they realized he was not particularly interested in helping them recapture their prime position on the coast. He did not offer them any help to "regain land they had lost to their 'strangers'" and made no effort to bring the Baga dream of a "'Baga Prefecture' with a capital in the industrial city of Kamsar" to reality.[111]

The emasculation of the Baga in Conakry is not particularly unique when one considers many of the new colonial cities in Africa. Rayfield has noted how they often have no visible host community, just as is the case with many American cities.[112] This is in contrast to the old cities of Africa, which usually had an established and powerful local community that played host to other settlers.[113]

ENTER THE REFUGEES

It was into this space that a bus driver deposited me one evening in early September 1997. The specific site was a bus stop in the neighborhood of Bambeto. I was only one of many people fleeing the joint Armed Forces Revolutionary Council/RUF government in Sierra Leone that was increasingly making life intolerable for people in that country as the civil war unraveled. My immediate task was to look for the compound of *Les Leonais* (The Sierra Leoneans) close to that bus stop. My French was practically nonexistent, but after much effort, a Guinean who had lived in Sierra Leone and spoke Krio fluently approached me and directed me to the compound, where my sister along with many other workers from their office in Sierra Leone had been temporarily relocated by their employer. I ended up staying in Conakry for a month before I made my way by road to N'Zérékoré in the southeast of the country. From there I traveled on to Abidjan in neighboring Cote d'Ivoire and then Accra, the capital of my country of birth, Ghana.

Upon my arrival in Bambeto, my sister introduced me to the head of the compound, another refugee who was the most senior staff member

---

[111] Ibid., 12.
[112] Rayfield, "Theories of urbanization," 174.
[113] Rayfield, "Theories of urbanization," 173; Jenkins, "African cities," 83; and Richard W. Hull, *African cities and towns before the European conquest* (New York: W.W. Norton & Company, 1976), 81–83.

present in the house. The house was crowded during the day but practically overflowed with people at night. Relatives, friends, and acquaintances
of the residents came in to look for food and a place to sleep before they
left early in the morning for various parts of the city. People slept on mats
spread on almost every conceivable space in the compound, including
outside of the house.

No one introduced me to the landlord, the neighbors, or *chef de quartier* of Bambeto. In fact, I never got to make a Guinean friend while there. I
never met the neighbors. My life degenerated into a rather boring routine.
After eating whatever I was lucky to find in the morning, I walked to the
neighborhood of Belleview, where the Embassy of Sierra Leone was located. I spent the whole day hanging out with other refugees. We talked
about events in Sierra Leone, looked for new arrivals, waited for briefings
from Embassy officials, and tried to cheer each other up. We also placed
as many phone calls as we could to people outside of Guinea seeking help.
In late September 1997, my former roommate from Fourah Bay College
who had traveled to the United States and was the recipient of many of
my calls sent me $100.00. This was what I used to pay for my trip to
Ghana. Once in a while we ventured to the market in Medina to take in
the spectacle and, on very rare occasions, actually buy things. As night
approached, I walked back to Bambeto. I took a taxi whenever I could
afford it, which was very rarely.

I was an autonomous refugee in Conakry. I was not symbolically
subjugated to the landlord, *chef de quarter*, or any of the notables in
the area. I did not symbolically exchange gifts with any Guinean notable
in the neighborhood, and no Guinean shared legal responsibility for my
actions. In fact, other than the trader from whose shop I used to buy
tapalapa (bread) in the morning and evening, I can say that I met none
of the people in the neighborhood during my presence there. The shop
owner was a Fulani who had lived in Sierra Leone for a while and so
spoke Krio, the lingua franca in Sierra Leone. We chatted sometimes.

My autonomous life as a refugee in Conakry was unexceptional. I
know this from my observation of and participation in the lives of many
of my refugee friends and acquaintances in Conakry at the time. This
was confirmed during interviews that I later did for this project with
people who had been refugees in Conakry during the wars in Sierra
Leone and Liberia. As refugees we arrived in a city that at that period
privileged residence over indigeneity in the apportionment of rights. The
distinction between those who belonged and those who did not did not
hinge on indigeneity. Conakry was the home of those who settled there.

As refugees, we were remarkable only in the circumstances of our arrival, not our arrival from elsewhere.

Because the distinction between indigenes and strangers was not salient, neighborhoods in the capital had no functioning institutions for normalizing the presence of non-indigenous residents. Furthermore, the society exerted no pressure on the refugees to seek to normalize their presence by establishing links with the indigenes. As noted by McGovern, President Lansana Conte had sought to activate the local level security apparatus of the Sekou Toure era by requiring that all strangers be taken to the *chef de quartier*.[114] Very few Guinean landlords in Conakry did this. However, even where they did so, the reporting did not form part of a broader effort to normalize the stay of new arrivals conceived of as residents who, by virtue of their lack of indigeneity, did not belong. None of the more extensive processes and structures for dealing with stranger residents that I write of in areas that privilege indigeneity existed in Conakry's neighborhoods. New arrivals just went on to live their lives like others in the city. People dealt with them without much consideration regarding whether they originated from the city or not. Although there was some half-hearted effort by the government to make sure refugees moved to the refugee camps located away from the capital, this had nothing to do with their not being indigenes of the area. Other non-Baga residents of the city did not face these restrictions.

In the absence of institutional mechanisms for linking strangers and natives in the city and lack of pressures on non-indigenes to normalize their stay through links with the indigenes, the refugees settled autonomously of local notables.[115] They did not symbolically subjugate themselves to local notables. Refugees did not report seeking friendships with Guinean notables in their neighborhoods, frequently visiting these notables or naming children after them. The exchange of gifts with local notables was also practically nonexistent. Refugees did not report routinely offering free labor to notables in their area. Local elites did not share legal responsibility for the refugees. One refugee put the relationship, or rather lack thereof, between them and the Guinean notables this way: "We had no business with the Guineans at all. We were there on our

---

[114] McGovern, "Conflit régional," 91.
[115] My characterization of the lives of refugees and their relations with Guineans in Conakry that follows is based on my observation of refugee life as a refugee in Conakry in 1997 as well as six formal interviews with former refugees in Conakry in 2009 and many informal conversations with people who were refugees in Conakry and have stayed on there after the wars ceased in their countries of origin.

own, for ourselves."[116] She also recalled the lack of an effort by either side to seek to create strong relations with the other: "No Guinean came to offer friendship to someone in our compound, and none of the people in our compound tried to make a Guinean friend. We did not know them."[117]

The landlords from whom the refugees rented tenements would have been the most likely people for refugees to establish such relations with because market relations between the two should have guaranteed some sort of initial contact. Almost all refugees in Conakry were self-settled, and the vast majority lived in rented private buildings from Guinean landlords. However, refugees often did not have much of a relationship with their landlords. Many never even got to meet those landlords. I lived in a compound in Bambeto for a month and never got to meet the landlord. In case you think this might have a lot to do with my being there for only a short while, my sister who lived there for more than two years also never got to meet the landlord.

The system of rental in Conakry was structured in a way that further alienated the refugees even from their landlords. One refugee would arrange the rental with the landlord and others will move in with him or her. Rents were often paid annually or biannually, limiting meetings between refugees and landlords. Landlords hardly ever visited the compounds. Even when they did, they did not necessarily meet most of the residents of the compound because most refugees spent the daytime outside of where they usually slept. Sometimes the only contact between the two parties was when the refugee who rented the house went to the landlord's house to pay the rent. There are refugees who reported staying in rental housing in Conakry for years and never meeting their landlords. The landlords very often did not introduce their refugee tenants to the *chef de quartier* or neighbors.

There were instances in which landlords also lived in the compounds they rented to refugees. This often guaranteed that, apart from the nightly sojourners, refugee tenants met the landlord. However, this did not result in the subjugation of the refugees to their landlords. I interviewed two refugees who lived in different parts of Conakry but who both stayed in the same compound as their landladies. Both were not subjugated to their landladies. Relations were almost purely confined to the market realm.

---

[116] Interview with a former refugee in Freetown, Sierra Leone (MRB 336), October 2, 2009.
[117] Interview (MRB 336).

They did not deliberately seek out their landladies to greet them in the morning, even though they said "hi" when they crossed paths. They did not routinely exchange gifts or food with the landladies. They exchanged food occasionally during Muslim holidays when most people exchange food with their neighbors. The landladies did not introduce them to the *chef de quartier* or anyone else in the neighborhood and certainly did not share legal responsibility for the refugees' actions.[118]

There were only a few refugees who created friendships with Guineans, and these were often Guineans who had stayed in Sierra Leone for a while. These relations were horizontal instead of patron–client ones in which the refugees were subjugated to the locals.

These friendships were exceptional. The refugees generally tended to look inward. The embassies of Liberia and Sierra Leone came to play central roles in their lives. Some of these are roles that are usually played by community leaders in indigeneity-privileging societies. The embassies evolved from places where refugees went to get various forms of travel documents and seek help with protection issues to the prime social sites for refugees. Later they even became the sites of first abode for many refugees in the city. Many new arrivals in the city first went to the embassies of their countries. Some went there because they had arranged to be met there by others who were already in Conakry. Some went there because they knew no one in Conakry. They slept there for a few days until they met someone or got enough money to find a place to live. The embassies became spots where refugee went to hang out. Many refugees spent most of their day in that vicinity. It was a place to get news about Sierra Leone, hang out with friends, seek new arrivals who you might have known previously, and make new friends.

Most refugees had no jobs. Some lived on remittances sent by relatives and friends abroad. Others survived by befriending and associating themselves with these more fortunate refugees. The embassies were the places where many of these friendships were formed. It was also where many housemates met each other. People met there, discussed housing, pooled resources, and rented a place. They then sometimes allowed their friends to either live with them on a full-time basis or just come to sleep at night. The refugees who could afford it often cooked and invited others to come and eat with them. Those who were going through immigration processes funded by relatives abroad were often relatively well off because some of

---

[118] Interviews with a former refugees in Freetown, Sierra Leone (MRB 335), October 2, 2009; and another refugee in Freetown, Sierra Leone (MRB 334), October 2, 2009.

their living expenses were met by the relatives sponsoring them. Some of these became the benefactors of many other refugees.

There were some refugees who worked. The garbage collection sector attracted a lot of refugees. These refugees were not subjugated to their employers in the manner defined here. Many refugees tried their hands at small-scale enterprises such as making and selling cakes and braiding hair, and some refugee women were known to have become prostitutes.[119]

The narrative of a former Liberian refugee on the autonomous life she led with her cousins in Conakry follows:

I was living in Concasseur in 1999 with my daughter, two cousins, and the family of my aunt's brother-in-law. We rented that place. My aunt in the United States sent money to her brother-in-law, who paid the landlord. None of us in the house worked. Our only job was to go to church. It was the Living Light Outreach Ministry led by one Sierra Leonean pastor. Most of the members of the congregation were from Sierra Leone. When we went to Conakry first, my aunt's in-law, who is Sierra Leonean, met us at the Sierra Leone Embassy, where he had told us to alight from the car. He took us to Concasseur, where he lived, and we stayed there for a few months. He did not show us to the landlord. The landlord lived somewhere else and came to the compound once in a while. Our in-law used to go to the landlord's house to pay the rent. We had no relationship with the landlord and never went to visit him or help him with work. No one showed us to the *chef de quartier* there.

Later the landlord began to complain that there were too many people in the house. He said he had rented it to a family of six and now there were thirteen people in the house. We moved. We first went to stay with some Liberian friends in Gbessia. Then my aunt sent money and my cousin went and rented another place in Concasseur. The landlord lived in the same compound and we saw them every day because our kitchens were close to each other. He even spoke Krio. We exchanged greetings sometimes. They were nice and did not bother us. But we did not do any housework for them other than cleaning the common spaces we shared once in a while. We were living on our own. We never tried to befriend the Guineans. . . . We were independent there and had nothing to do with the Guineans. I had many Sierra Leonean friends living in Hamdalaye, Belleview, and Concasseur. They were also renting and we visited each other often. I went to the Sierra Leone and Liberian embassies to get papers, participate in programs there, and just hang out. They were always full. Some Liberians lived in the embassy because they had nowhere to go to.[120]

A Guinean in Conakry gave his perspective on the autonomous lives of the refugees.

---

[119] Interview (MRB 342).
[120] Interview with a former refugee in Freetown, Sierra Leone (MRB 337), October 2, 2009.

I was in Conakry during the time of the refugees. We lived in my late father's house in Medina and there were a lot of Liberian refugees living there. I don't know if there was any house in Medina without refugees from Liberia and Sierra Leone. You could tell them apart from their accent. Some were cooking and selling fufu, some were polishing shoes, and some made a living by hailing passengers for public transport buses. Some had even better lives than the Guineans because they came with money. One refugee came and rented a place from my older brother in our house. After a short while a lot of other refugees moved in with him. Those people could crowd into little spaces. You could see over ten in one room. They will take a room and divide it up and both men and women will sleep together there. My brother introduced the renter to the *chef de quartier* but we did not do so for the others. Two of them became my friends and sometimes in the evening we talked and watched films from Sierra Leone. But generally they were not good people. They did not even greet us. They could see you sitting and just pass and go their way. They did not care. They did not do any work for us and the exchange of gifts was not between us. We used to just leave them on their own. We tried to comfort ourselves and said, "They don't know our language and that is why they are behaving this way."[121]

The short account of a Guinean landlord in Medina, Conkary, was similar.

When the refugees came I was living here in my dad's house. My dad was dead and I was the one controlling the house. Some Liberians were staying here. We introduced them to the *chef de quartier* but there were others who used to come and visit them here and play ludo. The tenants never came to greet me in the morning. If we met on the way we greeted each other. They did not help with housework here. If they met us eating we invited them but they never brought anything to us. I was very busy but sometimes if they were playing ludo and I had time I joined them. Most of them were not working. One was a carpenter and made a room divider for me. I just paid him.[122]

Just before September 2000, when the episode of generalized anti-refugee violence happened in Conakry, most of the refugees in the city did not know or have a relationship with their landlord, *chef de quartier*, or other notables in the neighborhoods in which they lived. They were autonomous of local notables. Pursuing lives that were often thoroughly separate from those of their Guinean neighbors, the Guineans knew little about the refugees. They saw them living in neighboring compounds, going about in groups, and hanging out around their embassies. To most Guineans, the refugees represented a largely mysterious quantity.

[121] Interview (MRB 387).
[122] Interview with a Guinean in Conakry (MRB 390), July 18, 2011.

Getting Rid of the 'Bedbugs'

It was against this background that rebels started to launch vicious attacks on Guinea. President Lansana Conte made a national broadcast ordering Guineans to rise and defend their country against foreigners, singling out the refugees as rebel collaborators. The state had withdrawn its protection from refugees. It went further to demonize the refugees and order its agents and citizens to attack them. A Sierra Leonean who was staying with Guinean relatives foresaw the violence to follow.

I saw Lansana Conte give the speech in Susu on TV. He said "Guineans we need to remove the bedbugs amongst us." He was referring to the refugees. This was after the rebels started attacking Guinea. I told my refugee friend that the refugees were going to suffer a lot in Conakry.[123]

This was a time of great tension in which the country faced a serious threat from rebels who were notorious for the terrible atrocities that they left in their wake.[124] There was a lot of fear in the capital. The possibility of refugees in Conakry collaborating with rebels was truly scary. The rebels in Sierra Leone were known to use infiltration as a key tactic. They often infiltrated towns and villages they were intent on attacking with ordinary-looking people who acted as couriers of information and joined in attacks later.

For many residents of Conakry, this fear and tension must have only been heightened by the lack of knowledge of the lives and activities of the large numbers of refugees living in their neighborhoods.[125] Many Guineans did not really know the refugees because of the autonomous lives the refugees led. Guineans' lack of knowledge of the daily lives of refugees had two consequences. There were many who bought into the allegations of the president. For these, attacking the refugees became a logical counterinsurgency activity. There were others who did not necessarily buy into the accusations of the president. However, they were still plagued by a fear of the unknown. Even if they did not buy into the president's account, they did not know enough about the refugees to reach a different conclusion. This was particularly important for those who might have felt some pity for the refugees and might have been in a position

---

[123] Interview (MRB 342).
[124] McGovern, "Conflit régional," 89.
[125] McGovern attributes even the tendency of many Guineans to believe denunciations of some citizens as rebel collaborators to the tense and uncertain situation in a country facing serious military threats. "Conflit régional," 92.

to protect them. For many of these, the dread of the threat the refugees' might possibly pose in a situation of great danger to their country was what drove them to join in the attacks or refrain from protecting them.

They faced a tough dilemma. If the president was wrong and the refugees were not rebel collaborators, they would have done a good deed in protecting the refugees. If the refugees turned out to be rebel collaborators, protecting them would have had terrible consequences for their country and for them as individuals. Others in society would have recognized them as offering protection to rebel collaborators. Not knowing much about the refugees, the safer option seemed to be the strategy of aiding the purging of the refugees. It is this sort of reasoning that must have driven many people in Conakry to attack or refrain from protecting refugees.

An extended quotation from a Guinean whose family owned a house in which refugees lived and who was one of the youths who hunted refugees follows.

We were afraid. There were rumors that rebels were coming from Sierra Leone, Liberia, and Cote d'Ivoire to attack Guinea. Lansana Conte called a meeting and told all the civil and military authorities to be vigilant and to pass the message down that all should be vigilant. They said "If you see someone you suspect tell the authorities about it because we are mixed. If someone comes to your house tell the authorities. If you don't know the person ask. If he is not in your family and is not Guinean tell the authorities to investigate."

Later they said the rebels were already amongst us and that we should catch all of them in the city one by one. In Belleview they arrested three rebels with arms. They showed them on TV. The captured rebels told the authorities of arms they were supposed to get through the port, and the weapons were confiscated upon arrival. They were rebels posing as refugees. They were infiltrators and they confessed. That is when we started arresting the refugees.

The landlords reported their refugee tenants to the youth, *chef de quartier*, and gendarmes. We did that because we doubted them. We reported them because we doubted them. In our house one came to rent and then many moved in with him. We were afraid and said to ourselves: "We hope he does not bring rebels here because these people only come at night. These people coming and going at night, we hope they are not rebels." We did not know them all. They spent little time in the house. My older brother called the guy who came to rent and asked him who all those people were. The refugee told us that they were all his relatives. My brother complained that his relatives were too many.

We knew the one who came to rent and introduced him to the *chef de quartier* but we began to doubt all of them. They came at night and went at night. They came and went in groups. We doubted them and thought they were doing something.

You had to report them to the authorities to seek clarity. The authorities will wait for them and arrest them all and ask them what they are up to. We reported our tenants to the soldiers and they came and took them early in the morning and investigated them. We never thought of just keeping them and not exposing them. You don't know a stranger. She just came and rented your place. If you hide her and there is a problem, as the landlord what will you do?

I was in eleventh grade then when the president gave his speech. He said since the wars in their countries were over, the refugees should go back home. Each neighborhood had its youth association. I was one of them here. We tied ropes across the roads and checked for IDs. We patrolled all night and there was a 10 pm curfew. We boiled *ataya*[126] and stayed up all night. If we saw someone suspicious, we called the soldiers. What we did is what prevented the rebels from conquering Guinea like they did in Liberia and Sierra Leone.[127]

The refugees had no local protectors. Disaffected youth who blamed the refugees for their circumstances and saw an opportunity to steal from and rape them while protecting their country from rebel attacks formed the main body of attackers. They systematically combed neighborhoods in search of refugees. Local notables in the form of landlords and *chefs de quartier* were eager to answer the call to patriotism. These were people who were benefiting economically from the presence of the refugees. However, their lack of clarity of what the refugees represented led some to embrace the view that the refugees were rebel collaborators. Others who did not necessarily believe that the refugees were rebels still chose the safe option of purging them given the uncertainty surrounding the refugees. Landlords were often the ones who invited the mobs into their compounds to attack the refugees.[128] A young man who actively participated in one of the youth groups that were looking for refugees and whose older brother rented rooms in their family house to refugees noted:

Money was never an issue in the whole thing. We were thinking about our lives. We never thought of money. These people were so many here. We were worried for our lives. We were afraid the war will come here. Some landlords were saying we will never rent places to refugees again and many evicted them. It was only after a TV announcement from the government that people stopped.[129]

---

[126] *Ataya* is a hot beverage that is consumed in many parts of West Africa. It is common for friends to boil and drink ataya while hanging out and discussing politics, football, and so forth.
[127] Interview (MRB 387).
[128] Interview (MRB 342); interview (MRB 337); and interview (MRB 335).
[129] Interview (MRB 387).

Even taxi drivers heeded the call to defend the country. They took many refugees trying to flee to their embassies or the port to gendarmeries.[130] At the height of the attacks, two young Sierra Leoneans boarded the taxi of a young Fulani driver and asked him to take them to the port to board the boat *MV Madam Monique*, which was a major link between Freetown and Conakry at the time. The driver instead took them straight to the notorious Seratay Police Station and told the officer at the counter: "Those rebels they are talking about, I have brought two of them."[131]

CONCLUSION

Some refugees escaped the attack in Conakry by running quickly to their embassies. Guinean landlords protected some really fortunate ones. These were the very few refugees who against all structural odds had formed deep relations with their landlords. Some of these landlords locked the refugees up and ran away with the keys, ensuring that people could not attack the refugees. However, the general pattern in Conakry was one of locals who knew little about the refugees attacking them out of fear of refugee collaboration with rebels. In Banie, Fangamandou, and Kondou Sub-Prefectures in the Forest Region of Guinea, the opposite general pattern prevailed. Almost all refugees were subjugated to local elites who did not buy into the state's denunciation of the refugees and kept their communities from attacking the refugees. In the next chapter, I present an account of events in these Forest Region communities.

---

[130] Interview (MRB 342).
[131] Ibid.

4

A Different Approach to Counterinsurgency in the Forest Region of Guinea

The village chiefs called a big meeting with the refugee chiefs and all the refugees. They said: "No one should go to Liberia and come back. If you see a stranger tell us. If we discover you did not we will send you all to Liberia." They said the refugees with farms near the river should not go there alone. When you wanted to go there you had to seek permission from the chief.[1]

On July 30, 2009, I sat with an elder of Dongueta in the verandah of his house for one of the many conversations that we had during my time doing research in Banie Sub-Prefecture in Guinea's Yomou Prefecture, on the border with Liberia's Lofa County. He was one of the village leaders in the year 2000 and recounted how a soldier came from Yomou to relay President Conte's orders that the community should gather, interrogate, and expel the refugees. Like many villagers of Dongueta and former refugees across the border in Salayea District in Liberia's Lofa County, he assured me that locals did not gather the refugees together or expel them. Because this amounted to disobedience of a direct presidential order, I asked him why they did not follow the president's orders. He first tried to hedge as many in these areas do when matters concerning their relations with state authorities arise in discussions. "Our refugees here all lived in one place so we did not need to gather them." I gently reminded him that the refugees in Dongueta did not in fact live in one place. Many lived in the town outside of the "camp," and like locals, others slept in temporary encampments in the forest during the active farming season.

[1] Interview with a former Liberian refugee in Doungueta, Yomou Prefecture, Guinea (MRB 214), July 30, 2009.

Anyway, why did they not expel the refugees even if they were all living in one place? "We did not have trucks to take them to the border," was the short reply.

I raised the facts that Dongueta is just a few miles from the border and that people walk to the border every day. Even I did that during my stay in the area. That is how most of the refugees came to Dongueta. His riposte was: "The order was just an informal verbal order. It was just word of mouth. If the government had sent a specific paper order we *might* have done it." I was pondering the use of "might" instead of the more definite "will" when, after a few seconds of silence, he finally confessed the unwillingness of the village elders to go along with the state's project:

The government brought them [the refugees] here and said we should take care of them and we did. If it later wanted them expelled, it should have done that itself instead of asking us to do it. If they were serious, they should have come and removed the refugees. We had a deep relationship with the refugees and so we did not respond like the people in Conakry. There is no way we could have done those things they did to the refugees in Conakry.[2]

During fieldwork in the Forest Region and neighboring Liberia and Sierra Leone, I found abundant evidence from talking to both Guineans and former refugees that true to the old man's words, counterinsurgency in many communities in the Forest Region took a decidedly different turn from that in Conakry. The response of local communities to the attacks on Guinea and President Conte's call to arms was more of a rights-based one than what we saw in Conakry. I call it a rights-based approach because it diverged from blanket attacks on all refugees with no effort at investigating their links with the insurgency. It was a more discriminatory method that tried in various ways to detect and punish the rebels and rebel collaborators within the refugee *and Guinean* population. Local authorities did learn of the orders of the president. Some heard it on the radio, and others received the orders from soldiers and administrators sent from prefecture headquarters.[3] The following is a sample of what *former refugees* and locals said were some of the measures taken by local communities around the same time that civilians were

---

[2] Interview (MRB 212).

[3] Interview (MRB 158); interviews with a villager elder in Dongueta, Yomou Prefecture, Guinea (MRB 201), July 30, 2009; a village elder in Dongueta, Yomou Prefecture, Guinea (MRB 209), July 29, 2009; a village elder in Dongueta, Yomou Prefecture, Guinea (MRB 211), July 30, 2009; and interview (MRB 212).

involved in an orgy of violence against refugees in Conakry in the name of counterinsurgency. I spend some time describing the nature of counterinsurgency efforts in these Forest Region communities to show their radically different character from what happened in Conakry.

In Yende Douane, Guéckédou Prefecture, soldiers put immense pressure on village elders to expel the refugees. The elders resisted and instead proposed a compromise to the soldiers. They would make meticulous records for each refugee household. Every week they would accompany a soldier around the village to check refugees against the list. If a refugee was not present, a household head would have to account for him. Failing this, that refugee would be regarded as a rebel. The soldiers reluctantly agreed to this arrangement.[4]

The rebels did not get to Kolomba, Guéckédou Prefecture, but people feared attacks, and many refugees and citizens ran away from the area. The locals formed a militia and imposed a curfew. Those caught breaking the curfew were arrested and beaten. Those who were not known by people in the area were sent to Guéckédou-Centre as rebel suspects. Those vouched for were released. Refugees who did not break the curfew were not physically harmed. Many Guineans complained that despite Guinea's hospitality to the refugees, the brothers of the refugees were attacking the country. They accused the refugees of belonging to nationalities that were ungrateful and untrustworthy. Some locals, especially the youth, accused the refugees of being rebels.[5]

In Kondou Lengo Bengou, Guéckédou Prefecture, newly arriving refugees were arrested and taken to refugee camp officials for identification. A curfew was imposed, and those arrested were given to the soldiers regardless of whether they were refugees or Guineans. The refugees were urged to form a militia to patrol the camp and were armed with hunting guns and knives. A pass was introduced for the refugees. It was jointly issued by military officials and refugee leaders and was valid for only a few days. It cost 500 Guinean francs, and all refugees who wanted to go out of the camp had to have a pass. Those caught without passes were taken to the military barracks. When it was confirmed that these arrested people were refugees, they were just beaten, fined, and released. Those whose identities remained unknown were often killed as rebels. The introduction of the pass was motivated by news that rebels had killed some

---

[4] Interview (MRB 231).
[5] Interview with a former refugee in Woroma, Penguia Chiefdom, Sierra Leone (MRB 255), September 11, 2009.

refugees and taken their cards and were posing as refugees to infiltrate towns and villages in Guinea. Those caught with tattoos that happened to be new in the area were killed if refugee leaders could not vouch for them. Some rebel groups were known to have used tattoos to mark their members.[6] Like in Kolomba, some decried the fact that despite Guinean hospitality to the refugees, rebels from Liberia and Sierra Leone were attacking Guinea. They said it was this ungrateful and untrustworthy character of Sierra Leoneans and Liberians that led to the wars in their countries in the first place.[7]

In Yomou-Centre, Yomou Prefecture, local militia members went from door to door in the camp every evening, counting refugees against lists that had been prepared earlier in conjunction with heads of refugee families. Refugees that could not be accounted for were considered rebels, and their families had a lot of problems. Locals suspected some of the refugees of being rebels, and many complained about how Liberians and Sierra Leoneans were repaying Guinean hospitality by trying to destroy the country.[8]

In Gotoye, Yomou Prefecture, many locals blamed refugees for what they saw as attacks on Guinea by the relatives of the refugees, but it did not lead to violence. Refugees were not included in the local militia. A curfew was passed, and refugees caught violating it were taken to the refugee leaders to confirm their identities. The locals assembled the refugees and told them not to go into the bush without first informing their hosts, who were supposed to accompany them. Then each refugee was asked to take a traditional oath that was supposed to kill all who had bad intentions for the town or hid suspicious activities they witnessed from the local leaders.[9]

In Forofonye, Yomou Prefecture, a militia was formed that included some refugees. They patrolled and manned checkpoints. All who sought to pass through, regardless of whether they were refugees or Guineans, were searched and checked for tattoos. The refugee militia members acted as translators when the militia encountered people from Liberia during patrols. The refugees were told not to go to the bush alone. They had to

---

[6] Paul Richards, *Fighting for the rainforest* (Oxford: James Currey, 1996), 5.

[7] Interviews Guéckédou (MRB 134); and interview with a Former Sierra Leonean refugee in Bambaro, Penguia Chiefdom, Sierra Leone (MRB 300), September 17, 2009.

[8] Interview with a former Liberian refugee in Gorlu, Salayea District, Liberia (MRB 311), September 25, 2009.

[9] Interview (MRB 327); interview (MRB 158); and interview with a Guinean in Gotoye (MRB 176), July 24, 2009.

be accompanied by a local person. The rebels were just across the water, and the leaders did not want them to use the refugees to enter the town. The attacks on Guinean towns led to some bad feelings toward the refugees, and some people used to say the rebels had followed the refugees into Guinea because the refugees' lives were entangled with those of the rebels. However, the locals did not attack refugees.[10]

In Dongueta, Yomou Prefecture, they formed a militia that had both locals and refugees. They controlled the crossing point on the Diani/St. Paul River border, patrolled the area, and manned checkpoints. The militia held a meeting with the rebels across the river and warned them that if they attacked the village, their relatives living as refugees there would be punished by the locals. Locals urged the refugees to go and advise their relatives who were rebels across the river. The militia helped soldiers search the camp for arms. They found nothing. They also checked both Guineans and refugees for tattoos at checkpoints. Male militia members searched men, and female villagers searched women. Travelers were asked for their ID cards and had their bags searched regardless of whether they were Guineans or refugees. Code words were used to determine the origins of people, and those with doubtful origins were sent to Banie for identification. A 10 pm curfew was in effect for all. The town leaders called a meeting and told the refugees they should report any suspicious activity they witnessed. They said if they found out one day that the refugees were conspiring to hide things that they knew would destroy the town, they would kill all the refugees. They announced this every time rebels invaded Guinean territory. However, they did not launch attacks on the refugees.[11]

The denial by refugees and Guineans that people in these communities in the Forest Region went along with the president's order in ways similar to the generalized anti-refugee attacks in Conakry goes against much of the literature on this episode in the history of the Mano River Basin. Authors tend to portray what happened in Conakry as a national phenomenon, a *Guinean* response to the president's prompting.[12] I see little

---

[10] Interviews with a former Liberian refugee in Forofonye, Yomou Prefecture, Guinea (MRB 189), July 27, 2009; an old Guinean in Forofonye (MRB 181), July 26, 2009; a leader in Forofonye (MRB 182), July 26, 2009; and a Guinean in Forofonye (MRB 188), July 27, 2009.

[11] Interview with a former member of the local militia in Dongueta (MRB 200), July 28, 2009; and interview (MRB 214).

[12] Arieff, "Still standing"; Gale, "The invisible refugee camp"; and McGovern, "Conflit regional."

reason why former refugees now living in their own countries would lie to exonerate Guineans in these communities of such anti-refugee attacks in September 2000. This is especially so because these former refugees spent long periods of time going into the gritty details of all the exploitation and harm they suffered at the hands of Guineans.

Beyond the general assertions by authors, a close examination of the literature lends credence to the claims of these Guineans and former refugees. It undercuts those who tend to portray what happened as a Guinea-wide phenomenon. Although there is very detailed description of the anti-refugee violence in Conakry,[13] it is extremely difficult to find any such description of generalized anti-refugee violence anywhere else in Guinea. There are accounts of violence involving refugees in many areas of Guinea, but as I show next, these do not amount to the sort of generalized anti-refugee violence seen in Conakry. Instead, we see in the literature indications that there was in fact no such violence. McGovern's account is important because he was living in a village in Macenta Prefecture when all of this was happening and gives us details of a response in an area other than those I studied. He paints a picture of a situation in which there was widespread verbal condemnation of the refugees in line with the President's speech, but he gives no indication of generalized attacks on refugees in the vicinity. Instead, what he paints is a picture of the sort of more measured and discriminating vigilante activity aimed at sniffing out both refugee and Guinean rebel sympathizers. Guineans in the villages where he lived threatened the punishment of non-return to all (not only refugees) who fled the village instead of helping to defend it.[14] Indeed, his work acknowledges the fact that only some areas of Guinea saw such generalized attacks.[15]

It is important to understand the claim I am making here. I am not rejecting the claim that some Guineans in these communities wanted to go along with the proposal to attack and expel the refugees. I am also not denying that many in these communities verbally vilified the refugees. The verbal vilification of refugees was widespread and even predated the president's speech, as I demonstrate later. People accused the refugees of all sorts of evils, including being prone to betrayal, being untrustworthy, being rebels, collaborating with rebels, theft, prostitution, drug abuse, defecating everywhere, and so forth. A refugee explained to me that one

[13] Human Rights Watch, "Refugee women in Guinea raped."
[14] McGovern, "Unmasking the state," 556, 576–577.
[15] Ibid., 555.

of the hardest things for her to take was when Guineans explained the plight of the refugees in terms of their national character. They would tell the refugees, "You Sierra Leoneans/Liberians are just ungrateful and untrustworthy people. That is why you people are killing each other in your country and that is why you are now refugees here. Since you people are not changing you will die as refugees here in Guinea because of those attitudes of yours."[16] However, such verbal vilifications, no matter how virulent and hurtful, do not amount to generalized anti-refugee attacks. As I note later, there were many youths in these communities who wanted to attack the refugees, but powerful people in these communities prevented these plans from coming to fruition.

The arrival of the refugees in Guinea coincided with outbreaks of civil violence, resulting in large numbers of deaths in towns and villages in the Forest Region such as N'Zérékoré, Macenta, and Guéckédou. Often some refugees ended up being victims as well as perpetrators of violence in these incidents. It is even plausible to argue that the arrival and activities of some of the refugees might have being part of the cause of the violence. However, these outbreaks were not anti-refugee in character. They all pitted certain Guinean communities such as the Loma, Kpelle, and Kissi against the Konianké/Maniang. Refugees were never the sole or even primary targets of such violence. Refugees fought and were killed in such attacks because they belonged to certain ethnic groups and not because they were refugees.[17]

Even deliberate efforts by locals to destroy certain refugee camps cannot necessarily be interpreted as anti-refugee violence. Most of this happened during the incursions when rebels were attacking camps, abducting refugees, and seeking to use refugees as guides and cover to infiltrate towns. Locals often sought to destroy camps not necessarily to harm the refugees but to prevent the rebels from exploiting the camps in these ways. For instance, at the height of the incursions in 2000, the elders in Koyama, Macenta Prefecture, urged the refugees to destroy their camp and move into the town proper. This was after town elders received a letter in which the rebels promised to attack the town and claimed to already have a presence in the camp. Many of the refugees did not heed the call to abandon the camp. After the attack, the elders insisted there

[16] Interview (MRB 327).
[17] McGovern, "Unmasking the state," 508–511.

would no longer be a camp and that all refugees who wanted to live in the area had to live with the locals in the town.[18]

Mine is not an effort to gloss over the harm done to refugees by Guineans in communities in the Forest Region. The rest of this chapter details the everyday exploitation and violence to which locals subjected refugees. However, those who paint the generalized anti-refugee attacks of early September as a national phenomenon provide us with a distorted history that makes it impossible to explain these events. It also unfairly condemns most Guinean societies for attacks that happened only in a tiny section of the country. Worse still, it fails to recognize the strenuous efforts made by some Guinean communities to ensure that such violence did not happen.

To understand why people in these Forest Region communities responded so differently to the president's speech, let us revert to the comment made by the elder of Dongueta at the beginning of the chapter: "We had a deep relationship with the refugees and so we did not respond like the people in Conakry." This response leaves us with three questions that I answer in the rest of this chapter. What exactly is this thing between refugees and locals that this elder called a "deep relationship"? How did this deep relationship obviate a violent assault on the refugees by the local population, even in the face of incitement to violence by the state? Why did this deep relationship exist between locals and refugees in these areas in the Forest Region but not in Conakry?

I suggest that the deep relationship he speaks of refers to the subjugation of refugees to elites in these communities. This subjugation obviated violence by providing local elites with a wealth of information about the refugees. Because they possessed such information, they did not buy into and act on the spurious claims of the president charging all refugees with collaboration. Also, the information ensured that they did not attack all the refugees out of uncertainty over what the refugees signified. Furthermore, because they knew most of the refugees were not guilty of the charges levied by the president, they were willing to prevent some local youth from exploiting the license provided by the president to attack refugees. I argue that this deep relationship existed in these Forest Region communities but not in Conakry because in the 1990s, when the refugees settled in Guinea, the societies in the Forest Region that I focused on

---

[18] Interview with a former refugee in Kpayea, Salayea District, Liberia (MRB 325), September 8, 2009.

privileged indigeneity in the apportionment of rights. This was opposed to Conakry, where residence was privileged over indigeneity. As new non-indigenous residents in these societies, the refugees had to normalize their stay by subjugating themselves to local elites.

INDIGENEITY OVER RESIDENCE

The settlements in Fangamandou, Kondou, and Banie sub-prefectures where I focused most of the research were places where indigeneity played a superior role relative to residence in the determination of rights of belonging *in the early 1990s* when many of the refugees arrived. Villages in Banie Sub-Prefecture were known to belong to certain lineages that mostly claimed to be Kpelle. Those in Fangamandou and Kondou were said to belong to autochthonous lineages that claimed to be Kissi. The privileging of indigeneity operated at two levels. At the most fundamental level, each of the settlements was seen as belonging to certain lineages, one of which was portrayed as more autochthonous than the others. This emphasis on autochthony based on lineages was increasingly embedded in a national one based on ethnicity. The settlements I studied in Banie Sub-Prefecture were seen as belonging to the Kpelle, whereas those in Guéckédou Prefecture were seen as the home of the Kissi.

The land-owning lineages in these communities historically granted land rights to other lineages. Lineage heads then allotted land to families, and it is family heads who were responsible for the routine management of land by granting parcels to family members. People who moved into these settlements were considered to be strangers who did not belong. This was so even when they belonged to the same ethnicity as that of the local lineages. They acquired land rights by approaching locals who could allocate land to them after consulting members of the leading lineage. Over time they could, through various mechanisms, acquire the status of indigenes and so access rights to belonging in these communities.

It is because of this that I lay more emphasis in this analysis on the localized understanding of indigeneity that emphasized lineage instead of the one focusing on ethnicity that is often deployed in national discourse and practice. This localized version was not limited to the Kpelle and Kissi. McGovern[19] paints a similar picture in his study of the Toma, who

---

[19] McGovern, "Unmasking the state," 236.

are sandwiched between Kissi and Kpelle areas in Guinea. Colson[20] made a similar point about the Tonga of Zambia.

The leading lineages often provided village leaders, including the administrative chief. It was from their ranks that the leading members of the Poro and Sande secret societies that regulate life off-stage in many of the communities in this part of West Africa came.

It is worth briefly reflecting on the history of these societies to understand some of these orientations toward identity and belonging that they demonstrated in the early 1990s when the refugees started arriving. For both the predominantly Kpelle- and Kissi-speaking areas of the Forest Region, studies conducted just before the French intervention describe societies marked by political organizations that were centered on villages and involved alliances between villages that were dictated by defensive needs. These alliances were, with rare exceptions, unstable and fleeting.[21]

Villages were often composed of people of diverse ethno-linguistic backgrounds that were gradually assimilated by the dominant language group in the area.[22] The diversity of the backgrounds of people in these settlements has been put down partly to migrations spurred by the decline of the Mali Empire in the fifteenth century. It was also the effect of active slave raiding and its consequent political economic instability that had characterized the area during the era of the Trans-Atlantic Slave Trade.[23]

Just before the intervention of the French, these societies privileged founding lineages that acted as the ultimate owners of land and exercised both secular and ritual leadership through the provision of the village chief and heads of the secret societies.[24] It is worth noting that founding or autochthonous lineages were not necessarily the first to settle in an area relative to all other existing lineages. As Murphy and Bledsoe noted, "the first comer status itself is not an outcome of actual first arrival,

[20] Colson, "The assimilation of aliens," 36.
[21] Suret-Canale, "La fin de la chefferie," 470 ; Denise Paulme, *Les gens du riz: Kissi de haute-Guinée Française* (Paris: Librairie Plon, 1954), 77–82; Yves Person, "Soixante ans d'évolution en pays Kissi," *Cahiers d'Etudes Africaines* 1 (1–1960): 82 ; Denise Paulme, "La société Kissi: son organisation politique," *Cahiers d'Etude Africaine* 1 (1–1960): 77; and Germain, *Peuples de la Foret,*' 100–102.
[22] Germain, *Peuples de la Foret*, 19; and Paulme, *Les gens du riz*, 14.
[23] Andreas Massing, "The Mane, the decline of Mali, and the Mandinka expansion towards the South Windward Coast," *Cahiers d'Etudes Africaines* 25 (97–1985): 44; Germain, *Peuples de la Foret*, 63–64 ; and Paulme, "La societe Kissi," 74.
[24] William Murphy, "Secret knowledge as property and power in Kpelle society: elders versus youth," *Africa: Journal of the International African Institute* 50 (2–1980): 194.

as jural rules would have it. Rather, being a first arrival is an outcome of various political transactions and semantic manipulations."[25] It was common for more powerful new arrivals to reshape political organizations, take power, assimilate, and gradually legitimize their power by cloaking it in the vestments of autochthony, redefining those they met there as "insignificant previous inhabitants."[26] These conquering newcomers turned autochthones could be from different ethno-linguistic origins than that of the people they came to dominate. In Farmaya, Kissidougou, the ruling lineage, which emphatically asserted its Kissi identity, was called *Keita* (which is a typical Malinké name) and traced its origins to a Malinké visitor that settled and took a local wife.[27]

The assimilation of new arrivals tamed the radically diverse and hybrid origins of these settlements. It helped them to accrue the wealth that settlers represented without subverting the insistence that only indigenes truly belonged and enjoyed primary rights over land and political power in these communities. This is what made possible the continued understanding of these places, characterized by an ongoing mixing of populations, as belonging to certain lineages whose members could trace their origins to founding ancestors.

The Forest Region of Guinea was the last area to be incorporated into the colony of French Guinea. The effort at putting down resistance and rebellions in the area lasted up to just before World War I.[28] Of primary importance is the fact that the colonial authorities never made an effort to take over the day-to-day administration of land in most of the area, including the Kissi and Kpelle settlements that are the focus of this study. This was the relevant primary difference in the approach of the colonial authorities to administration in Conakry and these settlements. The October 1904 decree giving all unused land to the French state covered these areas, but no effort was made to take over the powers of lineage and family heads in the allocation of land like we saw in Conakry.[29] Allowing these family and lineage heads to continue in their role as the main administrators of land in these areas went a long way

---

[25] Murphy and Bledsoe, "Kinship and territory," 142.
[26] Murphy and Bledsoe, "Kinship and territory," 129; and McGovern, "Unmasking the state," 236–237.
[27] Paulme, "La societe Kissi," 80; and Murphy and Bledsoe, "Kinship and territory," 131.
[28] Germain, *Peuples de la Foret*, 142.
[29] Claude Riviere, *Guinea: the mobilization of a people* (Ithaca: Cornell University Press, 1977), 116. See Jean Suret-Canale, *French colonialism*, 74–75.

to conserving the privileging of indigeneity as an organizing principle in these areas.

French attitudes toward chieftaincy also followed a path that tended to reinforce, instead of undermine, indigeneity in these areas. The penchant for preferring strangers to indigenes in the appointment of chiefs that characterized policies in Conakry during the key formative years of French rule there was largely absent in the Forest Region. Instead, policy tended to conserve the rights of the old ruling lineages. This was partly a function of the late period at which this area finally came under French rule relative to Conakry. By 1914, the most active days of the French radicals' cosmopolitan approach to chieftaincy that gave little respect to autochthony was over. The shift toward association for all it was worth was under way, and in 1909, William Ponty advocated a "policy of races," calling for the choice of chiefs from the ethnic groups that they were to govern.[30] In 1917, Governor-General Van Vollenhoven reemphasized the need to appoint chiefs that were indigenous to the areas they were supposed to rule.[31] So the continued resistance of French colonialism might have saved the ruling lineages in these areas. Many of the chiefs who had resisted French rule or rebelled against the French in the Kpelle areas fled south into Liberia. However, the French allowed their relatives to continue to rule.[32] In some instances, these former rulers even came back from Liberia later and were allowed to reassume their positions.[33]

There were a few instances in which people from outside of old ruling lineages were made chiefs. This often resulted from French ignorance of local realities and active scheming by those close to the French. There was also the fact that some chiefs in their continued covert resistance against the French fronted powerless community members as chiefs while they exercised power in the background. The French often quickly corrected these situations.[34]

We need to put the focus on the shift from assimilation to association in perspective. As I noted in my analysis of Conakry, the turn to association did not totally remove the French tendency to set aside indigeneity in shaping political units and making and unmaking chiefs when they thought other criteria were more important. This was evident

---

[30] Suret-Canale, *French colonialism*, 82.
[31] Goerg, "Chieftainships," 13.
[32] Germain, *Peuples de la Foret*, 143.
[33] Ibid., 143.
[34] Ibid., 143–144.

in the Forest Region too. The imposition of cantons and canton chiefs in the Kissi areas, including those under study here, is one example. Although the French tried to follow political realities in the initial designing of cantons in both the Kissi and Kpelle areas,[35] later reorganizations of cantons in the Kissi area had little to do with preexisting political realities.[36] Resistance against the creation of these cantons and their chiefs was, however, muted because the canton chiefs were often little more than glorified village chiefs. The French appointed canton chiefs from leading lineages. Their substantive power to interfere in land matters and other local affairs was limited to their role as lineage and family heads. They were mostly administrative instruments that implemented policies like tax collection and the recruitment of forced labor and soldiers.[37]

French deviation from custom occasionally went further. In 1914 the French administrator in the Kissi areas of Guinea, in a bid to revamp administration there, eliminated fourteen cantons. Furthermore, "wanting to create a well disciplined and effective chieftaincy he removed many chiefs [and] he did not hesitate to name chiefs that were strangers to the area."[38] The policy was however very short-lived. Using time-tested methods of resistance, many of these new chiefs were fatally poisoned or killed through other means. In 1917, the French reversed their policy and reverted to the old ruling families for chiefs.[39]

The arrival of Malinké in many areas of the Forest Region has always been one of the factors that held the potential of undermining indigeneity and privileging residence in the apportionment of rights in the Forest Region. This potential has been constantly thwarted by policies of partition that tended to transform the area into an ever more complex patchwork of spaces, with some belonging to Malinké and others to Kissi or Kpelle autochthonous people. Before the colonial era, arriving Malinké were not peculiar. Some of the ancestors of the people we call Kpelle today are known to have also arrived in the Forest Region from the same direction that many Malinké came from.[40] As I noted earlier, settlements in the Forest Region were intensely multiethnic, and the Malinké, like

---

[35] Germain, *Peuples de la Foret*, 228; and Person, "Soixante ans," 92.
[36] Person, "Soixante ans," 92.
[37] Ibid., 88–92.
[38] Ibid., 89.
[39] Ibid., 89–90.
[40] Germain, *Peuples de la Foret*, 46–69 & 87; and McGovern, "Unmasking the state," 183.

other new arrivals, were assimilated either as rulers or as subordinates to existing rulers.[41]

The advent of colonialism and the general effort at congealing and territorializing identities made the process of assimilation harder. A process of partition was what continuously subverted a movement to a situation that privileged residence over indigeneity. Malinké often acted as auxiliaries of the French in conquering and administering the Forest Region and so were no longer always willing to assimilate into these cultures. McGovern has shown how successful Malinké claims on canton chieftaincies in Macenta and local resistance to these claims led the French to adopt a policy of partition. They created cantons that belonged to Toma and some that belonged to Maniang.[42] In the Kissi areas, Malinké tended to concentrate in certain zones such as Yende Millimou that became trading centers.[43] Kissi autochthones in villages where Malinké settled often collectively fled to other places when they felt Malinké influence was too high.[44]

McGovern[45] has written of how in more recent times the Socialist government of Sekou Toure posed a serious challenge to the autochthonous control of land. It nationalized land, a move that was similar to the colonial decree of 1904. It then guaranteed rights to those who added value to land by putting it to rational use. As some of my interviewees told me, then "unused land had no owners."[46] The guarantee of land rights ceased to flow from indigeneity through autochthones. Instead it now accrued from the central authority through the "rational" use of land. Many Malinké acquired rights to land in the Forest Region through the development of cocoa, coffee, and kola plantations. As McGovern has pointed out, it was not the settlement of Malinké in these areas or their access to land that was new. It was their unwillingness to submit to the indigenes in the face of a state that guaranteed their rights to land and, sometimes, even political office.[47]

However, the potential of this to push society toward a system that privileged residence over indigeneity was again somewhat blunted by

41 Germain, *Peuples de la Foret*, 19; Murphy and Bledsoe, "Kinship and territory," 131–133; and Person, "Soixante ans," 87.
42 McGovern, "Unmasking the state," 389–396.
43 Person, "Soixante ans," 102.
44 Ibid., 104.
45 McGovern "Unmasking the state," 400–406.
46 Interview (MRB 378).
47 McGovern, "Unmasking the state," 406.

the practice of voluntary partition by many *Forestière* communities. As the Kissi did during the colonial days,[48] many *Forestière* communities facing increasing Malinké presence in their settlements left en masse to form new villages in the forest. This process, which a Toma interviewee described to McGovern,[49] is one that occurred also in the Kissi and Kpelle areas.

With the death of Sekou Toure in 1984, many of these *Forestière* communities had six years to reverse this privileging of residence over autochthony that his policies had encouraged before the refugees began to arrive in the 1990s. This reinforcement of indigeneity often involved violence and was aided by the new president, Lansana Conte. He was struggling to stem a challenge from Alpha Conde, a Malinké who posed a consistent threat during presidential elections. The president's encouragement of *Forestière* claims to privileged belonging in the Forest Region due to their indigeneity was aimed at undermining Malinké populations such as the Konianké and Maniang. This was because they were thought to be strongly supportive of Alpha Conde.[50] McGovern quotes a speech in N'Zérékoré in which the president asked: "You Malinkés, do you come from here? Were your ancestors born here? This is the ancestral land of the *Forestières* so if you have a problem, go back to your own homes."[51] In the Kpelle areas, the 1990s saw an outbreak of violent ethnic cleansing in which Malinkés were massacred in the city of N'Zérékoré and many outlying villages.[52] This was when the refugees were just arriving, and it must have left an impression on them.

Importantly, even Malinké resistance to these *Forestière* claims to privileged rights in the Forest Region during this time of Lansana Conte were often couched in the language of autochthony instead of one that emphasizes residence. They adopted the familiar strategy of making claims in the language privileged by the government of the day. During the days of Sekou Toure who privileged residence and "rational" land use, they emphasized their knack for putting land to rational use to make claims. During the time of Conte who played up indigeneity in his discourses on the Forest Region, Malinké often switched tactics and spoke in the language of the day that emphasized indigeneity. Where large numbers

---

[48] Person, "Soixante ans," 104.
[49] McGovern, "Unmasking the state," 508.
[50] Ibid., 511.
[51] Ibid., 574–575.
[52] McGovern, "Unmasking the state," 508–510; and Van Damme, "How Liberian," 49.

of Malinké had settled, they tended to reinforce indigeneity as the ultimate standard for defining who belonged. Their claim was not always that Guinea belongs to all Guineans and that they have rights to settle in these places just like everyone else. Theirs was often the more exclusionary claim that these areas in which they had settled belong to Malinké autochthones exclusively or that the Malinké were equally autochthonous in these areas as the Kpelle/Kissi/Toma/Mano.[53]

SUBJUGATING NEW ARRIVALS

Because these societies, in the 1990s, were mainly seen as belonging to indigenes, they had very elaborate and well-functioning institutions for dealing with settlers when the refugees arrived. Furthermore, refugees like other strangers were *forced* into normalizing their stay by going through these local institutional processes.

The acceptance of large numbers of people by these communities was dependent on a deliberate community decision. Strangers could not just go and settle in these communities. Although the village of Dongueta in Yomou Prefecture was to become host to a large number of refugees, the first Liberians who ventured to seek refuge there received a rather inhospitable reception. The villagers who were Kpelle had decided not to let any refugees in for fear of the rebels following the refugees. A Kpelle woman who was one of these refugees recalled what happened: "We were some of the first people to become refugees in Guinea. When we got to Dongueta, the villagers had a checkpoint at the entrance to the town and said they had decided not to let refugees in because the rebels might follow us. We begged and negotiated with them for three days. All those days we slept at the checkpoint. Finally we gave up and went on to Yomou."[54]

These villages also had very stringent policies requiring locals who received strangers to inform the chief before settling them. Visitors who knew no one in the community had to be taken to the home of the chief before they could stay anywhere in the village. People who hosted strangers without first informing the chief were often punished. People would generally not deal with or help strangers without first knowing

---

[53] Interview with an old man in Daro, Macenta Prefecture, Guinea (MRB 38), December 14, 2008; and interview with a Maniang youth in Macenta Centre (MRB 67), December 14, 2008.

[54] Interview with a Kpelle lady in Gorlu, Salayea District, Liberia (MRB 314), September 29, 2009.

whether they had been introduced to the chief. Usually, one of the first things people would ask a stranger is "Have you been to the home of the chief already?" Here is a man who fled with his family to Gotoye, also in Yomou Prefecture:

It was the dry season when we fled, and Gotoye was the first town on the way. When people asked us who we had come to visit, we mentioned the name of a friend, so they took us to his home. He told us we had to go and see the chief before he could take us in. When he got there he told the chief: "This is my stranger, and he and his family are going to be staying with me." The chief agreed and we stayed with my friend for two weeks before moving to the camp.[55]

Someone who had gone to Kelema, Fangamandou Sub-Prefecture, had this to say: "As soon as you entered Kelema, the person you came to had to take you to the chief and if you did not know anyone you had to go and see the chief. They controlled the entrance into their village tightly and did not allow people to just get in."[56]

There is a strong temptation to see this as a legacy of Sekou Touré's regime. It had encouraged people to inform on others and gotten neighborhood and village chiefs to keep tabs on people in their communities.[57] There is no denying that Sekou Touré encouraged this and that Lansana Conte's government sought to resurrect some of these practices in the face of the crisis that threatened Guinea during the wars in the Mano River Basin. However, there was a fundamental difference between the reporting of strangers to chiefs in Conakry and that in these villages in the Forest Region. In Conakry, the reporting of tenants to chiefs, on those rare occasions when it was done, was the beginning and end of what was a state-inspired effort at keeping tabs on new arrivals in communities. In the villages in the Forest Region that I studied, it was only a very initial step in a wide-ranging system that was meant to normalize and accommodate people seen as not belonging to these communities on account of their non-indigeneity.

Sekou Touré did not inspire these systems. They predated his rule. I can adduce two types of evidence in support of this claim. As many of my old informants told me, these were things their grandfathers used to

---

55 Interview with a former refugee in Kpayea, Salayea District, Liberia (MRB 328), September 28, 2009.
56 Interview with a former refugee in Tofawonde, Penguia Chiefdom, Sierra Leone (MRB 292), September 16, 2009.
57 McGovern, "Conflit régional," 91.

do long before Sekou Toure became president.[58] Furthermore, similar communities in neighboring countries that were not ruled by Toure and that had very different types of states and governments had the same practices. I did research in many villages in Liberia and Sierra Leone, and often I just could not get to the compound of the chief fast enough. People who wanted to know who I was visiting and whether I had gone to see the chief often intercepted me. I argue that there is something about the structure of these communities that better explains this orientation to strangers.

Another component of the mechanisms for dealing with strangers in these villages was the policy of putting strangers in care of locals. Strangers could not live on their own or for themselves in these communities. They had to be attached to a local person who was officially recognized as the host to whom they belonged. Refugees were often required to name the person they were visiting at checkpoints to villages. They would then be directed to the home of the person they named. Alternatively, the person they claimed to be visiting would be called to the checkpoint to receive them. Locals who took their visitors to the chiefs were recognized as the owners/hosts of those strangers.

When refugees knew no one in the village, chiefs sometimes distributed them to locals or adopted them as guests. In other instances, refugees were given some time to find and introduce hosts to the chief to continue living in the village. Locals were also instructed to host refugees with threats of fines for those who did not do so. Chiefs often called joint meetings of refugees and locals after the refugees had stayed in the area for a while. During these meetings, they asked refugees to publicly identify their hosts. Refugees who could not name a host were told to go seek refuge elsewhere or limit themselves to the United Nations High Commission for Refugees (UNHCR) camp. "After we arrived in Forofonye (Banie Sub Prefecture)," a former refugee recalled, "they called a meeting and said each refugee should show their stranger father (host).... If you did not show your stranger father they told you to move to another village."[59] Another recollected: "They told us there was no way you can be there [Komou, Yomou-Centre] as a stranger without a stranger father."[60] A

---

[58] Inerviews with Guineans in Dongueta, Yomou Prefecture, Guinea (MRB 360 and 362), July 8, 2011.
[59] Interview with a former refugee in Gorlu, Salayea District, Liberia (MRB 312), September 26, 2009.
[60] Interview (MRB 329).

Guinean who was a village leader then recounted during an interview in Dongueta, Banie Sub-Prefecture:

The refugees came in 1989. We had a meeting and we decided to accept them. It was a joint meeting. All gave their acceptance for the refugees to come and settle here. We had laws that we taught them. We also told our people "If a refugee comes to your farm or forest accept them. We have decided to accept them so be open to them." Some complained of refugees entering their bushes and we told them to take it easy.[61]

Some villages meticulously created records that formally linked refugees to their hosts. A refugee who lived in Komou confirmed this.

I was refugee vice president and then first secretary in Komou and I did all the registration of refugees there. When we got there, the town people held a meeting and told us that all refugee family heads should look for a local host. The host will be responsible for the refugee and give him land to farm. After a while, they called us again and said everyone should show their stranger father. When I was registering refugees, I wrote the name of the family head followed by the names of the other family members. And then above that I wrote the name of the stranger father (host). The villagers also kept records like that.[62]

Even when formal UNHCR camps existed, most refugees quickly sought to enter into these local incorporating institutions. The presence of these formal UNHCR camps created the possibility of refugees existing in these areas without subjecting themselves to these local institutions. However, sooner or later the few refugees who chose this path realized the lack of wisdom in their choice, for their lives became unbearable. They had to limit themselves to the camps and depend for all of their needs on humanitarian agencies. This was a mode of existence that was precarious, to put it mildly, given the inadequacy and uncertainty of this support.

A notable in Gotoye declared: "No one can live in this village without a host. All of them [refugees] had hosts."[63] Another explained: "The refugees had to have hosts. I told you my grandfather came and settled here long ago. It was the same then. If we find out that someone has hosted a stranger without telling the chief we will fine him. There is a law for that. You can't live here without a tutor. It has been that way for a very long time. My grand dad had a host."[64]

---

[61] Interview (MRB 362).
[62] Interview (MRB 329).
[63] Interview (MRB 378).
[64] Interview with a Guinean in Dongueta, Yomou Prefecture, Guinea (MRB 363), July 9, 2011.

Thus, in these societies that privileged indigeneity, a combination of strong local institutions for normalizing the stay of strangers and pressure on strangers to normalize their existence inevitably drove refugees en masse into relations of subordination to local elites.

For the vast majority of the refugees who knew no one where they had sought refuge or who ended up not striking it with the local they knew before their arrival, their subjugation often started with the deliberate seeking of friendships. Most often, the refugees were the ones who went on the offensive as they sought to court and capture well-off and powerful locals. These propositioning often happened after refugees had worked for locals, giving each an opportunity to observe the other. "You are now my uncle because you are Kissi and my mother is a Kissi from Sierra Leone" is how one refugee in Foedu-Kollet, Kondou Sub-Prefecture, pro-positioned the man who was to become his host.[65] Refugees who had good hosts were sometimes willing to share them with their refugee relatives. They would introduce these relatives to their hosts. A refugee who had fled to Dongueta late in the Liberian war went to live with his father-in-law, who had gone there as a refugee earlier. His father-in-law took him to his host and said, "This is my son-in-law and he is a refugee like us. I want to ask you to be his stranger father. If you give us one room in your house, we will all sleep there together."[66]

Refugees sometimes recruited through more aggressive means. Some followed people they were interested in to their farms, even when they were actively discouraged from doing so. They continued to follow the person around until he or she opened up to a relationship. Some adopted the tactic of sitting in front of the home of the person they were trying to recruit. This rarely used strategy exposed to all the advances of the refugee and threatened to paint the local person as one who was unwilling to host refugees. As one Guinean woman who had been recruited through this method in Yende Douane, Kondou Sub-Prefecture, told me in a rather bitter tone, "When people sit in front of your door you cannot jump over them to get into your house. You have to invite them in."[67]

Refugees were not the only ones recruiting. Guineans also courted refugees. In Banie, an old Liberian who belonged to the refugee committee was called on to pass judgment in a difficult case. After doing this, one of

[65] Interview in Kamiendor, Mafindor Chiefdom (MRB 223) September 3, 2009.
[66] Interview (MRB 306).
[67] Interview with an old woman in Yende Douane, Guéckédou Prefecture, Guinea (MRB 140), June 27, 2009.

the local elders told him: "You are a wise man and spoke the truth. Let us go and see your house. I will be your host."[68]

The Refugee–Host Relationship

The relationship between the subjugated refugee and host was marked by three relevant characteristics. These were constant performance of symbolic subjugation by the refugee to the host, the frequent exchange of gifts between the refugee and host, and the host's sharing of legal responsibility for the stranger. The relationship transformed the refugees into something akin to the minor children of their hosts. It is important in this regard to keep in mind that many refugees were far older than their hosts. There are many refugees who even had children that were older than their hosts. Next I discuss the three relevant aspects of this relationship.

Symbolic Subjugation

The refugees performed symbolic subjugation to their hosts by regularly going to visit them. Some went every morning and evening. They offered help with household chores and asked if there were other ways they could help. They made sure to address their hosts with titles of respect. A woman who was a refugee in Kolomba, Fangamandou Sub-Prefecture, recalled:

In Kolomba each refugee had a local friend. We used to cajole them [the locals] into becoming friends. In the morning you saw many refugees going up that hill to the village. It was to greet their hosts. They would talk to them nicely, help with housework, and ask if there was other work they could help with. It was only after this that they would go about looking for other work to survive on.[69]

These displays often had their desired effect. One Guinean noted: "I hosted many refugees, and some were far older than me. They used to call me 'Papay.' Those refugees really knew how to respect you. Even if you were a child, when they addressed you it made you feel good."[70] Sometimes the performance of subordination was to such an extent that some of its more humble beneficiaries felt embarrassed. A woman in

[68] Interview with an old man in Gorlu, Salayea District, Liberia (MRB 313), September 26, 2009.
[69] Interview with a former refugee in Kolomba, Guéckédou Prefecture, Guinea (MRB 108), June 20, 2009.
[70] Interview (MRB 160).

Gotoye recounted: "The refugees who lived with us used to call me 'Mother.' Sometimes I felt ashamed when they tried to do certain things for me like pounding my rice. They were old women doing this for a young girl like me. Occasionally I felt so embarrassed I told them to stop and not do it."[71]

These performances of symbolic acts of subjugation took other forms. Many refugees who had children in Guinea named those kids after their hosts or family members of their host. Both Guineans and refugees regarded this as a sign of gratitude and show of respect. Many refugees routinely consulted their hosts on various issues. When a refugee was going to send his or her children off to school or move to another area of Guinea were only two of many such occasions for consultations. Speaking of the refugees he hosted in Gotoye, a man recalled: "We were together. Even when they wanted to do contract work, they asked me first. When I told them to do something, they did it. When I told them not do something, they did not."[72]

Exchange of Gifts

Another element in the relationship between refugees and their hosts was the constant exchange of gifts. Initially a refugee would stay in the home of the host. This meant the host provided the refugee with lodging and food. In exchange, the refugee went along with the host to the host's farm and helped with farm labor free of charge like other minors in the household.[73] Hosts tended to be land-rich, and so in exchange for free labor, many provided refugees with land to use on a temporary basis to farm nonplantation crops such as rice and cassava. Even though refugees were often not required to give the host anything in exchange for the land, they offered some of their harvest to the host. Many hosts refused to take more than a little symbolic gift. There were only a few cases in which refugees were required to enter into sharecropping arrangements with their hosts. Where hosts lacked land, they helped their refugees to find land by arranging sharecropping arrangements and short-term leases with other locals. Many hosts also gave their refugees food items, employment, and help in getting jobs and allowed the refugees to gather sticks, palm

---

[71] Interview with a Guinea in Gotoye, Yomou Prefecture, Guinea (MRB 177), July 24, 2009.

[72] Interview with an old man in Gotoye, Yomou Prefecture, Guinea (MRB 159), July 22, 2009.

[73] Discussion with group of men in Kondou Lengo Bengou, Guéckédou Prefecture, Guinea (MRB 141), June 27, 2009.

thatch, wild fruit, and medicinal plants on their lands. Refugees, in, turn gave some of their humanitarian supplies to their hosts.

Shared Legal Responsibility

A key characteristic of the refugee–host relationship in these societies was the rule that hosts were legally responsible for the actions of their guests. One implication of this was that when refugees offended people in any way, their victims often did not even worry about tackling the refugees. They went and complained to the host of the refugee. It also meant that when the injury required compensation and the refugee could not afford it, the host was forced to pay. It buttresses the view of the stranger as a minor of his or her host in the indigeneity-privileging society.

A refugee in Kondou Lengo Bengou noted, "When I had a problem with people, many just went and told my host. They told him he is harboring thieves and that he should drive us away."[74] A former host in Foedu-Kollet mused, "I had to resolve problems created by my refugees. People used to come here to complain: 'Your strangers have done this and that to me.'"[75] In Vianga, Banie Sub-Prefecture, a former host complained about being forced by the village authorities to pay a fine on behalf of his indigent refugees who had refused to participate in communal work clearing the road to Yomou.[76] One former host in Dongueta recalled:

When people caught the refugees doing bad things, the aggrieved people came to me. Once, one of the women I hosted was walking in the bush and saw palm nuts that had been left where someone had extracted palm oil. She took some and was bringing them to the village when the owners caught her. They asked her "Who is your host?" and when she gave them my name, they said "Keep this on your head and let us go to him. He will pay for this." When they got here, they asked me "Is this your stranger?" I told them she was. They complained bitterly and said, "If you are in the business of giving away your palm nuts, we sell ours, so pay for what your stranger took." I was broke. I told her, "Please forgive her. She is my stranger so I am the one who took your palm nuts." After much begging the woman relented. After that I warned the refugee women to only collect palm nuts on my land.[77]

[74] Interview with a man in Kamiendor, Mafindor Chiefdom, Sierra Leone (MRB 225), September 3, 2009.
[75] Interview with a Guinean in Foedou-Kollet, Guéckédou Prefecture, Guinea (MRB 147), June 29, 2009.
[76] Interview with a Guinean in Vianga, Yomou Prefecture, Guinea (MRB 165), July 23, 2009.
[77] Interview with a Guinean in Dongueta, Yomou Prefecture, Guinea (MRB 208), July 29, 2009.

Refugees were not free of all responsibility for their actions. They were very often subjected to arbitrary and extrajudicial punishment for their perceived infractions. However, in the end, when there was compensation to be made, the host of the refugee was ultimately held responsible.

Complications in the System

They used to tell us "You people are now our slaves."[78]

Something has bitten these people [the refugees] that has really hurt them.[79]

It is these ties that the old man in Dongueta called a "deep relationship" and that some former refugees[80] referred to as "sitting at the feet" of their hosts. There were various tensions that occasionally affected the system because some hosts and strangers did not always meet their responsibilities. Some "bad hosts" did not help their refugees to access land. Others refrained from advocating on behalf of their refugees. In Yende Kombadu, Kondou Sub-Prefecture, the host of a certain refugee family did not only refuse to give them work in exchange for food, he also refused to plead on their behalf when they had problems.[81] In Kolomba, a woman whose host refused to give her rice on a day when she had nothing to feed her family ended the relationship.[82]

There were also "bad strangers" among the refugees. In Forofonye, when some refugees refused to help their host in whose house they were staying with his farm work, he denied them food. He told them, "Since you people say you won't help me because you are victims of war and do not know how to do farm work, I will only help my sister who assists me on the farm."[83]

Cases of refugees refusing to meet their duties as the strangers of certain hosts were rare. The big problem was with refugees who defected to wealthier and more powerful hosts, leaving their old hosts resentful, especially in cases involving hardworking and resourceful refugees. A

[78] Interview with a Sierra Leonean in Woroma, Penguia Chiefdom, Sierra Leone (MRB 296), September 16, 2009.

[79] This was a line in a song some Guinean work groups in Leobengou, Kondou Sub-Prefecture, used to sing while working to make fun of the refugees.

[80] Two interviews with former refugees in Kolomba, Guéckédou Prefecture, Guinea (MRB 101), June 19, 2009; and (MRB 109), June 20, 2009.

[81] Interview with a former refugee in Kamiendor, Mafindor Chiefdom, Sierra Leone (MRB 219), Septermber 3, 2009.

[82] Interview with a former refugee in Woroma, Penguia Chiefdom, Sierra Leone (MRB 297), September 16, 2009.

[83] Interview (MRB 312).

former host in Dongueta painfully recounted how his former guests who had stayed in his house for four years moved to the "camp" and started consorting with other locals. He reported the situation to the chief only to be told to just let them be.[84]

There is some evidence that Guinean hosts sometimes instigated such defections as they competed to recruit desirable refugees. The characteristics that made refugees desirable included being hardworking and skilled, having many youthful dependents, owning resources such as cows, and holding positions in the refugee community that gave one access to resources. A former refugee recounted how the chief of the village of Mano, Kondou Sub-Prefecture, and the chief's younger brother competed and quarreled over him.[85]

This competition by Guinean hosts created opportunities for cherry picking of hosts by highly sought after refugees.[86] There is evidence that villagers discussed and sometimes made inter-village pacts to prevent the defection of refugees from their hosts. A refugee who was victimized by such a pact recounted:

People from Gotoye, Gbamakama, Komou, and Yakpore had a meeting and decided that if a refugee could not get along with his stranger father, no one else should take him as their stranger. Once you had a stranger father, if you had problems with him and someone else tried to make you his stranger, your old stranger father could go to the new person and tell him "That refugee is with me. Don't be his stranger father or you will be responsible for him."[87]

These problems seem to have been isolated, and most refugees had such strong relations with their hosts that even after repatriating, they continued to visit and bring gifts to them. Because of this, it is tempting to idealize the experience of the subjugated refugee as an example of true integration. The subjugated refugees of the Forest Region were not totally free people enjoying the social, political, and economic rights that we normally associate with integration.[88] When you ask former refugees

---

[84] Interview with a Guinean in Dongueta, Yomou Prefecture, Guinea (MRB 203), July 29, 2009.

[85] Interview with a former refugee in Kardu, Mafindor Chiefdom, Sierra Leone (MRB 239), September 6, 2009.

[86] Writing of similar relations in Liberian Kpelle society, Bledsoe noted how "Though the subordinates are vulnerable to powerful people, they know to play high-status people off against each other to their own advantage." Bledsoe, *Women and marriage*, 54.

[87] Interview with a Liberian in Kpayea, Salayea District, Liberia (MRB 333), September 29, 2009.

[88] For definitions of integration, see Jacobsen, "The forgotten solution," 9; and Mushemeza, *Banyarwanda refugees*, 73.

about their lives in the places in which they sought refuge in the Forest Region, they almost always respond like this: "The people of that village were bad to us but my host was very good to me." The commitment of a Guinean in these communities in the Forest Region was not to the well-being of refugees; it was to the well-being of "his/her refugees." This drove refugees into the arms of their hosts, who protected them from the community. Many of the former refugees described their sojourn in these communities as one marked by suffering and servitude while express-ing profound gratitude to their former hosts. Next I reflect on some of the things that the former refugees I interviewed complained about the most.

Quotidian Slander: Fecal Matters

Former refugees complained bitterly about the quotidian slander they suffered at the hands of Guineans.[89] Refugees were blamed for many bad things in society, ranging from theft and drug abuse to prostitution and poor sanitation. The local discourse on fecal matters shows the level of imagination that locals deployed to slander and tease the refugees. The background to all of this was the fact that pit latrines did not initially exist in many of these villages and so people used the bush as a place of convenience.

Refugees were generally blamed when feces was discovered in places that were not supposed to be used as places of convenience. These attri-butions were often made in very colorful language. "*Nar den refugee den don kaka bad bad kaka nar ya so* [It is those refugees that have shit-ted such terrible shit here]" was how a former refugee translated it into Krio.[90] If they saw a refugee shitting somewhere, they did not always wait to reproach her. They tried to stop her while she was in the act. "When you went to the bush to shit if they saw you they gave you no peace. They began to scream at you: 'Get up, get up. Don't shit there. That place is not for shitting.'"[91] If the deed had already been done, then the unlucky refugee might be forced to remove it.[92]

The locals developed a rather sophisticated discourse on fecal mat-ters that focused on issues including soil fertility, cultural survival, food

---

[89] As Crisp showed, the slander of refugees is something that is prevalent across the con-tinent. Crisp, "Africa's refugees," 8.
[90] Interview with former refugee in Nyandehun village, Penguia Chiefdom, Sierra Leone (MRB 268), September 13, 2009.
[91] Interview (MRB 222).
[92] Interview (MRB 282).

quality, and what one might call "after-shitting rituals." Refugee fecal matter was portrayed as the ultimate threat to the survival of these cultures that are in many ways defined by rice growing.[93] "The Guineans used to say, 'The refugees are shitting undigested bulgur and it is going to destroy our bushes and make the soil infertile. We are in big trouble. We won't be able to make rice farms anymore!'"[94] They had explanations for the supposedly high toxicity of refugee fecal matter. "Some of the youth would strut in front of refugees saying: 'Bulgur does not digest. They shit it everywhere the same way they eat it, destroying our bushes.'"[95] They took some time to poke fun at the destitution of the refugees. "When the refugees shit it is pale because they eat their food with no ingredients."[96] "The feces of the refugees is white because they eat palm kernel oil. Ours is red because we eat palm oil."[97] Refugee after-shitting rituals were linked with what locals derisively portrayed as the spread of the text in their communities. "When we took our supplies we used the paper in which food was brought as toilet paper. We did not like to clean ourselves with leaves and water like them. They went around saying: 'Look they have food now. Go to the bush and see. They are shitting all over the place and writing notes to put by the side of the shit.'"[98] "They used to say a refugee is the only one that will shit and write a note and put it by the side of that shit."[99]

Debasement: Refugee the Dog

The discourse on feces was just one strand in what former refugees described as their general and routine debasement by host communities.

---

[93] In her book of the same name, Paulme noted that the people from the Sahel refer to the Kissi as *"Les gens du riz."* Paulme, *Les gens du riz*, 14. Also see the following for comments on the position of rice in Kpelle, Kissi, and neighboring cultures: Richards, *Fighting for the rainforest*, 65–66; Murphy, "Secret knowledge," 193; and Caroline Bledsoe, "The manipulation of Kpelle social fatherhood," *Ethnology* 19 (January 1980): 30.

[94] Interview with a former refugee in Kpayea, Salayea District, Liberia (MRB 331), September 29, 2009.

[95] Interview with a former refugee in Gorlu, Salayea District, Liberia (MRB 322), September 27, 2009.

[96] Interview with a former refugee in Kpayea, Salayea District, Liberia (MRB 324), September 28, 2009.

[97] Interview with a former refugee in Telemai, Salayea District, Liberia (MRB 350), December 8, 2010.

[98] Interview with a former refugee in Gorlu, Salayea District, Liberia (MRB 320), September 27, 2009.

[99] Interview (MRB 312).

Many complained that the Guineans treated them as less than human. Many who had sought refuge in Kondou Sub-Prefecture decried the fact that Guineans used to refer to them as "those things" (*nyaha* in Kissi). In Dongueta, both Guineans and former refugees told the story of Refugee the dog. To drive home the frequently and publicly expressed claim that refugees are dogs, one Guinean woman got a dog and named it Refugee. Tired of the debasement, one very bold refugee named her dog after the owner of Refugee the dog. The chief eventually got Refugee's owner to find another name for her pet, but the refugees then threatened to name their dogs after Guinean notables when they repatriated. There are rumors in some villages on the Guinean side of the border in Yomou Prefecture that a few Liberians have made good on these threats. When these Liberians who farm right next to the Diani/St. Paul River border see Guineans on the other side, they begin to call their dogs by the names of Guinean notables.

Reneging

If such verbal debasement wreaked psychological harm on the refugees, the practice of reneging on contracts by Guineans was a blow to refugees' material well-being. Many refugees worked as farm laborers to make a living. As in many of these refugee situations, wages were ridiculously low.[100] A day of work by a whole refugee family sometimes was rewarded with one kilo of rice.[101] However, some Guinean employers refused to pay even these low wages once the work was done. Unfortunately, refugees often had no way of seeking redress. A young former refugee recalled, "I broke a bag of palm nuts for three days for payment in rice. After the work the woman refused to pay, so I went and fetched my father to confront her. She came to her front door and told us 'If I come out again and see you people here I will scream that you are thieves.' We left quickly."[102] Such reneging was so common that it forced some refugees to stop doing such contract work altogether.[103]

We should resist the temptation to think of the subjugated refugees of the Forest Region as well-integrated people. Utas noted that "refugees in N'Zérékoré . . . experience powerlessness, including verbal and physical

---

[100] Doug Henry, "Thought and Commentary: The Legacy of the Tank: The Violence of Peace," *Anthropological Quarterly* 78 (Spring 2005): 446.

[101] Interview (MRB 219).

[102] Interview with a young lady in Nyandehun, Penguia Chiefdom, Sierra Leone (MRB 270), September 13, 2009.

[103] Interview (MRB 319).

maltreatment from Guinean citizens, harassment, and at times outright abuse from local authorities, in particular the military and the police."[104] A Liberian Kpelle lady in the town of Gorlu in Liberia reflected on the effects of this verbal and physical abuse on her psyche:

When I was in Dongueta [peopled almost entirely by Kpelle locals] I used to think a lot. I used to say to myself if it were not because of the war these people wouldn't be able to say things to us. But I could not do anything. I just used to talk to myself a lot. We were even older than them but they insulted us and spoke to us as they wished and we could do nothing. If there was a war in Guinea and the people of Dongueta came as refugees here, I am a Christian and would treat them well to show them we are good people here and that this is a good land. I can say that now but in those days I used to feel differently. Sometimes I felt like killing some of them. If I had power I would have killed some of them, but a refugee has no power. That is all that stopped me from harming some of them. But now I have had time to reflect and I am calm.[105]

Independent-Minded Refugees

Those people did not want us to be independent.[106]

I have given evidence in support of the claim that these indigeneity-privileging societies had well-functioning institutions for incorporating strangers. I have also provided some evidence indicating the pressures that refugees faced to submit to these incorporation processes. However, there were some refugees who were at various times not subjugated to elites in their local communities. Their stories tell us a lot about these societies' determination to rope in all strangers.

Some of the refugees had autonomy foisted on them. They, for one reason or another, were left for brief periods without hosts during their sojourn in these communities. The short way to put it is that bad things tended to happen to them. People irritated by their autonomy maliciously accused some of being rebels. Others, arrested for being rebels, ended up with no one to vouch for them because they lacked hosts who are supposed to do this. They were subjected to punishments that sometimes included death. A former refugee in Salayea District, Liberia, recalled:

In Guinea I had a stranger father who was very nice to me, but once his brother invited him to Conakry and he was there for five months. While he was away, I was just living on my own. I was independent, doing my own work and making

---

[104] Utas, "West African warscapes," 421.
[105] Interview (MRB 322).
[106] Interview (MRB 333).

my own farm. Those people did not want us to be independent. They used to see us as their slaves. They did not want us to do anything for ourselves. People knew I was his stranger and I had no problem with anyone in the village. But one man went to Yomou and told the leaders there that I was a rebel, that I had put poison in the village well and that I chased him with a knife and threatened to kill people in the village. I don't even know where he got that story. They came and arrested me and I was jailed in Yomou for three days. Fortunately, they allowed me to pay a soldier 25,000 Guinean francs to go and call the village chief to come and act as my witness. I was very lucky because the chief was a friend of my host and he said he knew me and that I was not a rebel and so I was set free. When my stranger father came he told me not to leave the town and that none of this would have happened to me if he had been around.[107]

There were rare cases of genuinely free-spirited people who tried at various times to maintain an independent existence. In the mid-1990s, a group of Sierra Leoneans fled from villages in Mafindor Chiefdom, Kono District, to the Guinean village of Cheseneh-Bolokodu, Kondou Sub-Prefecture, just across the Meli River border between the two countries. Instead of going to live in the village, they constructed a makeshift settlement close to the river and made a living by crossing to their villages to harvest crops. However, as one refugee noted, "The chiefs were not happy because we were not interacting with the villagers a lot." So when a group of soldiers came to visit the area, the chief is rumored to have told them to get rid of the refugee village. The soldiers told the refugees to move away from the border and set fire to their houses, beating those who tried to resist. Most of the refugees then moved a few meters into the village of Cheseneh-Bolokodu proper, where they came to outnumber the locals and assumed the normal life of subjugation to local notables. They lived peacefully with the locals after that.[108] What seemed like xenophobic attacks on the refugees were not meant to expel them from the body politic but to subjugate them to locals.

THE POSITIVE EFFECTS OF SUBJUGATION

When you go to a new place you have to become slippers for the big men. They might advocate on your behalf and save your life someday.[109]

The subjugation of refugees by the local elite in these communities in the Forest Region played a pivotal role in obviating violent attacks on

[107] Interview (MRB 333).
[108] Interview with a Sierra Leonean in Termessadou, Mafindor Chiefdom, Sierra Leone (MRB 248), September 7, 2009.
[109] Interview (MRB 300).

refugees by the local population when Lansana Conte gave his notorious orders in September 2000. It did so by providing the most powerful people in these societies with deep knowledge about the activities of the refugees. Because of this, they did not buy into the vilification of the whole refugee population as rebels and rebel collaborators. Furthermore, the refugees never came to represent the dangerous undefined quantity that struck fear into the hearts of so many in Conakry in this time of precarious uncertainty in Guinea and the rest of the Mano River Basin.

A key facet of the obligations that hosts have to their strangers is the duty to protect. However, this duty to protect does not constitute a workable causal mechanism here because of the recognition of the potential for betrayal by strangers in these societies. Strangers sometimes betray their hosts. History provides much evidence of people who came first as strangers and supplicated themselves to their hosts only for them to try to grab power from and dominate their erstwhile hosts later. Some were successful, assimilated into the culture of their hosts, and became the new autochthonous landowners.[110] Even though some hosts willingly handed over power to their more powerful guests, many were coerced against their will into doing so. The fact that the hosts fought back and sometimes defeated these efforts is evidence for this.[111]

McGovern has given a good account of how the discourse on betrayal reigned in various *Forestière* communities from 1984 onward. Many of these communities vilified and sought to root out their former Malinké strangers who had often used the rules of the state to shirk their duties as strangers. Strangers who betrayed their hosts were thought to have "put themselves beyond the pale of humanity."[112] They were seen as deserving of the worst forms of punishment.[113]

The duty to protect one's strangers could not therefore have guaranteed the refusal of these communities to heed the calls of President Conte. This is because the refugee who is welcomed and hosted by the community only to aid rebels to enter and destroy that community cannot but represent

---

[110] For an example of this, see Murphy and Bledsoe, "Kinship and territory," 131. Also see the case of the Keita lineage of Farmaya, Kissidougou. Paulme, "La societe Kissi," 80.

[111] We can understand the cleansing of Kpelle villages of Malinké families in 1990 as an instance of this. See McGovern, "Unmasking the state," 510. Also see Germain, *Peuples de la Foret*, 112, for an example of such resistance.

[112] McGovern, "Unmasking the state," 513.

[113] McGovern, "Unmasking the state," 540.

the epitome of betrayal. It is precisely this that the president was accusing the refugees of when he noted:

After all, no one in the world has ever taken better care of refugees than we have . . . nobody talks about the 400, 500 or 600 thousand refugees here. Even so we welcomed them as brothers. See how they repay us in chump change (monnaie de singe) . . . We thought they were brothers. Black like us! Their good-for-nothing compatriots came from the US and every other place and chased them out of their country. We accepted them here. And now they wage war against us. Well, let's see that they get the hell out of here![114]

Given what one might consider this national fascination with betrayal, it is all the more surprising that people in many of the communities in the Forest Region resolutely refused to bite the bait dangled in front of their noses by President Conte. To get at the link between the subjugation of refugees and the obviation of violent attacks on them by the local population, we need to answer two questions. First, why is it that the most powerful in these societies did not buy into the charges of betrayal leveled against the refugees by the president? Second, why were they not even overcome by fear of the refugees, even granted that they thought the accusation of the president was far-fetched?

The answer to both questions is that the subjugation of refugees to local elites provided these elites with deep knowledge about the refugees. They knew enough not to buy into the president's exploitation of the "particularly confusing and dangerous"[115] situation prevailing in the country to vilify all the refugees. They knew enough not to be motivated to attack the refugees out of uncertainty over what the refugees represented. This knowledge allowed them to adopt a more discerning and rights-respecting approach that tried to detect possible rebel collaborators within the refugee *and Guinean* population without resorting to large-scale and undiscriminating attacks on all refugees. It is also this knowledge that gave them the confidence to stick their necks out to protect the refugees by cracking down on youth in their communities that sought to exploit the President's orders.

[114] Cited in McGovern, "Unmasking the state," 554. For the same speech, see Gale, "The invisible refugee camp," 539–540. McGovern discussed the ways in which the discourse of Conte tapped into much earlier discourses on betrayal by his predecessor, Sekou Toure. McGovern, "Unmasking the state," 574–578.
[115] McGovern, "Conflit Regionale," 90.

Elites acquired extensive knowledge about the refugees because of the intense interactions between members of the two groups. Frequent visits, consultations, and time spent working together all facilitated this build-up of information about the lives of the refugees. In the Forest Region, time spent on paths walking to and from farms was one of the main facilitators of such knowledge. With farms that were sometimes up to ten kilometers from the village, local hosts and their refugee strangers had a lot of time to chat and get to know each other during these frequent trips. They often traveled these routes together because refugees helped their local hosts with farm labor. Locals also often gave their refugee guests land to farm that was adjacent to theirs. Stranger and host were in each other's presence most of the day spent on the farm. They ate together, set traps together, cut palm nuts together, and tapped and consumed palm and raffia wine together. Speaking of the host of his family in the Guinean village of Yowa in Yomou Prefecture, a Liberian former refugee noted, "We were together with him all the time. We traveled the same farm road. We did everything together. We went to his house at least three times a week."[116]

The fact that hosts were held legally responsible for their strangers gave the locals even more of an incentive to know and influence the behavior of their refugee guests. Some potential hosts propositioned by refugees asked for a probationary period to observe the character of the refugee before giving a response. Certain hosts cut off relations with refugees who turned out to be thieves. Others propositioned refugees only after closely observing their behavior. Refugees also had an incentive to contribute to this build-up of knowledge. They wanted to show off their good qualities to their (potential) hosts. The (potential) hosts wanted the refugees about them all of the time. Hosts complained when their strangers stayed away from them for a day or two. Such absence was frequently interpreted as a sign that the refugee had found or was looking for another host.

We do not have to believe that the locals knew all refugees to be innocent to understand their approach to the refugee issue in September 2000. It is only important that the hosts knew enough to conclude that the vast majority of the refugees were innocent, and that as hosts, they knew enough to discover the guilty refugees. The vigilant surveillance of the refugee populations in these villages indicates that these villagers were not under the delusion that they had totally figured out all the refugees.

---

[116] Interview with a Liberian in Passama, Zorzor District, Liberia (MRB 359), December 10, 2010.

The positive effects of their deep knowledge of the refugees on how they dealt with potential threats posed by the refugees was in evidence long before the president accused the refugees of grand betrayal. Soldiers deployed in areas around the border often cracked down hard on refugees out late. Although this was partly a ruse used to extract stuff from the refugees, soldiers had good reason to be concerned about infiltration, as rebels often crossed the border to cause mayhem. Elders in these societies tried to reign in the soldiers, advocating methods that did not victimize all refugees. A former refugee who was in Yende Douane, Kondou Sub-Prefecture, recalled how one soldier used to terrorize refugees at a checkpoint for being out late. The chief called a meeting of villagers, refugees, and soldiers to address the situation. He started by advising the refugees to return home earlier. However, he also had words for the soldier: "One out of ten refugees may be bad, but if we treat all ten badly, we also become bad people."[117]

The responses of elders during brief rebel incursions into Guinean territory, long before the attacks of 2000, confirmed their thoroughly discriminative approach to counterinsurgency. When rebels raided the Guinean village of Gbelemou, Yomou Prefecture, soldiers stationed in the nearby village of Komou decided to expel all refugees whose children were known to be rebels in Liberia. However, when they got to the Diani River border, some of the elders of the village stopped them from expelling the refugees in contravention of the international principle of non-refoulement refouling. They pointed out the problematic nature of holding people responsible for the actions of their adult children over whom they had no control and from whom they might have even fled. They told the soldiers, "You can kill refugees who are found to be rebels. We will support you in that. But we cannot harass innocent refugees just because their relatives are rebels in Liberia."[118]

Elders with deep knowledge of the refugees were already ensuring that state counterinsurgency did not degenerate into undiscriminating generalized attacks on refugees long before President Conte's speech in 2000. The announcements created an opportunity for youths who often detested the refugees to ratchet up demands for their expulsion. They began to increase opportunistic attacks on refugees. By assuming significant

[117] Interview with a Sierra Leonean in Kamiendor, Mafindor, Sierra Leone (MRB 250B), September 7, 2009.
[118] Interview with a Liberian in Kpayea, Salayea District, Liberia (MRB 332), September 29, 2009.

responsibilities in supplying farm labor to and caring for elderly hosts, refugees relieved local youth of back-breaking responsibilities. However, this also rendered such youth in some ways superfluous to their elders. This limited the influence the youth had on elders in what were already highly gerontocratic societies.[119] Resentful youth berated their elders and launched opportunistic attacks on refugees even before the president's speech.[120] When an old man in Leobengu, Kondou Sub-Prefecture, asked his sons on a rare occasion for some help, they told him, "Why don't you ask those refugees of yours since they are now your people?"[121] The allocation of land to refugees by the elders was often regarded with alarm by youths who wondered how much primary forest would be left for them to establish their own plantations in the future. Some of these youths saw the president's order as an opportunity to solve the refugee problem.

Beyond refusing to carry out the president's orders, elders stuck their necks out to defend the refugees. They tried to stamp out what they saw as bad behavior by youths eager to join the state project. A refugee in Komou recalls: "Some of the youths in the village were outlaws. They were attacking refugees they met in isolated places, but the elders condemned it. They told them, 'You people will make us look bad with this type of behavior.'"[122] A refugee in Kolifa, Kondou Sub-Prefecture, recalls a similar dynamic: "When the rebels attacked Guinea, I was in Kolifa, and the soldiers came and said all the refugees should be driven out of the village and sent to the camps. The youth were agitating against us and trying to drive us away, but the elders and chief told them to stop and assured us we did not need to worry."[123] In Sangedou, also in Kondou Sub-Prefecture, officials from sub-prefecture headquarters in Kondou Lengo Bengou held a meeting and told the villages to expel all the refugees from the village to the camps. However, as one refugee recalled: "The chief told us that we could stay if we wished to. Some of the young

---

[119] For discussions of the gerontocratic nature of these societies, see Murphy, "Secret knowledge," 193; James Gibbs, "Poro values and courtroom procedures in a Kpelle chiefdom," *Southwestern Journal of Anthropology* 18 (Winter 1962): 342; Paulme, "La societe Kissi," 77; Person, "Soixante ans," 88; Paulme, *Les gens du riz*, 82–83; and McGovern, "Unmasking the state," 61.

[120] Interview with a former refugee in Sambaya, Mafindor Chiefdom, Sierra Leone (MRB 227), September 4, 2009.

[121] Interview (MRB 227).

[122] Interview (MRB 332).

[123] Interview with a Sierra Leonean in Keseneh, Mafindor Chiefdom, Sierra Leone (MRB 233), September 5, 2009.

people were saying we should go and that we were all rebels but the elders told them to leave us alone."[124]

These conflicting positions of the elders and youth with regard to the refugees should be understood as part of intergenerational conflicts between youths and elders in these societies in which elders rule over and expropriate the labor of youth through various mechanisms.[125] Youth often respond through covert and, more rarely, overt resistance, including disruptive war-making, flight, and collaboration with external powers to undermine the authority of their elders.[126]

The ability of elders to crack down on youths who were seeking to embrace the state's project has to be understood from both a secular and ritual perspective. The elders and chiefs could enforce local rules as the secular authorities recognized by the state. However, in a situation in which they were enforcing rules that did not have the backing of the state, it is even more important to look at the roles that local sources of power played. The resort to ritual power is paramount here.

The Kissi and Kpelle, like many other communities in this area, have "powerful, well-organized secret societies."[127] The best known of these are the Poro for men and Sande for women into which all community members are supposed to be initiated.[128] These societies have internal gradations that tend to reserve the most powerful positions for the elders, and among them, the elders of the landowning lineages.[129] Oaths during initiation ceremonies and the control of secret knowledge by elders facilitate the control of youth initiates and junior members by the elders. It creates in the minds of the youth what Gibbs calls a "deeply ingrained

[124] Interview (MRB 239).
[125] McGovern, "Unmasking the state," 63–83 and 433–466; Person, "Soixante ans," 100; Paulme, "La societe Kissi," 75; Caroline Bledsoe and William Murphy, "The Kpelle negotiation of marriage and matrilineal ties," in *The versatility of kinship*, ed. Linda Cordell and Stephen Beckerman (New York: Academic Press, 1980), 148; Richards, *Fighting for the rainforest*, 104; Stephen Ellis, *The mask of anarchy: the destruction of Liberia and the religious dimension of an African civil war* (New York: New York University Press, 2007), 285–290; and Caroline Bledsoe, *Women and Marriage*, 95–98.
[126] Person, "Soixante ans," 100; McGovern, "Unmasking the state," 442–445.
[127] James Gibbs, "The Kpelle of Liberia," in *Peoples of Africa*, ed. James Gibbs (New York: Hold, Rinehart and Winston, 1965), 199.
[128] McGovern, "Unmasking the state," 116; Murphy, "Secret knowledge," 194; and Person, "Soixante ans," 93–94.
[129] William Murphy, "The rhetorical management of dangerous knowledge in Kpelle brokerage," *American Ethnologist* 8 (November 1981): 671; Murphy and Bledsoe, "Kinship and territory," 140; Gibbs, "Poro values," 342; and McGovern, "Unmasking the state," 116.

willingness to submit to authority."[130] Scholars have also noted the very physical nature of these instruments of control.[131] Murphy emphasized how threats from "physical punishment or death from mysterious powers of the secret societies... serves to inculate [*sic*] respect for the elders' control of knowledge."[132] He also noted how "the persistent threat of beatings [and] poisonings... intensif[y] respect for the elders and their apparent knowledge of the mystical powers of the secret society."[133]

The effort at protecting the refugees from blanket condemnation and attacks pitted the elders not just against segments of their youth population, but often, also against state officials pressing for the execution of the president's orders. Although they were not about to fight state agents who wanted to attack refugees, these elders were not willing to do the dirty job of the government. Their position generally was that which was enunciated by that elder in Dongueta: "If [the state] wanted [the refugees] expelled, it should have done that itself instead of asking us to do it."[134]

A Sierra Leonean who had sought refuge in Mano, Kondou Sub-Prefecture, recalled: "My host was one of the owners of the village. When the rebels attacked Guinea, people came from Kondou Lengo Bengou and said all the refugees should go. The chief told them 'The refugees are now citizens and we cannot drive them away if they do not want to go.'"[135] Another Sierra Leonean who had sought refuge in Leobengu, Kondou Sub-Prefecture, recalled: "During the attacks, soldiers came from Kondou Lengo Bengou every day and were saying we should all go to the camp. But the chief told them: 'There are no refugees here. These people have been here since the beginning of the war and are Guineans now. They have farms and houses here. We cannot drive them away.'"[136]

These elders sometimes preferred to guarantee the good behavior of the refugees. There is evidence of leaders asking the state to punish them if the refugees were later found to have aided the rebels. The chief of Kholifa, Kondou Sub-Prefecture, told the authorities to hold him responsible in the event that refugees in his town turned out to be rebel collaborators.[137]

---

[130] Gibbs, "The Kpelle of Liberia," 222.
[131] Ibid., 222.
[132] Murphy, "Secret knowledge," 199.
[133] Ibid., 200.
[134] Interview (MRB 212).
[135] Interview with a Sierra Leonean in Kardu, Mafindor Chiefdom, Sierra Leone (MRB 241), September 6, 2009.
[136] Interview with a former Sierra Leonean refugee in Sambaya, Mafindor Chiefdom, Sierra Leone (MRB 227), September 4, 2009.
[137] Interview with a former refugee in Keseneh, Mafindor Chiefdom, Sierra Leone (MRB 233), September 5, 2009.

They knew the refugees well enough to stake their reputations and lives on the refugees' good behavior.

This resistance of the state's project was not always without costs. The village elders had called on the state to hold them accountable if anything went wrong, and some nearly lost their lives on account of this. Rebel attacks on areas in Guéckédou Prefecture intensified in late 2000 and early 2001. Citing elders' request to be held accountable for the behavior of the refugees in their settlements, soldiers arrested many chiefs and elders in Fangamandou Sub-Prefecture and took them to Nongoa, also in Guéckédou Prefecture, for execution in March 2001, blaming the refugees for the attacks. It took serious intervention by locals to save their lives.[138]

CONCLUSION

Beyond its contribution to the overall argument of this book, this chapter constitutes an important contribution to the historiography of the conflicts and refugee crises in the Mano River Basin. It departs from other works on this period[139] in explicitly recognizing that the 2000 anti-refugee violence was a Conakry phenomenon, not a Guinean one. This paves the way for me to explore why it is that many Guineans did not respond to the president's call with attacks on refugees like their counterparts in Conakry did. This is a task that no one else has undertaken. I believe I have marshaled enough evidence to support this suggested amendment to this important section of the Mano River Basin's historiography. Pointing out that many Guinean communities did not attack but actually sought to protect refugees during this period is important. It absolves of blame many communities that have come in for blanket condemnation in works on this period.[140] However, more importantly, we cannot have a complete understanding of what happened during that period without understanding why some people decided not to heed President Conte's call. We cannot even understand why people attacked refugees in Conakry without understanding why their counterparts elsewhere did not attack refugees.

---

[138] Interviews with a man who went to Nongoa to plead on behalf of the elders taken there for execution in Kolomba, Guéckédou Prefecture, Guinea (MRB 103), June 19, 2009; and with one of the elders sent to Nongoa for execution in Tombou, Guéckédou Prefecture, Guinea (MRB 128), June 24, 2009.
[139] McGovern, "Conflit régional"; Arieff, "Still standing"; and Gale, "Bulgur marriages."
[140] Ibid.

5

On Two Competing Explanations

Co-Ethnicity and Population Numbers

They [The Guinean hosts] insulted us and treated us very badly. Since we returned home, some of them who used to come here often before the war cannot visit this place anymore because of the bad things they did to us. Those **Kpelle** people are bad![1]

(*A* **Kpelle** *former Liberian refugee*)

I don't care what happens with numbers. If you come to me, you can't have more power than me. They had bush, their own houses, plantations, palm, etc.; we had nothing. How could we be more powerful than them? It is all these things that gave them power over us.[2]

In 1990, Fanta Conde fled with her family from Salayea District in Liberia into Yomou Prefecture Guinea. The National Patriotic Front of Liberia (NPFL) forces of Charles Taylor were approaching these areas of Lofa County, and news spread of the brutality with which the Kpelle, Mano, and Gio fighters who were operating in the area treated Mandingos.[3] Many Mandingos like Fanta fled into Guinea. However, instead of seeking refuge in Malinké-dominated areas of Guinea in the Forest Region or *Haute Guinée*, Fanta and her family settled just across the border in the village of Dongueta, where the population was almost one hundred percent Kpelle. Even though Fanta's parents were born in Macenta and Beyla prefectures in the Forest Region of Guinea and had only migrated to

---

[1] Interview with a *Kpelle* former Liberian refugee in Yarpauah, Salayea District, Liberia (MRB 349), December 8, 2010.

[2] Interview (MRB 312).

[3] For more on the ethnic dimensions of the conflict in Liberia, see Van Damme, "How Liberian," 36–53 and 49; Ellis, *The mask of anarchy*, 128.

Liberia as young adults, Fanta did not move to those places. She stayed on in Dongueta even when murderous violence broke out between Kpelle and Konianké populations in nearby N'Zérékoré Prefecture later in 1990.[4] A summary of Fanta's life in Dongueta in her own words follows:

I was born in Bong County [Liberia] and I am Mandingo. During the war I came straight to Dongueta. My stranger father was an old Kpelle man. He was really good to us. It is not just giving things to people that is important. That man also treated us with respect. We lived in his house for some time before we built in the camp. He gave us food, palm nut to make oil, etc. Sometimes we decided on our own to go and help him farm, and when we were ready to come back, he gave us rice from his granary. He was so simple. I used to call him by his first name and we joked with him all the time. When his sons joined the Poro society we assisted because of how their dad had taken care of us. When we needed raffia to roof our houses, he took us to his swamp to help us cut raffia. To this day we go to collect kernel on his land. One day I will name a grandson after him. Our children play together now. As a Malinké in a Kpelle village, I never noticed that I was treated worse because of my ethnicity. Our host was very good to us, though he was Kpelle and we are Malinké. My father is from Guinea and his relatives came and took me to his home in Beyla once but I did not go there again. He is dead and I prefer to stay here in Dongueta.[5]

As I conducted research in the Mano River Basin and the Great Lakes Region, I heard many stories like that of Fanta Conde that led me to question an influential and blindingly obvious explanation that tends to crop up when people think of refugee–host relations in Africa. It concerns co-ethnicity and the role that it plays in facilitating positive relations between refugees and hosts. This chapter takes up this competing explanation and another that focuses on refugee–host population numbers to account for intergroup relations. The analysis here is meant to reinforce the arguments made in the preceding chapters and also clear the way for the analysis on the Great Lakes Region that follows.

There is little evidence that co-ethnicity or refugee–host numbers had a significant influence on the occurrence and patterns of anti-refugee attacks in Conakry or their absence in the Forest Region. There is no evidence of an ethnic component to the anti-refugee violence in Conakry. Refugees of all ethnicities were attacked in Conakry. Those who could convincingly pass as Guineans had the highest chance of escaping the

---

[4] For more on these intercommunal conflicts, see Van Damme, "How Liberian," 36–53 and 49.
[5] Interview (MRB 214).

violence, and language ability was the greatest determinant of people's ability to pass as Guineans. The Guineans organizing, facilitating, and carrying out the attacks were drawn from many of Guinea's ethnic groups in what one might call a veritable cross-ethnic alliance. This lack of salience of ethnicity also characterized refugee–host relations in the Forest Region of Guinea. There, generalized anti-refugee violence did not happen regardless of whether or not there were relations of co-ethnicity between refugees and Guinean host populations.

The refugee–host population argument similarly helps us little in understanding patterns of anti-refugee violence in Guinea. Despite various permutations of refugee–host numbers, anti-refugee violence failed to occur in these Forest Region communities.

One cannot generalize to the rest of Africa based on research in the Forest Region. However, I employ insights from secondary literature to show that the results from Guinea at least require us to rethink our understanding of refugee–host relations in other parts of Africa. In the rest of this chapter, I explore why these arguments offer us little help in understanding refugee–host relations in Guinea. This serves to reinforce the explanation focusing on refugee links with opposition movements and the characteristics of the areas in which they settle that I build in this work.

THE LIMITED SALIENCE OF CO-ETHNICITY: REFLECTIONS FROM THE FOREST REGION

The Argument

There is an abundance of work citing co-ethnicity as an explanation of the nature of refugee–host relations in Africa. Co-ethnicity is said to increase the ability of refugees *to blend into host communities*. Studying self-settled Angolan and Zairean refugees in the Northwestern Province of Zambia, Freund and Kalumba[6] noted that they "blend easily into the host community because of shared ethnicity." Hansen[7] similarly attributed the survival and ability of self-settled Angolan refugees to hide in Zambian villages to "shared kinship and ethnic identity." Coethnicity is also said to *ease the sense of loss* experienced by refugees. Writing of ethnic Somali

---

[6] Paul Freund and Katele Kalumba, "Spontaneously settled refugees in Northwestern Province, Zambia," *International Migration Review* 20 (Summer 1986): 301.
[7] Hansen, "Once the running stops," 370.

Ethiopian refugees in Somalia, Kibreab[8] noted how the "severity of the loss suffered was to a large extent mitigated and the process of recovery telescoped considerably" by the fact that the locals among whom they settled belonged to the same ethnicity and sometimes even the same clan. Nelder[9] noted that "in some instances, such as when refugees have fled a minority regime or colonial rule, tribal kinship across a border has eased the trauma of being a refugee."

Locals are said to be *more willing to receive and treat refugees with kindness* when they are their coethnics. Reflecting on Senegalese populations that received refugees from Guinea Bissau, Zartman[10] wrote of their "simply receiving large numbers of fellow tribesmen" and of their being "oblivious of international frontiers and national citizenship." Holborn[11] made the bold claim that rural refugees usually have co-ethnic hosts, "with the result that their personal legal status is the same as that of the people around them." Westin[12] wrote of how "the cultural and ethnic affinity between the Rwandan refugees and the local Tanzanian communities close to the Rwandan border generally prevented manifestations of conflict." He continued: "refugees from one country will generally be treated kindly by ethnic or tribal compatriots on the other side of the border. So while the deviation of state boundaries from ethnocultural boundaries is part of the problem, it has, to date, also been part of the solution."[13]

The warm reception of refugees by co-ethnic host populations is said to make some refugees unwilling to settle in areas in which they lack co-ethnics. Aall[14] wrote of Mozambican refugees resisting efforts at relocating them because "they were of the same tribe as the locals" among whom they were already settled. Gerdes invoked Grovogui[15] in asserting that during the wars in the Mano River Basin in the 1990s and

---

[8] Kibreab, "The myth of dependency," 338.

[9] Brian Neldner, "Settlement of rural refugees in Africa," *Disasters* 3 (4–1979): 394.

[10] Zartman, "Portuguese Guinean refugees," 144.

[11] Holborn, *Refugees*, 292.

[12] Charles Westin, "Regional analysis of refugees movements: origins and response," in *Refugees: perspectives on the experience of forced migrants*, ed. Alistair Ager (London: Pinter, 1999), 28.

[13] Westin, "Regional analysis," 29.

[14] Cato Aall, "Refugee problems in Southern Africa," in *Refugee problems in Africa*, ed. Sven Hamrell (Uppsala: The Scandinavian Institute of African Studies, 1967), 29.

[15] Siba Grovogui, "L'impact socioculturel et politico-Economique de l'arrivee des refugies dans le district de Nzinigrozou (Macenta)," (Mémoire de maitrise, Option Sociologie, Annee Universitaire 1994/1995, Universite de Conakry, 1996).

2000s "the refugees chose their place of refuge according to criteria of ethnicity."[16]

Although many of these works are more than twenty years old, the co-ethnicity thesis is still alive and well today. More recently, Crisp[17] and Polzer[18] highlighted shared ethnicity as facilitating the integration of refugees in various parts of Africa. Gerdes[19] and Grovogui[20] made similar arguments. Elsewhere, Banki invoked a similar argument in explaining difficulties with the integration of recent Afghan refugees in Pakistani cities. She noted that "Decreasing ethnic similarity generates Pakistani reluctance to host such a massive population."[21] She asserted that "the link between ethnicity and integration" is "well established."[22]

Some United Nations High Commission for Refugees (UNHCR) officials have bought into the co-ethnicity argument as well. When locals in North Kivu Province in Zaire attacked refugees in the 1960s, the Aga Khan, then head of UNHCR, in an effort to explain the attacks, noted that the locals were ethnically different from the refugees.[23] When UNHCR decided to move Southern Sudanese refugees away from Azande areas close to the border with Sudan due to insecurity, "ethnic affinities" were considered in addition to characteristics such as topography, land availability, and ecology in choosing a place.[24]

Three Pathways

We can identify three plausible pathways that could link co-ethnicity to the positive effects on refugee–host relations highlighted by authors previously.

The language pathway focuses on the common language that co-ethnics share and its positive impact on relations. When refugees and locals share the same language, it makes it easier for them to avoid conflicts that arise from common misunderstandings. For example, refugees may not follow rules just because they are not aware of them. A common

---

[16] Felix Gerdes, "Forced migration and armed conflict: an analytical framework and a case study of refugee-warriors in Guinea," *University of Hamburg, Research Unit of Wars, Armament and Development Working Paper* No. 1 (2006), 107.

[17] Crisp, "The local integration," 12.

[18] Tara Polzer, "Invisible integration: how bureaucratic, academic and social categories obscure integrated refugees." *Journal of Refugee Studies* 21 (December 2008): 480.

[19] Gerdes, "Forced migration," 107.

[20] Grovogui, "L'impact socioculturel."

[21] Banki, "Refugee integration," 10.

[22] Ibid., 15.

[23] Holborn, *Refugees*, 1022.

[24] Ibid., 1102.

language will also help in the management and resolution of conflicts when they do arise. Furthermore, a shared language might facilitate interactions that enhance refugee well-being, such as the employment of refugees by locals.[25] Sharing a language with the host population could also make it easier for refugees to pass as locals, thus enhancing their welfare when nonlocals are targeted for discrimination.

The familiarity pathway maintains that co-ethnics share a similar culture and language and enjoy familiarity with each other. The shared culture in itself prevents conflicts. It takes away some of the reasons for which groups sometimes fight each other by ensuring that they share similar values and tastes. It might also provide co-ethnic refugees and hosts with shared instruments for preventing and managing conflicts. Furthermore, it can help refugees pose as locals to access benefits that are reserved for locals. This is in addition to the possible psychological benefits of operating in a familiar culture.

The ethnic nationalism pathway posits that people possess particular warmth for members of their ethnic group. This motivates them to treat members of their ethnic group with a high level of cordiality that is denied nonmembers of their group. This is so even when those co-ethnics happen to be refugees who are citizens of another country. Because of this, locals will have better relations with co-ethnic refugees than with non–co-ethnic ones. For example, when land rights are reserved for members of the ethnic group, we can expect refugee ethnic group members to access such rights, whereas non–co-ethnic refugees are denied these rights.

Design and Methods

To assess the impact of coethnicity on refugee–host relations, I interviewed Liberians and Sierra Leoneans who had been refugees in two pairs of villages in Guinea. These are Gotoye and Dongueta in Banie Sub-Prefecture, Yomou Prefecture, and Kolomba and Kelema in Fangamandou Sub-Prefecture, Guéckédou Prefecture. I also interviewed Guineans in these villages who had played host to the refugees. In the Gotoye-Dongueta area, the ethnic Kpelle who constituted almost one hundred percent of the local population received refugees who were overwhelmingly their Liberian Kpelle co-ethnics. They also hosted a few refugees from other Liberian groups such as the Lorma, Mandingo, Gbandi, and Bele. In the Kolomba-Kelema complex, the Kissi Guineans, who

---

[25] Noel Calhoun, "UNHCR and community development: a weak link in the chain of refugee protection?" *New Issues in Refugee Research* 191 (October 2010): 12.

TABLE 5.1. *Ethnic Profile of Hosts and Refugees*

Host Community	Dominant Host Ethnicity	Dominant Refugee Ethnicity	Other Refugee Ethnicities	Former Refugees Interviewed In
Kolomba-Kelema, Fangamandou, Guinea	Kissi	Mende	Kissi, Limba, Susu, Mandingo	Penguia Chiefdom, Sierra Leone
Dongueta-Gotoye, Banie, Guinea	Kpelle	Kpelle	Lorma, Gio, Vai, Mandingo, Bele, Mano	Salayea and Zorzor Districts, Lofa County, Liberia

constituted nearly one hundred percent of the population, received refugees who were overwhelmingly Sierra Leonean Mende non–co-ethnics. However, a few of the refugees were Kissi co-ethnics of the locals.

This configuration allowed me to exploit comparison within each pair of cases as well as across these two pairs. The ethnic diversity of refugees in each village allowed me to ask people to reflect on how they thought refugees who were co-ethnics of the predominant local population got along with the locals and fared relative to those who were not co-ethnics of the local population. I then used these answers and other observations from the field to reflect on refugee–host relations in Kelema-Kolomba and Dongueta-Gotoye. This comparison across cases enabled me to get at the broader question of the nature of refugee–host relations in areas predominantly characterized by co-ethnicity between refugees and locals (Dongueta-Gotoye) as opposed to areas that are not (Kolomba-Kelema).

I focus on interviews conducted with former refugees here because Guineans as potential perpetrators of discrimination in favor of their co-ethnics might have an incentive to lie. This is because of what Posner speaks of as "a strong social norm against open confessions of ethnic motivations."[26] Unsurprisingly, Guineans I interviewed in Kolomba, Kondou Lengo Bengou, Foedou Kollet, Dongueta, and Gotoye, among other places, all insisted that ethnicity was not significant in how they related to the refugees.[27]

---

[26] Daniel Posner, *Institutions and ethnic politics in Africa* (New York: Cambridge University Press, 2005), 94.

[27] Interview (MRB 103); interview (MRB 141); interview (158); and interviews with a Guinean in Foedou Kollet, Guéckédou Prefecture, Guinea (MRB 149), June 29, 2009; a Guinea in Gotoye (MRB 170), July 23, 2009; and a Guinea in Dongueta, Yomou Prefecture (MRB 207), July 29, 2009.

FIGURE 5.1. Map of Kono, Kailahun, and Guéckédou[28]

I met the former refugees who had stayed in Kolomba-Kelema in villages such as Njalah, Woroma, Nyandehun, Bambaro, and Tofawonde in Penguia Chiefdom in Sierra Leone's Kailahun District.

[28] This map was created by Rita Effah, using the following resources: FAO-Africover, "Multipurpose Africover"; GADM, "Database of Global"; and WRI, "Waterbodies in Uganda."

FIGURE 5.2. Map of Banie, Salayea, and Zorzor [29]

I found the Liberians who were formerly refugees in Dongueta-Gotoye in villages such as Gorlu, Kpayea, Telemai, Passama, and Yarpauah in Salayea and Zorzor Districts in Liberia.

[29] This map was created by Rita Effah, using the following resources: FAO-Africover, "Multipurpose Africover"; GADM, "Database of Global"; and WRI, "Waterbodies in Uganda."

I spoke to both former refugees who self-identified as co-ethnics of host communities and some who described themselves as not being co-ethnics of Guinean host populations. The refugees who were co-ethnics of the predominant local population were supposed to be the beneficiaries of the presumed discriminatory system that made life better for some more than others. As scholars of discrimination have for long noticed, the beneficiaries of prejudice often under-report it.[30] This might be because they notice it less, seek to mask it,[31] or expect the system to favor them even more than it does. The victims are expected to over-report discrimination due to their greater ability to see it and their higher levels of sensitivity.[32] Therefore, statements by supposed victims indicating that there was little discrimination should be taken as strong evidence that there was indeed little discrimination. Statements by supposed beneficiaries indicating that there was a lot of discrimination against the victims should constitute strong evidence of the existence of discrimination.

In addition to long semistructured interviews, I asked interviewees to answer seven standardized questions concerning specific issues that former refugees mentioned often during earlier interviews. These questions forced refugees to reflect on very specific aspects of refugee–host relations. They are as follows:

1. *Access to land*: Did refugees who were co-ethnics of host populations have easier access to land for cultivation than those that were not?
2. *Access to employment*: Did refugees who were co-ethnics of locals have better access to jobs? These jobs were mostly short-term farm labor contracts, and refugees were paid with either money or food items such as rice and cassava.

---

[30] Glen Adams, Teceta Tormala, and Laurie O'Brien, "The effect of self-affirmation on perception of racism," *Journal of Experimental Social Psychology* 42 (September 2006): 616–626; Don Operario and Susan Fiske, "Ethnic identity moderates perceptions of prejudice: Judgments of personal versus group discrimination and subtle versus blatant bias," *Personality and Social Psychology Bulletin*, 27 (May 2001): 550–561; and Derek de la Pena et al., "Reexamining perceived discrimination between blacks and whites following Hurricane Katrina: a racial-conciliatory perspective," *North American Journal of Psychology* 12 (June 2010): 366.

[31] Glen Adams, Laurie O'Brien, and Jessica Nelson, "Perceptions of racism in Hurricane Katrina: a liberation psychology analysis," *Analysis of Social Issues and Public Policy* 6 (December 2006): 215.

[32] Adams, O'Brien and Nelson, "Perceptions of racism," 215.

3. *Wage discrimination*: Did refugees who were co-ethnics of the local population receive higher wages than those who were not co-ethnics of the locals for the same jobs offered by Guinean employers?

4. *Reneging*: The contracts discussed previously in (2) were often preceded by wage negotiations. The problem was that Guineans did not always deliver the agreed-on payment once the work was done. Did refugees who were co-ethnics of the locals experience reneging less?

5. *Persecution of gatherers*: Rural refugees depended a great deal on gathering things such as sticks, wild food, and medicinal plants in the bush. Sometimes, Guineans harassed refugees who they caught gathering. Were the refugee co-ethnics of the local population harassed less for gathering?

6. *Access to hosts*: Refugees often established relations with locals who became their hosts or friends in the area in which they lived. Was it easier for the refugee co-ethnics of the local community to get hosts?

7. *Quotidian slander*: Refugees reported being subjected to rampant verbal insults, taunts, and accusations at the hands of locals. Refugees were blamed for theft, prostitution, and so forth. Did the locals slander refugees who were their co-ethnics less than those who were not?

Responses

The interviewees raised serious doubts over whether refugees who were co-ethnics of the local population fared much better than those who were not. I posed these questions to four ethnic Kissis who had been refugees in Kolomba-Kelema where the locals were their co-ethnics. Three noted no differentiation between refugees who were the co-ethnics of the locals and those who were not on all seven indicators. Only one claimed refugees who were co-ethnics of the Guinean hosts had better access to jobs and got better wages than those who were not. I also interviewed eighteen former refugees who were not co-ethnics of the local population in Kolomba-Kelema. Only three of the eighteen former refugees thought refugees with co-ethnics had more access to land, got better wages, were harassed less for gathering, had easier access to a host, and were slandered less than those without co-ethnics. Only two of the eighteen thought refugees without co-ethnics were reneged on more than refugees with co-ethnics. The most significant result was the question of employment discrimination, where five of eighteen interviewees thought refugees with co-ethnics had easier access to jobs. All of them attributed this to their ability to speak the language of the Kissi locals.

I interviewed nine Kpelle Liberians who had been refugees in Dongueta-Gotoye where members of the local population were their co-ethnics. All nine of them responded that there was no differentiation between co-ethnics and non–co-ethnics on any of the seven indicators. I also interviewed eleven Liberians who had sought refuge in Dongueta-Gotoye but were not co-ethnics of the Guinean Kpelle hosts. Ten of them asserted that there was no difference between co-ethnics and non–co-ethnics of the local population on any of the seven indicators. One thought Kpelle refugees had easier access to land but fared the same as the other refugees on all other counts.

The results of these interviews were corroborated by the semistructured interviews and observations during field work in Guinea, Sierra Leone, and Liberia. The results mirror the stubborn insistence by many Guineans that ethnicity was not significant in how they related to the refugees.[33] The results provide us with a window into arguments about why various versions of the co-ethnicity argument do not help us understand refugee–host relations in Guinea and why we should be doubtful of their efficacy further afield in the rest of Africa.

The Limited Promise of the Co-Ethnicity Argument

The Language Thesis

After just a day of talking to locals in Kolomba and Kelema, I began to understand why the language hypothesis of the co-ethnicity argument might be flawed. It is possible that refugees who share a language with locals get along with them and fare better than those who do not. However, for this to support the language hypothesis, language ability and ethnicity have to neatly overlap. The problem is that language ability and ethnicity hardly neatly overlap in most areas in Africa. Many Africans are multilingual.[34] People often know the language of neighboring groups that they are in contact with but may not be ethnic members of.

---

33 Interview (MRB 103); interview (MRB 141); interview (MRB 149); interview (MRB 158); interview (MRB 170); and interview (MRB 207).

34 Adama Oane and Christine Glanz, *Why and how Africa should invest in African languages and multilingual education: an evidence- and practice-based advocacy brief* (Hamburg: UNESCO Institute for Lifelong Education, 2010), 6–24; and Amina Mama,

So many refugees who settle among neighboring groups that are not their co-ethnics often still speak the language of their hosts. This also means that many hosts know the language of neighboring non–co-ethnic groups whose members end up coming as refugees. Cohen and Middleton noted that "It is clear that multilinguality is a widespread aspect of African social life" and that language hardly ever acts as an impediment to interethnic relations.[35]

Furthermore, in protracted refugee situations, many refugees and hosts learn each other's language during the course of the refugee crisis. People who grow up speaking multiple languages, as many Africans do, are thought to find it easier to learn new languages as adults than those who grow up speaking only one language.[36] There is also the fact that there are many ethnic groups that share mutually intelligible languages in Africa. For example, in Uganda, even though the Bakiga, Banyankore, Batoro, and Banyoro are thought to constitute different ethnic groups, their languages are all mutually intelligible.[37] Recently, these languages have come to be collectively called Runyakitara.[38]

Thus, even if it were true that a shared language makes relations between refugees and hosts better, it will not offer much support for the co-ethnicity thesis. Many of the self-described Guinean Kissi of Kolomba-Kelema in Guinea's Fangamandou Sub-Prefecture spoke Mende long before their areas received refugees in the early 1990s. Living deep inside the Kelema Isthmus of Guinea and bordered on almost all sides by Mende-speaking people in Sierra Leone, they had to learn Mende to facilitate interactions with their neighbors. Many of the Mende Sierra Leoneans who sought refuge in Kolomba-Kelema from areas such as Penguia Chiefdom in Kailahun District also spoke Kissi already before they went to Guinea as refugees. This is because of their relations not only with the Kissi of the Kelema Isthmus in Guinea, but also with the Sierra Leonean Kissi populations in Kailahun District that they share villages and towns with.

"Challenging subjects: gender and power in African contexts," *Identity and beyond: rethinking Africanity, Nordic Africa Institutite Discussion Paper* 12 (2001), 12.

[35] Ronald Cohen and John Middleton, "Introduction," in *From tribe to nation: studies in incorporation processes*, ed. Ronald Cohen and John Middleton (Scranton, PA: Chandler Publishing Company, 1970), 23.

[36] European Union, "Study on the contribution of multilinguality to creativity final report," *Study commissioned by European Commission, Directorate General Education and Culture* (July 16, 2009), 11.

[37] Chretien, *The great lakes of Africa*.

[38] Jan Bernsten, "Runyakitara: Uganda's 'new' language," *Journal of Multilingual and Multicultural Development* 19 (2–1998): 93.

This leads us to wonder whether the few claims that Kissi refugees got jobs more easily because they spoke the Kissi language of the Guinean hosts gives much support to the co-ethnicity thesis.

The Familiarity Thesis

The familiarity from shared practices mechanism suffers from the same flaw as the language mechanism. People often share practices with neighboring groups even when they are not co-ethnics. I saw very strong evidence of this in the relationship between the Guinean Kissi of Kolomba and Kelema and the predominantly Mende people who live on the other side of the border in Sierra Leone's Kailahun district. These are two ethnic groups with distinct languages.[39] However, the close proximity of the Mende of Sierra Leone and the Kissi of Sierra Leone and Guinea and the necessities of daily life in an area where everyday survival has often required much inventiveness mean the two groups have come to share many practices. This has created a deep sense of familiarity that long preceded the refugee crisis in that area.

These two peoples have long shared markets both legal and nonlegal. Whenever distance, roads, and prices in their country made trading there unfavorable, they crossed the border to markets in the other country.[40] What many Guineans saw as the abusive rule of President Sekou Toure motivated some Guineans to move to Sierra Leone.[41] This flight from Toure's government mirrors similar flight from oppressive colonial and precolonial rulers all over the African continent.[42] The Mende and Kissi

---

[39] David Dwyer, "The Mende problem," in *Studies in African comparative linguistics with special focus on Bantu and Mande*, ed. Koen Bostoen and Jacky Maniacky (Tervuren, Belgium: Royal Museum for Central Africa, 2005), 29–42; and McGovern, "Unmasking the state," 183.

[40] Interviews with a Guinean in Kelema, Guéckédou Prefecture, Guinea (MRB 115), June 21, 2009; a Guinean in Kelema, Guéckédou Prefecture, Guinea (MRB 116), June 21, 2009; and a Guinea in Kelema, Guéckédou Prefecture, Guinea (MRB 117), June 21, 2009.

[41] Interview (MRB 116); interview with a Guinean in Kolomba, Guéckédou Prefecture, Guinea (MRB 100), June 19, 2009; interview (MRB 101); interview (MRB 134); interviews with a Guinean in Yende Douane, Guéckédou Prefecture, Guinea (MRB 136), June 27, 2009; and a Sierra Leonean in Tofawonde, Penguia Chiefdom, Sierra Leone (MRB 291), September 16, 2009.

[42] Mamdani, *When victims become killers*, 163–247; Catherine Newbury, *The cohesion of oppression: clientship and ethnicity in Rwanda 1860–1960* (New York: Columbia University Press, 1988), 48; Thomas Turner, *The Congo wars: conflict, myth and reality* (London: Zed Books, 2007), 79; and Oliver Bakewell, "Repatriation and self-settled

straddling the two sides of the border have had a long history of very deep interactions. These interactions facilitated intermarriages that led to the sharing of marriage, birth, and funeral rites. These people had for long exploited what Merkx called the "interplay between restrictions and opportunities"[43] that this borderland represented.

Of even greater significance was the fact that these people have for long shared Poro and Bondo secret society initiations and rituals. These secret societies form the deepest core of the political and cultural life of each of these groups. Important decisions in society are still often taken in the secret society bushes. People who are not initiated into them are unlikely to ever hold any important positions in these societies.[44]

It was very instructive to find out that Mende from Sierra Leone have often crossed into Guinea at the invitation of the Kissi Guineans to participate in Poro initiations and ceremonies. One of the more detested policies of former Guinean President Sekou Toure in these areas was his injunction on Poro initiations in Guinea. It prompted many Kissi Guineans to take their children across the border to Sierra Leone for initiation during Mende Poro initiations.[45]

Given the depth of familiarity from shared practices between these two communities, it is unsurprising then that Guineans as well as former refugees in Kolomba-Kelema did not report much of a difference in how Kissi Guineans got along with Mende and Kissi refugees. Shared practices along with the familiarity they breed do not neatly overlap with co-ethnicity and so do not offer much support for this thesis.

Further undermining the familiarity thesis is the fact that people belonging to the same ethnic group may not have shared practices along with the familiarity that it brings. This is something that this variant of the co-ethnicity thesis wrongly automatically assumes. For instance, many Kpelle Guineans in Dongueta and Gotoye engage in traditional religious practices and self-identify as traditionalists. Their Liberian co-ethnics from Salayea District in Liberia also dabble in these traditional religious practices but conscientiously and proudly self-identify as Christians.

refugees in Zambia: bringing solutions to the wrong problems," *Journal of Refugee Studies* 13 (4–2000): 359–360.

43 Jozef Merkx, "Refugee identities and relief in an African borderland: a study of northern Uganda and southern Sudan," *New Issues in Refugee Research* 19 (June 2000): 4.

44 Richard Fulton, "The political structures and functions of poro in Kpelle society," *American Anthropologist* 47 (October 1972): 1218–1233.

45 Conversation with a leader in Kolomba, Guéckédou Prefecture, Guinea, (MRB 133), June 24, 2009.

These Liberians often saw the Guinean Kpelle as unreconstructed heathens. What this points to is the importance of national cultures that McGovern[46] has written about. However, these intra-ethnic differences sometimes exist even within groups on the same side of the border. Conflict between Toma Christians and traditionalists of the same village in Macenta Prefecture, Guinea, degenerated into violence in the 1990s.[47]

The Ethnic Nationalism Thesis

The ethnic nationalism version of the co-ethnicity argument ties a direct link between co-ethnicity and more positive relations between refugees and their host. The main question we can pose here is whether the warmth for in-group members actually exists and whether it makes a difference in the type of refugee–host relations that are the subject of this study. Guinean former hosts and both their co-ethnic and non–co-ethnic refugee guests mostly poured doubt on the idea of ethnic nationalism. On the whole, the former refugees, regardless of their ethnicity, seemed to think of the Guineans as equal opportunity oppressors. A former Liberian refugee who was a co-ethnic of the local Kpelle population among whom she sought refuge put it succinctly: "They treated us all the same way. Badly."[48] One Mende refugee who vehemently rejected any suggestions that the Kissi Guineans among whom she sought refuge treated the Kissi refugees better than the Mende ones put it in a short but interesting way: "They treated all of us the same way. With those Kissi [Guinean] people you could be a Kissi and speak Kissi until your teeth got sweaty and they still won't give you a job."[49] A Vai former Liberian refugee who was not a co-ethnic of the Kpelle Guineans among whom she was a refugee noted: "They treated us all the same way. You did not have rights as long as you were a refugee. A refugee is a refugee."[50]

Analyzing the more detailed answers of the interviewees led me to conclude that ethnic nationalism seemed to have an influence on people mostly when they were speaking in abstract terms or were involved in

---

[46] McGovern, "Unmasking the state," 598–601.

[47] Ibid., 450–65.

[48] Interview (MRB 349).

[49] Interview with a former refugee in Woroma, Penguia Chiefdom, Sierra Leone (MRB 283), September 14, 2009.

[50] Interview with a former refugee in Telemai, Salayea District, Liberia (MRB 350), December 8, 2010. For similar accounts of refugee suffering and powerlessness in another context see Inhetveen, "'Because we are refugees,'" 7–9.

arms-length relations with others. When it came to intimate relations with people involved in their daily lives, as was the case when they hosted refugees, they seemed to put character above ethnicity. Furthermore, once you pushed people to go beyond abstract considerations to think in contextual terms, the history of their relations with people always seemed to trump ethnicity.

The two interviews below with former Sierra Leonean refugees who had insisted that refugees with co-ethnics fared better on some of the previously mentioned indicators than those without co-ethnics demonstrate the points made earlier. The first was an interview with a Mende man in the village of Woroma in Penguia Chiefdom, Kailahun District.

> Author: Do you think the Kissi Guineans treated the Kissi refugees better than the refugees who were not Kissi?
>
> Interviewee: Of course they did. I am Mende. If I were here and a Mende and a Limba came to ask for something which of them do you think I will give a room to? The Mende, of course.
>
> Author: So are you saying ethnicity is the most important factor that you will consider in how to treat the two people? Did you feel like that was what always motivated how people treated you in Kolomba?
>
> Interviewee: Well, maybe not always. It all depended on your relationship with people. If you were friends with people there you could ask and they would give you many things. For example, I am Mende but as I told you earlier, when I was in Kolomba I was a blacksmith and had a lot of Kissi [Guinean] friends who I made machetes for. Because of this I was given land everywhere. I had farms in Tombu, Kolomba, all over. I got land because of the good relations I had with those people even though I was Mende and they were Kissi. When their tools were broken I fixed it for them. A lot of the time they had no money but wanted tools and I made it for them free of charge I was even sharpening knives for their wives.[51]

The second was with a man in Tofawonde, Penguia Chiefdom.

> Interviewee: Refugee life makes you do all sorts of things. When I was in Guinea I became a Kissi even though I am Mende. I used to tell people I am Kissi.

---

[51] Interview with a former refugee in Woroma, Penguia Chiefdom, Sierra Leone (MRB 265), September 12, 2009.

Author: Why did you tell people you were Kissi?

Interviewee: Because I thought since the Guineans were Kissi, I will be treated better if I were Kissi. I told my stranger father called Sahr that even though he knew I was Mende he should tell everyone who asked that I am Kissi. I spoke Kissi well so I became a Kissi. As we are sitting here if we were members of the same ethnic group and I ask you for something you will give it to me because we belong to the same group.

Author: But your stranger father, Sahr, was a Kissi and knew you were Mende. Did he treat you worse than he treated the Kissi refugees because of that? Why did you think he would mislead his Kissi co-ethnics about your identity and treat you well even though he knew you were Mende?

Interviewee: My relationship with Sahr was very different. He knew that I was Mende but he treated me better than even the Kissi refugees. I can say that he saved my life in Kolomba and I knew he would never tell people I was Mende. He knew my character and that was what mattered most in our relationship. He always defended me. He used to settle disputes even between my wife and me.

Author: So let us say, God forbid, there is a war in Guinea and Sahr came along with Mende refugees from Guinea. Will you give a house and food to the Mende refugees before you think about helping Sahr because they are Mende like you and he is not?

Interviewee: God forbid! I already told you Sahr saved my live. Yes, I can say he saved my life with all the things he did for me even though I am Mende and he is Kissi. If he came here with Mende refugees, I will take care of him before I even look at the Mende refugees. Because of the way he treated me and his character I will treat him better than even Mende people.[52]

When it comes to the contextual and intimate relations between refugees and hosts that we are talking about, hosts tended to be influenced less by ethnic nationalism and more by issues of character. They wanted a trustworthy person they could leave their coffee plantation with without fear of pilfering or entrust their children to who would not sexually abuse

---

[52] Interview with a former refugee in Tofawonde, Penguia Chiefdom, Sierra Leone (MRB 295), September 16, 2009.

them. They wanted to host refugees who would not seduce their spouses. Such trustworthy people could be co-ethnics but they could also be non–co-ethnics.

There are times when these considerations of character neatly overlap with considerations of ethnicity. Situations in which ethnic cleavages have been poisoned with hate and a history of violence and atrocity are examples. Here, ethnicity would stand as a somewhat efficient proxy for character. However, these situations make up only a minute subset of relations between ethnic groups. So when it comes to refugee–host relations, it is better to speak in terms of the nature of relations between individuals and groups than simply in terms of co-ethnicity and its absence.

The Spatial Component

A spatial comparison of the Kolomba-Kelema complex characterized by refugee–host co-ethnicity and the Gotoye-Dongueta complex not characterized by it further supports the critique in this chapter. Relations between the Kpelle refugees from Liberia and their Guinean Kpelle hosts in Dongueta-Gotoye and those between the Mende refugees from Sierra Leone and their Guinean Kissi hosts in Kolomba-Kelema were very similar. Like the Kpelle co-ethnics in Dongueta-Gotoye, many of the Mende and Kissi could understand and speak each other's language. Like the Kpelle co-ethnics, the Mende and Kissi have had a long history of legal and extralegal market relations across their common border. When the Government of Sekou Toure cracked down on secret society initiations in the Forest Region of Guinea, many Kpelle Guineans took their kids for initiation among their Kpelle neighbors in Liberia.[53] The Kissi Guineans in Kolomba District did the same among their Mende neighbors in Sierra Leone.[54] Intermarriages proliferate across both frontiers. In short, deep relations and the familiarity they breed are not the preserve of co-ethnics.

An Objection: Measurement Validity

One might object that this work suffers from a severe flaw of measurement validity. Maybe Guineans did not treat the refugees I call their co-ethnics any better because contrary to my assumption, they did not even recognize them as their co-ethnics. Perhaps the separation of group members by

[53] Interview (MRB 309).
[54] Interview (MRB 133).

colonial and postcolonial borders eroded the sense of co-ethnicity across borders, making the critique developed here baseless. The Kpelle and Kissi of Guinea saw themselves as hosting refugees, all of whom were their non–co-ethnics and so, as expected by the co-ethnicity argument, did not extend to any of them the privileges they reserve for their co-ethnics.

The simple answer to this objection is that people readily recognize the existence of members of their ethnic group on the other side of national borders. Sierra Leoneans, Guineans, and Liberians who I interviewed all routinely talked about their co-ethnics on the other side of national borders. Many who have worked on the recent socio-politics of these areas, including van Damme, Gerdes, Ellis, the International Crisis Group, Gale, and McGovern,[55] all point to the existence of this cross-border co-ethnic awareness in the 1990s and 2000s.

However, there is a deeper sense in which we could understand this objection. One might argue that in the precolonial period, these ethnic groups that now straddle borders were conscious of their shared ethnicity and had the peculiarly thick ties that ensured they privileged each other over non–co-ethnics. It might further be argued that the introduction of colonialism and postcolonial states eroded these ties. This is particularly true because Guinea was colonized by France, Sierra Leone by Britain, and Liberia, with its links to freed slaves from the United States, was never colonized by a European power. Thus in the 1990s, even where people recognized others across the border as their co-ethnics, national culture may have severely rendered such recognition irrelevant. National culture might have eroded the sentiments that accompanied such awareness in the precolonial period. The significance of national cultures in refugee–host relations is one that McGovern has highlighted.[56]

The problem with this objection is that it saves an argument that no one really makes. None of the proponents of the co-ethnicity argument cited earlier argue that the thesis applied in the precolonial period but is no longer relevant. They all study postcolonial and, in a few cases late colonial, refugee crises and argue that co-ethnicity helps us understand the reception of refugees. The fact that the impact of co-ethnicity

[55] Van Damme, "How Liberian," 49; Gerdes, "Forced migration," 106–110; Ellis, *The mask of anarchy*, 179; International Crisis Group, "Stopping Guinea's slide," 20–21; International Crisis Group, "Liberia and Sierra Leone: rebuilding failed states." *ICG Africa Report* No. 87 (2004): 25; Gale, "The invisible refugee camp," 544–45; and McGovern, "Unmasking the state," 513, 516.

[56] Ibid., 524.

exists despite colonial and postcolonial disruptions is what impresses those who make the co-ethnicity argument.[57] Thus Zartman[58] wrote of Senegalese "simply receiving large numbers of fellow tribesmen" from Guinea Bissau and of their being "oblivious of international frontiers and national citizenship." Westin's words also capture this: "Refugees from one country will generally be treated kindly by ethnic or tribal compatriots on the other side of the border. So while the deviation of state boundaries from ethnocultural boundaries is part of the problem, it has, to date, also been part of the solution."[59]

The possibility that the development of colonial and postcolonial states and national cultures have eroded the bonds between co-ethnics across borders only reinforces the argument in this book. This is the point that the co-ethnicity argument holds little promise for understanding refugee–host relations in the Mano River Basin crisis of the 1990s and 2000s as I argue. However, there is doubt over whether co-ethnicity helps us understand intercommunal relations even during the precolonial and colonial eras in Africa. Next I cite studies that lead us to question whether focusing on presumably stronger precolonial and colonial bonds of co-ethnicity helps us understand interpersonal and intercommunal relations in precolonial and colonial African societies.

Colson's work on stranger–host relations among the Tonga of Zambia in the precolonial and colonial period is one example. She asserted that among the Tonga, new arrivals from outside of a local community were regarded as strangers, regardless of whether they happened to be Tonga or non-Tonga speakers.[60] Furthermore, she made the point that local processes of incorporation routinely transformed such strangers, regardless of their ethnicity, into Tonga members of the local community within a few years. These incorporated members came to exercise all the rights of the community members among whom they had settled.[61]

In his study of the Forest Region of Guinea, McGovern made similar observations. People were known to switch between ethnicities from Malinké to Toma and from Toma to Malinké.[62] Toma people who

[57] Hansen, "Once the running stops," 369–370.
[58] Zartman, "Portuguese Guinean refugees," 144.
[59] Westin, "Regional analysis," 29.
[60] Colson, "The assimilation of aliens," 36.
[61] Ibid., 36, 39.
[62] McGovern, "Unmasking the state," 181–216, 411.

moved from one village to another might be classed as strangers even when the autochthonous members of the village in which these migrants settled were also Toma.[63] Many others who have studied precolonial and colonial societies *across Africa* have noted similar processes of fluid and mobile identities, syncretism, and the nonprivileging of ethnicity in interpersonal and intergroup relations.[64]

These insights help us understand why people in the Mano River Basin did not seem to put as much weight on ethnicity in their dealings with refugee strangers as we might expect. The ethnicity of a refugee or stranger generally might not count for much, even when he or she moves to another village inhabited by co-ethnics. This is because indigeneity and all of its privileges are often defined in far more local terms than that assumed by Holborn[65] and other proponents of the co-ethnicity argument. Furthermore, for the non–co-ethnic stranger (refugee or national) who comported herself in an appropriate manner, there was the possibility of receiving rights and benefits that were not automatically accorded to co-ethnic stranger nationals or refugees.

During my research, I met Guineans whose lives exemplified these processes. In what locals describe as the Kpelle village of Gotoye in Yomou

[63] Ibid., 383.

[64] Mamdani, *When victims become killers*, 163; Geschiere, *The perils of belonging*, 9; Audrey Richards, "The assimilation of the immigrants," in *Economic development and tribal change: a study of immigrant labour in Buganda*, ed. Audrey Richards (Cambridge: W. Heffer and Sons Ltd, 1952), 166–171; Kibreab, *Ready and willing*, 150; Tim Allen, "Ethnicity and tribalism on the Sudan-Uganda border," in *Ethnicity and conflict in the horn of Africa*, Fukui Katsoyoshi and John Markakis (London: James Currey, 1994), 134; Martin Doornbos, *Not all the king's men: inequality as a political instrument in Ankole, Uganda* (The Hague: Mouton Publishers, 1978), 75; Clay, *The eviction of Banyarwanda*, 18; Randall Packard, "Debating in a common idiom: variant traditions of genesis among the Ba Shu of eastern Zaire," in *The African frontier: the reproduction of traditional African societies*, ed. Igor Kopytoff (Bloomington: Indiana University Press, 1987), 149–52; Aidan Southall, "Ethnic incorporation among the Alur," in *From tribe to nation: studies in incorporation processes*, ed. Ronald Cohen and John Middleton (Scranton, PA: Chandler Publishing Company. 1970), 71–72; R. G. Abrahams, "The political incorporation of non-Nyamwezi immigrants in Tanzania" in *From tribe to nation: studies in incorporation processes*, ed. Ronald Cohen and John Middleton (Scranton, PA: Chandler Publishing Company. 1970), 95–101 and 109; Germain, *Peuples de la Foret*, 19; Massing, "The Mane," 44; Paulme, *Les gens du riz*, 77–82; Ellis, *The mask of anarchy*, 32–28, Richards, *Fighting for the rainforest*, 73, 95; and Yves Person, "Ethnic movements and acculturation in Upper Guinea since the fifteenth century," *African Historical Studies* 4 (3–1971): 677.

[65] Holborn, *Refugees*, 292.

Prefecture, I met a very old Toma Guinean man whose reflections on life are summarized here:

I was born here and can really only speak Kpelle, even though if someone speaks Toma near me, I can understand it. My grandfather came from a Toma village to settle here. My uncle also came to settle here because of war. He had a very strong war medicine. He came here and they kept him so he would work on people when there was war. When they went fighting, he led the fighters and no one died. The Gbanamou landowners here hosted them and gave them land. I have a Kpelle name now and we have our own quarter that carries our Kpelle name. We see here as our home. We have plantations here. We were born here. People know us as Toma people and we know we are Toma but it is here that we are. We know we came from somewhere but this is our home. We have become the same as the Kpelle here. They treat us as autochthones. We have a lot of land here. We are citizens here and no one has ever challenged our citizenship.[66]

His account was corroborated by the recognized landowner of the village, the leading living descendant of the founders of Gotoye.[67]

Given the scope of the fieldwork carried out for this study, I can make the firmest claims about the effects of co-ethnicity on refugee–host relations only for the Mano River Basin. One might even be tempted to restrict this further to the Forest Region of Guinea. However, the arguments concerning language and language abilities, familiarity, ethnic nationalism, mobile identities, and the assimilation of strangers apply to other parts of the continent, as shown in the secondary literature cited. This certainly gives us reason to question the alleged promise of co-ethnicity as an explanation of refugee–host relations on the African continent.

Although not dedicating significant attention to it, several scholars have questioned this thesis. Harrell-Bond, whose insightful work contributed in no small way to the creation of the burgeoning field of Refugee Studies, raised questions about the promise of co-ethnicity in her 1986 work on refugee situations in Sudan and Uganda.[68] De Montclos and Kagwanja, writing of a refugee situation in Kenya, have

---

[66] Interview with a Guinean in Gotoye, Yomou Prefecture, Guinea (MRB 385), July 14, 2011.
[67] Interview (MRB 373).
[68] Harrell-Bond, *Imposing aid*, 67.

expressed similar reservations.[69] Jacobson, writing of refugees in Malawi and Sudan, has noted that the "goodwill" of local communities and leaders, rather than co-ethnicity, is determinant in how refugees are treated.[70] Chambers, commenting on Burundian refugees in the Democratic Republic of Congo (DRC) and Bakongo Angolan refugees in DRC, noted that "Neither moving a short distance, nor settling among ethnic kin, necessarily assures acceptable self-settlement."[71] Adepoju et al., in writing of refugees in West Africa during the 1990s wars in the Mano River Basin, make similar reservations. They noted: "Notwithstanding that refugees in West Africa often share significant ethnic, linguistic and other affinities with the populations of their host states, they are perhaps as often scapegoats for ills in West African societies as they are for the same sorts of ills in European, North American or other societies."[72]

NUMBERS AND REFUGEE–HOST RELATIONS

The lack of generalized violence against refugees in all of the communities in the Forest Region poses a fundamental challenge to another influential argument in the study of intercommunal violence. This is the argument that focuses on population numbers. The numbers argument would posit that refugee–host relations are dependent on refugee and host population numbers. There are two variants of this argument. A simple version posits a linear correlation between refugee numbers and the probability of such violence happening. The greater the number of refugees, the more likely it is that locals will undertake large-scale attacks against them. The work of Spilerman on riots by blacks in the United States posits such a version of the argument.[73] A more nuanced version of this theory focuses on ratios instead of absolute numbers and posits a "curvilinear relationship"[74]

---

[69] Marc-Antoine de Montclos and Peter Kagwanja, "Refugee camps or cities? The socio-economic dynamics of the Dadaab and Kakuma Camps in Northern Kenya," *Journal of Refugee Studies* 13 (June 2000): 206.

[70] Karen Jacobson, "Refugees' environmental impact: the effect of patters of settlement," *Journal of Refugee Studies* 10 (March 1997): 27.

[71] Chambers, "Rural refugees in Africa," 386.

[72] Adepoju, Boulton, and Levin, "Promoting integration," 17.

[73] Seymour Spilerman, "The causes of racial disturbances: tests of an explanation," *American Sociological Review* 36 (June 1971): 429.

[74] Steven Wilkinson lays out both versions of this argument, which he rejects, in his work, *Votes and violence*, 332.

between refugee–host ratios and the propensity for violence. It is argued that violence is most likely to happen when the opposing communities are relatively equal in number.[75] This "proportions"[76] version of the argument predicts less likelihood of violence when locals far surpass refugees because the refugees are low in number and do not constitute an actual or potential threat. Violence is also unlikely to happen when refugees far outnumber locals because even though the refugees may become insolent and locals may want to violently put them in their place, locals will not try to do so. This is because of the low chances of success. In this situation, locals can be understood to have "accepted a subordinate political position"[77] out of necessity.

Both the absolute numbers and proportions variants of the numbers argument are based on a strong association of numbers and empowerment.[78] It is understood that the larger a group gets, the more powerful it becomes. Refugees believe this, and that is why they are tempted to be less subservient as their numbers increase. Locals also believe this, and that is why they pay attention to refugee numbers. It is for this reason that they avoid attacking refugees when the refugees far outnumber them or they far outnumber the refugees. This very close association of group size with group power and sense of empowerment is at the core of the numbers argument.

The Poverty of the Numbers Argument

Villages in Fangamandu, Kondou, and Banie prefectures presented a good opportunity to assess this argument for two reasons. They displayed significant spatial as well as temporal variation in refugee–host population

---

[75] Wilkinson, *Votes and violence*, 33; Roger Jeffery and Patricia Jeffery, "The Bijnor Riots, October 1990: Collapse of a mythical special relationship?" *Economic and Political Weekly* 29 (March 5, 1994): 551; Richard Lambert, *Hindu-Muslim riots in India* (PhD diss., University of Pennsylvania, 1951), 25; Ghosh, *Riots: prevention and control* (Calcutta: Eastern Law House, 1971), 53; and Naresh C. Sexana, "The nature and origins of communal riots in India," in *Communal riots in post-independence India*, ed. Asghar Ali Engineer (Hyderabad: Sangam Books India, 1984), 55.

[76] Jeffery and Jeffery, "The Bijnor riots," 551.

[77] I am again borrowing the terminology of Jeffery and Jeffery here. "The Bijnor riots," 551.

[78] It is worth noting that there are other causal stories that can be superimposed on these arguments beyond the empowerment one taken previously. Some argue that larger minority members create a greater possibility of "contact and, therefore, for conflict between the majority and minority communities." I focus on the empowerment version of the numbers argument because I find it to be the most plausible and compelling.

ratios. Some, like Fandou, Saadou (Kondou Sub-Prefecture), Vianga, and Forofonye (Banie Sub-Prefecture), had far fewer refugees than locals. Others, like Kolomba, Kelema (Fangamandou Sub-Prefecture) Gotoye, and Dongueta (Banie Sub-Prefecture), had far more refugees than locals. In others yet still, like Yende Douane and Kiligbema (Kondou Sub-Prefecture), refugee–host numbers were relatively equal.

Many of these villages also displayed variation over time. Refugees started arriving slowly, constituting only a tiny fraction of the local population. However, their numbers kept increasing until they sometimes became equal to those of the locals. Sometimes they then went on to far surpass the host population. In some communities, refugee numbers were again drastically reduced when many moved to newly created camps established in other communities. Kolomba is a good example. Refugees started arriving as a mere trickle in the early 1990s in the village of Kolomba, which had about 500 people. Then they were badly outnumbered by the locals. As the war got closer to areas of Kailahun District in Sierra Leone from where many of the refugees were fleeing to Kolomba, there was a flood of refugees that came to outnumber the local population. However, things got even more dramatic when UNHCR and the government of Guinea decided to locate a camp for refugees living in all the nearby villages in Kolomba. Kolomba Camp eventually came to host up to 42,000 refugees. The local population had still not surpassed a thousand by then.

Research in Fangamandou, Kondou, and Banie Sub-Prefectures in Guinea revealed that despite the wide variation in refugee–host ratios and absolute refugee numbers across space and time, all of these villages had escaped generalized anti-refugee violence. The hard part was figuring out why variations in absolute refugee numbers and refugee–host ratios over time and space seem to have made little difference in the outbreak of violence on refugees.

My initial interviews began to cast light on this. They suggested that the key assumption on which the numbers argument is based was problematic and that this might account for its failure to explain generalized anti-refugee attacks in Guinea. This is the assumption that both refugees and locals associate population numbers with empowerment. Early interviews cast doubt on this close association. My initial Guinean interviewees in Kolomba often laughed when I asked them which group was more powerful in their town, given the fact that refugees at one point outnumbered locals by forty-two to one. "The locals, of course," was the answer I got. This response was important because if both refugees and locals did not

TABLE 5.2. *Refugee–Host Ratios*

Host Community	Proportion of Refugees to Locals	Former Refugees Interviewed In
Kolomba	42:1	Penguia, Sierra Leone
Kelema	10:1	Penguia, Sierra Leone
Dongueta	2:1	Salayea District, Liberia
Gotoye	3:1	Salayea District, Liberia

necessarily associate group size with group power, then the interpretation of the numbers argument I lay out earlier will fall apart. Refugees who outnumbered locals would not necessarily get uppity and disobey locals, provoking anti-refugee attacks. Locals seeing refugee numbers soar will not necessarily fear a loss of power and so use violence to keep refugee numbers down.

In an amendment of my interview plans, I decided to ask people in a more systematic manner about their sense of power relations given the refugee–host population configurations in their areas. The goal was to assess whether locals and refugees associated higher numbers with more power, as the numbers argument suggests. Did the locals feel like they had lost or were losing power to refugees in cases where they thought the refugees outnumbered them or were in the process of outnumbering them? Did refugees feel like they had or were acquiring more power than locals in cases where they thought they outnumbered or were outnumbering the locals?

I posed these questions to locals in four Guinean villages. In all four villages, refugees went from being just a few people in a sea of locals to outnumbering locals. In Kolomba in Fangamandu Prefecture, refugee numbers were to rise up to 42,000 to less than 1,000 locals. In Kelema, locals estimated that at some point the refugee population was at least ten times that of the local population. In Gotoye, there were three times as many Liberian refugees as Guineans. In Dongueta, around 2,000 refugees lived with 1,000 locals. I also posed these questions to people in Penguia Chiefdom in Kailahun District, Sierra Leone, who had been refugees in the villages of Kolomba and Kelema in Fangamandou Sub-Prefecture. Liberians from Gorlu and Kpayea in Salayea District, Liberia, who had been refugees in the villages of Gotoye and Dongueta in Banie Sub-Prefecture, Guinea, also responded to these questions.

The responses I got from both Guineans and former refugees further undermined the basic assumption of the numbers argument. This is the supposition that both refugees and locals closely identify population numbers with power and the sense of empowerment.

The former refugees claimed they were powerless relative to the local hosts even in situations in which they far outnumbered their hosts. All eleven people who were formerly refugees in Kelema stated that despite the larger refugee numbers, the Guineans in Kelema had more power. All thirteen who were formerly refugees in Kolomba claimed locals had more power in Kolomba, even though the refugees far outnumbered them. All eight residents of Salayea District in Liberia who were formerly refugees in Dongueta stated that the locals had more power despite the larger refugee numbers. When I went to Salayea District to interview Liberians who had been refugees in Gotoye, all five claimed that the locals had more power even if the refugee population was higher.

Locals were less categorical but also undermined the link between numbers and the sense of power that underpins the empowerment version of the numbers argument. Four of six locals in Kolomba said that superior refugee numbers did not mean superior refugee power relative to the local population. In Kelema, five of seven respondents claimed that the locals were more powerful than the refugees, even when the refugees were more than twice the population of the locals. In Gotoye, five of six interviewees said the locals were more powerful than the refugees, even though the refugees far outnumbered the locals. The story in nearby Dongueta was similar; all four locals interviewed asserted that the locals were more powerful than the refugees even when the refugees outnumbered the locals.

In most of these interviews, locals expressed having initial fears when the refugees started arriving. However, these fears went away so that even when refugee numbers swelled, they did not look on them as powerful. The most revealing aspects of these interviews were the explanations of why both refugees and locals did not seem to equate numbers with power. Here I list a few of the responses by Guineans hosts.

The refugees outnumbered us here but we had more power. This is our country. The refugees had money but it got finished without a way of replenishing it. We had wealth that could replenish itself like plantations. We had social networks here that they did not have. If I had a case with a refugee and we had to go to Fangamandou, I would have an advantage because I already knew people there. We knew this area better than the refugees. Their supplies were not always sufficient or on time, and they always ended up depending on us for food and health care.[79]

When we saw them coming, first we were afraid, but the government sent a military contingent to Kolomba to be with us, and that erased our fears. We depended on the soldiers and went to them with our problems. We were more powerful than the refugees, but we did not use this power to abuse or threaten them.[80]

There were more Liberians than Guineans in this quarter. We were worried that the rebels would follow them here, and they were worried we would drive them away. But we had more power here. When you receive a stranger, even if they are more numerous, they can't be more powerful. When they want to drink, get cassava, take a bath, it is you they approach. They can't be more powerful than you when they depend on you for all of their needs.[81]

The responses of the refugees were similarly revealing.

Even though we were far larger in number, we had less power than the Guineans. Are you joking? We were living at their feet; how could we have had more power? We were strangers. We could not say no when they made a demand. They gave us a big place to bury our dead and to build houses to stay in so how could they not have power over us?[82]

We outnumbered them but we could not have been more powerful than them. They were the hosts and could fulfill all their needs. We could not fulfill any of our needs and depended on them for all sorts of things, including pots and pans.[83]

Of course they were more powerful than us even though there were more of us. It was not our area. They gave us a place to build our houses. We had to abide by what they said. Did they not tie and imprison my brother-in-law, saying he is a rebel? The soldiers came and pointed a tank at the camp, saying they would kill all of us if the war spilled over into Guinea. How could we have been more powerful?[84]

An Anatomy of Power

The insight we can draw from these answers is the complex and rounded understanding of power that they reveal. The responses lay bare the

[79] Interview (MRB 115).
[80] Interview with a Guinean in Kolomba, Guéckédou Prefecture, Guinea (MRB 100), June 19, 2009.
[81] Interview (MRB 159).
[82] Interview with a former refugee in Gotoye, Yomou Prefecture, Guinea (MRB 161), July 22, 2009.
[83] Interview (MRB 306).
[84] Interview (MRB 319).

weaknesses of the numbers argument. A close examination indicates that population size is only one determinant of power. Another is the nature of in-group networks. This determines, among other things, the extent to which group members can engage in collective action in the group's interest. The nature of out-group links is also important. As scholars of inter-state war know, a small group with thick positive ties with other groups might have more power than that a bigger one with no ties or hostile relations with neighboring groups.[85]

The resources of a group are also important. These resources include weapons and money. In a situation of violence, the possession of superior weaponry might make even a small group very powerful. Some groups are powerful because of their wealth. Wealth can be transformed into political resources through the purchase of weapons, votes, professional rioters, allies, and so forth. Many interviewees pointed to the relative destitution of the refugees and their economic dependence on the locals.[86]

The knowledge possessed by a group is similarly important in determining its power and the sense of empowerment of its members. This knowledge may take the form of specialized technical knowledge that gives a group disproportionate influence on policy making and implementation in a specific area. The technocratic change teams that are sent by the International Monetary Fund to institute economic reforms in aid-receiving countries often exercise a lot of influence on those countries.[87] It might also include knowledge of a terrain that magnifies the military power of a small group relative to larger ones that lack similar knowledge. Superior

---

[85] Brett Ashley Leeds, "Alliances and the Expansion and Escalation of Militarized Interstate Disputes," in *New directions in international relations*, ed. Alex Mintz and Bruce Russett (Lanham, MD: Lexington Books, 2005), 117–134; James Morrow, "Alliances, credibility and peacetime costs," *Journal of Conflict Resolution* 38 (June 1994): 270–297; Alastair Smith, "Extended deterrence and alliance formation," *International Interactions* 24 (October–December 1998): 315–343; Alastair Smith, "Alliance Formation and War," *International Studies Quarterly* 39 (December 1995): 405–425; and Paul Huth and Bruce Russett, "Deterrence Failure and Crisis Escalation," *International Studies Quarterly* 32 (March 1988): 29–45.

[86] Interview (MRB 115); interview (MRB 159); interview with a former refugee in Woroma, Penguia Chiefdom, Guinea (MRB 284), September 14, 2009; and interview (MRB 306). As Jacobson points out, many refugees leave their assets behind when they flee to host countries. *The economic life of refugees*, 10–11.

[87] Ferguson, *The anti-politics machine*, 258–259; Thandika Mkandawire, "Crisis management and 'choiceless democracies,'" in *State, conflict and democracy in Africa*, ed. Richard Joseph (Boulder: Lynne Rienner Publishers), 119–122; and Adebayo Olukoshi, *The elusive Prince of Denmark: structural adjustment and the crisis of governance in Africa* (Uppsala : Nordiska Afrikaninstitutet, 1998).

fighting skills and what the French called a *tempérament guerrier*[88] often attracted French and British colonial authorities to certain groups that were heavily recruited into colonial forces and then sometimes went on to play roles out of all proportion to their size.

Given all of these determinants of power and a sense of empowerment, the overreliance on population size as a determinant of power is clearly problematic. One might argue that democratic settings represent a space where population size is a privileged determinant of power and a sense of empowerment. However, even this claim is problematic. Money is influential in determining winners in many democracies in that it influences how many followers a politician might eventually have.[89]

It is because of all of these reasons that the numbers argument, whether in the study of refugees or in the more general study of civil relations, as seen in the work of Posner,[90] is problematic. Even if the numbers argument worked well in the democratic context, it is not certain that it will apply well to refugee–host relations because most refugees do not vote in their host countries or participate in local political campaigns.

CONCLUSION

A serious engagement of these arguments is necessary because they carry a lot of influence in the explanation of intergroup relations. This is particularly true of the co-ethnicity argument, which has a profile almost second to none in the explanation of refugee–host relations across Africa. We cannot justifiably generalize to the rest of the continent these studies of the Forest Region of Guinea. However, the theoretical insights and evidence from farther afield, drawn from secondary literature, lead us to

---

[88] Claude Riviere, "La toponymie de Conakry et du Kaloum," *Bulletin de l'IFAN. Notes et Documents. Senie B: Sciences Humaine, Dakar* xxvii. (Juillet-Octobre 1966): 1009–1018.

[89] See the edited volume by Frederic Schafer, *Elections for sale: the causes and consequences of vote buying* (Boulder, CO: Lynne Rienner Publishers, 2007); Bruce Ackerman and Ian Ayres, *Voting with dollars: a new paradigm for campaign finance* (New Haven: Yale University Press, 2002); John Samples, *The fallacy of campaign finance reform* (Chicago: University of Chicago Press, 2006); Rodney Smith, *Money, power and elections: how campaign finance reform subverts American democracy* (Baton Rouge: Louisiana State University Press, 2006); and David Donnelly, Janice Fine and Ellen Miller, *Are elections for sale?* (Boston: Beacon Press, 1999).

[90] Daniel Posner, "The Political Salience of Cultural Difference: Why Chewas and Tumbukas Are Allies in Zambia and Adversaries in Malawi," *American Political Science Review* 98 (November 2004).

take another look at the promise of these arguments in other contexts on the African continent. This chapter plays the key role of clearing the path for the analysis that follows by providing us with strong enough reasons to jettison these key counterarguments that would otherwise constantly be at the back of our minds.

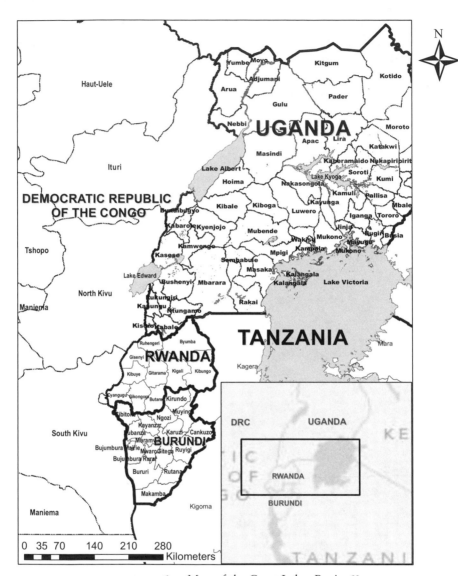

FIGURE 6.1. Map of the Great Lakes Region[91]

[91] This map was created by Rita Effah, using the following resources: FAO-Africover, "Multipurpose Africover"; GADM, "Database of Global"; and WRI, "Waterbodies in Uganda."

6

Not "Chasing" Banyarwanda in Southwestern Uganda

> When Obote came back to power [in 1980], his youths started seizing our cows and started attacking us. Many refugees ran to the settlement and some went to Rwanda. But some of the local people told the youth to leave us alone because we were their friends.[1]

The month of October 1982 brought with it an episode of refugee cleansing in areas of southwestern Uganda that previously constituted the colonial kingdom of Ankole. When the Rwandese Social Revolution broke out in 1959, Uganda was a big destination for fleeing predominantly Batutsi refugees. In October 1982, local chiefs, youth wingers from the ruling Uganda People's Congress (UPC), and a unit of the state's Special Force violently evicted Rwandese refugees from areas outside of the official United Nations High Commission for Refugees (UNHCR) settlements of Oruchinga and Nakivale, in what is today Isingiro District. Systematically and openly, they went to the homes of the refugees, forced them out, looted any properties they desired, and set the houses on fire. Many refugees were beaten and tortured, and some were killed. Some refugee women were raped. As a result of the exercise, approximately 30,000 people were forced into the UNHCR camps, whereas 40,000 ran to Rwanda, where they were settled in camps. Thousands also fled into Tanzania. When Rwanda closed its border with Uganda, about 4,000 displaced people were trapped at Mirama Hill, on the Ugandan side of the border.[2] This exercise, which popularly became known as "The chasing

---

[1] Interview (GLR 88).
[2] Zolberg, Suhrke, and Aguayo, *Escape from violence*, 68.

of the Banyarwanda," swept away even many Ugandan citizens. Eventually, only about thirty percent of its victims were thought to have been Rwandese refugees.[3]

Although much has been written about what happened during the exercise, it is what did *not* happen that is of interest here. The local population of Ankole seems to have largely refrained from participating in the exercise. After the evictions, various state officials tried to present it as a spontaneous and popular local uprising against the refugees.[4] The then minister of culture first explained the violence as "clashes between the refugees and the local population resulting from cattle rustling."[5] The state-owned *Uganda Times* newspaper portrayed the flight of refugees as the result of mere panic from rumors of forced evictions of Banyarwanda who had killed local residents searching for stolen cattle.[6]

There is evidence that this was not so. None of the many people who have studied the situation mention participation by people other than state officials, state security forces, and the UPC Youth Wing.[7] By then the UPC Youth Wing had evolved into a state militia that was also deeply involved in intelligence work. Many local Banyankore who I interviewed denied that there was popular participation in the attacks.[8] Of even greater significance is the fact that the victims of the attacks denied that there was popular participation in the exercise. This was so even when I interviewed former refugees in their home country where they had repatriated and had little to fear from speaking their minds.[9] Some comments on the eviction by some of these evictees follow.

The people who drove the refugees were the ones called the *bayouths* [UPC youth wingers]. They sent the refugees away and took their properties. Then they came

---

[3] Zolberg, Suhrke, and Aguayo, *Escape from violence*, 68.
[4] Clay, *The eviction of Banyarwanda*, 3; Mamdani, *When victims become killers*, 168.
[5] Cited in Clay, *The eviction of Banyarwanda*, 36.
[6] Cited in Clay, *The eviction of Banyarwanda*, 50. Also see Charles Meynell, "Uganda and Sudan," *Minority Rights Group Report 66* (December 1984), 11.
[7] Mamdani, *When victims become killers*, 168–169; "The political diaspora," 315; Hamilton, "Human rights in Uganda," 19–20; Watson, "Exile from Rwanda," 10–11; Zolberg, *Conflict and the refugee crisis*, 67; Zolberg, Suhrke and Aguayo, *Escape from violence*, 67–68; and Khiddu-Makubuya, "Voluntary repatriation," 150.
[8] Interviews with a Munyankore in Ntungamo (GLR 8), March 27, 2010; and with another Munyankore in Ruhaama, Ntungamo District (GLR 17), March 31, 2010.
[9] Interview (GLR 86); interview (GLR 87); interview (GLR 88); interviews with a former refugee in Nyabitekeri, Nyagatare District, Rwanda (GLR 89), May 23, 2010; with a former evictee in Ntungamo Town (GLR 6), March 27, 2010; and with a former evictee in Ruhaama Town, Ntungamo District (GLR 16), March 30, 2010.

to the settlement and took cows from people. If the camp were not protected they would have come in to kill us. They had the plan of taking all our properties.[10]

I was a victim of the evictions. The UPC Youth Wing leader met me in Ntungamo town and put a pistol to my stomach and said: "All of you Banyarwanda should leave this place." Our neighbors did not do the evictions. It was the Youth Wing and the chiefs that did it. I had a friend in the local community who was a bishop and he drove my family to Kamwezi near the border with Rwanda. The youth wingers chased my son around town but he ran and hid under the bed of an old friend of mine. That man saved my son's life. Our neighbors helped us. They did not evict us. When I was in a camp in Rwanda after my eviction, eighteen of my neighbors went to visit me there. When I came back they celebrated and gave me milk and some cows to start my herd again. The youth wingers had eaten all 150 of my cows. The youth wingers had power.[11]

All the Banyarwanda settled outside of camps were evicted in 1982. The chiefs and youth wingers told us to go. They drove us and torched grass houses. They beat us and threw us out of our houses and we went with nothing. When some of our neighbors tried to help us, they were also harassed. One of our neighbors drove us to the border. In Rwanda we went to Kibondo Camp.[12]

Like in the communities in the Forest Region of Guinea, this nonparticipation of the local population in the attacks was not for want of trying by state agents to get them involved. The perpetrators cajoled, encouraged, threatened, and even victimized locals, all in a bid to get them to participate. The large land parcels and significant cattle herds of some of the refugees were dangled as attractive rewards for those who participated in "chasing" the refugees away.[13] However, instead of a rush to participate, the opposite often happened. Some locals tried to protect the refugees, offer them help with surviving the ordeal, forewarned them of impending attacks, and helped them to secure their properties before raids. It is on account of this that "one Mbarara [District] UPC official, Mr. L.R. Makatu proclaimed that it would be anti-Ugandan for anyone to provide food or water to the evicted refugees."[14] State agents and youth wingers physically "prevented local non-Banyarwanda inhabitants from giving food or water to those in flight."[15] They pointed out that there was nothing stopping those who were saddened by the evictions

---

[10] Interview (GLR 89).
[11] Interview (GLR 6).
[12] Interview (GLR 16).
[13] Mamdani, *When victims become killers*, 168.
[14] Mushemeza, "Politics and the refugee experience." Also see Clay, *The eviction of Banyarwanda*, 35.
[15] Hamilton, "Human rights in Uganda," 19.

from going along with the evicted to Rwanda.[16] As one woman recalled: "If you pleaded for a refugee you knew, they told you: 'If you feel you are pained by the evictions go with them.'"[17]

Those caught trying to help refugees were victimized.[18] I was told of a Ugandan who was caught hiding refugees during the exercise. He was expelled along with the refugees he had being protecting and died close to the border with Rwanda.[19]

This chapter explains why the local population in southwestern Uganda did not join state agents in their attacks on the refugees. Like in the Forest Region of Guinea, the involvement of a few refugees in opposition activities is what explains the state's hostile attitude toward the refugee population. UPC officials blamed the refugees for supporting the National Resistance Movement (NRM) Bush War, the former government of President Amin, and the opposition Democratic Party (DP).[20] Some of these accusations were particularly potentially damaging to the refugees. These were the accusations of participation in Amin's abusive security forces and cattle theft to aid the NRM rebellion. The problem for the state was that the powerful people in the communities whose participation they sought in the attacks knew enough to discern the lack of substance in blanket accusations about refugee participation in the Amin regime, in the NRM rebellion, and cattle theft. They thus refrained from joining in the undiscriminating assault on the refugees. Their nonparticipation and subtle efforts at subverting the exercise dissuaded the rest of the predominantly Bairu Banyankore underclass, who held real grudges against the refugees from joining the attacks.

THE STATE AND THE EVICTIONS

Like in Congo and Guinea, the UPC's decision to clamp down on the refugees was due to the links of some of the refugees to major opposition groups that posed a serious threat to the UPC leadership. The UPC

---

[16] Interview (GLR 8).

[17] Interview (GLR 17).

[18] Mushemeza, "Politics and the refugee experience," 153.

[19] Interview with a Uganda in Kabingo, Isingiro District, Uganda (GLR 42), April 16, 2010.

[20] Elijah Mushemeza, "Politics and the refugee experience in the Africa Great Lakes Region" (paper prepared for presentation at the MASSPM Seminar, Kampala, Uganda, November 1999), 15; and Republic of Uganda, *The report of the Commission of Inquiry into Violations of Human Rights: findings, conclusions and recommendations* (Kampala, Uganda, October 1994), 501.

leadership had for long viewed the Banyarwanda refugees and Ugandan Banyarwanda citizens as opponents. The Banyarwanda were thought to heavily support the DP, which posed the most significant electoral threat to the Obote government before its removal in 1971. There are indications that without widespread rigging, the DP will have won the 1980 elections that saw the return of Obote to power. Some refugees were thought to have registered and voted for the DP, an offense that the UPC never forgave.[21] Obote had called for a census of all Banyarwanda, including Ugandan citizens, in the country before his ouster in 1971. Many believe this was to make sure they did not participate in elections.[22]

It was on account of this that many of the refugees were probably not saddened when Amin removed Obote from power in 1971. A commission of inquiry later found that a few of the refugees even joined his State Research Bureau, which perpetrated some of that regime's worst abuses.[23] The UPC cast blanket blame on the refugees for the abuses of the Amin government[24] and even accused them of fighting with his troops against the invading force from Tanzania that eventually toppled Amin. The fact that some Banyarwanda refugees were actively involved in the armies that removed Amin was overlooked.[25]

Because of its ability and demonstrated willingness to rig elections, one would suspect that support by the refugees for the DP did not pose too much of a concern to the UPC in the early 1980s. Refugee involvement in the armed insurgency was a more serious threat. The UPC accused the refugees of joining the NRM movement led by Yoweri Museveni, which started its Bush War in 1981 and was eventually to topple Obote in 1986.[26] Two of the thirty-four people who staged the initial attack were Rwandese refugees – Fred Rwigyema and Paul Kagame.[27] There was no indication of widespread participation by refugees in the movement. Despite this, Obote and the UPC began to call it "a Banyarwanda rebellion" and portrayed the whole refugee community as NRM collaborators.[28]

[21] Mushemeza, "Politics and the refugee experience in the Africa Great Lakes Region," 15; and Republic of Uganda, *The report of the Commission*, 501.

[22] Mamdani, *When victims become killers*, 167.

[23] Hamilton, "Human rights in Uganda," 19; and Watson, "Exile from Rwanda," 10.

[24] Mushemeza, "Politics and the refugee experience in the Africa Great Lakes Region," 15; and Republic of Uganda, *The report of the Commission*, 501

[25] Mushemeza, "Politics and the refugee experience," 165.

[26] Mushemeza, "Politics and the refugee experience in the Africa Great Lakes Region," 15; Republic of Uganda, *The report of the Commission*, 501.

[27] Mushemeza, "Politics and the refugee experience," 166.

[28] Mushemeza, "Politics and the refugee experience in the Africa Great Lakes Region," 15.

Playing on fears of the very sensitive issue of cattle theft in a region of widespread cattle ownership, they sought to translate this demonization into a local idiom by accusing the refugees of stealing cattle to support the rebellion.[29] At rallies, they urged Ugandans to prevent the refugees from overthrowing the government.[30] In a speech printed in the *Uganda Times*, Obote noted that "A visitor who does that [dabbling in opposition politics as noted above] is inviting himself to be sent away."[31]

If the accusations sound exaggerated, it is because like in Guinea, the UPC was interested not just in punishing refugee opponents and dissuading refugee participation in opposition politics. UPC leaders seized on the involvement of some refugees in opposition politics to achieve wider political objectives. The campaign sought to fan nationalist flames against the NRM insurgency by delegitimizing it as made up of foreigners and stooges of foreigners. As Mushemeza noted, Obote branded the NRM's Bush War a rebellion by Rwandese refugees. In the Luweero Triangle, "UNLA (Uganda National Liberation Army) graffiti denounced Museveni and the NRA as Banyarwanda."[32]

Mamdani has pointed out that this UPC move became a self-fulfilling prophecy. The large-scale attacks on Banyarwanda for what the UPC saw as their collaboration with the opposition is what ended up driving hordes of Banyarwanda youth into the grateful arms of the NRM. By 1986 when the NRM took power, Banyarwanda constituted around a quarter of their fighters.[33]

The UPC was putting the campaign to even more sinister ends. Under the guise of evicting Rwandese refugees, they evicted ethnic Banyarwanda citizens of Uganda who were deemed to be opponents of the UPC.[34] It needs to be emphasized that the eviction of these other Banyarwanda was not an unfortunate side effect of a move that was primarily targeted at the refugees. It was deliberate. When people claimed that they were not refugees but Banyarwanda who had come to the area earlier, the response of the evictors was, "Those who came earlier should go early. Those who came later will go later."[35] Even Bakiga and Banyankore, who were

---

[29] Interview with an old man in Kazia, Isingiro District, Uganda (GLR 72), April 27, 2010.
[30] Clay, *The eviction of Banyarwanda*, 33.
[31] Cited in Clay, *The eviction of Banyarwanda*, 33.
[32] Watson, "Exile from Rwanda," 11.
[33] Mamdani, *When victims become killers*, 169–170.
[34] Ibid., 168.
[35] Interview with a former refugee couple in Nyabitekeri, Nyagatare District, Rwanda (GLR 94), May 24, 2010.

known to be strong opposition members, were often evicted.[36] Although some of these Ugandans ran into the refugee settlements at Nakivale and Oruchinga, others were forced across the border into Rwanda, where they became refugees.[37]

There is abundant evidence that officials at the highest levels of government were actively involved in the eviction program and that it was a state program. The chiefs, UPC Youth Wing members along with police and a unit of the Special Force, carried out the evictions.[38] Three senior government officials were heavily involved in and are thought to have directed and authorized the exercise. These were Chris Rwakasisi, minister of state for security affairs; Patrick Rubaihayo, minister of state for agriculture; and Gersom Kagurusi, MP for Mbarara Southwest, one of the areas that were heavily affected by the evictions.[39] A local official was to claim later that when they tried to stop the evictions after the murder of a teacher, Minister Rubaihayo instructed them to continue.[40]

THE PUZZLING NONPARTICIPATION OF THE LOCAL COMMUNITY

The nonparticipation of the civilian nonstate population in southwestern Uganda is baffling. This is because there are many reasons for which one would expect that a majority of the population there would have wanted the refugees gone. Part of the reasons for this is related to the general inconvenience that the arrival of large numbers of refugees tend to place on less privileged members of local communities all across Africa.[41] Beyond these, there were reasons that were specific to intergroup relations in southwestern Uganda and neighboring Rwanda, from where the refugees originated.

---

[36] Mamdani, *When victims become killers*, 168.
[37] Interview with a Ugandan who was expelled to Rwanda during the evictions in Ntungamo Town, Uganda (GLR 80), May 3, 2010.
[38] Zolberg, Suhrke and Aguayo, *Escape from violence*, p. 68; Mushemeza, "Politics and the refugee experience," 151; and Clay, *The eviction of Banyarwanda*, 56.
[39] Republic of Uganda, *The report of the Commission*, 498; Clay, *The eviction of Banyarwanda*, 3; Chretien, *The great lakes of Africa*, 299; and Marian Kankunda, "Land tenure and changing pastoral practices in Kashari County 1962–1993" (M.A. diss., Makerere University, 1996), 67.
[40] Republic of Uganda, *The report of the Commission*, 504.
[41] For more on how the arrival of large numbers of refugees tend to burden the least privileges members of society the most see Whitaker, "Refugees in Western Tanzania"; and Chambers, "Rural refugees in Africa," 388–389.

FIGURE 6.2. Map of Ntungamo, Isingiro, and Nyagatare[42]

There was much resentment over refugees' acquisition of land outside of the UNHCR settlements by both cultivator and pastoralist

[42] This map was created by Rita Effah, using the following resources: FAO-Africover, "Multipurpose Africover"; GADM, "Database of Global"; and WRI, "Waterbodies in Uganda."

Banyankore locals experiencing land shortage.[43] There was also much antipathy toward the refugees for competing with citizens for jobs.[44] Many refugees who moved outside of the settlements acquired jobs by pretending to be Ugandans.[45] This was in the context of a declining national economy that made it impossible for many locals to get jobs.

Beyond these general issues that plague refugee–host relations in most places, intergroup relations in Rwanda and southwestern Uganda bedeviled interactions between the refugees and the vast majority of the local population. The Social Revolution in Rwanda had pitted the minority pastoralist Batutsi, from which the leadership of the country had been drawn for a long time, against the majority, oppressed Bahutu cultivators.[46] The Banyankore society the refugees entered into from 1959 had a similar demographic divide between a pastoralist and dominant but minority Bahima Banyankore population and the majority Bairu Banyankore cultivator population.[47] Pumped up on myths of their superiority,[48] some of the arriving Batutsi refugees tended to view and treat the ordinary Bairu with the same disdain that they had treated the Bahutu in Rwanda. This angered many Bairu.[49] Their resentment was partly due to the fact that intergroup relations in precolonial as well as colonial southwestern Uganda never assumed the oppressive character that Belgian rule had meticulously engineered in Rwanda.[50]

---

[43] Virginia Bond, "Identity crisis: Banyaruanda refugees in Uganda" (M.A. diss., University of Edinburgh, 1988), 17; For more on land problems in southwestern Uganda see Martin Doornbos, "Land tenure and political conflict in Ankole, Uganda," *Journal of Development Studies* 12 (October 1975): 54–74; and Kankunda, "Land tenure."

[44] Robina Namusisi, "The plight of Rwandese refugees in Uganda" (LLB diss., Makerere University, 1988), 40; and Mushemeza, "Politics and the refugee experience in the Africa Great Lakes Region," 14.

[45] Namusisi, "The plight of Rwandese refugees," 40; and Clay, *The eviction of Banyarwanda*, 17.

[46] See Mamdani, *When victims become killers*.

[47] Doornbos, *Not all the king's men*, 77–79.

[48] For an account of how the colonial educational system further heightened Batutsi belief in their inherent superiority over Bahutu, see Mamdani, *When victims become killers*, 79–102. For an account of the troubled and troublesome history of the Hamitic Hypothesis which the belief in Tutsi and Hima superiority was based on see Sanders, "The Hamitic Hypothesis."

[49] Interview with a former district councillor in Ngoma sub County, Ntungamo District, Uganda (GLR 36), April 7, 2010.

[50] For more on the nature of Bahima-Bairu relations in southwestern Uganda, see Samwiri Rubaraza Karugire, *A history of the Kingdom of Nkore in western Uganda to 1896* (Oxford: Clarendon Press, 1971); Doornbos, *Not all the king's men*; and Martin Doornbos, "Images and reality of stratification in pre-colonial Nkore," *Canadian Journal of African Studies* 7 (3–1973): 477–495.

Many accused the refugees of treating Bairu disdainfully.[51] One comment about this from a Muiru follows:

I can tell you that what people say about Batutsi arrogance is true. They despised others. That is why they refused to eat with us. Even if they were your friends they could not eat in your house. Even when they were extremely hungry they would take what you gave them home and eat there. If you asked why, some would respond that the Batutsi don't eat with Bahutu. Whenever they got drunk they began to call the Bairu *Bahutu*. They will say to you: "Hey, you Muhutu, you Muhutu."[52]

Conversations with former refugees confirmed this disdain for ordinary Bairu. Two of many such views of former refugees on the subject follow.

Our parents who came here as refugees were very proud and very determined. Some were from the royal families in Rwanda. When we were children they did not want locals to even enter their houses. They would go out and talk to them. They did not eat with locals. In Rwanda they separated themselves from the Bahutu, who were their servants and did the worst jobs. Here they said the Bairu were the same as the Bahutu and tried to treat them in the same way. They referred to people here as *Bahutu*. As kids we knew if they found you eating with locals they will beat or punish you.[53]

We met the locals here very dirty. They did not bathe and smelled like fish. We taught them how to bathe and be clean. We used to despise the locals because of their lifestyle. We did not eat with them even if we were close friends because of that. In the early days we did not even want them to touch us. We found them in a very bad state. They had jiggers. That is why we despised them.[54]

Related to this arrogance was what many saw as the unwillingness of the Batutsi refugees to intermarry with the Bairu Banyankore masses. This was an allegation that many former refugees confirmed. When I asked a former refugee whether the allegation was true, he looked me straight in the eye and gave a terse response. "In Rwandese culture you don't give your daughter to a Mutwa[55] unless the girl runs to them."[56] He later elaborated:

---

[51] Interviews with Muiru Munyankore in Kikagate Sub County, Isingiro District, Uganda (GLR 51), April 20, 2010; and with a Muiru Munyankore in Kikagate Sub Country, Isingiro District, Uganda (and GLR 53), April 20, 2010.

[52] Interview (GLR 53).

[53] Interview with a former refugee in Isingiro District, Uganda (GLR 71), April 27, 2010.

[54] Interview with a former refugee in Isingiro District, Uganda (GLR 65), April 24, 2010.

[55] In Rwanda the Twa who were previously predominantly hunter-gatherers were thought to be even socially lower than the Bahutu.

[56] Interview (GLR 88).

The refugee girls that eloped with Banyankore were mad. We did not allow our daughters to marry them. Our boys did not marry them. We liked the Banyankore, shared many things with them, but when it came to marrying our children we said no. The Banyankore don't respect their wives. They beat them on the road. Those who married them came back after a few days saying they had been beaten. The Banyankore treated their wives badly.[57]

One of the refugee women who had married a Munyankore noted:

When I got married to a Munyankore I broke a taboo. Other young Banyarwanda laughed at me that I had married a Muhutu. That is how they called the Bairu. They despised and made fun of the Bairu. The Banyankore never went to Banyarwanda families to ask for the hands of their daughters because the Banyarwanda families always refused. They just stole the ladies and later went to introduce themselves. My husband took me to Mbarara for two months and my parents were desperately looking everywhere for me. One Munyankore had gone to ask for my hand before but my parents refused. He had shops around and was not poor but my parents still refused. The Banyankore men wanted to marry Banyarwanda girls. The Banyarwanda men did not marry Banyankore [Bairu] women. I never saw that.[58]

The majority of the Bairu who constituted most of the population in the area thus held a lot of grievances against the Banyarwanda refugees by 1982.[59] UPC leaders expertly played on these popular feelings.[60] An old Munyankore who lived very close to one of the refugee settlements asserted that Bairu did not take action on these grievances and expel the refugees only because they were held in check by the state. "The government guaranteed peace between us and the Banyarwanda" was how he put it.[61] So why did the Bairu not seize on the opportunity presented by the state's campaign against the refugees to vent their fury?

The Land of the Banyankore

To begin to unravel this puzzle, we need to recognize that many of the areas in which the refugees settled in southwestern Uganda beginning in 1959, at the time privileged indigeneity over residence in the apportioning of rights to belonging. These areas were parts of the Kingdom of Ankole,

---

[57] Interview GLR 88).
[58] Interview with a former refugee in Isingiro District, Uganda (GLR 56), April 21, 2010.
[59] Hamilton, "Human rights in Uganda," 2; and Watson, "Exile from Rwanda," 10.
[60] Mushemeza, "Politics and the refugee experience," 150.
[61] Interview in Kajaho, Ntungamo District, Uganda (GLR 59), April 22, 2010.

a colonial creation that was made up of the precolonial Kingdom of Nkore and other neighboring entities such as Mpororo, Buhweju, and Igara.[62] These areas were all seen as the home of mostly Banyankore and, to a more limited extent, Bahororo indigenous communities. These communities controlled chieftaincies and exercised extensive powers over access to land rights.

Precolonial Nkore was a centralized Banyankore kingdom with a *Mugabe* – king – who exercised the power to appoint and dismiss chiefs in various areas of his realm.[63] New chiefs were mostly appointed from amongst the heirs of previous chiefs. Deviations from this principle were rare.[64] Although the King could move chiefs around his realm, such movement was also atypical.[65] The principle of the control of chieftaincy by indigenous ruling lineages was also present in new areas that were brought under Nkore to create the Kingdom of Ankole by the British colonial authorities at the advent of colonialism. In areas with strong ruling lineages like Buhweju and Igara, the king of Ankole appointed chiefs from the old ruling lineages.[66]

Local chiefs exercised great control over the settlement of land in their areas. Even though there was the idea that the *Mugabe* owned all land in Nkore,[67] the occupation of new lands required the consent of the local chief, not the *Mugabe*.[68] The passage of a Crown Lands Ordinance by the British in 1903[69] did not change this greatly. In most areas, arriving migrants and locals just sought the approval of local chiefs to open up new lands for settlement, cultivation, and grazing.[70]

The fact that indigeneity was still privileged in the area in 1959 when the refugees began to arrive has to be understood from the perspective of its colonial history. In southern Uganda, the British had divergent attitudes toward states where elites opposed their rule and those where rulers

---

[62] Doornbos, *Not all the king's men*, 62–66.
[63] Karugire, *A history of the Kingdom of Nkore*, 201; and Audrey Richards, *East African chiefs: a study of political development in some Uganda and Tanganyika tribes* (London: Faber and Faber Limited, 1960), 149–150.
[64] John Roscoe, *The Banyankole* (Cambridge: Cambridge University Press, 1923), 14.
[65] Richards, *East African chiefs*, 157.
[66] H.F. Morris, *A history of Ankole* (Kampala: East African Literature Bureau, 1962), 35–37.
[67] Kankunda, "Land tenure," 28.
[68] Doornbos, "Land tenure," 58.
[69] W. Kisamba-Mugerwa, "Rangeland tenure and resource management: an overview of pastoralism in Uganda," *Access to Land and other Natural Resources in Uganda: Research and Policy Development Project Research Paper* 1 (January 1992), 7.
[70] Doornbos, *Not all the king's men*, 132.

agreed to submit to and even aid British rule. This marked the divergent paths that the Kingdoms of Ankole and Buganda developed along, as opposed to the neighboring Kingdom of Bunyoro. Where elites accepted their rule and agreed to collaborate with them, as in Buganda, the British assumed a superordinate position in relation to rulers but reinforced the control that these rulers had over their societies. They reinforced the rights of these indigenous ruling lineages over the control of land and political power. In areas such as Bunyoro, where they were met with opposition, the British undermined the ruling elites' control over power and land. They often fundamentally subverted the privileged role of indigeneity in the distribution of rights by imposing foreign rulers on these communities. It was these foreign leaders who came to exercise significant control over land. These non-indigenous chiefs and the colonial authorities then regulated the settlement of immigrants in these areas dissociating land rights from indigeneity.

Ankole fell squarely in the category of kingdoms whose rulers decided to collaborate with the British. The colonial authorities on one hand, and the *Mugabe* and his senior chiefs on the other, signed the Ankole Agreement in 1901.[71] In exchange for the allegiance of the Ankole ruling elite, the British guaranteed the *Mugabe* and his senior chiefs certain privileges that perpetuated their control over their area. With regard to chieftaincy, the chiefs were allowed to keep their jobs and were also guaranteed the right to choose their successors. This ensured the continued control of chieftaincy by indigenous elites.[72]

The agreement also maintained, and in some ways even further strengthened, the control of land rights by the indigenous elite. One way in which it did so was by granting freehold rights in large (*mailo*) parcels to these rulers. The initial grants were extensive and were further enlarged on exertion of pressure by the chiefs. The *Mugabe* was given fifty square miles, his most senior chief, the *Enganzi*, got sixteen, and the other senior chiefs got ten each. Apart from these private allocations, official grants were also made that were the property of the offices that these chiefs occupied. New chiefs were also awarded *mailo* grants.[73] Even though the Crown Lands Ordinance (1903) transformed land in Ankole into Crown lands, local chiefs continued to play a central role in managing the

[71] Morris, *A history of Ankole*, 38.
[72] Ibid., 38.
[73] Kankunda, "Land tenure," 32–35; Doornbos, *Not all the king's men*, 80–82; and Morris, *A history of Ankole*, 38.

settlement of land. People had to seek their consent before opening up new areas for settlement and use.[74]

One needs to address a few things that either held the potential to boost residence over indigeneity in the determination of belonging in Ankole or seemed to indicate the superior relevance of residence over indigeneity in the area. One of these was the presence of many chiefs in Ankole who originated from other areas of the colony. Twenty-seven of the eighty-four county and sub-county chiefs in Ankole were of non-Banyankore extraction in 1907. Of these "foreigners," twenty-five were Baganda.[75] This presence of non-indigenous chiefs raises questions about the extent to which indigenous elite indeed controlled chiefly authority and with it, control over land in the area. In addition to chiefs, many Baganda administrators, catechists, and policemen were deployed to Ankole.[76]

In rebellious Bunyoro, the Baganda were imposed on the elite as well as the general population.[77] In Ankole the story was very different. "The Baganda chiefs recruited to the district turned out to be supportive of the new Bahima establishment," which ruled Ankole.[78] The Baganda chiefs were "specially recruited"[79] by Nuwa Mbaguta, the most senior chief of the *Mugabe* of Ankole. He also sent Baganda as counselors to some chiefs and even organized some Baganda into a mercenary militia in his conflict with other members of the ruling elite.[80] The Baganda were never imposed on the Banyankore elite. They never threatened to undermine the privileged hold on political power by those who claimed to be the indigenous elite. They were mere instruments of a section of the ruling elite. When people complained about misrule by chiefs, Baganda chiefs as the "'alien' elements," were summarily dismissed in the 1930s.[81]

Colonial land policy also held the potential for boosting residence over indigeneity in Ankole. However, the actualization of this potential was often minimized by the overarching colonial support for the indigenous ruling elites. The Crown Lands Ordinance of 1903 was blunted by the fact that local chiefs continued to act as those whose consent was

---

[74] Doornbos, "Land tenure," 58.
[75] Martin Doornbos, "Ethnicity, Christianity, and the development of social stratification in colonial Ankole," *The International Journal of African Historical Studies* 9 (4–1976): 560–561.
[76] Chretien, *The great lakes of Africa*, 229.
[77] Ibid., 231.
[78] Doornbos, *Not all the king's men*, 77.
[79] Doornbos, "Ethnicity, Christianity," 559.
[80] Chretien, *The great lakes of Africa*, 229.
[81] Doornbos, "Ethnicity, Christianity," 562.

required to open up new space in many areas. Even the experimentation with freehold titling[82] did not fundamentally undermine the authority of these chiefs. The system only sought to document rights that chiefs were instrumental in creating in the first place.[83] These chiefs sat on the land boards and played significant roles in adjudicating claims before they could be documented.[84] People sought letters from them to have their rights documented.[85] This was in fundamental ways not different from the practice of seeking their consent to open new land.

The granting of *mailo* land to a few World War I veterans[86] and settlement of some Banyarwanda and Bakiga[87] in Ankole by the British are moves that in some ways mirror the settlement of Banyarwanda in Kivu by the colonial administration there.[88] In Ankole, however, such settlement was done on a very limited basis. Furthermore, because the colonial authorities were intent on rewarding the rulers of Ankole for their collaboration, engaging in such settlement without the agreement of, or even in the face of opposition by, the ruling elites was unlikely.

The subjugation of areas like Buhweju and Mpororo under the *Mugabe* of Nkore to create the Kingdom of Ankole also held some potential for driving parts of Ankole down the path that privileged residence over indigeneity. It gave the *Mugabe* the possibility of imposing leaders on these areas and appropriating control over land rights from them. This is significant because many in these areas resisted incorporation and did not self-identify as Banyankore. Some in the incorporated areas of Mpororo still call themselves Bahororo and their areas Mpororo today.[89]

The British as well as Nuwa Mbaguta avoided aggravating resistance to their rule by appointing chiefs from the ruling lineages.[90] The British were intent on using the collaborating elite to rule Ankole. They also wanted to use Ankole "as a center from which stable government could

---

[82] Doornbos, *Not all the king's men*, 132.

[83] Interview with a former chief in Ngoma Sub county, Ntungamo District, Uganda (GLR 40), April 9, 2010.

[84] Interview (GLR 36).

[85] Interview (GLR 36); and interview (GLR 40).

[86] Doornbos, "Land tenure," 62.

[87] Kankunda, "Land tenure," 37.

[88] Koen Vlassenroot, "Reading the Congolese crisis," in *Conflict and social transformation in Easter DR Congo*, ed. Koen Vlassenroot and Timothy Raeymaekers (Gent: Academia Press, 2004), 41; and Bucyalimwe Mararo, "Land conflicts in Masisi, eastern Zaire: the impact and aftermath of Belgian colonial policy [1920–1989]" (PhD diss., Indiana University, 1990), 163–165.

[89] Karugire, *A history of the Kingdom of Nkore*, 232–233.

[90] Morris, *A history of Ankole*, 36–37.

be introduced to an area that was of special significance because it lay on the borders of Belgian and German territory, adjacent to the troublesome Nyoro...."[91]

The assertion that, in most of Ankole, indigeneity was privileged over residence in the determination of rights of belonging when the Banyarwanda refugees began to arrive in 1959 is not to make any assertions about the ethnic purity of the local population. There were a lot of Bakiga, Banyarwanda, and others who migrated to Ankole.[92] The claim is that these places were seen as uniquely belonging to indigenes in whose hands rested chieftaincy and control over land. These indigenes were distinguished from newly arriving settlers who were thought of as not belonging. The new arrivals came to acquire primary rights to power and land by converting over time into indigenous status. So, as in the Forest Region of Guinea,[93] the Banyankore, the putative natives, should not be thought of as an "uncontaminated" group. What we now call the Banyankore have always been a mixed and mixing population. Doornbos tells us, for instance, that the ruling Bahima elite of Ankole was a thoroughly hybrid population that continuously assimilated pastoralists from areas such as Mpororo, Karagwe, Rwanda, and Toro.[94] Furthermore, arriving cultivators such as Bahutu from Rwanda and Bakiga often just became Bairu Banyankore, whereas pastoralists from neighboring areas became Bahima Banyankore.[95] This exercise of switching identities was facilitated by similarities between many of the languages in the interlacustrine area.[96]

Sitting at the Feet of Local Notables

Because communities in Ankole privileged indigeneity over residence in determining belonging, they possessed functioning institutions for dealing with strangers. These institutions subjugated strangers to locals through whom these strangers could access rights, including those of residence. Like in the Forest Region of Guinea, these communities put great pressure on strangers to submit themselves to these local institutions. Many of the

---

[91] Richards, *East African chiefs*, 156.
[92] Kankunda, "Land tenure," 87; and Clay, *The eviction of Banyarwanda*, 18.
[93] Germain, *Peuples de la Foret*, 19; and Paulme, *Les gens du riz*, 14
[94] Doornbos, *Not all the king's men*, 75.
[95] Clay, *The eviction of Banyarwanda*, 18.
[96] On the similarity of languages in the area see Doornbos, *Not all the king's men*, 19; and Chretien, *The great lakes of Africa*, 47.

refugees felt there was a general unwillingness among the locals to deal with strangers who were not attached to locals. They had to be connected to locals to enjoy interactions, including market ones. The following are some of the ways in which the former refugees I interviewed spoke of this pressure to subjugate themselves to the locals.

When we got there first we had nothing. We could not have survived without befriending them. When we got there we had only cows. We did not have money. It was later that we sold our cows in the cattle market and got money. We could not have done other than befriend them. We had to work to get food. You could not get a job from someone without being his or her friend. We went to the locals and showed them how needy we were. They had mercy on us and friendships happened. Then they said come and work if you need things. After working we talked and then we were paid and went home. They also visited us and got things. You could not work for them without being their friend. After one day they would tell you not to come back.[97]

We thought we would have to stay there for a long time and so wanted to create relationships with the local people. The country did not belong to the UN. It belonged to the locals, and the leaders came from among them, so having a settlement did not mean we should not seek relationships with the locals. We did not want to stay in the settlement. We wanted to live in the villages. . . . You don't have land and can't conquer land by force in an area so how can you settle there without befriending people there?[98]

When you go from one country to another it is a must for you to befriend the local people you meet. When you befriend locals you can settle with them and have one heart. Without friends life would have been hard. If you lack friends in a place, you have not settled there. If you lack friends, if you lose a relative no one will help you bury the person. If your cow falls in a well or a hole, no one will help you take it out. If you have a large farm, you won't be able to call people to help you. That is why we felt like making friends with the local people even though we had cattle, humanitarian supplies, and settlement land.[99]

The Lion Learns to Eat Grass
Arriving in such an environment, the refugees quickly set about systematically creating relationships with the relatively well off and powerful in society. These were powerful and wealthy Bahima *and* Bairu. Although

[97] Interview with a former Rwandese refugee in Nyabitekeri, Nyagatare District, Rwanda (GLR 90) May 23, 2010.
[98] Interview with a former refugee in Nyabitekeri, Nyagatare District, Rwanda (GLR 83), May 21, 2010.
[99] Interview with a former refugee in Kahirimbi, Isingiro District, Uganda (GLR 46), April 19, 2010.

some of them were chiefs, many were just wealthy and powerful locals. Many of the refugees confessed to actively and deliberately seeking relationships with notables in the villages in which they settled or operated.

There were multiple ways in which the refugees made contact with local notables. Some started relations with the notables first as laborers. They approached them seeking work or were introduced to the notables by acquaintances. Where refugees reported to chiefs, these chiefs often looked for wealthy locals with whom they could place the refugees.[100] Refugees frequently went to work herding cattle. The pastoralist Batutsi refugees were thought to be expert cattle herders. However, many Batutsi refugees who could not find work as cattle herders became farm laborers.[101] Some refugees who went to Uganda with their cows approached local cattle owners with a proposition: in exchange for the right to graze their cattle on the land of the local, they would look after the cattle of the landowner.[102]

These workers often stayed in the compound or on the land of their employers. Some offered help with domestic chores and other work. The employer in turn treated the herdsman as more than a mere employee and provided him with other help beyond the money and/or milk to which the worker was entitled. The employer introduced the employee to local leaders, and it became known that the employee was with him. Often interactions became like father–son or mother–daughter relationships, in which the refugee was subservient to the employer and he or she in turn took care of and was responsible for the refugee. Refugees who were particularly endeared to their employers were sometimes given plots of land to farm temporarily or to keep permanently. Employers sometimes gave favored herdsmen cows. When such workers wanted to get married, their employers led the group that went to ask for the hand of the bride. Occasionally, the employer even provided the cows for the dowry. Eventually, the refugees amassed enough resources to move away and live on their own.[103]

This move did not always sever links between the two. Often, the refugees continued to maintain relations with and seek help from their former bosses. They sought their help with concluding land transactions.

---

[100] Interview with a former chief in Rweikiniro Sub-County, Uganda (GLR 38), April 8, 2010; and interview (GLR 83).

[101] Interview (GLR 38).

[102] Interview (GLR 87).

[103] Interview with a former chief in Ruhaama, Ntungamo District, Uganda (GLR 12), March 29, 2010.

A good employer will help the refugee find land and negotiate rights. She will also witness transactions entered into by the refugee. Refugees continued to visit these former employers and brought them gifts of milk, bananas, and cattle. The former employer and employee often maintained a strong relationship, even though the refugee was less dependent on the local than before.[104]

The labor path described previously was not taken by all of the refugees. Some of the refugees succeeded in crossing the border with sizable herds of cattle and took care of those instead of selling their labor. However, this did not preclude them from establishing relations with local notables. The main means by which they did this was through gifts of cows to notables. The giving of cattle is a practice that has a long history and is very common in southwestern Uganda as well as Rwanda, where the refugees came from. The practice itself takes multiple forms and is used to serve diverse ends, as is evident by the end of this chapter. In establishing and maintaining relations with local elites, cows were one of the main instruments deployed by the refugees. Although some of the notables approached the refugees to ask for cows, it was often the refugees who went and offered cows to these local leaders.

This approach of notables by refugees had a very strategic character. A refugee would sometimes do it after consultations with the rest of his family over the need to build relations with a certain notable. Sometimes refugees formed groups that went around actively recruiting elites and offering them cows. A few of the refugees were quite open in describing this as a deliberate method of befriending the chiefs. One refugee put it thus: "We used tactics to get chiefs to give us places to settle. Otherwise you did not get a place to settle. We visited them and gave them cows so they would give us land to settle."[105] A refugee who moved out of Nakivale settlement to establish a life elsewhere in Isingiro District put it this way:

When we got there we befriended the chiefs and gave them bulls. We did not just give away our cows to ordinary people. It was a way of introducing ourselves to the chiefs. We wanted them to know us. It was so the chiefs would know us and help us with our problems. You could not live in that place if you did not

[104] Interviews with a former Rwandese refugee in Nyabitekeri, Nyagatare District, Rwanda (GLR 91), May 23, 2010; and with a Ugandan in Ruhaama, Ntungamo District, Uganda (GLR 21), April 1, 2010.
[105] Interview with a former refugee in Nyabitekeri, Nyagatare District, Rwanda (GLR 93), May 23, 2010.

introduce yourself to the big people there. Who would show you free land to occupy if chiefs did not know you?[106]

This strenuous effort at roping in notables was not just the preoccupation of the refugees who abandoned the settlements to live in local communities. Even the refugees in the official UNHCR settlements of Nakivale and Oruchinga were involved in the rush to befriend locals. One refugee who stayed in Nakivale settlement during all of his time in Uganda put it thus:

We used tactics with the leaders. We respected them because they were in their country and we were refugees. We worked with them and had no problems with them. When we got there we formed a group. I did not go alone. We formed a group and visited them. We gave them cows. I gave cows to three people. We befriended them through various means. When your country expels you and you go elsewhere, you have to befriend the people there so they will give you what you want. Some of the refugees were very well educated. We held a meeting and the educated refugees advised that we form a group to go and meet and befriend the leaders. We visited them and sat and talked with them and then we invited them to visit us. It was all so that we could live there in peace.[107]

Many locals were also aware of the very strategic nature of the refugees' efforts at befriending and giving cows to local notables. One noted: "The refugees were wise. If they wanted something from you they befriended you and gave you animals until they put you in a position where you could not say no to their request. This is how they treated the chiefs."[108] Another put it thus: "The refugees used cow-giving to get close to the leaders here and get what they wanted. The Bairu leaders were the most susceptible to this because they were poor and had few cows and wanted the cows of the refugees."[109]

There is a tendency in the literature to infuse relations between refugees and locals in southwestern Uganda with a high dose of co-ethnic automatism. Many would agree with the description of relations between refugees and locals given previously but restrict it to relations between the Batutsi refugees and the Bahima Banyankore. The Batutsi refugees who were predominantly pastoralists are said to have developed close relations with

---

[106] Interview with a former refugee in Kabingo, Isingiro District, Uganda (GLR 44), April 17, 2010.
[107] Interview (GLR 88).
[108] Interview (GLR 53).
[109] Interview (GLR 36).

the pastoralist Bahima of Ankole but not the Bairu cultivators, who were like the Bahutu that the refugees were fleeing from.[110]

I argue that the Batutsi refugees in many ways adhered to equal opportunity standards in seeking and roping in powerful local allies. They subjugated themselves to both powerful Bahima and Bairu. They also avoided doing this with both powerless and poor Bahima and Bairu. Thus it is better to use the lens of political economic stratification rather than ethnicity to understand relations between refugees and locals.

Former refugees and Bahima cast doubt on this assumed natural identity of interest and affinity between Batutsi refugees and Bahima. They pointed to the latent conflicts and hostilities that existed between the two groups. Land was one source of such conflict. As land became scarce, many poorer Bahima who had been rendered almost landless[111] resented the entrance of refugee cattle herds into the few areas where they could graze.[112] Many fled to areas such as Nyabushozi to "escape" from advancing refugees.[113] Some claim that land-hungry Bahima rejoiced when the refugees were evicted in 1982 because they could return to graze on old pastures that the refugees had occupied.[114] Even old Banyarwanda migrants feeling a land squeeze tried to keep the refugees at arm's length. They were aware that close association with the Banyarwanda refugees would cause people to begin to think of them as refugees instead of citizens.[115] Some allege that the Ugandan Banyarwanda used to surreptitiously report the presence of the refugees in their localities to the authorities so they would be transported to the refugee settlements.[116]

Beyond this, the refugees stereotyped the Bahima as dull-minded.[117] They in turn stereotyped the Banyarwanda as hard-hearted, cunning people, prone to betraying trust and addicted to cattle theft.[118] A Muhima

---

[110] Clay, *The eviction of Banyarwanda*, 19; and Mushemeza, "Politics and the refugee experience," 117.

[111] For more on how many Bahima are feeling the land squeeze, see Kankunda, "Land tenure," 121–125.

[112] Interview with a Muhima in Ngoma Sub-County, Ntungamo District, Uganda (GLR 37), April 8, 2010.

[113] Interview (GLR 90).

[114] Interviews with a Ugandan in Ntungamo town, Uganda (GLR 82), May 4, 2010; and a Ugandan in Kampala, Uganda (GLR 1), March 24, 2010.

[115] Interview (GLR 83); and interview (GLR 89).

[116] Interview (GLR 37).

[117] Interview (GLR 56).

[118] Interviews with a Muhima in Rushenyi sub county, Ntungamo District, Uganda (GLR 33), April 6, 2010; and with another Muhima in Ngoma subcounty, Ntungamo District, Uganda (GLR 35), April 7, 2010; interview (GLR 57).

told me of their being advised by their parents from childhood against marrying Banyarwanda.[119]

Under pressure to seek local patrons through whom they could access rights in these societies that privileged indigeneity, the refugees, like powerless strangers in many African societies that privilege indigeneity, sought the most attractive patrons they could find.[120] These were ideally rich, powerful, and kind people. Sometimes they happened to be Bahima. At other times they turned out to be Bairu. Subjugating themselves to these Bairu was only one of the many adjustments that most of the refugees made to survive outside of their country. Many who had never cultivated and disdained the activity became farm hands who worked on farms for payment in bananas. An old man who made the sudden transition from cattle owner and pastoralist to farm hand told me: "When you are in need you do all people ask of you even if it means cultivating when you were a pastoralist. We had to work to get food."[121] A former refugee noted: "When life changes you have to change with it. We Banyarwanda say that when a lion loses meat it learns to eat grass."[122]

Some Dimensions of Subjugation

A key aspect of the subjugation of Banyarwanda refugees to Banyankore elites was the performance of symbolic acts of subservience to elites by the refugees. This often started with the formal seeking of relationships noted previously. Frequent visits and greetings were also a part of this symbolic performance of subjugation.[123] This was complemented by the symbolic consultation of elites by refugees on important events in the life of the refugee.[124] Some refugees also showed their respect for elites by temporarily placing their children with them. It is important to understand the symbolic meaning of this act. Refugees did not place their children because they could not care for them. The wife of a local Muiru notable in

---

[119] Interview (GLR 33).

[120] See Colson, "The assimilation of aliens," 43; Murphy and Bledsoe, "Kinship and territory," 126; and McGovern, "Unmasking the state," 193.

[121] Interview (GLR 83).

[122] Interview with a former refugee in Nyabitekeri, Nyagatare District, Rwanda (GLR 95), May 24, 2010.

[123] Interview with a former Rwandese refugee in Nyabitekeri, Nyagatare District, Rwanda (GLR 85), May 22, 2010; interview (GLR 83); interview (GLR 86); interview (GLR 91); and interview (GLR 21).

[124] Interview (GLR 91); and interview with a Tutsi former refugee in Ntungamo Town Council area, Uganda (GLR 78), April 29, 2010.

Kazia, Isingiro District, told me: "The refugee who brought his daughter to live with us was not poor. He had a lot of cows. He just wanted to show his trust in and respect for us. The girl lived with us for three years and then went back to her family in the settlement."[125]

Another aspect of this subjugation of refugees to local notables was the frequent exchange of gifts between the refugees and local leaders. The Banyarwanda refugees were often endowed in terms of cattle and labor. The locals often had land and plantations. These resources served as the major gifts that were exchanged. Many refugees gave cows to the locals they had formed relationships with.[126] Their wives took milk, meat, and butter to the wives of these elites.[127] Those refugees who could not afford such gifts often had labor that they offered. They sometimes went to work free of charge for their local friends or brought firewood they had collected in the settlement for them.[128] The locals offered refugees land to graze cattle on or cultivate.[129] Many of the locals had banana plantations and offered their refugee friends bananas. Others gave sections of their plantations to the refugees to care for and harvest for as long as they remained in the area.[130]

Local elites who had such relations with refugees introduced the refugees to the chiefs and people in the area and were then seen as being the "owners" of the refugees during the time the refugees spent in the area. This ownership involved the local sharing legal responsibility for the actions of the refugee, even though this did not absolve the refugee of all responsibility for what he or she did. People wronged by the refugees often reported to the patrons of the refugees. When the refugee could not pay his or her debts, the local was required by law to pay on behalf of the refugee. Otherwise, the local had to stand as guarantor and ultimately pay in the instance in which the refugee could not. These "owners" of refugees were sometimes punished for wrongs committed by "their" refugees. For instance, there was a spate of cattle theft in Rweikiniro Sub-County, Ntungamo District, in the early 1960s after the arrival of

---

[125] Interview with a Ugandan in Kazia, Ntungamo District, Uganda (GLR 57), April, 21, 2010.

[126] Interview with a former refugee in Nyabitekeri, Nyagatare District, Rwanda (GLR 84), May 22, 2010; interview (GLR 88); and interview (GLR 91).

[127] Interview with a former refuge in Nyabitekeri, Nyagatare District, Rwanda (GLR 85), May 22, 2010.

[128] Interview (GLR 91).

[129] Interview (GLR 87); interview (GLR 90).

[130] Interview (GLR 85).

refugees in the area. Many believed the refugees were responsible for the thefts. The parish chief of Kabungo at the time recalled announcing the decision to punish locals whose refugees were caught stealing cattle. "We told the hosts: 'If your refugee misbehaves we will punish you.' They started to control the refugees after that."[131]

The Effect of the Subjugation on Elites

As I noted at the beginning of this chapter, local notables refused to join the chiefs, youth wingers, and state security forces in the evictions. Although they could do nothing overtly to help the refugees, elites, including some of the chiefs, tried to aid them in surreptitious ways. They forewarned them of impending attacks, giving them an opportunity to escape or hide their properties before the marauding gangs arrived. Even some of the local chiefs who are rightly blamed for leading the youth wingers in attacks on the refugees subtly subverted the eviction exercise. A former refugee who lived in Kikagate, Isingiro District, recounted:

I got married to a Munyarwanda who had stayed in Kikagate for a long time. His parents had migrated there long ago in search of pasture. I moved from Nakivale [refugee settlement] to live there with him. When the evictions started, the town people held a meeting to which Banyarwanda were not invited. Then the chief came to me quietly after the meeting and said: "A decision has been taken that all Banyarwanda should go to the camps and leave their properties. You should run away now with your things before bad things happen to you." I told him I had a sick child that I needed to take to the hospital, but he insisted saying: "Go immediately because in a few hours they will come to drive you from here." He came again when I returned from hospital and asked, "Why are you still here?" That is when I asked him: "Why are you doing this? You were the best friend of my late husband. You shared deep secrets and you are a godfather to our child. Why are you sending me away?" He responded: "You know your appearance is that of a true Mututsi. You can't hide your identity. If I don't send you away, those people will think I am trying to help you. They are my people so I can't do otherwise." Later the Bayouths [UPC Youth Wingers] came and destroyed my house and took my animals as I hid nearby. The chief was with them. But he came later that night and said: "I am sorry I could do nothing to help you because people know you are a Munyarwanda." I still refused to leave Kikagate and he allowed me to stay in my compound till the evictions ended.[132]

---

[131] Interview (GLR 38).
[132] Interview (GLR 95).

Many recognize that some local notables showed leniency toward the refugees and tried to shield them from the worst of the attacks despite instructions and urgings from local MPs and the youth wingers. However, people often wrongly put this down to bribery. One local who is still angry about the inability of the eviction exercise to rid his area of Banyarwanda complained: "When the government said to drive them (the Banyarwanda refugees) out, the leaders let them stay in exchange for bribes."[133] However, this explanation of the attitudes of some of the local leaders in terms of bribery underestimates and misdiagnoses the nature of the "deep relationship" [to use the term of the local leader in Dongueta, Guinea, cited in Chapter 4 [134]] between the refugees and most of the local notables in southwestern Uganda. The refugees did not have to bribe local notables then to discourage elites from participating in the attacks. They had been ensuring that since they first arrived in Uganda by firmly roping in these notables as "special friends" and patrons through interactions that provided these notables with a lot of information about the lives of the refugees.

Local notables knew the refugees well enough not to buy into the two most damaging charges that the UPC used to demonize the refugees and incite local participation in the attacks. These were the charges that held the refugees responsible for most of the atrocities under President Amin and implicated them in the NRM rebellion against the ruling UPC government,[135] which had a significant following in Ankole. The refugees were accused not only of fighting with the NRM but of stealing the cattle of the Banyankore to fund the NRM war.[136] Cattle theft always raises passions among these cattle owners. Notables, who were often cattle wealthy, did not buy into these blanket denunciations of refugees and were not plagued by fear due to uncertainty about what the refugees represented.

One former chief even recalled arguing before the Mbarara District Council that although some refugees may be guilty of cattle theft, most of them were cattle owners themselves and not cattle thieves.[137] Given the close relations between locals and most of the refugees, they must

---

[133] Interview with a Ugandan in Ntungamo town, Uganda (GLR 7), March 27, 2010.
[134] Interview (MRB 212).
[135] Mushemeza, "Politics and the refugee experience," 15; and Republic of Uganda, *The report of the Commission*, 50.
[136] Interview (GLR 72).
[137] Interview (GLR 38).

have known that very few refugees had been involved in the security and intelligence forces of Amin, despite allegations to the contrary.[138] Furthermore, even many Bairu notables who were UPC supporters must have known then that most of the refugees were neither involved in the NRM nor stealing cattle to fund its operations. It has subsequently been shown that it was the evictions that drove many refugees into the NRM.[139] I talked with a man who was evicted in 1982 and worked to recruit Banyarwanda expelled across the border into camps in Rwanda for the NRM.[140]

If elites did not buy into the allegations, it was because of their relations with the refugees. Like in the Forest Region of Guinea, the subjugation of the refugees to local leaders facilitated the systematic transfer of information about the daily lives of the refugees to a large segment of the local elite. The frequent visits, consultations, and exchanges of gifts that outlasted the employment of refugees by many locals ensured that the refugees did not constitute an unknown quantity to local notables. Subjugation did not tell them all there was to know about the refugees. However, it gave them enough information to recognize that the refugees did not constitute the grave threat to their existence that the government tried to conjure.

One evening I went to a settlement close to Kabingo to interview a self-styled retired herdsman. The shortened version of what he told me gives a sense of the relations that existed between many refugees and their patrons. It shows why these notables did not buy into the anti-refugee fear-mongering of the UPC government, even when it dwelled on cattle theft, a highly sensitive issue to cattle owners.

I was born in Rwanda in the 1930s and came here as a refugee. I have been a pastoralist all my life and never did anything else. When I came, first I was herding cattle for a Muiru in Kajara, but we had a dispute so I came and started working for my boss here. He introduced me to the chiefs. He lives just on the other side of the hill there and is a very rich businessman. He is a Muiru and is far younger than I am. I treat him like a father and he treats me like a son. Every morning he came to look at his cows and we talked. He gave me a cow. He fed me. When I saw a woman I wanted to marry I told him and he went to arrange the

---

[138] Hamilton points out that little evidence has been found of the sort of widespread participation by refugees in the Amin government and its security forces that was alleged by the UPC government. Hamilton, "Human rights in Uganda," 19; and Watson, "Exile from Rwanda," 10.

[139] Mamdani, *When victims become killers*, 168–170.

[140] Interview (GLR 6).

marriage and gave me a cow to pay the dowry. Even though I am old now, I still live on his land. His herdsmen look after my cows on his land and they bring me milk every day. I was with him when they were driving away the Banyarwanda. The chiefs and youth wingers wanted to drive me away and told him he should tell me to go. But he kept pleading with the sub-county chief until they left me alone.[141]

Why the Masses Did Not Participate

Although the nonparticipation of local notables is understandable given their relationship with the refugees, the fact that even the underclass did not join in the attacks does come as a surprise. The refugees did not subjugate themselves to these less-advantaged members of society who were mostly Bairu cultivators that the refugees sometimes treated with the same disdain that they had often soured relations between Batutsi and Bahutu in Rwanda. As I noted earlier in this chapter, these people had a lot of grievances against the refugees and were largely supportive of the evictions. An old Muiru lady who had played a leading role in her community put it this way: "The majority of Bairu supported the evictions in their hearts even if they did not participate in the attacks. Most Bairu supported the evictions but they did not want to reveal their true intentions."[142]

The combination of this antipathy toward the refugees along with the license to attack them granted by state agents who encouraged and led the evictions makes the nonparticipation of most Bairu in the evictions baffling.

The Rural Political Economy

The answer to their nonparticipation in the attacks can be found in the organization of the rural political economy. The response lies in the ways in which it afforded the Banyankore notables, to whom the refugees were subjugated, control over members of the underclass who were predominantly Bairu. It is this control that inhibited the Bairu masses and ensured that even though they supported the evictions, they did not participate in them. As one old woman told me, "I think most Bairu supported the evictions but did not participate because of fear."[143] Another observer

---

[141] Interview (GLR 78).
[142] Interview with an old Munyankore community leader in Rushyeni Sub-County, Ntungamo District, Uganda (GLR 81), May 4, 2012.
[143] Interview (GLR 81).

noted, "The Bairu did not drive them away despite their insolence because the Bairu did not have power."[144] State agents made it difficult for local notables to offer overt aid to the refugees. However, the nature of the rural political economy ensured that prudent Bairu seeing local notables' displeasure with and subtle subversion of the exercise also stayed away.

By 1982, society in Ankole was stratified between a fairly well-integrated elite comprising of both Bairu and Bahima and an underclass that was mostly made up of Bairu. This was the result of colonial and postcolonial transformations in the social stratifications that existed in precolonial Nkore society. There is a rather robust debate on the nature of social relations between Bahima and Bairu in precolonial Nkore. Oberg has portrayed it as a feudal one in which Bahima lords ruled over Bairu serfs.[145] Karugire has taken an opposite view in seeing it as an "open" class system based on the "mutual exchange of goods."[146] He noted that:

Nkore society was a class society in which the possession of cattle counted for much. The class system was an open one, but it was a class system all the same, in which the Bairu were of lower social standing than the Bahima. Nkore's governing class was drawn from the wealthy section of the Bahima, and the criterion for belonging to that class was wealth in cattle.[147]

Doornbos' view occupies a middle ground, portraying the society as indeed a hierarchical one with Bahima at the top and Bairu at the bottom, even if it did not constitute a feudal system.[148]

British colonial officials tended to act on assumptions about society that approximated the interpretation of Oberg and ended up putting in place such a system regardless of whether or not it in fact characterized the precolonial polity.[149] They made movement between the two groups more difficult through censuses. They also reinforced Bahima rule and taught the Hamitic Hypothesis, which praised Bahima innate superiority and Bairu inferiority.[150]

Bairu protest against this system through the Kamunyana Movement in the 1950s as well as the fact that Bairu tended to be more interested in

---

[144] Interview (GLR 36).

[145] K. Oberg, "The kingdom of Ankole in Uganda," in *African political systems*, ed. Meyer Fortes and Edward E. Evans-Pritchard (Oxford University Press, 1940), 121.

[146] Karugire, *A history of the Kingdom of Nkore*, 41 & 50.

[147] Karugire, *A history of the Kingdom of Nkore*, 66.

[148] Doornbos, *Not all the king's men*, 47–48.

[149] Ibid., 77–79.

[150] Doornbos, Not all the King's men, 77–79 & 85; Karugire, *A history of the Kingdom of Nkore*, 70; and Doornbos, "Ethnicity, Christianity," 563–566.

pursuing Western education had begun to open up opportunities to them toward the end of the colonial era.[151] The formation of the UPC and its rise to national domination further enhanced the power of the burgeoning Bairu elite. Many Bairu had converted to Protestantism and threw their support behind the UPC, whereas Bahima and Catholic Bairu supported the DP.[152] In fact, the Uganda Peoples Union, one of the two parties that united to form the UPC, had roots in western Uganda.[153] As protestant Bairu began to take over chieftainships from Bahima and occupy more positions in national and local administration, they acquired land and cattle, thoroughly integrating the Ankole elite.[154]

It was this integrated elite to whom the Banyarwanda refugees got subjugated. Excluding the chiefs, many of these notables refused to participate in the anti-refugee violence. Their negative attitude toward the evictions dissuaded the Bairu masses from joining in the attacks because of the politics of land and cattle-giving in the Ankole countryside.

This control of the elite over Bairu masses was partly rooted in the rural land tenure system. Bahima along with a few Bairu tended to own the largest chunks of land in the countryside, and the growing land scarcity in Ankole had made poor Bairu and Bahima increasingly dependent on these elites for their land rights.[155] This dependence made it extremely unwise for ordinary Bairu to join the attacks that their landlords noticeably frowned on.

It was the Bahima, who were earlier described as being uninterested in land ownership,[156] who initiated the accumulation of large parcels in Ankole. Eleven of the first twelve recipients of freehold *mailo* parcels from the British after the signing of the Ankole Agreement in 1901 were Bahima. Bahima domination of the chiefly ranks during the colonial era made them the biggest beneficiaries of subsequent freehold *mailo* grants as well.[157] Once the registration of land began, Bahima employed their connections with chiefs to register large parcels that they had used as pasture. Some used various strategies to push neighboring Bairu off land

[151] Martin Doornbos, "Kumanyana and Rwenzururu: two responses to ethnic inequality," in *Protest and power in Black Africa*, ed. Robert Rotberg and Ali Mazrui (New York: Oxford University Press, 1970), 1093–1094; Doornbos, "Ethnicity, Christianity," 572; and Doornbos, *Not all the king's men*, 90.
[152] Doornbos, *Not all the king's men*, 146–147.
[153] Ibid., 147.
[154] Ibid., 137.
[155] Kankunda, "Land tenure," 13 & 121–125;
[156] Martin Doornbos, *Not all the king's men*, 49.
[157] Doornbos, "Land tenure," 61–62; and Kankunda, "Land tenure," 34.

to enlarge their parcels. One strategy involved letting their cattle destroy the crops of a cultivator, apologizing, and paying compensation and then letting the cattle destroy the crop again. Sooner or later, the Muiru realized they had to move to avoid damage to their crops.[158] Bairu elites were to later join the chiefly and administrative classes, and as they entered into the elite, many acquired land and cattle.[159]

Elite domination of land was to become increasingly politically salient as land became scarce in Ankole. Landlords subjected their *mailo* tenants to all sorts of demands. In addition to rents, tenants often had to give gifts of food crops, submit themselves to courts constituted and presided over by these landlords, and adhere to their political choices.[160] The Ankole Landlord and Tenant Law passed in 1957[161] to save tenants from these impositions did not succeed in sweeping them away.

A Muiru community leader[162] told me that even those Bairu who were not *mailo* tenants began to fall under the influence of their landed neighbors. This happened as soil fertility declined and people with small land parcels found themselves needing to enter into rental or sharecropping arrangements with their landed neighbors. Sharecroppers particularly desired the land of large cattle owners because they were continuously fertilized by cow dung. Although some landlords asked for money, others sought a share of the produce of the sharecroppers. One thing that has remained constant about this arrangement is that landlords give land only to people in their good books. The poor know this and so are wary of disobeying or showing disrespect to their landed neighbors lest their next request for temporary rights to farm be rejected.

Another way in which cattle-wealthy Banyankore exercised control over poor Bairu and Bahima Banyankore was through the institution of cattle giving. As I talked to both pastoralists and cultivators in southwestern Uganda and Rwanda, I realized that the exchange of cows was a delicate and complicated dance that could become one of the ultimate instruments through which a rich and powerful cow giver could dominate a poor and powerless recipient.

The poor person seeking cattle often had to obey, show respect to, work for, and give gifts to the cow giver before he received a cow. This was

---

[158] Interview (GLR 36); and interview with a large land owner in Nyaburiza, Ntungamo District, Uganda (GLR 39), April 9, 2010.

[159] Doornbos, *Not all the king's men*, 137.

[160] Doornbos, "Land tenure," 65–67; and Kankunda, "Land tenure," 13.

[161] Doornbos, "Land tenure," 65.

[162] Interview (GLR 81).

necessary because being in the good graces of the cattle owner influenced many key decisions that came before the cow was delivered. First the cattle owner had to decide whether to grant the request or not. Even when he decided to grant the request, the cultivator hoped for a heifer that would produce milk and offspring instead of a bull. Also, a mature cow was always preferable to a calf that could die before it matured.

Unlike in the case of the elites who often received cows they did not even ask for, the poor sometimes had to ask repeatedly while supplying a steady stream of gifts. Finally, the would-be cow giver would tell the person seeking a cow: "Come and visit me with brew," suggesting an intent to give the person a cow. The person would then bring along friends and family members to the home of the cow giver. Although most will offer a cow then, some really mean ones will not even broach the topic of the cow gift during the first visit and will pretend not to have heard if the visitor brought up the topic. One Muiru who had received cows described it as a dating exercise in which the man had to ask multiple times to get the attention of the woman. Eventually, the giver would declare publicly: "I have given you a cow."

The control and domination of the recipient by the giver did not end once the declaration was made. The poor recipient continued to work for, offer gifts to, and show respect to the cow giver long after the declaration was made. In many ways it became like a lifetime commitment that tied the poor cow recipient to the rich cattle giver as a subordinate.

There are many reasons for the continuing servitude of these poor cow recipients. The main one is that it is an integral and well-known part of this tradition that the giver of the cow has a right to demand a cow in return from the recipient at a later date. This right is enforceable in a court of law, and that is partly why both the giver and the recipient arrange for the presence of their friends and family when cows change hands. However, beyond this legal enforceability, the person who refuses to give a cow back can be sure that his or her reputation will be damaged to the point where he or she will find it almost impossible to get a cow from anyone else. Even after the cow, the giver, and recipient had all died, the children of the cow giver could demand a cow from the children of the recipient.

Cow givers did not have to ask for a cow in return, and some had been known to instruct their children not to ever demand a cow back from the family of a cow recipient with whom they were very happy. Because of this, recipients worked for and gave gifts to the cow giver, hoping that they would not demand a cow from them. Others worked just to put off the date of the request. Givers could usually go to ask for a cow after the second delivery of a heifer gift. They could also wait for the fifth or sixth delivery. It was up to them. Also, the cow recipient hoped to influence the giver into requesting a bull instead of a heifer. Furthermore, in the event of the death of a cow, the recipients hoped to influence the givers into replacing the cow, something they were not obligated to do.

The description of the relationship by a former refugee who had witnessed the giving and receiving of cows between poor Banyankore and their wealthy neighbors was striking for its honesty.

Pastoralists give cows to poor Bairu here. Even our refugee parents gave cows to Bairu. Sometimes the pastoralist will give a man a young bull that was about to die. The man will have to work a lot for that dying calf. They will fetch water, dig pit latrines, renovate kraals and houses for the pastoralist, etc. The recipient became a friend and a child in the house of the giver. He brought *matookes* (bananas) almost every week. He did a lot before the cow was given to him. Even after receiving the animal, he continued to work. They asked for animals in bars. They asked many times. They went to the home of the pastoralist so the family of the pastoralist would know them. They took their wives carrying calabashes of brew and *matookes*. They went many times. Then they will be shown a breastfeeding calf as a gift and they worked 'til it was strong enough to be taken away. They became part of the family of the pastoralist and a family friend. When the pastoralist had a party, he called them and they had to bring *matookes* and come and offer labor. It was the same when the pastoralist had to renovate his house. Even kids of the Muiru knew the pastoralist family is their family friend and that they should go and work there. After the Muiru is given a cow, it cannot be taken back from him but they still worked because it was just like a loan. They knew the pastoralist could ask for a cow back at any time. So they worked to put off the demand for the cow. Sometimes when they kept working hard our parents would tell us: "Look at that poor man. How can he get a cow to give me? Leave him alone and don't ask him for a cow back. He will keep working for me. He is a friend."[163]

Even some Banyarwanda refugees got involved in these relationships as cow givers. The Bairu could potentially have freed themselves from the shackles of these refugees by driving them away. However, that would still have angered the local elites to whom the refugees had subjugated themselves.

It was this strong hold of the Banyankore elite on the masses that led the Bairu masses to desist from joining the government's project to attack the refugees. The antics and proclamations of youth wingers and parliamentarians who were often not even resident in villages were not

---

[163] Interview (GLR 71).

going to break this very strong and enduring hold of the elite on the underclass. The fact that even many of the old chiefs who on the surface went along with the eviction actually undermined it in various subtle ways must have further made plain to the masses the desires of the elite.

The new chiefs who were installed by the UPC in the run-up to the evictions did not stand a chance of breaking this hold of local elite on the Bairu masses. These chiefs often lacked a strong position in the rural political economy prior to their appointment and assumed the positions only because of their sympathy for the UPC.[164] They lacked a strong hold on the underclass. Furthermore, their behavior frequently alienated the masses even further. Being rather poor, many of them seized on their appointments to speedily enhance their economic positions. They are accused of extortion of gifts from even poor peasants and exploitative and overzealous enforcement of tax laws. People who refused to give them gifts had their taxes hiked or were invited for communal work. Poor peasants lacking money to pay taxes had to turn to the same elite at whose feet the refugees had sat for loans to avoid imprisonment or end their stints in jail.[165]

CONCLUSION

It is true that many ordinary Banyankore detested the refugees and were sympathetic to the evictions, but they did not participate because of fear of rural notables to whom the refugees had subjugated themselves. Rural notables did not want to participate in the evictions. The rural poor could not.

---

[164] Interview with a Uganda in Ntungamo District, Uganda (GLR 33), April 6, 2010.
[165] Interview (GLR 33); and Interview with a Muhima in Rugarama Sub-County, Ntungamo District, Uganda (GLR 32), April 6, 2010.

7

The Eviction of 59ers in Kivu, Democratic Republic of Congo

We started noticing the Congolese holding meetings. They distributed letters inviting people to meetings. If you tried to join them, they said, "Go away. We are having a private meeting." Then the villagers and chiefs came with sticks, pangas, and spears. They took properties, destroyed houses, and drove people away. The villagers participated heavily in the evictions. We were later released but those who went to their villages were again attacked there. Many left prison and ran to Uganda. I ran to Masaka [Uganda].[1]

Uganda's neighbor, the Democratic Republic of Congo, was another big destination for many of the refugees who fled Rwanda after the Social Revolution of 1959. Most of these refugees went to Kivu, and by 1961 their numbers were estimated to be approximately 60,000.[2] Many self-settled, whereas some went to United Nations High Commission for Refugees (UNHCR) settlements such as Bibwe and Ihula.[3] However, the sojourn of many of these refugees was to be a short one. In 1964, the refugees were violently evicted from some of the settlements as well as many local communities in which they had settled. There were mass arrests and imprisonment of refugees and the burning, destruction, and seizure of their properties. Many refugees were brutally beaten and sometimes killed. Female refugees were often subjected to rape and other forms of sexual assaults. Like in Conakry, the security officers guarding refugees in prisons subjected them to further mistreatment. When

[1] Interview with a former Rwandese refugee in Bwijanja Sub-County, Masindi District, Uganda (GLR 98), May 11, 2010.
[2] Holborn, *Refugees*, 1078.
[3] Holborn, *Refugees*, 1079–1082.

they were released, those who returned to their homes were sometimes attacked again. There were attacks on refugees both in local communities and in the refugee settlements. Many refugees fled to Uganda, Burundi, and Tanzania and the UNHCR had to organize an aerial evacuation of some of the refugees to the newly created Mwesi Settlement in Tanzania.[4]

Although state agents such as soldiers were heavily involved in the attacks, the local population also participated in large numbers and with much zeal, unlike in Southwestern Uganda. Like in Conakry, Guinea, attacking groups were often composed of a few soldiers or policemen along with many local civilians. State agents often had guns while locals carried sticks, machetes, hoes, and other blunt instruments. These were not state-affiliated militias. They were ordinary civilians. Their participation extended well beyond the identification of their refugee neighbors to state security agents. They were involved in arresting, beating, and sexually assaulting refugees and the destruction and seizure of refugee properties. A former refugee who I interviewed in Uganda put it thus: "In Congo the local people actively participated in the attacks on us. The local people and soldiers took our cows, raped our women, and killed many people. They attacked the camps and I had to walk to Kisoro in Uganda."[5] Another claimed: "the Bahunde burnt our houses and beat up people."[6] As one exasperated former refugee put it, "Most of the people who came to evict us were our own neighbors who we knew very well, and they did not even come at night to do these bad things. They came in broad daylight."[7] Many others who were formerly Rwandese refugees in Congo told a similar story of widespread and enthusiastic local participation in the attacks on refugees in Kivu in the early 1960s.[8]

The participation of the local population was on such a massive scale that some of the refugees who were attacked sometimes portrayed the

---

[4] Johan Pottier, "Modern information warfare versus empirical knowledge: framing 'the crisis' in Eastern Zaire, 1996," in *Negotiating local knowledge: power and identity in development*, ed. Johan Pottier, Alan Bicker, and Paul Sillitoe (London: Pluto Press, 2003), 225; Holborn, *Refugees*, 1092–1093 and 1161; interview (GLR 86); and interview (GLR 97).

[5] Interview (GLR 86).

[6] Interview (GLR 97).

[7] Interview (GLR 99).

[8] Interviews with former Rwandese refugees in Kiryandogo Sub-County, Uganda (GLR 101), May 16, 2010; (GLR Nyangaya Sub-County, Masindi District, Uganda (GLR 103), May 20, 2010; (GLR 104), Kigumba Sub-County, Masindi District, Uganda (GLR 104), May 14, 2010.

whole exercise as a local initiative, denying the involvement of state security agents in the exercise.

We did not see soldiers during the evictions. Maybe they were in civilian clothes. The Bahunde and Banande got together and evicted us. . . . Those evicting us had no guns. They had sticks, spears, and pangas. There were only a few people with guns. They did not destroy crops because they probably wanted to harvest our crops. They were not trained soldiers.[9]

One of the victims of the evictions was something of a serial evictee. He was initially forced to flee Rwanda due to attacks on Batutsi that followed the Social Revolution in 1959. He went through Burundi, Tanzania, and Uganda to the Ihula refugee settlement in the Democratic Republic of Congo. However, shortly after his arrival, he was part of the Banyarwanda refugees evicted from Kivu in 1964. He fled and found a home in Rubaare in what was then Mbarara District in Uganda. In 1982, he was again evicted from Rubaare. This rather "rich" experience allowed him to share his comparative insights on the anti-refugee violence in Kivu and Uganda with us.

I was evicted in Congo and ran to Rubaare [Uganda]. Unfortunately, I was again chased from Rubaare in 1982 and settled in Kibondo camp in Rwanda for some time. They took all my stuff and told me to go and find my relatives in Rwanda. If they saw you with a cow, they took it and said you did not come to Uganda with a cow. It was the soldiers of Obote that did it. They were uniformed and had guns. The locals did not participate in the attacks in Uganda. The Bakiga and Banyankore protected us and tried to protect our properties and cows by claiming it was theirs. But in Congo the local community participated very much in the attacks.[10]

Scholars, including Holborn and Lemarchand, support the idea of popular local participation in the attacks on the refugees in Kivu.[11]

The goal of this chapter is to explain why the local population in Kivu visited such violence on Banyarwanda refugees in 1964. I argue that the state's permission of attacks on and demonization of the refugees was a necessary condition for the campaign of violence launched by the local population. Despite the grievances against the refugees by sections of the local population, these generalized and systematic attacks will not have been possible without the permission of the state. Like in Guinea and

---

[9] Interview a former Rwandese refugee in Kimengo Sub-County, Masindi District, Uganda (GLR 105), May 17, 2010.
[10] Interview (GLR 86).
[11] Holborn, *Refugees*, 1087–1089; and Lemarchand, *Rwanda and Burundi*, 210–211.

Uganda, the state ordered the attacks on the refugees because of links between some of the refugees and the armed Lumumbist rebellion in the east of the country.[12] However, why did the locals in Kivu exploit the permission granted by the state to attack refugees when locals in southwestern Uganda refrained from undertaking similar violence against Banyarwanda refugees fomented and led by the UPC state?

Unlike the Banyarwanda in southwestern Uganda, those who sought refuge in Kivu settled in an area in which Belgian colonial policies had sought with some success to privilege residence over indigeneity in the apportionment of rights to power and land. This meant that refugees were not subjugated to local elites in the areas in which they settled, ensuring that the locals knew little about their lives and activities. When state officials began to accuse the refugees of all sorts of evil, including participating in the Lumumbist rebellion and seeking to dominate local groups, residents bought into the campaign. All of this happened in a situation of increasing national and local political volatility, and local elites who were benefiting from cheap refugee labor did not only participate in the attacks, but they also organized the masses to undertake it.

AN EXPULSION AND SEQUESTRATION ORDER

It was concern over politics in their home country that led some of the 1959 Banyarwanda refugees into involvement in Congolese politics. The refugees were composed partly of ordinary people fleeing the violence that characterized the Social Revolution. Among them, there were also former members of the ruling class who fled not necessarily because of the violence but because of their unwillingness to submit to the Party of the Hutu Emancipation Movement (PARMEHUTU) government in the country. Many of these state-in-exile refugees had no intention of resorting to quiet lives as refugees. They were intent on returning to Rwanda, but only as rulers. The overthrow of the new dispensation in Rwanda was a necessity for them.[13] They quickly formed a government in exile in 1962 under the banner of the Rwanda National Union (UNAR). They had Francois Rukeba as prime minister, Pierre Mungalurire as finance minister, Gabriel Sebyeza as information minister, and Hamoud Ben Salim as defense minister.[14]

---

[12] Holborn, *Refugees*, 1093.
[13] Lemarchand, *Rwanda and Burundi*, 201; and Holborn, *Refugees*, 1083.
[14] Lemarchand, *Rwanda and Burundi*, 201–203.

Lischer has noted the propensity of such state-in-exile and persecuted refugees to militarize.[15] In all of the countries neighboring Rwanda to which they went, they quickly began to organize, train, and arm themselves for a violent return to Rwanda. Their fighting bands, which came to be known by the derogatory term *Inyenzi* (cockroaches, in the Kinyarwanda language), launched multiple invasions into Rwanda from many neighboring countries. On December 21, 1963, they undertook the spectacular Bugesera Invasion into Rwanda. The plan was to launch simultaneous attacks from the neighboring countries of Tanzania, Burundi, Congo, and Uganda. Even though attacking parties from Uganda and Tanzania were stymied, an invasion was launched from Congo, and the *Inyenzi* fighters from Burundi came to within 12 miles of Kigali before they were repulsed by Rwandese and Belgian troops. Bahutu killed approximately 10,000 Batutsi who were still resident in Rwanda in retaliatory attacks after this invasion.[16]

A big problem that the *Inyenzi* faced was the clamp down on their activities by host governments in Congo, Tanzania, and Uganda.[17] Unlike Burundi,[18] these neighboring countries were hostile to militarization by the refugees and the use of their soil as bases from which attacks were launched on Rwanda. These attacks damaged relations between Rwanda and these governments, and led leaders in Congo, Tanzania, and Uganda to undertake measures to curb the military activities of the refugees.[19]

In Congo, it was this frustration of their efforts by state authorities that encouraged some of the more militant refugees to join the Lumumbist rebellion in the eastern areas of the country, adjacent to Rwanda. The goal of the refugees was what Lemarchand called "reciprocal assistance in the course of military engagements."[20] The refugees would help the Lumumbist rebels in their fight against the government in Kinshasa. In the case in which the Lumumbists succeeded, they would then help the refugees to overthrow the PARMEHUTU government in Rwanda.

The Peoples Liberation Army (APL) of the Congolese National Movement–Lumumba (MNC-L) party launched the Lumumbist rebellion in Eastern Congo in 1964. It was one of two rebellions that were

[15] Lischer, *Dangerous sanctuaries*, 21–28.
[16] Lemarchand, *Rwanda and Burundi*, 216–225.
[17] Ibid., 209–210.
[18] Ibid., 215.
[19] Ibid., 209–210.
[20] Ibid., 214.

to seriously threaten to overthrow the national government in Kinshasa in the early 1960s.[21] The other rebellion – the Mulelist uprising based in Kwilu Province – was to die out quickly.[22] The Lumumbist rebellion was far more successful, and its fighters, locally known as Simbas, swept through the east of the country. In August 1964, they captured Stanleyville after overrunning many towns in July, including Baudoinville and Kindu. "On September 5, with the proclamation of a revolutionary government in Stanleyville, the eastern rebellion reached its high water mark: almost half of Zaire and seven local capitals out of twenty-one were in rebel hands."[23] The rebellion became an international affair, with the rebels attracting support from left-leaning governments in the Union of Soviet Socialist Republics, China, and Algeria, among others.[24] Che Guevara and a band of Cuban internationalists joined the rebels in 1965.[25] It was only put down with aid from foreign mercenaries, U.S. and Belgian troops, and Cuban counterrevolutionaries supplied by the United States. The United States increased military aid to the Congolese government and provided it with trainers, bombers, trucks, tanks, and transport planes.[26]

Banyarwanda refugees became involved at high political levels in the rebellion.[27] The refugee leader Francois Rukeba, who was former UNAR prime minister, participated in discussions by the MNC-L leadership in Uvira in 1964. Colonel Louis Bidalira was for a while the MNC-L's "Chief of Staff of the Eastern Territories" and Jerome Katarebe became the *Chef de Cabinet* of Gaston Soumialot, the leader of the eastern section of the rebellion.[28]

Refugees were heavily involved in combat[29] and in "guidance and leadership" in military matters.[30] In the diary that Che Guevara

[21] Crawford Young, "Rebellion and the Congo," in *Rebellion in Black Africa*, ed. Robert Rotberg (London: Oxford University Press, 1971), 209–214.

[22] Crawford Young, *Politics in the Congo: decolonization and independence* (Princeton, NJ: Princeton University Press, 1965), 585.

[23] Lemarchand, "Historical setting," 41; and Didier Gondola, *The history of Congo* (Westport, CT: Greenwood Press, 2002), 128.

[24] Stephen Weissman, *American foreign policy in Congo 1960–1964* (Ithaca: Cornell University Press, 1974), 221.

[25] Galvez, *Che in Africa*.

[26] Weissman, *American foreign policy*, pp. 205–247; and Galvez, *Che in Africa*, 14.

[27] Mathews, "Refugees and stability," 72; and Holborn, *Refugees*, 993.

[28] Lemarchand, *Rwanda and Burundi*, 214.

[29] Galvez, *Che in Africa*.

[30] Lemarchand, *Rwanda and Burundi*, 214.

maintained during his days fighting with the APL rebels in eastern Congo, he makes frequent mention of visits to frontline positions manned by Rwandese fighters.[31] He paints them as generally more disciplined, organized, and dedicated to fighting than their Congolese counterparts.[32] He wrote of how one Major Mundandi, the leader of "the first battalion of Rwandans," sent him a letter:

complaining that he wouldn't have any combatants left for making the revolution in his own country, because many men had been killed in the last actions.... He also said that he had been planning that, once Albertville had been taken, he would return to his own country to begin the struggle, but, with so many losses in his ranks, it would be impossible.[33]

The Congolese government formally responded to the involvement of Rwandese refugee fighters in the Simba rebellion on August 19, 1964. It issued an order expelling *all* Rwandese refugees and sequestering their properties.[34] This went along with a general campaign that demonized the refugees. Local politicians came to blame the refugees without discrimination for all sorts of evil.[35] These refugees, the vast majority of whom were not only pacific but also uninvolved in local politics, were blamed for all the problems of the region. This was achieved by identifying them with the old resident Banyarwanda (especially Batutsi) of North Kivu, who were already attaining the status of bogeymen for Congolese communities such as the Banande and Bahunde.[36] The refugees were accused of evils that included plotting to dominate the local population and seeking to turn the area over to the government of Rwanda.[37]

It is worth remembering that the vast majority of these refugees were in fact not militarized. Most were uninvolved in Congolese politics, local or national, and were mostly consumed with eking out a living and hoping for a quick return to Rwanda.

The motivations of state officials in this campaign were similar to those of their counterparts in Lansana Conte's Guinea of the year 2000 and those of Obote's UPC government of 1982. Calls for the expulsion of all of the refugees served to punish those among the refugees who were

---

[31] Galvez, *Che in Africa.*
[32] Ibid., 143.
[33] Ibid., 110.
[34] Holborn, *Refugees,* 1093; Zolberg, Suhrke and Aguayo, *Escape from violence,* 46; and Bustin, "The Congo," 187.
[35] Holborn, *Refugees,* 1088.
[36] Jackson, "Sons of which soil?" 109.
[37] Lemarchand, *Rwanda and Burundi,* 211.

involved in rebel activities. It also fanned nationalist flames in favor of the state and against the Lumumbists, who were cast as pawns of foreigners.

EMBRACING THE STATE'S PROJECT

Unlike in southwestern Uganda, where residents refused to embrace the state's violent anti-refugee campaign, locals in Kivu responded enthusiastically to the Congolese state's call to attack the Banyarwanda refugees. The following section explains why many locals were predisposed to buying into the state's narrative that portrayed the refugees as dangerous betrayers of the national and local trust.

Subverting Indigeneity as an Organizing Principle

The enthusiasm with which the local community embraced and took advantage of the state's effort at attacking the Rwandese refugees is deserving of explanation. As we saw in Uganda and in the Forest Region of Guinea, the local population sometimes does not go along with the project of the state. They sometimes even seek to protect refugees in the face of attacks by state agents. Why did the local population in Kivu so enthusiastically participate in the attacks on the Rwandese refugees? I argue here that the answer lies in the legacy of contradictory Belgian policies that ended up reinforcing residence over indigeneity as an organizing principle in Kivu. These efforts only truly ended when Congo attained independence in 1960, a year after the refugees began to arrive. The subversion of indigeneity and reinforcement of residence as an organizing principle in Kivu under Belgian rule blunted local instruments for subjugating strangers. This had an impact on the levels of information that local elites had about the daily lives and activities of the refugees. This is what made it easy for many locals to blame the mostly innocent refugees for all of the grievances that local communities such as the Bahunde and Banande had over decades of Banyarwanda settlement in Kivu.

The colonial history of Kivu that is of relevance here in many ways resembles that of the Guinean capital, Conakry. By 1959 when Rwandese refugees started arriving in Kivu, very significant blows had been dealt to indigeneity as the organizing principle in society by decades of Belgian rule. The colonial state had done a lot to divorce issues concerning land rights and even political leadership from questions of indigeneity. This had undermined the extent to which the area was seen as belonging in unique ways to indigenous communities such as the Hunde and Nande.

Much has been written about the colonial tendency to ethnicize territory by carving out areas as homelands of various groups.[38] Mamdani and Jackson have each written about such ethnicization of territory in Eastern Congo.[39] However, in Kivu, like in Conakry, there was an aggressive countervailing tendency in colonial policy that blunted indigeneity and reinforced residence in determining belonging. In effect, the Belgian efforts at ethnicizing territories in ways that privileged indigeneity were severely undercut by countervailing Belgian policies that granted recognized stranger Banyarwanda migrants all the privileges of indigeneity. They in effect proclaimed that indigenes had certain privileges and then also added "But you can have these privileges even if you are not indigenous as long as you reside here." This tended to reinforce residence as an organizing principle.

After the formal creation of the Congo Free State in August 1885, Belgian colonial authorities were impressed by the agricultural potential of Kivu and sought to transform it into a settler plantation economy. Their effort at bringing settlers to the area was successful, as many Europeans were eventually attracted to Kivu by its fertile soils and good rainfall.[40] By 1925 there were 192 European settlers in the area. This number shot up to 943 in 1929. They established coffee, tea, quinine, and pyrethrum plantations. Mining activities in the area were to follow later.[41]

The land policies established to cater for these European settlers represented the initial blows to efforts at privileging indigeneity as an organizing principle in the area. Colonial authorities imposed their institutions as the grantors and guarantors of land rights to the European settlers. This was a first step toward divorcing land rights from questions of indigeneity. Generous land policies were made that gave settlers easy access to land and safeguarded these rights. Like in other colonial settler economies in Africa, the colonial authorities took land away from the local Bahunde community that they specifically set aside for European settlement.[42] The Fundamental Law of 1908, for instance, distinguished between

---

[38] Mamdani, *Citizen and subject*, 21–23; and Mamdani, *When victims become killers*, 30–31.

[39] Jackson, "Sons of which soil?" 100; and Mamdani, *When victims become killers*, 237–239.

[40] Newbury, *The cohesion of oppression*, 159.

[41] Ibid., 160.

[42] Koen Vlassenroot, "Land and conflict: the case of Masisi," in *Conflict and social transformation in Easter DR Congo*, ed. Koen Vlassenroot and Timothy Raeymaekers (Gent: Academia Press, 2004), 84.

indigenous lands and state lands in the area.[43] Beyond lands that were expropriated outright, the Belgians acquired more lands for settlers by buying it from some traditional chiefs, who were only too happy to get money for land that was then in abundance.[44]

By 1925 European settlers and their plantations had become part of the Kivu landscape. Their arrival in and acquisition and continued enjoyment of land rights in the area were all predominantly negotiated with and guaranteed by the colonial state instead of local communities. This severely undercut the rights of indigenous communities to dictate the terms of settlement in "their homelands" as autochthones to whom later arrivals must be subjugated. The Belgians had begun to insert themselves as alternatives to local institutions for dealing with strangers like the French authorities did in the early years of the city of Conakry.

Like in Conakry, the labor problem was what compelled the colonial authorities to land further blows against indigeneity and in support of residence as an organizing principle in Kivu. As noted previously, the Belgians did succeed in attracting European settlers to Kivu. However, as in many colonial plantation economies, the authorities and settlers soon realized there was a vital ingredient that was missing. The grand project of transforming Kivu into a settler plantation economy faced a big labor problem. Many areas in Kivu were underpopulated at the beginning of the twentieth century.[45] Like in many other places in Africa, even the few locals in the area were not particularly interested in entering the cash crop economy as laborers. Many were involved in subsistence farming, hunting, and gathering. They had access to a lot of land and were in no hurry to make the transformation to wage labor. Like the rubber collectors of King Leopold's Congo and colonial authorities across Africa, the Belgians experimented with a regime of forced labor. Peasants resorted to the nonconfrontational resistance strategies of "dissertion of villages, hiding in the bush and emigration towards remote areas"[46] that have proved a headache for many state makers around the world.[47] Desperate officials even tried forcibly recruiting women and children for plantation work. However, this did little to solve the labor problem.[48]

---

[43] Mararo, "Land conflicts in Masisi," 62.
[44] Ibid., 165.
[45] Ibid., 53.
[46] Ibid., 65.
[47] Hyden, *Beyond Ujamaa*, 209; and James Scott, *Seeing Like a State* (New Haven: Yale University Press, 1998), 49.
[48] Mararo, "Land conflicts in Masisi," 66.

Like their French counterparts in Conakry, the Belgians finally settled on the solution of attracting labor to Kivu from elsewhere. The neighboring Belgian territory of Ruanda-Urundi, which was to later become the independent countries of Rwanda and Burundi, fit the bill for this perfectly. Like French colonial officials in Conakry, the Belgians did not initially envision the permanent settlement of Banyarwanda and Barundi in Kivu. The goal was to get them to temporarily come and sell their labor in Kivu and then return home.[49] Ruanda-Urundi was one of the most densely populated areas in Africa and was already a major supplier of labor migrants to the neighboring territories of Uganda and Tanganyika (which later united with the island of Zanzibar to form the country of Tanzania).[50] There was a combination of push and pull factors that led to this labor migration. On the push side was harsh Belgian rule, which often included corporal punishment. Ruanda-Urundi also experienced droughts and its related famine.[51] On the pull side one could count the less harsh British and German colonial regimes higher wages, and better working conditions in the neighboring territories.[52] The Belgian authorities and European settlers set their eyes on diverting some of these labor migrants to Kivu.

Many European settlers sought permission to employ workers in Ruanda-Urundi.[53] By 1924 they had started recruiting such migrant laborers with offers of relatively high wages.[54] The colonial authorities tried to facilitate these recruitment drives by passing a decree on July 19, 1926, that permitted the people of Ruanda-Urundi to legally migrate in search of labor outside of their territory. The same decree also permitted colonial enterprises to recruit laborers in Ruanda-Urundi.[55] People began to trickle into various areas of Kivu from Ruanda-Urundi as well as other areas of Congo.[56]

---

[49] Ibid., 100.
[50] Newbury, *The cohesion of oppression*, 157; Archie Mafeje and Audrey Richards, "The commercial farmer and his labor supply," in *Subsistence to commercial farming in present-day Buganda*, ed. Audrey Richards, Ford Sturrock and Jean Fortt (Cambridge: Cambridge University Press, 1973), 179.
[51] Audrey Richards, "The travel routes and the travelers," in *Economic development and tribal change: a study of immigrant labour in Buganda*, ed. Audrey I. Richards (Cambridge: W. Heffer and Sons Ltd., 1952), 67–70.
[52] Newbury, *The cohesion of oppression*, 157–158 and 177.
[53] Ibid., 166.
[54] Mararo, "Land conflicts in Masisi," 64.
[55] Ibid., 135.
[56] Mararo, "Land conflicts in Masisi," 100; and Newbury, *The cohesion of oppression*, 161–164.

This trickle did not develop into the massive flow that the settlers and colonial officials had hoped for. Neighboring British colonies such as Uganda and Tanganyika continued to be the preferred destinations for labor migrants.[57] There was the fact that moving to Congo from Ruanda-Urundi did not represent an escape from harsh Belgian rule, unlike the flight to Uganda and Tanganyika. Many of the migrants were motivated by the desire to flee severe Belgian colonial policies.[58] Furthermore, employers and colonial authorities in Uganda, mindful of the heavy need for farm laborers in central Uganda, sought to aggressively defend their advantage in attracting and keeping labor migrants. They employed attractive wages, perks, and even temporary land rights.[59] The importance of networks in migration flows also meant that the presence of large Banyarwanda and Barundi migrant populations in Uganda might have made it easier for Uganda to attract later migrants who might be acquaintances of earlier migrants.

It was against this background that the Belgian authorities resorted to a solution that the French also eventually employed in Conakry. They embraced the radical idea of permanently settling people from Ruanda-Urundi in various areas of Kivu.[60] The plan was to lure Banyarwanda from densely populated Ruanda-Urundi with offers of permanent land rights in Kivu. The hope was that these settled populations would then constitute a dependable and stable source of labor for the plantations. The formal offer of land rights to would-be migrants also countered one of the key advantages that Uganda, where many labor migrants in Buganda got parcels to cultivate, held over Congo. Apart from solving the labor problem in Kivu, the Belgian authorities also saw it as a way of decongesting the densely populated Ruanda-Urundi. This would partly solve the incessant problem of famine in Rwanda. Many chiefs in Rwanda

---

57 Mararo, "Land conflicts in Masisi," 137.
58 Powesland, "History of the migration," 46; and Mararo, "Land conflicts in Masisi," 137.
59 Richards, "The travel routes," 70–74; J.M. Fortt, "The distribution of the immigrant and Ganda population within Buganda," in *Economic development and tribal change: a study of immigrant labour in Buganda*, ed. Audrey Richards (Cambridge: W. Heffer and Sons Ltd., 1952), 79; R.I. Richards, "Methods of settlement in Buganda," in *Economic development and tribal change: a study of immigrant labour in Buganda*, ed. Audrey Richards (Cambridge: W. Heffer and Sons Ltd., 1952), 125; and Audrey Richards, "The problem for Buganda," in *Economic development and tribal change: a study of immigrant labour in Buganda*, ed. Audrey Richards (Cambridge: W. Heffer and Sons Ltd., 1952), 197.
60 Mararo, "Land conflicts in Masisi," 137.

envisaged it as a way of ridding themselves of troublesome subjects, and people who had problems often saw such migration as an escape.[61]

It was in pursuit of this resettlement goal that the Belgian authorities established the *Mission d'Immigration des Banyarwanda* (MIB) in 1948. This body was later renamed *Mission d'Immigration des Populations* (MIP) to account for its work in the settlement of non-Banyarwanda migrants. Its main function was to oversee the resettlement of migrants in Kivu. From 1937 to 1956, large numbers of Banyarwanda were permanently settled in various areas of what is now North Kivu such as Masisi and Rutshuru.[62] Like they did for European settlers, the colonial authorities and their MIB expropriated some lands without compensation from Bahunde and Banyaga communities that they distributed to the Banyarwanda settlers. They also bought land from local chiefs for the Banyarwanda.[63] The Belgians also created "Zones of free migration" where migrants could buy land from the chiefs by offering them "cows, beer and goats."[64]

Batutsi initially constituted the biggest number of settlers. This was later to change, and Bahutu settlers came to outnumber Batutsi by a large margin.[65] Banyarwanda came to constitute large sections of the population in Kivu. In Masisi in North Kivu, they came to make up seventy percent of the population by the end of the transmigration program.[66]

There are certain characteristics of this population movement that tended to undermine indigeneity as the predominant organizing principle in society. First, the goal of the Belgians was to *permanently* settle the immigrants in Kivu and they made this known to both the immigrants and the indigenes.[67] This was very different from the widespread promotion of temporary migration by colonial authorities to facilitate production, construction, and mining activities in other parts of Africa. In these cases of temporary settlement, migrants were seen and often saw themselves as temporary sojourners. In Kivu, the insistence on permanent settlement was the first step in granting settlers a sense of belonging that would

[61] Ibid., 139–142.
[62] Ibid., 7.
[63] Vlassenroot, "Reading the Congolese crisis," 41; Chretien, *The great lakes of Africa*, 279; and Mararo, "Land conflicts in Masisi," 163–165; and Emizet Kisangani and F. Scott Bob, *Historical Dictionary of the Democratic Republic of Congo 3rd Edition* (Lanham, MD: Scarecrow Press, 2010), 43–44.
[64] Mararo, "Land conflicts in Masisi," 166.
[65] Ibid., 149–150.
[66] Vlassenroot, "Land and conflict," 91.
[67] Mararo, "Land conflicts in Masisi," 137.

raise questions about the superior rights of indigenes to belonging in the area.

Second, the colonial authority and its MIB/MIP hijacked the traditional roles for welcoming, settling, and incorporating strangers that are the privileged rights of autochthones in indigeneity-privileging societies. The Belgians played a big role in acquiring land rights for and settling the migrants. Like the European settlers, many Banyarwanda migrants got land directly from the colonial authorities who had acquired the land from the locals through expropriation and market transactions.[68] In other instances where migrants got land from chiefs, the colonial authorities still intervened in the process by demarcating these areas as zones of free migration set aside for settlers. All of this had implications for the rights of settlers and the claims that indigenous populations could then make on them.[69]

One relevant effect of this was that it tended to give the migrants land rights that they saw as independent of and impervious to the authority and opinions of the local population that they found there. They saw themselves as having land rights that were just as good as any in the area. Furthermore, by appropriating the role of settling strangers, the colonial authority and its MIB rendered local institutions that played these roles redundant, leading to their gradual corrosion.

Third, the colonial authorities reinforced the political rights of migrants. This further fueled the view among both the settlers and locals that the newly arrived Banyarwanda had acquired rights that were as solid and independent as those of the indigenous populations. Although the settlers appreciated this fact, the indigenes greatly resented it. The main means by which the Belgians achieved this reinforcement of the political rights of the settlers was by appointing chiefs for migrant communities who were themselves migrants instead of indigenes.[70]

The fact that these lesser chiefs were under higher indigenous chiefs lessened its impact. However, the Belgians even went to the extent of creating a customary authority for some of the migrants that was not subjugated to, but co-equal with, those of the locals. For almost twenty years (1936–1957), the Belgians established and defended the *Chefferie*

[68] Ibid., 163.

[69] Ibid., 166.

[70] Vlassenroot, "Land and conflict," 225; and Mararo, "Land conflicts in Masisi," 144; interviews with a former Rwandese refugee in Masindi District, Uganda (GLR 100), May 19, 2010; and with a Rwandese whose parents had migrated to the Democratic Republic of Congo in Masindi District, Uganda (GLR 106), May 17, 2010.

de Gishari for Banyarwanda migrants in Masisi. The *Mwami* of Rwanda was given the right to select the head of this customary authority, and he duly selected Bideri a Munyarwanda as chief.[71] Two years before the refugees began to arrive and three years before Congolese independence, the non-indigenous Banyarwanda migrants of Masisi enjoyed what Mamdani[72] has listed as one of the ultimate privileges of indigeneity and autochthony – their own customary authority.

The state's reinforcement and guarantee of the land and political rights of settlers had a predictable effect. It weakened the links between belonging and indigeneity. It eroded the connection between autochthony and the enjoyment of local citizenship rights. It put into question the privileged rights that indigenes had to belonging in the area by divorcing the Banyarwanda migrants' origins from their enjoyment of some of the most fundamental benefits of autochthony in the indigeneity privileging society. These are a customary authority and its appendages of customary land rights, justice, and political authority. It made this dependent solely on their residence.

This empowered and delighted the new arrivals. Banyarwanda settlers began to assert their rights to belonging early. They resisted paying tributes to local chiefs.[73] This was a sign not only of their refusal to part with money, animals, and produce, but also unwillingness to concede any privileged right of the indigenous communities. This greatly angered local communities because it meant the passing of their privileged positions in these communities as autochthones. Like other communities thus imposed on by central state authorities,[74] they harbored grievances against the circumstances surrounding the settlement of Banyarwanda. However, before independence in 1960, they could do little about it in the face of colonial support for the rights of the settlers in Kivu.

After independence, many of these indigenous communities began to take steps to undercut the rights of the migrants. They urged them to "Go home like the Europeans."[75] However, local communities in Kivu have never been able to attain clear success in this effort. Buoyed by decades of colonial policies and strategic alliances, Banyarwanda settlers in Kivu

---

[71] Mamdani, *When victims become killers*, 241; and Turner, *The Congo wars*, 111–112.
[72] Mamdani, "Political identity," 10.
[73] Vlassenroot, "Land and conflict," 85.
[74] See Herschelle Challenor, "Strangers as colonial intermediaries: the Dahomeyans in Francophone Africa," in *Strangers in African societies*, ed. William Shack and Elliott Skinner (Berkeley: University of California Press, 1979), 67.
[75] Turner, *The Congo wars*, 85.

have tried to defend their rights in Kivu and have even attacked other communities in defense of those rights in violent outbreaks that continue today.[76] The first large-scale conflict between Banyarwanda migrants and indigenes over what the migrants saw as efforts at subverting their rights in Kivu was the *Guerre de Kanyarwanda* that broke out in 1963 and lasted for two years.[77] From 1960 Bahunde chiefs started a campaign to restore indigeneity as the privileged organizing principle in Kivu. They began to replace Banyarwanda chiefs with Bahunde ones[78] and to "take back" Bahunde rights to "land, houses, shops, cattle, and plantations" owned by Banyarwanda settlers. In 1963, the Banyarwanda launched a violent rebellion against these measures.[79]

It was in this environment where belonging had increasingly become an "open question," to borrow a phrase from Diagne in an unrelated context,[80] that the 1959 refugees settled in Kivu. Local mechanisms for dealing with strangers had been blunted by decades of Belgian immigration policy, and resistance that was sometimes violent was making the reassertion of these local mechanisms difficult. Like previous migrants to the area, refugees settled and lived autonomously of the local elites. Importantly, the MIP, which had settled earlier Banyarwanda migrants, ended up playing a significant role in the settlement of the refugees.[81]

The claim that Belgian colonialism undermined indigeneity as the privileged organizing principle for distributing rights to power and land in Kivu will raise consternation in the minds of some. After all Mamdani, Jackson, and many others[82] have rightly noted that a key cause of the ongoing problems in eastern Congo is the ethnicization of territory and

---

[76] Vlassenroot, "Reading the Congolese crisis," 41; Vlassenroot, "Land and conflict," 85; Koen Vlassenroot, "The promise of ethnic conflict: militarization and enclave-formation in South Kivu," in *Conflict and ethnicity in Central Africa*, ed. Didier Goyvaerts (Tokyo, Insitute for the study of the languages and culture of Asia and Africa, 2000), 67; Turner, *The Congo wars*, 114–25; and Mararo, "Land conflicts in Masisi," 180.

[77] Vlassenroot, "Land and conflict," 85; and Turner, *The Congo wars*, 115.

[78] Mamdani, *When victims become killers*, 241–242.

[79] Turner, *The Congo wars*, 117; Mamdani, *When victims become killers*, 241–42; and Vlassenroot, "Land and conflict," 85.

[80] Souleymane Bachir Diagne, "Africanity as an open question," *Identity and beyond: rethinking Africanity, Nordic Africa Institutite Discussion Paper* 12 (2001).

[81] Holborn, *Refugees*, 1080.

[82] Jackson, "Sons of which soil?" Mamdani, *When victims become killers*; Mahmood Mamdani, "Understanding the crisis"; Vlassenroot, "Reading the Congolese crisis"; Vlassenroot, "Land and conflict"; Vlassenroot, "Identity formation," 499–515; and Turner, *The Congo wars*, 64–66.

the exclusionary politics of autochthony that tends to give little ground to residence in the apportioning of rights.

While acknowledging the validity of claims by scholars like Jackson and Mamdani, consternation over my assessment of the situation in Kivu in 1959–1964 is likely to be based on two problematic moves. One of these is the transposition of the characteristics of Kivu today or the Kivu of the 1990s unto the Kivu of the late 1950s and early 1960s. The Kivus of these periods are very different. Belgium was still the colonial power in 1959 when the Rwandese refugees began to arrive. As I noted previously, it was only two years after they had eliminated the *Chefferie de Gishari* created for the Banyarwanda migrants. Indigenous communities in the area were only then beginning to assert their rights in a bid to reverse the subversion of autochthony's privileged position in Kivu. Almost to forty years had passed by 1996 when Rwanda invaded Kivu, leading to the conflagration that is still destroying lives and property today. It should be expected that much has happened in the region since then. It is thus extremely problematic to assume that the Kivu of today where indigeneity may be privileged over residence is the same as the Kivu of 1959.

There is another problem with this objection. It mistakes the strength of the backlash against Belgian subversion of indigeneity for the lack of such subversion. However, the backlash should instead alert us to the fact that there was something that it was meant to counter. Where the privileges of indigeneity are not being seriously contested, one does not really hear much of a discourse of autochthony. The privileging of indigeneity in such a society is a matter of course that operates quietly in the background raising little attention to itself. It lacks the anxiety that serious challenges cause and that motivates vociferous assertions and violent defense. De Soto[83] made a similar point about property rights when he noted that in places where such institutions are deeply rooted and function well, people take them for granted not just because they are effective and efficient, but also because they operate quietly without attracting much attention.

There are clearly pervasive discourses and assertions of autochthony and violent efforts at challenging residence as a principle for determining belonging in Kivu that Mamdani and Jackson[84] have written about. However, this should be seen as evidence of the extent to which Belgian

---

[83] Hernando de Soto, *The mystery of capital* (New York: Basic Books, 2000).
[84] Jackson, "Sons of which soil?" and Mamdani, *When victims become killers.*

colonial policies had put the privileges of indigeneity in question in the area. It should not be understood as a sign that indigeneity had never been fundamentally challenged as the main organizing principle in the determination of belonging in the area. A few phrases from Bauman can help us describe the situation better. The raucous and violent "vigilance" that the defenders and promoters of autochthony display in Kivu is evidence of the "incurable fragility and shakiness"[85] of their position in the face of decades of Belgian colonial policies. These policies created a transgressive tendency that pitted residence against indigeneity in the determination of citizenship rights in eastern Congo. Putting the non-indigenes in their place regardless of how successful such an effort has been implies that the non-indigenes were out of what is supposed to be their place as subordinates of autochthones in the first place. It is not evidence that the non-indigenes have always occupied their place. One does not need to put what is already in its place in its place. For as Bauman noted, it is those things that "will not stick to their assigned place"[86] that require vigilant and violent policing and raucous denunciation.

The Autonomous Lives of the Refugees

This residence-privileging character of Kivu in the late 1950s and early 1960s militated against the subjugation of the refugees to local elites. By 1959, many of the indigenous institutions for dealing with strangers had been significantly undermined by the colonial creation of the MIB/MIP as the institution that oversaw transmigration in Kivu. Furthermore, the refugees felt no pressure to seek alliances with local notables. After all, they had arrived in an area where the fact of their being from elsewhere was not peculiar. There were large numbers of others who came from elsewhere but were granted rights of belonging that were considered to be just as deep as those of everyone else. The distinction between strangers and indigenes had been rendered increasingly insignificant. The refugees settled into a mode of existence that was very autonomous of the local elite in the area. Like the refugees in Conakry, they were not subjugated to the notables in the areas in which they settled. They did not symbolically subjugate themselves to these elites or engage in the frequent exchange of gifts with them. Also, these elites did not share legal responsibility for the actions of the refugees.

---

85 Bauman, *Postmodernity*, 6.
86 Ibid., 6.

Some of the former refugees interviewed for this work seemed to have taken notice of the dazzling diversity of the areas in which they settled and the little significance that indigeneity seemed to have in the allocation of rights. One former refugee who I interviewed had stayed in Ihula Camp and worked in a tea factory twelve miles away. This is how he described the area in which he settled:

It was the home of the Banyarwanda. There were Bahunde and Banande around but that area mostly had Banyarwanda. There were Batutsi, Bahutu, and Batwa. Even the king we dealt with there was a Munyarwanda. He had many other little kings under him and most were Banyarwanda. I heard there was a Congolese king over him but we never met him.[87]

Another recounted all the groups that lived in the general area. "The Bashi, Bahunde, Banande, Bahave, and Banyarwanda all lived in that place. All of these groups had chiefs. I lived in Rutshuru and it was like Rwanda."[88] Another was even clearer on the openness of the question of belonging in the area where he settled. "The local people where we settled were Bahunde, Banande, and Banyarwanda Bahutu and Batutsi. The Banyarwanda were just like the indigenous people there."[89] Another former refugee buttressed her remarks. "I lived for a year with my relatives who had migrated to Masisi earlier. That place had a lot of Banyarwanda migrants. It was like a district for the Banyarwanda. I don't even know which other people lived there. Some of my relatives were even chiefs there in Nyamitabo in Masisi."[90]

Beyond the fact that the refugees lived autonomously of local elites, their existence in many ways mirrored those of the rural refugees in the Forest Region of Guinea. The following sketch of the lives of the refugees is gathered from interviews in 2010 with former refugees who had since returned to Rwanda or resettled in Uganda. Although some lived in the refugee settlements such as Bibwe and Ihula created by UNHCR, many others self-settled. Some had relatives who had migrated to Congo earlier and went straight to them on their arrival from Rwanda. Others first went to the settlements and then sought employment in local communities. It was through these jobs that some moved out of the settlements into local communities.

---

[87] Interview (GLR 87).
[88] Interview (GLR 96).
[89] Interview GLR 100).
[90] Interview (GLR 101).

There were a few refugees who escaped with some resources and were able to set up shops in towns such as Goma and Bukavu. Most of the refugees lost their properties and went to Congo with almost nothing. Many survived by farming. The refugees in the settlements had enough land to farm there. Those who lived outside of the UNHCR settlement got small parcels to farm through relatives. Many refugees emphasized that accessing land in Kivu was very easy then. An old Munyarwanda migrant to Kivu who observed the arrival and short stay of many of the refugees pointed out that many of the refugees did not acquire large land parcels because of the short time they stayed in Congo.[91] To this we have to add their fixation on a quick return to Rwanda in those early days.[92]

Many refugees survived by selling their labor. Some worked for locals as farm hands. This included even those refugees who were in the settlements. Like in southwestern Uganda, this was often done to acquire staples such as bananas, cassava, and potatoes that the UNHCR did not supply the refugees. It was also done to get money to purchase clothes and other necessities. Refugees also worked as farm hands for early migrant Banyarwanda as well as Banyarwanda who were already in Kivu before the formation of the Congolese state. The early migrants had acquired significant parcels of land and were more involved in farming than the populations they met in Congo and so tended to employ more labor. It was common for Bahunde, Banande, and early Banyarwanda migrants and indigenes of the area to pay refugee laborers with food items such as bananas and potatoes instead of money. Some of the more fortunate refugees got jobs in the European plantations, which were thought to pay more. These workers often stayed on the plantations along with other laborers and visited the refugee settlement and self-settled relatives only occasionally.

However, the similarity between the refugees in the Forest Region of Guinea and Kivu is limited. When it came to their relationship with the local elite, these refugees were more similar to those in the Guinean capital of Conakry. The deliberate courting of friends that characterized relations between refugees and locals in the Forest Region of Guinea and southwestern Uganda did not exist. Neither were the frequent visits and the (sometimes exaggerated) shows of respect by refugees toward local elites. Also absent were the placing of refugee children with locals, naming of refugee children after locals, and frequent consultation of locals by

---

[91] Interview (GLR 96).
[92] Holborn, *Refugees*, 1078 and 1084.

refugees. Like in Conakry, the frequent exchange of gifts between refugees and locals did not exist, and local elites did not share legal responsibility for refugees.

There was a lot of contact between refugees and locals as I indicated earlier. Like in Conakry, there were some refugees who made Congolese friends. However, these relationships were not as deep as the friendships created in indigeneity-privileging areas like southwestern Uganda and the Forest Region of Guinea. They were devoid of the depth of subjugation that is causally relevant here. Many of the refugees seemed to have had no Congolese friends at all. The following quotes by a few former refugees drive home the point:

We met with the Bahunde in bars and made friends there sometimes. But we lacked the friendship that included visiting each other. We did not invite each other to social occasions. They were in their place and we were in ours. It was not common for refugees to visit the Congolese. They saw us walking around and said: "Those are Banyarwanda. Those are Batutsi."[93]

I used to go and work for the Banande and Bahunde in exchange for food. It was impossible to get a Congolese guardian. You only worked for them for the day and returned to the settlement. You did not have a strong relationship with them beyond working and getting paid. Relations with the chiefs were bad. No one cared about you. Some refugees got Congolese friends and they visited each other once a while. But there was not a strong culture of making friendships in Congo as there is here in Uganda. You only related with the Congolese by doing odd jobs for them. We did not give gifts to the chiefs while we were in the camps. We met the local people in public places. I worked in plantations with them.[94]

We used to buy brew from the Bahunde. We were friends with them since we went to buy their brew but we did not make strong friendships. We did not give gifts to chiefs in Masisi. We did not introduce ourselves to chiefs. I met Banande in the tea plantations where I worked. We picked tea leaves together. They were good people. They were like us and we ate and drank together.[95]

DEMONIZATION, UNCERTAINTY, AND ANTI-REFUGEE VIOLENCE

People stick the goat's ears on you so that the lion will eat you.[96]

Given the nature of these refugee–host relations in Kivu, the local Bahunde and Banande elites knew very little about the daily lives of the refugees

---

93 Interview (GLR 98).
94 Interview (GLR 101).
95 Interview (GLR 103).
96 Interview (GLR 6).

compared with the sort of information that Banyankore elites had about the Banyarwanda refugees in southwestern Uganda. Like in Conakry, the refugees were an unfamiliar quantity to locals, which made them very vulnerable to demonization.

Like in southwestern Uganda, state agents cleverly exploited this situation by couching their national program against the refugees in a locally relevant idiom. They saddled the newly arriving refugees with the baggage of what locals saw as the long history of infractions and impositions on them by Banyarwanda migrants in the area. I have already detailed these local grievances against and conflict with the Banyarwanda transmigrants in this chapter. State agents accused the refugees of aiding the Lumumbist rebels with the intention not only of overthrowing the Congolese government but also of eventually joining with early Tutsi migrants to dominate political life in North Kivu.[97] This raised the dire possibility of what many locals saw as the ongoing expropriation of their lands and domination of politics in the area by Banyarwanda migrants. The final end sought by the refugees and their migrant co-conspirators was said to be the formal transfer of Kivu from Congolese authority to the government of Rwanda. This was in a way similar to the UPC not only charging Banyarwanda refugees in Uganda with participation in the NRM struggle to overthrow the government of Uganda, but also with the even more locally sensitive offense of stealing the cattle of Banyankore to fund the NRM struggle.

I argue that the subjugation of Banyarwanda refugees to Banyankore elites in southwestern Uganda meant that these elites had enough information about the lives and activities of the refugees not to buy into the accusation. They knew enough about the refugees to conclude that most of them were neither cattle thieves nor NRM collaborators. This was not so for the counterparts of these refugees who went to Kivu. Because they were not subjugated to local elites, these elites knew little about the lives of the refugees. They were uncertain about what the refugees represented, and many swiftly bought into this demonization. Given how little they knew about the refugees, it did not appear particularly wise to most locals, even when they did not entirely believe in the state's denunciations, to wager their future on the innocence of the refugees. This is why Bahunde and Banande, like Guineans in Conakry, eagerly participated in attacks on the refugees.

It is tempting to explain the attacks on the refugees in terms of general interactions between Rwandophones and other populations in Kivu.

[97] Holborn, *Refugees*, 1088.

The argument here will be that locals seized on the opportunity to attack the refugees simply because of the long history of general resentment against Banyarwanda populations. I have already explored the ways in which the manner of the settlement of Banyarwanda in Kivu sparked local resentment and protests. The refugees, in local eyes, it could be said, represented just more of their enemies.[98] The resort to an argument about the refugees' autonomous lives will then be redundant. They were doomed from the start because of their identities as Banyarwanda in an environment characterized by high levels of xenophobia against Rwandophones.

This counterargument sounds appealing but has a significant flaw. The Banyarwanda refugees did not share a common past with the early migrants. Also, they had very different living conditions. And beyond this, in very significant ways, the refugees had a different vision of the future from long-term Banyarwanda residents of Kivu. So why did so many of the local people come to believe in this equation of refugees with early migrants? Why did they imagine these two *very different* populations as one that was guilty of the same sins and designs for the future? Why did this strategic superimposition of the Munyarwanda early migrant's ears on the head of the Munyarwanda refugee fool the indigenous population? This counterargument does not answer this question, and one cannot truly understand the attacks on the refugees without resolving this puzzle.

The need to understand this local embrace of the homogenization of the Banyarwanda refugees and Banyarwanda early migrants is important because there were very glaring distinctions between the two groups. The two populations occupied very distinct economic positions. Most of the early migrants had accumulated a lot of land and property in Congo and were mostly better off than the locals.[99] Many had huge plantations and some cattle. It is thus plausible to portray local resentment against such accumulation as the cause of conflicts with the early migrants. However, most of the refugees before 1964 were poorer than the locals and owned very little. The few who got land outside the refugee settlements most often had only small parcels. They came as refugees with little and had not accumulated much by 1964, when the expulsions happened. This was partly because of the short length of time they spent in Congo before the expulsions happened. Some arrived only a few months before the evictions. Also, these refugees, like many others across the continent,

---

[98] Lemarchand, *Rwanda and Burundi*, 210.
[99] Mararo, "Land conflicts in Masisi," 216.

believed they would return home quickly and were initially generally uninterested in accumulating wealth or making any long-term economic investment in Congo.[100] They were notoriously fixated on their past. When some of them were sent to Mwesi Settlement in Tanzania, they refused to accept ID cards issued by the government of Tanzania despite all of their benefits because they viewed acceptance of the cards as denial of their Rwandese nationality.[101]

Like refugees elsewhere on the continent, most of the refugees were destitute and sold their labor cheaply to farmers, including poor indigenous Bahunde, Banande, and Banyarwanda. One former refugee noted that the Bahunde used to call them "our poor people."[102] Another recalled that the Bahunde were greatly appreciative of the cheap refugee labor and spent their days drinking and saying "Thank God for giving us laborers."[103]

Unlike the early migrants who were asserting their political independence from indigenous populations,[104] the vast majority of refugees were involved in no such activity before 1964 when the expulsions happened. Even the refugee fighters who were involved in the Simba rebellions were not in a struggle to assert their rights against local populations. The lack of subjugation was not due to any resistance of local efforts at subordinating them. Like most civilian refugee populations, the vast majority of the Banyarwanda refugees were powerless people relative to their hosts.[105]

The two groups also had very different visions of the future. The early migrants were people who had fled Rwanda and generally had no intention of going back. They were in a struggle to ensure secure access to and enjoyment of Congolese citizenship. They were intent on building a life in their "new" country. Most of the refugees left Rwanda against their wishes and were hoping for a quick return. Acquiring secure Congolese citizenship was not a priority for most of them. As noted above, even the involvement of some of these refugees in the Lumumbist rebellion had nothing to do with a struggle for a secure future in Congo. It was for them a means of facilitating their armed and quick return to Rwanda. Unlike the early migrants and Tutsi Banyamulenge of South Kivu who were fighting

---

[100] Interview (GLR 97); and interview (GLR 101); Holborn, *Refugees*, 1078.
[101] Holborn, *Refugees*, 1165.
[102] Interview (GLR 97).
[103] Interview (GLR 96).
[104] Turner, *The Congo wars*, 117; Mamdani, *When victims become killers*, 241–242; and Vlassenroot, "Land and conflict," 85.
[105] Lemarchand, *Rwanda and Burundi*, 212.

to stay in Congo, the refugees were struggling to flee Congo and return to Rwanda.

These divergent visions led these populations to make very different choices on key issues. I already noted the participation of some of the predominantly Batutsi refugees in the Lumumbist rebellion. Importantly, the vast majority of the Batutsi Banyamulenge population of South Kivu who participated in the war fought on the side of the government and contributed significantly to defeating the rebels who included Tutsi refugees.[106] The Banyamulenge fled Rwanda toward the end of the 1800s under duress from what they considered excessive exactions from the Rwandese King *Mwami* Rwabugiri.[107] Like the early migrants, they had accumulated a lot of property in Congo and were dedicated to protecting their Congolese citizenship.[108] As Vlassenroot noted, "Banyamulenge were not very keen on the egalitarian discourse produced by the Simba, especially where their herds were concerned. For the Banyamulenge pastoralists, the ideology of the APL came down to... the free distribution of their cattle with the Babembe [Lumumbist rebels]."[109] The newly arriving refugees had little property to speak of, and it was understandable that they were not particularly concerned about the redistributive schemes of the Simba rebels.

The fact that Rwandophones in Kivu do not always share the same past and designs for the future or have the same interest is not one that escaped the non-Rwandophone populations in the area. The struggle of the Tutsi Banyamulenge and some of the Batutsi refugees on different sides of the Lumumbist rebellion was an obvious demonstration of this to those involved in the struggle. Also, in the early 1960s, Bahunde politicians in Kivu often were involved in denunciations and protests that did not group all Rwandophones together. They often singled out the Batutsi for demonization and identified the Bahunde and Bahutu Rwandophones as joint victims of Batutsi scheming.[110] This differentiation between Bahutu and Batutsi Rwandophones was to become stronger when predominantly Bahutu Rwandese refugees arrived in Congo in 1994. The Hutu ex-FAR and *Interahamwe* collaborated with local *Mayi Mayi* militias to attack

---

[106] Turner, *The Congo wars*, 86; Vlassenroot, "Identity formation," 504; and Pottier, "Modern information warfare," 223.

[107] Pottier, "Modern information warfare," 221; and Vlassenroot, "Identity formation," 502.

[108] Turner, *The Congo wars*, 87.

[109] Vlassenroot, "Identity formation," 503.

[110] Lemarchand, *Rwanda and Burundi*, 211.

Banyamulenge in South Kivu.[111] The Tutsi-dominated army of Rwanda, the Rwandan Patriotic Army (RPA), and Tutsi Banyamulenge fought each other and the RPA was even suspected of aiding *Mayi Mayi* militia to attack Banyamulenge communities in a bid to bring the Banyamulenge under the influence of the RPA.[112]

If locals, rightly, do not always automatically assume a unity of interest among all Rwandophones, then one has to account for why they were willing to heap all of their frustrations against old Banyarwanda migrants on the Batutsi refugees in 1964. It is important to keep in mind that the vast majority of these refugees were poor and powerless people selling their labor to locals, including Bahunde and Banande peasants. Why were many Bahunde and Banande willing to believe that these "refugees, who [were] peacefully resettled in the virgin forest" and fixated on a quick return to Rwanda were guilty of "murder, arson, violence"[113] and of planning to expropriate and ultimately dominate local communities? I argue that the opacity of the refugees' lives due to their non-subjugation to local elites made it highly likely that locals will buy into such charges against the refugees. It made it likely that they will at least entertain enough doubt about what the refugees represented not to want to place their bets on their innocence.

To make this argument is not to deny the fact of anti-Rwandophone sentiments in Kivu at the time. It is to assert that these sentiments and the real history of expropriation and political conflicts that they were based on cannot help us understand the attacks on the refugees. One has to account for why, despite all of the glaring and highly salient differences between the vast majority of the refugees and the early Banyarwanda migrants, many locals viewed these two communities as one and heaped all the "sins" of the migrants on the refugees. One has to explore imaginaries and their structural conditions, and this is what I try to do here. The history of Rwandophones and anti-Rwandophone sentiments in Kivu is important because it acted as the fulcrum on which the eloquent narratives about Banyarwanda refugee plots were constructed. However, given that these narratives were mostly fictional, even if highly eloquent and imaginative, we have to account for why locals embraced and acted on them nonetheless. My argument is that the paucity of local knowledge about the daily lives of the refugees and the Belgian promotion of

---

[111] Vlassenroot, "Identity formation," 512.
[112] Ibid., 512–513.
[113] Lemarchand, *Rwanda and Burundi*, 212.

residence as an organizing principle in the area that caused it constitute promising explanations.

On August 11, 1964, the Congolese Army started to arrest all refugees around Bukavu, and this was followed on the 19th by the formal order to expel and seize all properties of the Banyarwanda refugees.[114] Like in Conakry, this was during a period of dangerous political uncertainty. The Simba rebels who were sweeping across the east of the country had a fearsome reputation as both ill-disciplined and brutal in their treatment of perceived opponents.[115] They subjected Rega people, who were seen as opponents of the Bembe who heavily participated in the rebellion, to murderous violence.[116] In towns that they conquered, they routinely killed many people, "including government officials, political leaders of opposition parties, provincial and local police, school teachers, and others believed to have been westernized."[117]

It was in this context that locals to whom the refugees mostly represented an unknown quantity received the messages about refugee scheming against locals and their participation in the rebellion. It was easy for many of the locals to believe in the accusations levied by government authorities given the little that they knew about the refugees. Even when they did not entirely buy the story, it must have been hard for them to wager their future on the innocence of the refugees, given the opacity of the lives of the refugees.

Many Bahunde and Banande opted for what seemed like the safer path of expelling the refugees. They zealously joined state security agents in the attacks on the refugees. Villages held meetings and sometimes distributed weapons to be used in the operations. Like in Conakry, despite the autonomous lives of the refugees, some of them had succeeded against all odds to cultivate deep friendships with locals. These locals warned the refugees of the impending violence and told them to flee.[118] However, also like in Conakry, the vast majority of the refugees did not enjoy similar benefits. There were mass arrests, killings, rapes, and the destruction and seizure of properties. The refugees who were fortunate to escape the ordeal often walked to the borders of neighboring countries.

---

[114] Holborn, *Refugees*, 1093.
[115] Turner, *The Congo wars*, 33; and Weissman, *American foreign policy*, 220.
[116] Koen Vlassenroot and Timothy Raeymaekers, "Conflict and artisan mining in Kamituga (South Kivu)," in *Conflict and social transformation in Easter DR Congo*, ed. Koen Vlassenroot and Timothy Raeymaekers (Gent: Academia press, 2004), 126.
[117] Lemarchand, "Historical setting," 41.
[118] Interview (GLR 96).

ON SETTLEMENT PATTERNS AND RESOURCE COMPETITION

Settlement Patterns

The fact that these evictions targeted camp as well as self-settled refugees brings into focus some of the implications that are sometimes drawn from refugee self-settlement as opposed to settlement in camps. It has been argued that the ways in which refugees settle has a determinate effect on their chances of integration and the nature of their interactions with the host community.[119] In making this argument, scholars often focus on the distinction between refugees who live in camps and those who self-settle among local populations. Some claim that settlement in camps is a better way of ensuring positive refugee–host relations, whereas others argue the opposite.[120,121]

I contend here that this debate is problematic because the critical characteristics that are said to distinguish camp refugees from self-settled ones and that have differential effects on refugee–host relations do not necessarily exist. Because we cannot always make these distinctions between camp and self-settled refugee life, we cannot draw strong conclusions

[119] Liisa Malkki, *Purity in exile: violence, memory, and national cosmology among Hutu refugees in Tanzania* (Chicago: University of Chicago Press, 1995); Art Hansen, "Refugee dynamics: Angolans in Zambia 1966 to 1972," *International Migration Review* 15 (Spring–Summer 1981): 175–194; Hansen, "Once the running stops"; Khiddu-Makubuya, "Voluntary repatriation"; Tom Kuhlman, "Organized versus spontaneous settlement of refugees in Africa," in *African refugees: development aid and repatriation,* ed. Howard Adelman and John Sorenson (Boulder: Westview Press, 1994); Jacobson, "Refugees' environmental impact"; Kibreab, "Local settlements"; and Chambers, "Rural refugees in Africa."

[120] Kibreab, "Local settlements'; Kuhlman, "Organized versus spontaneous"; and Jacobson, "Refugees' environmental impact,' reflect on both sides of this debate. The following works offer strong support for the benefits of self-settlement. Hansen, "Refugee dynamics," pp. 192–194; Hansen, "Once the running stops," pp. 369–370; Khiddu-Makubuya, "Voluntary repatriation"; 378–379; Zartman, "Portuguese Guinean refugees," 158; Malkki, *Purity in exile,* p. 16. For an opposing view, see Chambers, "Rural refugees in Africa." Barbara Harrel-Bond, "Are refugee camps good for children," p. 1.

[121] Kibreab, "Local settlements"; Kuhlman, "Organized versus spontaneous"; and Jacobson, "Refugees' environmental impact," reflect on both sides of this debate. The following works offer strong support for the benefits of self-settlement. Hansen, "Refugee dynamics," 192–194; Hansen, "Once the running stops," 369–370; Khiddu-Makubuya, "Voluntary repatriation"; 378–379;\in le dectures de s..pytoff eds Zartman,\in le dectures de s..pytoff eds "Portuguese Guinean refugees," 158; Malkki, *Purity in exile,* 16. For an opposing view, see Chambers, "Rural refugees in Africa" and Barbara Harrel-Bond, "Are refugee camps good for children," 1.

about the nature of refugee–host relations based on whether refugees live in camps or are self-settled.

There are various reasons why camp life may be said to reduce the chances of refugee–host conflict in comparison with self-settled life. Refugees in camps are said to be secluded from the local population, reducing interactions and thus the possibility of conflict. Furthermore, because they are secluded, they are unlikely to compete economically with locals for jobs and other resources.[122] The lower competition is also due to the fact that refugees in camps are more likely to receive aid than self-settled ones because they are usually more visible. Often they are placed in such camps either by or with the help of international agencies like UNHCR. Their concentration also facilitates the delivery of aid and services.[123] Such aid reduces the need of these refugees to depend on local resources and thus annoy locals who may be even more impoverished than refugees. Self-settlement, it is argued, often leads to the impoverishment of both refugees and locals,[124] creating a conflict-prone environment.

The congregation of refugees in camps also creates a very visible situation that host states and nongovernmental organizations (NGOs) can use to appeal for help that goes beyond aid for refugees to development aid touching the host population and the country as a whole.[125] This aid to the wider population could enhance local goodwill toward the refugees. Such aid also creates a flow of resources that powerful state and local officials can dip their hands into for private gains. This might motivate leaders to protect refugees on whose presence all of these benefits depend. In comparison, self-settled refugees largely maintain a low profile and so are hard to use as arguments for aid by host states and NGOs. Aid agencies sometimes deliberately neglect helping these refugees because of the assumption that they are receiving help from their hosts, unlike those in camps.[126]

---

[122] Kibreab, "Local settlements," 474; and Jacobson, "Refugees' environmental impact," 23.

[123] Kuhlman, "Organized versus spontaneous," 123; and Shelly Dick, "Liberians in Ghana: living without humanitarian assistance," *New Issues in Refugee Research* 57 (February 2002): 2.

[124] Chambers, "Rural refugees in Africa," 386 and 388.

[125] Harrell-Bond, *Imposing aid*, 8; Kibreab, "Local settlements," 485; and Kuhlman, "Organized versus spontaneous," 122.

[126] Chambers, "Rural refugees in Africa," 286.

The partisans of self-settlement reject such arguments. They point out that because self-settled refugees are forced to deal with locals, they learn through repeated interactions how to fit into host communities.[127] This should lead to lesser possibility for violent conflict in the long run. Secluded camp refugees often do not learn how to deal with locals,[128] making the possibility of violence resulting from any conflicts higher. Also, because self-settled refugees most often do not receive aid, unlike camp refugees, they are less likely to arouse jealousy and violence from local communities who may feel unjustly marginalized. Some have pointed to such local jealousy over aid received by refugees as central to anti-refugee sentiments and violence.[129]

The partisans of self-settlement may concede that self-settled refugees are more likely to compete with locals for jobs. However, they would argue that because they most often do not receive aid, they are unlikely to undercut wages as badly as aid-receiving camp refugees. This limits resentment toward them from local workers. Because camp refugees receive aid, they usually can afford to sell their labor at extremely low rates. Their wages are in effect subsidized by the aid they receive. This makes life much worse for locals who do not receive aid but have to compete for the same jobs.[130] The resulting desperation among local workers can spur violence against refugees.

The supporters of self-settlement even counter that, in the long run, it better aids the achievement of self-sufficiency by refugees in that they assume responsibility for their own lives and get integrated into local economies in more permanent ways.[131] Camp refugees often do not really get integrated into local economies in ways that will survive the cessation of aid.[132]

A Problematic Argument

The problem with this debate is that it is based on dichotomies that often do not characterize actual processes on the ground in

---

[127] Malkki, *Purity in exile*, 16; and Jacobson, "Refugees' environmental impact," 26.
[128] Jacobson, "Refugees' environmental impact," 26.
[129] Duncan, "Unwelcome guests," 29; and Jacobson, "Refugees' environmental impact," 26.
[130] Chambers, "Hidden losers?" 252.
[131] Jacobson, "Refugees' environmental impact," 122.
[132] Kibreab, "Local settlements," 470–472.

refugee-affected areas. This "compartmentalized"[133] approach to camp and self-settlement frequently largely deviates from social realities. One of these distinctions claims that camp refugees are secluded from local communities unlike self-settled ones that are dispersed in them. As Van Hear noted, "camps may also be sites of connection and link. People in camps, or at least some people in some camps, are plugged into transnational networks."[134]

Many camp refugees interact freely with neighboring local communities.[135] For many refugees, belonging to a camp and being self-settled are not mutually exclusive. Many not only are registered in and do spend time in camps but also spend a lot of their time living in local communities where they seek to build their lives. Some split up their families, leaving the older and less able refugees in camps while sending the more able ones to self-settle among local communities.[136] Accounts from Guinea, eastern Sudan, southwestern Uganda, Tanzania, Kenya, and my own observations from Ghana, among others, provide evidence that refugee camps have not always secluded refugees from local populations.[137] Whether camps separate refugees from local populations or not should be an empirical question, not an a priori one. It is dependent on the type of camp, its distance from local population centers, state refugee policies, and so forth. The implications for refugee–host relations drawn from this presumed distinction between camp and self-settled life are thus problematic.

A second problematic dichotomy is that which portrays camp refugees as recipients of aid who thus do not have to compete with locals for resources and jobs, unlike self-settled refugees. Camp refugees very frequently also compete for resources and jobs with locals. This is because due to corruption and dysfunctional aid agency policies, some deserving refugees do not get any aid at all or do not get as much as they need. Furthermore, supplies are sometimes irregular and hard to predict. Food meant to last for a month might have to serve for two or three months as supply dates get postponed. Furthermore, refugees often are not provided

---

[133] Van Hear, "From durable solutions," 3.
[134] Ibid., 3.
[135] Jacobson, *The economic life of refugees*, 7.
[136] Van Damme, "How Liberian," 50; Jacobson, *The economic life of refugees*, 7; and Dick, "Liberian in Ghana," 8.
[137] Kibreab, *Ready and willing*; Whitaker, "Refugees in Western Tanzania"; Watson, "Exile from Rwanda"; Van Damme, "How Liberian"; and de Montclos and Kagwanja, "Refugee camps or cities?" 212.

with all their needs, so they sometimes work to get money to buy things like clothes, soap and so forth. All of this means that camp refugees regularly work to ensure their survival just like self-settled refugees.

A third dichotomy distinguishes between aid-receiving refugees that severely undercut wages and self-settled ones who do not. This dichotomy is very problematic because it reduces the amount of wages refugees receive to a question of the will of refugees and removes issues of power and destitution from consideration. Self-settled refugees do not undercut wages too badly because they cannot afford to, it is implied. Aid-receiving camp refugees undercut wages badly because they can afford to.[138]

Contrary to this account, wage levels are heavily dependent also on issues of power and destitution and not just on the will of refugees. When I interviewed aid-receiving Sierra Leonean and Liberian refugees who were in Guinea, they did not put the low wages they received down to their willingness to accept these wages because they were receiving aid. They put them down to their powerlessness and destitution. They wanted and would have gladly received higher wages but could not exert the necessary influence to get those wages. Self-settled refugees may need and want higher wages, but if they lack the power to extract such wages, local employers are not going to hand it to them anyway. The lack of legal rights to work, organize in support of their interests, and engage in forceful advocacy often puts refugees at the mercy of employers.[139] This lack of rights is often the very reason why employers tend to prefer such workers.[140] The economic destitution of refugees is likely to compromise their ability to negotiate the higher wages that they need. I was shocked by how little many self-settled refugees were paid for a day's labor in

---

[138] Whitaker, "Refugees in Western Tanzania," 348; Walter Kok, "Self-settled refugees and the socio-eocnomic impact of their presence on Kassala, Eastern Sudan," *Journal of Refugee Studies* 2, No. 4 (1989): 435 and 438; Catherine Brun, "Not only about survival: livelihood strategies in protracted displacement," in *In the maze of displacement: conflict, migration and change*, ed. N. Shanmugaratnam, Ragnhild Lund and Kristi Anne Stolen (Kristiansand S., Norway: HoyskoleForlaget, 2003), 36; Chambers, "Hidden losers?" 252; and Kuhlman, "Organized versus spontaneous," 134.

[139] Kok, "Self-settled refugees," 438.

[140] Kok, "Self-settled refugees," 433; F. Zackariya and N. Shanmugaratnam, "Moving into the extra household domain: survival struggles of displaced Muslim women in Sri Lanka," in *In the maze of displacement: conflict, migration and change*, ed. N. Shanmugaratnam, Ragnhild Lund, and Kristi Anne Stolen (Kristiansand S., Norway: HoyskoleForlaget, 2003), 57; and Jonathan Bascom, "The peasant economy of refugee resettlement in Eastern Sudan," *Annals of the Association of American Geographers* 83 (June 1993): 337.

Guinea. A kilo of rice was often enough to get a father, mother, and their children to work on a farm for the whole day. Aid-receiving camp refugees in the area were given the same wage. The employers who were generous would often throw in an afternoon meal. If those refugees did not get higher wages, it was not because they did not want it. They lacked the power to extract the sort of wages that would have improved their lives.

A final dichotomy that I want to explore here is that between aid-receiving camp refugees that attract jealousy from local populations and non–aid-receiving refugees who do not. What those who make this argument often overlook is that frequently, locals consume some of the aid meant for refugees. Sometimes, many deserving refugees are deprived of this aid, whereas locals who have no claim to refugee status enjoy them. One resident of Njalah in Sierra Leone who was a refugee in Kelema, Guinea, told me:

> When the registration and supplies started, the Guineans also went and got registered and took supplies. They told us: "You people are here under us so you should know that the supplies do not taste sweet only in your mouths. We are going to eat it together." If any refugee dared protest they had big problems. Sometimes they even took your own supply card from you.[141]

Reports of local people registering for and collecting refugee supplies were widespread and were confirmed by both former refugees and Guineans in those communities.[142] Many refugees aided their Guinean friends and hosts to get registered and access supplies.[143] When locals were not registered to collect supplies, their refugee friends often gave them part of the supplies they received.[144] Even when locals did not get some of the supplies, they often appreciated it because the arrival of supplies saved them from the job of feeding and caring for the refugees out of their own

---

[141] Interview with a Sierra Leonean in Njalah, Penguia Chiefdom, Sierra Leone (MRB 285), September 15, 2009.

[142] Interviews with a Guinean in Kolomba, Guéckédou (MRB 102), June 19, 2009; interview (MRB 100); interview Guéckédou (MRB 115); interview with a Guinean in Komou, Yomou Prefecture, Guinea (MRB 157), July 21, 2009; and interview (MRB 160). Robert Chambers describes a similar situation in Zambia's Eastern Province, which had received Mozambican refugees in the 1960s. "Rural refugees in Africa," 388.

[143] Interview (MRB 165); interview Guéckédou (MRB 100); and interview with a Guinean in Vianga, Yomou Prefecture, Guinea (MRB 168), July 23, 2009.

[144] Interview Guéckédou (MRB 103); interview (MRB 159); interview with a Guinean in Kelema, Guéckédou Prefecture, Guinea (MRB 118), June 21, 2009; and interview with a Guinean in Foedou-Kollet, Guéckédou Prefecture, Guinea (MRB 146); June 29, 2009.

meager stocks.[145] The portrayal of aid uniquely targeted at refugees as something that locals always resent[146] is a mistaken one.

Of critical importance here is that although ordinary locals can also dip into the pot of benefits, it is often the most powerful locals who benefit the most from the system. In Guinea, well-placed people were known to have tens of ration cards each for multiple dependents. They collected large quantities of supplies that they then traded in stores in towns such as Guéckédou, Kissidougou, and N'Zérékoré.[147] These people can use their power to prevent even those disadvantaged by the presence of refugees from using violence against the refugees. The suggestion thus that locals would be jealous of and would use violence against refugees just on account of their receipt of aid is somewhat exaggerated and might be a conclusion drawn from the examination of only a few cases whose circumstances may not apply to many other contexts.

The camp versus self-settlement debate sheds little light on why locals undertake generalized anti-refugee violence in some situations but not in others because it is built on too many problematic dichotomies.

Scarcity and Resource Competition

A reflection on the circumstances surrounding the eviction of Banyarwanda refugees in Kivu and southwestern Uganda raises questions about the promise that one of the key theories deployed to account for intercommunal violence has for understanding refugee–host relations. This is the argument that focuses on scarcity and competition over economic resources. The arrival of hordes of refugees in an area often increases the use of natural resources like water, grazing and arable land, and firewood in significant ways. This is almost always true when refugees arrive first and lack any institutionalized system of support.[148] Where such a system is created it can act as an alternative source of livelihood for refugees, thus easing the pressure they put on local resources. In cases in which this pressure on resources persists and threatens the livelihoods of local populations, it can spur local resentment against the refugees that can

---

[145] Interview with a Guinean in Kiligbema, Guéckédou Prefecture, Guinea (MRB 143) June 28, 2009.

[146] Bakewell, for instance, asserted that "The focus of aid efforts on refugees immediately drives a wedge between local hosts and the refugees, especially when the refugees arrive in very remote areas of great poverty." "Refugee aid and rural protection," 4.

[147] Interview (MRB 276).

[148] Jacobson, "Refugees' environmental impact," 19–21.

lead to anti-refugee violence.[149] The extent to which competition arises will depend on the skill sets, assets, and resource use patterns of refugees and locals.[150]

The scarcity and economic competition that results from the arrival of refugees can sour relations with locals even when they were at first very friendly. It is partly in an effort to prevent the dangerous consequences of such scarcity and competition that some advocate the seclusion of and provision of aid to refugees. It is argued that this reduces the extent to which refugees depend on local resources, thus lessening local discontent over refugees.

Many scholars of the refugee situation in Uganda have pointed to increasing refugee access to land and jobs and the pressure that this puts on the local population as part of the explanation for the eviction of Banyarwanda.[151] Many locals and former refugees in southwestern Uganda also resort to the economic competition argument to account for the evictions.[152]

On close inspection the circumstances of the anti-refugee attacks in Uganda and Kivu severely undermine this resort to economic competition. On one hand the local population participated heavily in the evictions of the refugees in Congo. Importantly, these refugees had stayed there for at most five years and most had stayed for far shorter. Most of them were destitute and poor, uninterested in accumulating wealth and land in Congo, and acted as cheap labor for locals. Few had acquired any parcels of land outside of the refugee settlements. Their access to public sector jobs was rather limited. Despite all of this, locals embraced the anti-refugee attacks. This was not limited to lower class locals who might have been disadvantaged by refugees who competed with them for work as farm hands. Even the chiefs and peasants who employed refugees as cheap farm hands joined in the attacks.

On the other hand, the locals refrained from joining state agents to attack refugees in southwestern Uganda. Unlike their counterparts in

---

[149] Bascom, "The peasant economy," 336; Jon Unruh, "Refugee resettlement on the horn of Africa: the integration of refugee and host land use patters," *Land Use Policy* 10 (January 1993): 49–50.

[150] Belinda Dodson and Catherine Oelofse, "Shades of xenophobia: in-migrants and immigrants in Mizamoyethu, Cape Town," in *Transnationalism and new African immigration to South Africa*, ed. Jonathan Crush and David McDonald (Cape Town: Southern African Migration Project and Canadian Association of African Studies, 2002), 138.

[151] Mushemeza, *Banyarwanda refugees*, 90–91; Twine Said, "The Banyarwanda citizenship question in Uganda: a case study of Ntungamo district 1959–2002" (M.A. diss., Makerere University, 2008), 87; and Clay, *The eviction of Banyarwanda*, 7.

[152] Republic of Uganda, *The report of the Commission*, 503.

Kivu, many of the refugees in southwestern Uganda had been resident there for more than twenty years. With time, many came to acquire land outside of the refugee settlements, and some of them became large landholders. Many acquired jobs in both the public and private sectors.[153] There were many in educational institutions. This was all in a situation in which employment and access to education were becoming increasingly difficult for locals. It caused a lot of resentment against the refugees.[154] The UPC leaders who masterminded the evictions spent a lot of time reminding locals of the economic stress they faced on account of the refugees.[155] In 1969, President Obote ordered that all Banyarwanda refugees be removed from public service jobs.[156] Just before the exercise he even accused the refugees of forcing locals into becoming "refugees in their own country" through their abuse of the hospitality granted them.[157] Despite all of this, the local population refrained from getting involved in the evictions.

Scarcity and economic competition do not provide a good explanation of generalized anti-refugee violence by local communities for two reasons. One of these is that it is too deterministic. It sees increasing scarcity and competition, inevitably leading to violence. This determinism is a frightening aspect of the Malthusian environmental security literature, which generates the specter of increasing resource scarcity, inevitably causing civil and international wars.[158] The ironclad determinism gives too little credence to variations in how people manage and adapt to these situations of increasing scarcity and competition.[159] It is plausible to see situations in which people try to manage such competition in peaceful ways and even collaborate to increase resilience and invent survival strategies.

The second and bigger problem of this scarcity and resource competition explanation is that it is at best an incomplete one. It suffers from a necessary account of power dynamics in local communities. This account of power dynamics is necessary because the local community is not one homogenous entity. It is made up of different groups with diverse

---

153 Namusisi, "The plight of Rwandese refugees," 31; and Clay, *The eviction of Banyarwanda*, 17.
154 Mushemeza, *Banyarwanda refugees*, 90–91.
155 Clay, *The eviction of Banyarwanda*, 7.
156 Republic of Uganda, *The report of the Commission*, 498.
157 Cited in Clay, *The eviction of Banyarwanda*, 33.
158 Thomas Homer-Dixon, *Environment, scarcity and violence* (Princeton, NJ: Princeton University Press, 1999), 177.
159 Nancy Lee Peluso and Michael Watts, "Violent environments," in *Violent environments*, ed. Nancy Lee Peluso and Michael Watts (Ithaca: Cornell University Press, 2001), 5.

and sometimes conflicting interests that are affected in different ways by the scarcity and competition that might result from the presence of refugees.[160] One example here makes this point clear. Refugees frequently constitute a reserve of low-wage laborers who compete with locals for work. This often leads to the reduction of jobs available for locals as well as the undercutting of wages, as refugees lacking much bargaining power work for lower wages. This tragedy for local low wage laborers is, however, often a boon for local employers. They get a larger labor pool to hire from at lower wages. Furthermore, they no longer have to bother with "troublesome" locals, as they employ more pliant and powerless refugees.[161]

Seen from this point of view, the problem of the scarcity and competition argument is that the presence of competition does not really tell us much about the likelihood of violence against refugees. If the most powerful members of society who have a lot of control over the use of violence in these societies are the beneficiaries of the scarcity and competition caused by refugees, why should we expect them to allow the less fortunate members of society to attack refugees? We can expect these powerful people to use their influence to protect refugees from violent attacks. Scarcity and competition on their own do not constitute a good explanation of these attacks because of this.

CONCLUSION

In presenting us with a rural setting where residence had overshadowed indigeneity as an organizing principle and where the civilian population launched large-scale attacks on refugees, this chapter serves very important functions in this book. It shows that rural spaces do not necessarily privilege indigeneity as an organizing principle and that refugees are not necessarily safe from such attacks at the hands of their local neighbors in rural settings. The distinction drawn between indigeneity and residence-privileging societies is not just a more fancy way of distinguishing between rural and urban areas.

---

[160] Kuhlman, *Burden or boon*, 63; and Whitaker, "Refugees in Western Tanzania"; and Chambers, "Rural refugees in Africa," pp. 388–389.

[161] Brun, "Not only about survival," 36.

8

Conclusion

Then we had nothing. We wore the same clothes for days. We had to go to the stream, wash our clothes, and wait for them to get dry before putting them back on.[1]

ON GENERAL LESSONS

It is important to once again delimit the outcomes under study here as large-scale campaigns of violence against refugees. This study does not seek to make statements about opportunistic attacks on individual refugees or the well-being of refugees in general. I have already noted the ways in which the absence of large-scale anti-refugee violence can coincide with the presence of more particularized victimization of refugees. This explanation will probably not work for more particularistic attacks. This is because even highly capable states and local notables are unlikely to have the capacity to deter such violence.

It is important then not to read this book as a glorification of areas that privilege indigeneity as an organizing principle. There is literature indicating that refugees in indigeneity-privileging areas, far beyond the cases I focus on here, are subjugated to local notables in ways that compromise their rights to an autonomous existence on a daily basis.[2] They are deprived of the right to personal autonomy and in many ways are reduced to the position of minors. They are marked out as strangers

---

[1] Interview (MRB 219).
[2] Harrell-Bond, *Imposing aid*, 90–94; Art Hansen, "Refugee dynamics," 185–187 and 191; and Hansen, "Once the running stops," 370–371.

and sometimes subjected to various acts of discrimination. However, it is this very subjugation and the infringements it is constituted of that ensure their safety from generalized attacks at the hands of local elites. Similarly, the claim about how settlement in residence-privileging areas contributes to the autonomy of refugees is one that is attested to in many cases beyond those studied here.[3]

The argument that settlement in such residence-privileging areas contributes more to such generalized attacks than refuge in indigeneity-privileging ones is counterintuitive. This book shows the trade-offs that are involved in settlement in these two types of areas. The refugees in residence-privileging societies are autonomous of local notables, can mix with the local population relatively easily, and can more easily escape the everyday discrimination that comes with being marked out as a stranger. However, they are more susceptible to rare outbreaks of large-scale violence. Although the indigeneity-privileging society does not represent an unmitigated evil, the residence-privileging one also does not constitute a good without significant shortcomings. Each of these spaces has its advantages and disadvantages for the refugee.

This means that the push to transform societies that privilege indigeneity toward the privileging of residence and vice versa is not a policy recommendation that this book puts forward to better the lives of refugees and refugee–host relations. This is partly because the shift from one type of society to another is a long structural process that is not easily susceptible to short-term tinkering. Furthermore, a successful campaign at pushing societies from either end of the continuum to the other will not come without its own costs to refugees and society as a whole.

The insight into the often-elided positive possibilities of spaces that privilege indigeneity is not new. Authors, including McGovern, Murphy, Bledsoe, and Colson,[4] have all commented on the ways in which the principle of autochthony undergirded highly incorporative societies in precolonial Africa. Latecomers in these societies were subjugated to earlier arrivals. However, through various incorporative processes, they over time got assimilated by the host populations and acquired citizenship rights that were often as unimpeachable as those of earlier arrivals.[5] This

---

[3] Marc Sommers, *Fear in Bongoland: Burundi refugees in urban Tanzania* (New York: Berghahn Books, 2001).

[4] Colson, "The assimilation of aliens"; Murphy and Bledsoe, "Kinship and territory"; and McGovern, "Unmasking the state."

[5] Colson, "The assimilation of aliens," 36.

point needs to be repeated, for recent work tends to highlight the exclusionary potential of autochthony and nativism without emphasizing their incorporative possibilities.[6]

Recognition of the contradictory potential of both indigeneity and residence-privileging societies is what this work calls for. Like many social institutions and ordering principles, these two modes of distributing rights in society do not each guarantee only one outcome when it comes to relations between refugees and local populations.

What this work contributes to the literature is establishment of an original causal path through which residence-privileging and indigeneity-privileging societies tend to affect the chances that refugees will suffer generalized attacks at the hands of local populations. In pointing out the relative effects of these two types of societies on local knowledge of what refugees represent, I contribute to the literature that emphasizes the roles that knowledge, uncertainty, and doubt play in outbreaks of intercommunal violence.[7]

This explanation, which focuses on knowledge and uncertainty, is particularly suited to the explanation of violence against civilian refugees. Because of their relatively disempowered character and the rarity of their involvement in local politics, issues such as struggles over power and economic competition that might be effective in explaining intercommunal violence between citizens offer only limited promise for understanding violence against refugees.

WEALTH IN PEOPLE

The recourse to a distinction between indigeneity and residence-privileging societies to explain the subjugation or autonomy of refugees is one that might be questioned from the standpoint of the rich literature on wealth in people.[8] This literature points out that in Africa, unlike in Europe, because of low population densities, people tended to privilege wealth in people over wealth in things. Wealth in people transformed

[6] For example, see Geschiere, *The perils of belonging*; Nyamnjoh, *Insiders and outsiders*, 141.

[7] Appadurai, "Dead Certainty"; Hoffman, *Doubt, time, violence*; and Bauman, *Postmodernity*.

[8] For contributions to this literature, see Jane Guyer, "Wealth in people and self-realization in Equatorial Africa," *Man* 28 (2–1993): 243–265; Ceuppens and Geschiere, "Autochthony," 396; Geschiere, *The perils of belonging*, 23; Bledsoe, *Women and marriage*, 81; and Bledsoe, "The manipulation," 31.

readily available land into productive farms, engaged in economic activities that generated income that could be taxed, and reinforced the political positions of patrons. This explained why societies coveted strangers and sought to lure, welcome, and incorporate them. Bledsoe adds to this literature by pointing out how this covetousness of people has declined in economically depressed urban areas where the possibilities for transforming a large following into money and power were limited.[9]

This literature provides a competing explanation for why some refugees are subjugated and others autonomous. It could be that refugees who settle in areas where land is abundant like the Forest Region of Guinea and southwestern Uganda are subjugated because of the operation of the principle of wealth in people. The autonomous lives of the refugees in Conakry might then be put down to the cost of maintaining a following in an urban area and the limited possibility of squeezing gains and power out of clients in such a land and job scarce environment. The resort to whether societies privilege indigeneity or residence in apportioning rights will then be misleading or at best redundant.

The design of the study immediately reveals a problem that this argument runs into. Kivu was largely rural with low population densities like southwestern Uganda and the Forest Region of Guinea. Despite this, the refugees indicated that they lived autonomously of local elite.

The wealth in people argument cannot account for the ways in which hosts embrace strangers. It can only account for whether or not they embrace strangers. In other words, the political–economic need for people cannot explain the specific institutional design that the harnessing of people takes in societies. This is because there are always multiple ways of embracing strangers. Bledsoe noted a few:

Because land in traditional areas of Africa is generally plentiful human labor here largely determines productive success. Wealth and security therefore rest on the control of others.... Subordinates in Kpelle society may be acquired through institutions such as marriage, filiation, wardship, clientage, slavery (in the past), pawnship, and secret societies.[10]

To these we can add pure wage relations. The form that the embrace of strangers takes depends on sociopolitical factors that go beyond the mere political economic need for people and the labor and political support they represent.

---

[9] Bledsoe, "The manipulation," 35.
[10] Bledsoe, "The manipulation," 31. Also see Bledsoe, *Women and marriage*, 60–79.

In the Forest Region of Guinea as well as southwestern Uganda, I noticed a phenomenon that was rather puzzling given the literature on wealth in people. This literature had led me to believe that villagers in these land-rich areas would queue to host strangers, that there would be a mad rush to take in strangers. Colson captured this expectation brilliantly in her exploration of stranger–local relations among the Tonga of Zambia:

> The newcomer in a Tonga neighborhood is fair game to the first comer, and the first comer arrives rather promptly. He views the stranger as a treasure trove, as an asset to be used in advancing his own interests . . . Alliance is the common tool for subjugating the stranger, but the stranger may be viewed as patron, equal, or client depending upon his strength and status. The poor man is given accommodation and food for a limited period and is then expected to begin working for his host, who in turn, sponsors him before the rest of the community.[11]

It is with such ideas in the back of my mind that I noticed the rather "weird" fact that in the Forest Region of Guinea, many communities had laws requiring villagers to host refugees. They often threatened to punish those who were found not hosting refugees. Furthermore, chiefs sometimes had to go from house to house to negotiate the hosting of refugees with locals. This is how the then chief of the village of Dongueta in Banie Sub-Prefecture put it:

> When the refugees started arriving, I was the chief here. We had to take care of them and feed them. We told everyone in the town "We have strangers and we have to take care of them, give them places to stay, and help them build." We gave them a place to build their camp. But before they went to the camp, they used to live in people's houses. All these rooms you see here were full of refugees. We had an obligation to feed them and care for them. I went from house to house telling people: "You have to give your room to the refugees." When we got a group of refugees, I went and told the heads of households they had to take in some of the refugees. When they agreed I brought the refugees to them. No one refused to take them. If someone had refused to host refugees, he would have been fined.[12]

If people were so eager to subjugate the refugees as clients, then why were there laws threatening locals who failed to establish such patron–client relations with them? We can begin to unravel this puzzle if we note that locals were not necessarily rejecting relations with the refugees.

---

[11] Colson, "The assimilation of aliens," 41.
[12] Interview with a Guinean in Dongueta, Yomou Prefecture, Guinea (MRB 195), July 28, 2009.

They were not refusing to embrace or exploit the wealth in people that the refugees represented. They were just trying to employ certain methods of exploitation instead of others. In a situation in which poor and vulnerable refugees could be easily employed for starvation wages, some villagers found the establishment of pure market relations, without all the patron–client trappings that tended to impose obligations on the patron, more attractive. In these market-based employment relationships, employers did not bear legal responsibility for the refugees they employed. This spared them the significant economic burdens that came with being ultimately legally responsible for the acts of a stranger. We can imagine that the same sort of alternative possibilities existed for harnessing the political possibilities of refugees. Refugees could be motivated in cash and kind for services during rallies and voting instead of cultivating deep long-term patron–client relations. These unencumbered market relationships were pervasive as even refugees who had hosts spent a lot of their time working for others with whom they had only market relations. What some villagers may have being trying to do was to escape the system of subjugation all together.

In the village of Forofonye in Guinea's Forest Region, which never had a refugee camp or even a separate refugee quarter, I encountered a woman who seemed to have successfully evaded the establishment of patron–client relations with the refugees in favor of market-based ones.

I was born and raised here and was here when the refugees came. I was living with my husband and we hosted no refugees. I used to farm rice, cassava, and corn and I employed refugees to work for me. I just paid them money. I had refugee friends and we helped each other work sometimes and gave each other gifts once in a while but we were never their hosts. They were all from Gorlu and sometimes when they go to market in Yomou they pass here and bring me gifts. They invited me to visit them but I have not had the time to go there.[13]

What this woman did was akin to what some employers and landlords in the Guinean capital of Conakry did. In Conakry, as I point out in Chapter 3, Guineans entered into relations with the refugees that were predominantly market-based by renting tenements to them or employing them.

The problem here is not that the idea of wealth in people is flawed. It is that there is always the temptation to place on its shoulders a causal burden it cannot possibly carry. The idea of wealth in people *can* account for

---

[13] Interview with a lady in Forofonye, Banie Sub-Prefecture, Guinea (MRB 192), July 27, 2009.

the eagerness of many African societies to incorporate strangers. What it cannot tell is why societies incorporate strangers in certain ways instead of others. Here, as in other situations, there existed multiple ways of solving the same political–economic problem that we can call people scarcity. Thus the mere fact of the existence of the political economic problem cannot explain the ways in which actors sought to solve it. Instead, we need to resort to wider sociopolitics to understand why societies and individuals tried to incorporate refugees in certain ways but not in others.

Knight,[14] in his conflict-oriented study of the origins of institutions, made this very point. Although institutions such as property rights provide certain collective benefits, these collective benefits cannot explain why institutions are designed in certain ways instead of others. This is because there are always multiple institutional designs that can provide the same social benefits. The difference lies in how they distribute benefits among members of society. Each design distributes burdens and costs in different ways, and it is these distributional consequences and the relative power of actors that determine which designs are adopted and which are discarded.

Brenner and Dobb made a similar point in the literature on the transition from feudalism to capitalism in Europe. There was the tendency to use the rise of a money economy and spread of markets to explain the jettisoning of feudal relations and adoption of capitalist ones in various areas of Europe. Lords, it is argued, realized the relative efficiency of capitalist production relations for meeting increasing market demands and were further attracted by the commutation fees serfs paid for their freedom.[15] Both Brenner and Dobb[16] argued convincingly that this argument is flawed because it is predicated on the assumption that there was one best way of extracting the gains promised by the spread of markets and the money economy. However, this assumption was faulty because what worked depended on the specific sociopolitical milieu in which lords operated, which varied across Europe.[17] Converting to capitalist relations

---

[14] Jack Knight, *Institutions and social conflict* (New York: Cambridge University Press, 1992), 42. Also see Terry Moe, "Power and Political Institutions," *Perspectives on Politics* 3 (2–2005): 1.

[15] Paul Sweezy, *The transition from feudalism to capitalism; a symposium* (New York: Science and Society, 1954), 44–45.

[16] Robert Brenner, "The origins of capitalist development: a critique of neo-Smithian Marxism," *New Left Review* 104 (1977); and Maurice Dobb, *Studies in the development of capitalism* [2d (rev.)] (London: Routledge & Kegan Paul, 1963).

[17] Brenner, "The origins," 43; and Dobb, *Studies in the development*, 43.

made sense in certain contexts. However, those who could afford it could just squeeze more labor and rent out of their serfs.[18] This, Dobb contended, explains the otherwise bizarre fact of the reinforcement of feudal socioeconomic relations in areas of Europe where markets and money had gained the most influence and where one would therefore have expected capitalist relations to occur fastest.[19]

My contention here is that the subjugation of refugees and strangers, more generally, in patron–client relations is only one possible design for accessing wealth in people. To understand why some African societies chose this whereas others tended to emphasize market relations, we cannot just look at the importance of wealth in people. We have to look beyond that to other sociopolitical facts that concern the distribution of power and resources. In this case my contention is that the subjugation of strangers to locals is a means of solving the problem of the stranger in an indigeneity-privileging society. Indigenes constitute the primary holders of rights in such a society, and they hold such rights because of their autochthony.

One way of dealing with strangers in such a society is to exclude them altogether as people who, due to their lack of indigenous status, lack rights in such a society. This possibility was not chosen because of the importance of wealth in people. Wealth in people meant that societies wanted strangers. The question in the indigeneity-privileging society then is how these non-indigenes, who do not belong, can access the rights necessary to survive in society. My contention is that the subjugation of strangers to locals in these societies is a means of harnessing wealth in people that also solves the problem of the stranger in the indigeneity-privileging society. The stranger is given the status of an appendage of the native. And it is through this connection that rights flow from their primary holder – the indigene – to their secondary holder – the stranger – until the stranger somehow acquires the status of an indigene.

This mode of harnessing wealth in people privileges certain members of society. These are the indigenes considered as a general category. However, as Murphy and Bledsoe[20] pointed out, there is differentiation even within the broad category of indigenes. For in many of these societies, certain lineages hold the status of first-comers and have privileged symbolic and real rights to land and political office relative to other

---

[18] Brenner, "The origins," 42; and Dobb, *Studies in the development*, 41.
[19] Dobb, *Studies in the development*, 39.
[20] Murphy and Bledsoe, "Kinship and territory."

indigenous lineages.[21] They are first-among-equals, so to speak. They have the greatest investment in the perpetuation of indigeneity as an organizing principle in these societies.[22] The fact that in the Forest Region of Guinea it is precisely these chiefs and elders who made it their business to enforce the subjugation of the refugees and prevent others from choosing alternative modes of harnessing wealth in people was not coincidental.

Like Knight's[23] actors, the landowning lineages were choosing a very specific design of an institutional solution to a political economic problem in their communities that reinforced their dominance. Their superior power made this choice stick. Less privileged local lineages and youth who often benefited less from the privileging of indigeneity can be understood as those who occasionally tried to opt for more market-oriented relations with the refugees and had to be dissuaded through the threat of punishment. Even though this would have deeply unsettled the indigeneity-privileging character of their communities, it would also have allowed them to exploit the refugees without bearing many of the responsibilities that indigeneity-privileging patron–client relationship imposed on them.[24]

GENDER AND THE REFUGEE EXPERIENCE

As I conducted research for this work in the Mano River Basin and Great Lakes Region, gender kept coming to the fore, even though it was not the focus of my investigations. It was clear that in many ways men and women refugees and locals experienced the refugee situation and the violence that caused, surrounded, and resulted from it in significantly different ways. It is worth reflecting on some of these differences. Women were more likely to be victims of sexual violence in these refugee situations and the violence that caused them. The rape, sexual abuse, and sexual enslavement of women and girls were common in the wars in Sierra Leone and Liberia.[25] However, escaping to Guinea as refugees did not

---

[21] Murphy and Bledsoe, "Kinship and territory," 124; and Murphy, "The rhetorical management," 671.

[22] Murphy, "Secret knowledge," 202.

[23] Knight, *Institutions and social conflict*, 42.

[24] A very short conversation with Paul Richards during dinner with an invited speaker in New Haven enabled me to better formulate my thoughts on this subject.

[25] Physicians for Human rights, "War-related sexual violence in Sierra Leone: a population-based assessment" (a report by Physicians for Human Rights, 2002), accessed

necessarily save women from such violence. Rape was one of the most commonly employed methods of victimization of women during the anti-refugee violence in Conakry in September 2000.[26] Even in the Forest Region where such attacks did not take place, the sexual abuse and exploitation of women was common. Refugee women were sometimes forced to offer sexual favors to cross checkpoints, acquire documents, and access refugee supplies.[27] The perpetrators ranged from Guinean security personnel to humanitarian agency officials.[28]

In Mafindor Chiefdom, many former refugees complained about the sexual harassment they suffered at the hands of ordinary Guinean men when they were refugees. They often gave the example of the response that groups of young men would jokingly give when refugees went seeking work in the morning. In response to "Work, work, is there work?" some Guinean boys would shout "There is work in the bedroom?" and break out in hearty laughter.[29]

Of particular importance was the marked difference in the psychological impact that refugeehood *seemed* to have had on men and women. As I conducted research, I noticed that even though men did not experience any more physical or structural violence than women, they tended to express more hopelessness and despair than women. They generally thought of the life of refugeehood as more destabilizing than women. For some it almost seemed like the world had, for a while, come to an end. Women were no less graphic in their depiction of the difficulties and trauma of refugee life, but they tended to exude less of a sense of hopelessness, despondency, and despair than men. This difference was interesting because if anything women had rampant sexual violence and exploitation to deal with in addition to many of the other problems that they shared with male refugees.

October 13, 2012, https://s3.amazonaws.com/PHR_Reports/sierra-leone-sexual-violence-2002.pdf.

[26] Human Rights Watch, "Refugee women in Guinea raped"; and Agnes Callamard, "Refugee women: a gendered and political analysis of the refugee experience," in *Refugees: perspectives on the experience of forced migrants*, ed. Alistair Ager (London: Pinter, 1999), 205.

[27] Utas, "West African warscapes," 205.

[28] UNHCR and Save the Children-UK, "Note for Implementing and Operational Partners by UNHCR and Save the Children-UK on Sexual Violence & Exploitation: The Experience of Refugee Children in Guinea, Liberia and Sierra Leone based on Initial Findings and Recommendations from Assessment Mission 22 October – 30 November 2001," accessed October 13, 2012, http://www.savethechildren.org.uk/sites/default/files/docs/sexual_violence_and_exploitation_1.pdf; and Utas, "West African warscapes," 421.

[29] Interview (MRB 270).

As I reflected on this puzzle, I began to realize that it might be understandable only if one goes beyond a focus on what happened to people as refugees to look at their prewar lives. This in turn required an insertion of reflections on the refugee situations into a broader reflection on sociopolitical economies, especially in rural areas of the Mano River Basin and the Great Lakes Region. Luckily I had experiences from my earlier research on property rights in various parts of the continent to draw on.

Male former refugees I spoke with in the Mano River Basin tended to emphasize three areas when they reflected on the hopelessness of refugee-hood. These were their subjection to extra-legal arbitrary violence at the hands of locals, the rather flimsy nature of the very limited land rights they could access, and their loss of control over family members. The loss of control over members of their households like children, wives, and other adult male relatives was one that many dwelt on in their commentary on the despondency that characterized their lives as refugees.

The fact that women tended to suffer less from such despondency became slightly less puzzling when I reflected on the lives of men and women before they became refugees in many rural areas in the Great Lakes Region and the Mano River Basin. I realized that for women, the lack of secure property rights, lack of control over household members, and exposure to extra-legal arbitrary violence at the hands of others were not things that afflicted their lives only when they became refugees. In many ways these were things that characterized their lives in various forms and to various extents even before they became refugees.

In many rural societies in Sierra Leone and Liberia, where the refugees in Guinea came from, men tend to be the primary holders of land rights.[30] The preponderance of men as heads of families, lineages, and communities ensured that they were the key controllers of land, and male offspring tended to inherit land rights.[31] The strength of indigeneity in many of these

---

[30] Roy Maconachie, "New agricultural frontiers in post-conflict Sierra Leone? Exploring institutional challenges for wetland management in Eastern Province," *BWPI Working Paper* 24 (January 2008): 7; IRIN, "Sierra Leone: fighting for women's rights to land," *IRIN*, June 22, 2012, accessed August 2, 2012, http://www.irinnews.org/Report/95705/SIERRA-LEONE-Fighting-for-women-s-right-to-land.

[31] Acord, Oxfam and Action Aid, "The right to land and justice for women in Africa," (report of the African Women's Land Rights Conference, Red Court Hotel, Nairobi, Kenya, May 30–June 2, 2011), accessed October 5, 2012, http://www.acordinternational.org/silo/files/the-right-to-land-and-justice-for-women-in-africa.pdf; and Maconachie, "New agricultural," 8.

communities ensured that for women who got married to men in other communities and moved to settle with them, land rights were dependent on their relationship with their husbands. They were "strangers" who were not entitled to land rights on their own account. Thus, for many adult female refugees, the fact that they had to depend on friendships with locals to acquire highly tentative land rights, which depended on the goodwill of locals, was not as new as it was for many men.

A similar story can be told for exposure to extra-legal and arbitrary violence, or "slaps," as many refugees spoke of it. For many refugee men, the fact that they could be slapped around as adults was mind-boggling and very disturbing. Many decried the fact that they could be beaten up even by youths the age of their children for trespassing, cutting sticks without permission, or just speaking "rudely" to a local.[32] Often it was not the physical pain that was disturbing. It was the infantalization implicit in the subjection of an adult to extra-legal corporal punishment.

Given the fact of domestic violence against women in many societies around the world, it is unsurprising that such violence was not as new to adult female refugees as it was to adult male refugees. As an adult female in many communities in the Mano River Basin, like in many parts of the world, getting slapped by a partner is not necessarily unheard of. It may well be possible that women suffered more physical violence as refugees than before they fled their homes. After all, they had to contend with violence from locals as well as violence from their refugee partners. However, this was more a difference in degree compared to what many adult male heads of households suffered as the completely new phenomenon of getting slapped around in public. In a sense, in the eyes of these refugee men, they were not only being infantilized, they were also being "feminized" (because women were the ones who were usually subjected to such domestic violence), and this might have partly accounted for the psychological shock and trauma.

It is similarly unsurprising that women did not decry the lack of control over household members as much as men in refugee situations. Men in many Mano River Basin communities, where they happen to be family heads, exercise control over at least one partner, children, and adult unmarried relatives who live in their compound. Wives did not exercise as much control over other adults in the household, and this meant that

---

[32] Interview with a former refugee in Gorlu, Salayea District, Liberia (MRB 348), December 7, 2010; and interview (MRB 282).

TABLE 8.1 *A Gendered View of Changes Wrought by Refugeehood Here*

| Domain | Extralegal Violence | | Property Rights | | Power/Control | |
| | Pre-Refugee | Post-Refugee | Pre-Refugee | Post-Refugee | Pre-Refugee | Post-Refugee |
Period						
Men	Limited exposure to such violence as adult males	High exposure to such violence by hosts, soldiers, police, etc.	Significant ability to control land as heads of clans, families, etc.	Dependent on others for temporary land rights	Ability to control women, children, and dependent males as heads of households	Inability to control children, women, and other males due to absence of structures that facilitate such control
Women	High exposure as many suffer domestic abuse as adult daughters and wives	High exposure to such violence by partners, soldiers, police, others in host community	Patriarchal societies often limit women's rights to property	Highly dependent on hosts for temporary land rights	Limited ability to control adult males; slightly more ability to control children	Limited ability to control adult males and children

for them the lack of control over others during the refugee situation did not represent as much of a break as for men.

Refugeehood eroded many of the material bases on which men's control over women, children, and other men were based. The erosion of their privileged access to land rights as family, lineage, and clan heads dealt a severe blow to this social control. The need to access land caused strangers and others with less-recognized claims on land to prostrate themselves to lineage heads that controlled land.[33] Control over land provided

[33] Maconachie, "New agricultural frontiers," 8; Germain, *Peuples de la Foret*, 221; Murphy and Bledsoe, "Kinship and territory," 126; and James Gibbs, "The Kpelle of Liberia," 200–201.

tribute from lenders of land, creating wealth and control over others.[34] The reduction of the activities of secret societies among refugees also meant the loss of one of the primary instruments of domination by male members of leading families in the Mano River Basin. The rather egalitarian basis on which aid agencies distributed humanitarian supplies also meant that men no longer had privileged control over economic resources. In many instances, women were even privileged in the distribution of resources as particularly vulnerable people.[35]

There is clearly need for further work here. Given the prevalence of sexual violence and exploitation, it is hard to accept that women indeed suffered less psychological despondency than men.[36] It is highly likely that, given the sensitive nature of issues surrounding sexual violence, a different study design and methodology would have led to different results and/or suggested different explanations.[37]

SOME POLICY IMPLICATIONS

There are a few policy implications and recommendations that we can draw from this study. One is that there is a lot that can be done to reduce structural violence against refugees in Africa. This is particularly true in indigeneity-privileging societies. To address structural violence in these places, we have to step back from what Agblorti rightly noted as the tendency to over-romanticize refugee–host relations in Africa,[38] which is particularly true in the case of self-settled refugees.[39] As I demonstrated earlier, self-settled refugees are often the victims of pervasive structural violence. I have shown how some of this is core to the indigeneity-privileging logic of many communities and its consequent subjugation of refugees to locals. However, there are many aspects of this structural violence that are not necessary parts of the ordering logic of these communities. These include the pervasive reneging on contracts by locals that I write about. There is also the wanton subjection of refugees to extra-legal verbal and physical abuse.

---

[34] Maconachie, "New agricultural frontiers," 8.
[35] Gale, "Bulgur marriages," 361.
[36] Kibreab, *Ready and willing*, 61–62; and Gale, "Bulgur marriages," 356–358 and 365–366.
[37] Anita Spring, "Women and men as refugees: differential assimilation of Angolan refugees in Zambia," *Disasters* 3 (4–1979): 425.
[38] Agblorti, "Refugee integration," 2.
[39] Art Hansen, "Refugee dynamics," 192–194.

Local activists and organizations, national refugee agencies, and international organizations can all work toward reducing this structural violence. Local judicial structures can be reinforced to deal with the tendency of locals to renege on contracts with, and to physically abuse refugees. Such institutional reform has to be done with the peculiar characteristics of refugees in mind. Many of them are poor, lack confidence in their own legal status, and are heavily dependent on the goodwill and collaboration of local communities. Local communities should be involved in the establishment of tribunals so they do not see it as a pro-refugee move aimed at undermining local control. If this happens, they might target refugees in other ways that will end up making these courts not particularly useful. They may refrain from giving refugees contracts, for example.

Those presiding over such tribunals could be drawn from both refugee and local communities. Tribunals should be placed in close proximity to refugees so they are accessible even to poor refugees who cannot afford the cost of transportation. Roving tribunals could also be good alternatives. The conduct of proceedings in languages the refugees understand and banning of legal representation that costs money are all elements of design that will make these tribunals useful.

This reinforcement of local judicial structures can go along with advocacy campaigns aimed at changing local attitudes toward the abuse of refugees and respect of contracts with refugees.

Societies that privilege residence hold different challenges for refugees. Although structural violence is not as accentuated in these societies, they hold significant possibilities for outbreaks of large-scale anti-refugee violence by local populations, as we saw in Conakry and in Kivu. There is much that local and international agencies can do to prevent the outbreak of such violence. First, they could work with state officials to curb the tendency for such officials to demonize and withdraw protection from whole-refugee populations when they see signs of refugee involvement in opposition activities. Second, work has to go into keeping refugees away from opposition politics in their host countries because it is the reason why state leaders promote anti-refugee violence. Much effort goes into preventing militarization among refugees, but as I show here, even the involvement of refugees in nonmilitarized opposition politics in the home country can be disastrous for refugee protection. Sensitization campaigns and efforts at keeping refugees who get involved in such opposition groups from extending their activities to refugee settlements can help.

These preventive efforts have to be backed up by plans for minimizing harm to refugees in the event that such attacks break out. Conakry and southwestern Uganda offer a lot of practical lessons here. It is always wise to have sanctuaries that are well known by, and easily accessible to refugees. The Embassies of Liberia and Sierra Leone in Guinea and the United Nations High Commission for Refugees (UNHCR) camps in southwestern Uganda played this protective role. If the UNHCR had had easily accessible safe houses around Conakry, many more refugees would have escaped the violent outbreaks of September 2000. Knowledge of where refugees are concentrated and means of reaching those areas at short notice would also have helped refugees who were trapped for days in certain areas waiting for help that never came. Evacuation plans are also worth investing in. When the security of sanctuaries is not guaranteed or space in these sanctuaries is not enough, moving refugees to areas unaffected by the violence can save many from harm. In Conakry, many refugees sought to flee on their own, primarily through the sea route with the vessel MV *Madam Monique*. Unfortunately, many were not even able to make it to the port, and gangs of civilians and security personnel operating around the port sometimes attacked those refugees who successfully made it there.

As I indicated in an earlier section, refugee situations can destabilize gender relations. Although this creates psychological trauma, it also presents opportunities for increasing gender equality. There are some concrete steps that can help us transform this instability into gains for gender equality. First, refugee men should be targeted for counseling that involves conversations on gender equality and the gains that it can bring them and their communities. This is vital for the prevention of a resort to violent reprisals against women who are seen to be stepping out of patriarchal confines. Second, steps should be taken to ensure that repatriation does not amount to the reinstatement of patriarchy. To ensure that repatriation does not whittle away the gains that women made while in exile, one important step that could be taken is to reorganize property relations to increase women's access to land rights. Land reform should go along with repatriation and resettlement. Campaigns against domestic violence in the form of programs aimed at changing attitudes and boosting the capacity of judicial mechanisms to deal with such abuse should be undertaken.

CONCLUSION

This project is an attempt to subject rare but very deadly generalized anti-refugee violence by local populations to a sustained comparative gaze. The general task is to understand why such outbreaks characterized by open and systematic violence, massacres, beatings, rape, and forcible evictions happen in some cases but are absent in most refugee–host situations in Africa.

The core of the argument here is that civilian refugees are subjected to such attacks by the host population because of a combination of the demonization of and encouragement of attacks against the refugees by the state and limited local knowledge of what the refugees represent. I account for the propensity of states to demonize and encourage attacks on refugees in terms of whether sections of the refugee population get linked to opposition groups that threaten the host government. The extent of local knowledge about what the refugees represent is dependent on whether the refugees settle in areas that privilege indigeneity or residence in the determination of rights of belonging. While indigeneity-privileging areas ensure that locals accrue significant information about the daily lives and activities of refugees by subjugating them to local elites, residence-privileging ones work to hide the lives of refugees from local populations by ensuring the autonomy of refugees from local elites.

Refugees do not suffer such attacks in the vast majority of cases because they enjoy the protection of host states. Even where such protection is withdrawn, their settlement in areas that privilege indigeneity ensures that locals do not engage in such attacks on them.

A key theoretical contribution of this project is its response to a question that arises from a lot of work that deals with the effects of globalization on exclusionary politics and violence.[40] This book contributes to our understanding of why essentially similar circulations of refugees generate different levels of "uncertainty in social life" in different places and affect the likelihood of deadly violence against refugees in divergent ways. It sheds some light on why globalization seems to coincide with order and peace in some areas but with disorder and violence in others.

---

[40] Appadurai, "Dead Certainty," 228; and Geschiere and Nyamnjoh, "Capitalism and autochthony."

Bibliography

Aall, Cato. "Refugee problems in Southern Africa." In *Refugee problems in Africa*, edited by Sven Hamrell. Uppsala: The Scandinavian Institute of African Studies, 1967.

Abrahams, R. G. "The political incorporation of non-Nyamwezi immigrants in Tanzania." In *From tribe to nation: studies in incorporation processes*, edited by Ronald Cohen and John Middleton. Scranton, PA: Chandler Publishing Company, 1970.

Ackerman, Bruce and Ian Ayres. *Voting with dollars: a new paradigm for campaign finance*. New Haven: Yale University Press, 2002.

Acord, Oxfam and Action Aid. "The right to land and justice for women in Africa." Report of the African Women's Land Rights Conference, Red Court Hotel, Nairobi, Kenya, May 30–June 2, 2011. Accessed October 5, 2012. http://www.acordinternational.org/silo/files/the-right-to-land-and-justice-for-women-in-africa.pdf.

Adama Oane and Christine Glanz. *Why and how Africa should invest in African languages and multilingual education: an evidence- and practice-based advocacy brief*. Hamburg: UNESCO Institute for Lifelong Education, 2010.

Adams, Glen. "The effect of self-affirmation on perception of racism." *Journal of Experimental Social Psychology* 42 (2006): 616–626.

Adams, Glen, Laurie O'Brien and Jessica Nelson. "Perceptions of racism in Hurricane Katrina: a liberation psychology analysis." *Analysis of Social Issues and Public Policy* 6 (2006): 215–235.

Adelman, Howard. "The use and abuse of refugees." In *Refugee manipulation: war, politics, and the abuse of human suffering*, edited by Stephen Stedman and Fred Tanner. Washington, DC: Brookings Institution Press, 2003.

Adepoju, Aderanti, Alistair Boulton and Mariah Levin. "Promoting integration through mobility: free movement and the ECOWAS protocol." *New Issues in Refugee Research* 150 (December 2007): 1–27.

Agblorti, Samuel. "Refugee integration in Ghana: the host community's perspective." *New Issues in Refugee Research* 203 (March 2011): 1–24.

Allen, Tim. "Ethnicity and tribalism on the Sudan-Uganda border." In *Ethnicity and conflict in the horn of Africa*, edited by Fukui Katsoyoshi and John Markakis. London: James Currey, 1994.

Appadurai, Arjun. "Dead certainty: ethnic violence in the era of globalization." *Public Culture* 10 (1998): 225–247.

Arieff, Alexis. "Still standing: neighborhood wars and political stability in Guinea." *Journal of Modern African Studies* 47 (2009): 331–348.

Atfield, Gaby, Kavita Bahmbhatt and Therese O'toole. "Refugees' experiences of integration." *Refugee Council Integration Report 2007* (September 2007): 1–73.

Bakewell, Oliver. "Repatriation and self-settled refugees in Zambia: bringing solutions to the wrong problems." *Journal of Refugee Studies* 13 (2000): 356–373.

Bakewell, Oliver. "Refugee aid and protection in rural Africa: working in parallel or cross-purposes." *New Issues in Refugee Research* 35 (March 2001): 1–12.

Bakewell, Oliver. "Returning refugees or migrating villagers? Voluntary repatriation programmes in Africa reconsidered." *New Issues in Refugee Research* 15 (December 1999): 1–29.

Banki, Susan. "Refugee integration in the intermediate term: a case study of Nepal, Pakistan and Kenya." *New Issues in Refugee Research* 108 (October 2004): 1–24.

Barret, Michael. "Social landscapes and moving people: the mysterious meaning of migration in western Zambia." *New Issues in Refugee Research* 78 (February 2003): 1–18.

Bascom, Jonathan. "The peasant economy of refugee resettlement in Eastern Sudan." *Annals of the Association of American Geographers* 83 (1993): 320–346.

Bates, Robert. *Markets and states in tropical Africa: the political basis of agricultural policies*. Berkeley: University of California Press, 1981.

Bates, Robert, Avner Grief, Margaret Levi, Jean-Laurent Rosenthal and Barry Weingast. "Introduction." In *Analytic narratives*, edited by Robert Bates, Avner Grief, Margaret Levi, Jean-Laurent Rosenthal and Barry Weingast. Princeton: Princeton University Press, 1998.

Bates, Robert. "Probing the sources of political order." In *Order, conflict and violence*, edited by Stathis Kalyvas, Ian Shapiro and Tarek Masoud. New York: Cambridge University Press, 2008.

Bates, Robert. *When things fell apart: state failure in late century Africa*. New York: Cambridge University Press, 2008.

Bauman, Zygmunt. *Postmodernity and its discontents*. New York: New York University Press, 1997.

Bayart, Jean-François, Stephen Ellis, and Beïatrice Hibou. *The criminalization of the state in Africa*. Bloomington: Indiana University Press, 1999.

Bernsten, Jan. "Runyakitara: Uganda's 'new' language." *Journal of Multilingual and Multicultural Development* 19 (1998): 93–107.

Berry, Leah. "The impact of environmental degradation on refugee–host relations: a case study from Tanzania." *New Issues in Refugee Research* 151 (January 2008): 1–25.

Bledsoe, Caroline. *Women and marriage in Kpelle society*. Stanford: Stanford University Press, 1980.

Bledsoe, Caroline. "The manipulation of Kpelle social fatherhood." *Ethnology* 19 (1980): 29–45.

Bledsoe, Caroline and William Murphy. "The Kpelle negotiation of marriage and matrilineal ties." In *The versatility of kinship*, edited by in Linda Cordell and Stephen Beckerman. New York: Academic Press, 1980.

Bond, Virginia. "Identity crisis: Banyaruanda refugees in Uganda." M.A. diss., University of Edinburgh, 1988.

Brenner, Robert. "The origins of capitalist development: a critique of neo-Smithian Marxism." *New Left Review* 104 (July–August 1977): 25–92.

Brooks, George. *Landlords and strangers: ecology, society, and trade in Western Africa, 1000–1630*. Boulder: Westview Press, 1993.

Brown, Michael. "The causes and regional dimensions of internal conflict." In *The international dimensions of internal conflict*, edited by Michael Brown. London: MIT Press, 1996.

Brun, Catherine. "Not only about survival: livelihood strategies in protracted displacement." In *In the maze of displacement: conflict, migration and change*, edited by N. Shanmugaratnam, Ragnhild Lund and Kristi Anne Stolen. Kristiansand S., Norway: HoyskoleForlaget, 2003.

Bustin, Edouard. "The Congo." In *Refugees south of the Sahara: an African dilemma*, edited by Hugh Brooks and Yassin El-Ayouty. Westport, CT: Negro Universities Press, 1970.

Calhoun, Noel. "UNHCR and community development: a weak link in the chain of refugee protection?" *New Issues in Refugee Research* 191 (October 2010): 1–19.

Callamard, Agnes. "Refugee women: a gendered and political analysis of the refugee experience." In *Refugees: perspectives on the experience of forced migrants*, edited by Alistair Ager. London: Pinter, 1999.

Caplan, Lionel. "Creole world, purist rhetoric: Anglo-Indian cultural debates in colonial and contemporary Madras." *Journal of the Royal Anthropological Institute* 1 (1995): 743–762.

Ceuppens, Bambi and Peter Geschiere. "Autochthony: local or global? New modes in the struggle over citizenship and belonging in Africa and Europe." *Annual Review of Anthropology* 34 (2005): 385–407.

Chabal, Patrick, and Jean Pascal Daloz. *Africa works: disorder as political instrument*. Bloomington: Indiana University Press, 1999.

Challenor, Herschelle. "Strangers as colonial intermediaries: the Dahomeyans in Francophone Africa." In *Strangers in African societies*, edited by William Shack and Elliott Skinner. Berkeley: University of California Press, 1979.

Chambers, Robert. "Hidden losers? The impact of rural refugees and refugee programs on poorer hosts." *International Migration Review* 20 (1986): 245–263.

Chambers, Robert. "Rural refugees in Africa: what the eye does not see." *Disasters* 3 (December 1978): 381–392.

Chretien, Jean-Pierre. *The great lakes of Africa: two thousand years of history*. New York: Zone Books, 2003.

Clay, Jason. *The eviction of Banyarwanda: The story behind the refugee crisis in southwest Uganda.* Cambridge, MA: Cultural Survival, 1984.

Cohen, Ronald and John Middleton. "Introduction." In *From tribe to nation: studies in incorporation processes,* edited by Ronald Cohen and John Middleton. Scranton, PA: Chandler Publishing Company, 1970.

Collier, Paul. "Doing well out of war: an economic perspective." In *Greed and Grievance: economic agendas in civil wars,* edited by Mats Berdal and David Malone. Boulder: Lynne Rienner Publishers, 2000.

Colson, Elizabeth. "The assimilation of aliens among Zambian Tonga." In *From tribe to nation: studies in incorporation processes,* edited by Ronald Cohen and John Middleton. Scranton, PA: Chandler Publishing Company, 1970.

Crisp, Jeff. "Africa's refugees: patterns, problems and policy changes." *New Issues in Refugee Research* 28 (August 2000): 1–22.

Crisp, Jeff. "Local integration and local settlement of refugees: a conceptual and historical analysis." *New Issues in Refugee Research* 102 (April 2004): 1–8.

de la Pena, Derek, Christine Bachman, Rose Mary Istre, Michelle Cohen and Michelle Klarman. "Reexamining perceived discrimination between blacks and whites following Hurricane Katrina: a racial-conciliatory perspective." *North American Journal of Psychology* 12 (2010).

de Montclos, Marc-Antoine and Peter Kagwanja. "Refugee camps or cities? The socio-economic dynamics of the Dadaab and Kakuma Camps in Northern Kenya." *Journal of Refugee Studies* 13 (2000): 205–222.

de Soto, Hernando. *The mystery of capital: why capitalism triumphs in the West and fails everywhere else.* New York: Basic Books, 2000.

Dick, Shelly. "Liberians in Ghana: living without humanitarian assistance." *New Issues in Refugee Research* 57 (February 2002): 1–71.

Diagne, Souleymane Bachir. "Africanity as an open question," *Identity and beyond: rethinking Africanity, Nordic Africa Institute Discussion Paper* 12 (2001): 19–24.

Diagne, Souleymane Bachir. "Keeping Africanity open." *Public Culture* 14 (2002): 621–623.

DiPasquale, Denise and Edward Glaeser. "The LA riot and the economics of urban unrest." *National Bureau of Economic Research Working Paper* 5456 (February 1996): 1–25.

Dobb, Maurice. *Studies in the development of capitalism.* London: Routledge & Kegan Paul, 1963.

Dodson, Belinda and Catherine Oelofse. "Shades of xenophobia: in-migrants and immigrants in Mizamoyethu, Cape Town." In *Transnationalism and new African immigration to South Africa,* edited by Jonathan Crush and David McDonald. Cape Town: Southern African Migration Project and Canadian Association of African Studies, 2002.

Donnelly, David, Janice Fine and Ellen Miller. *Are elections for sale?* Boston: Beacon Press, 1999.

Doornbos, Martin. "Kumanyana and Rwenzururu: two responses to ethnic inequality." In *Protest and power in Black Africa,* edited by Robert Rotberg and Ali Mazrui. New York: Oxford University Press, 1970.

Doornbos, Martin. "Images and reality of stratification in pre-colonial Nkore." *Canadian Journal of African Studies* 7 (1973): 477–495.

Doornbos, Martin. "Land tenure and political conflict in Ankole, Uganda." *Journal of Development Studies* 12 (1975): 54–74.

Doornbos, Martin. "Ethnicity, Christianity, and the development of social stratification in colonial Ankole." *The International Journal of African Historical Studies* 9 (1976): 555–575.

Doornbos, Martin. *Not all the king's men: inequality as a political instrument in Ankole, Uganda.* The Hague: Mouton Publishers, 1978.

Dorjahn, V.R. and Christopher Fyfe. "Landlord and stranger: change in tenancy relations in Sierra Leone." *Journal of African History* 3 (1962): 391–397.

Dryden-Petersen, Sarah and Lucy Hovil. "Local integration as a durable solution: refugees, host populations and education in Uganda." *New Issues in Refugee Research* 93 (September 2003): 1–27.

Duncan, Christopher. "Unwelcome guests: relations between internally displaced persons and their hosts in North Sulawesi, Indonesia." *Journal of Refugee Studies* 18 (2005): 25–46.

Dwyer, David. "The Mende problem." In *Studies in African comparative linguistics with special focus on Bantu and Mande*, edited by Koen Bostoen and Jacky Maniacky. Tervuren, Belgum: Royal Museum for Central Africa, 2005.

Ellis, Stephen. *The mask of anarchy: the destruction of Liberia and the religious dimension of an African civil war.* New York: New York University Press, 2007.

European Council on Refugee and Exiles, "The way forward: towards the integration of refugees in Europe." *European Council on Refugees and Exiles Report* (July 2005): 1–53.

European Union, "Study on the contribution of multilinguality to creativity final report." *Study commissioned by European Commission, Directorate General Education and Culture* (July 16, 2009): 1–24.

Evans, Peter. *Embedded autonomy: states and industrial transformation.* Princeton: Princeton University Press, 1995.

Ferguson, James. *The anti-politics machine: "development," depoliticization, and bureaucratic power in Lesotho.* Minneapolis: University of Minnesota Press, 1994.

Fielden, Alexandra. "Local integration: an under reported solution to protracted refugee situations." *New Issues in Refugee Research* 158 (June 2008): 1–21.

Fortt, Jean. "The distribution of the immigrant and Ganda population within Buganda." In *Economic development and tribal change: a study of immigrant labour in Buganda*, edited by Audrey Richards. Cambridge: W. Heffer and Sons Ltd., 1952.

Fourchard, Laurent. "Dealing with 'strangers': allocating urban space to migrants in Nigeria and French West Africa, end of the nineteenth century to 1960." In *African cities: competing claims on urban spaces*, edited by Francesca Locatelli and Paul Nugent. Lieden: Brill, 2009.

Freund, Paul and Katele Kalumba, "Spontaneously settled refugees in Northwestern Province, Zambia." *International Migration Review* 20 (1986): 299–312.

Fulton, Richard. "The political structures and functions of poro in Kpelle society." *American Anthropologist* 47 (1972): 1218–1233.

Gale, Lacey Andrews. "Bulgur marriages and 'Big' women: navigating relatedness in Guinean refugee camps." *Anthropological Quarterly* 80 (2007): 355–378.

Gale, Lacey Andrews. "The invisible refugee camp: durable solutions for Boreah 'residuals' in Guinea." *Journal of Refugee Studies* 21 (2008): 537–552.

Galvez, William. *Che in Africa: Che Guevara's Congo Diary*. Melbourne: Ocean Press, 1999.

Gberie, Lansana. "Destabilizing Guinea: diamonds, Charles Taylor and the potential for wider humanitarian catastrophy." *Partnership for Africa Canada Occasional Paper* 1 (October 2001): 1–16.

Gerdes, Felix. 'Forced migration and armed conflict: an analytical framework and a case study of refugee-warriors in Guinea,' *University of Hamburg, Research Unit of Wars, Armament and Development Working Paper* No. 1 (2006): 1–144.

Goerg, Odile, *Commerce et colonization en Guinée 1850–1913*. Paris: Editions L'Harmattan, 1986.

Georg, Odile. "Chefs de quartier et 'tribal headman:' deux vision des colonises en ville." In *Les ethnies ont une histoire*, edited by Jean-Pierre Chretien and Gerard Prunier. Paris: Editions Karthala, 1989.

Georg, Odile. "La genese du peuplement de Conakry." *Cahiers d'etudes Africaines* 30 (1990): 73–90.

Goerg, Odile. "La Guinée Conakry." In *Rives colonial: architectures de Saint-Louis a Doula*, edited by Jacques Soulillou. Marseiles: Editions Parentheses, 1993.

Goerg, Odile. "From Hill Station (Freetown) to Downtown Conakry (First Ward): comparing French and British approaches to segregation in colonial cities at the beginning of the twentieth century." *Canadian Journal of African Studies* 32 (1998): 1–31.

Goerg, Odile. "Chieftainships between past and present: from city to suburb and back in colonial Conakry, 1890s–1950s." *Africa Today* 52 (2006): 3–27.

Germain, Jacques. *Peuples de la Foret de Guinée*. Paris: Académie des Sciences d'outre-Mer, 1984.

Geschiere, Peter and Francis Nyamnjoh. "Capitalism and autochthony: the seesaw of mobility and belonging." *Public Culture* 12 (2000): 423–452.

Geschiere, Peter. "Funerals and belonging: different patterns in South Cameroon." *African Studies Review* 48 (2005): 45–64.

Geschiere, Peter. *The perils of belonging: autochthony, citizenship, and exclusion in Africa and Europe*. Chicago: The University of Chicago Press, 2009.

Ghosh, Srikanta. *Riots: prevention and control*. Calcutta: Eastern Law House, 1971.

Gibbs, James. "Poro values and courtroom procedures in a Kpelle chiefdom." *Southwestern Journal of Anthropology* 18 (1962): 341–350.

Gibbs, James. "The Kpelle of Liberia." In *Peoples of Africa*, edited by James Gibbs. New York: Hold, Rinehart and Winston, Inc, 1965.

Glissant, Edouard. *Caribbean Discourse: selected essays*. Charlottesville: University Press of Virginia, 1989.

Gondola, Didier. *The history of Congo*. Westport, CT: Greenwood Press, 2002.

Grare, Frederic. "The geopolitics of Afghan refugees." In *Refugee manipulation: war, politics, and the abuse of human suffering*, edited by Stephen Stedman and Fred Tanner. Washington, DC: Brookings Institution Press, 2003.

Grindle, Merilee. *Challenging the state: crisis and innovation in Latin America and Africa*. Cambridge: Cambridge University Press, 1996.

Grovogui Siba. "L'impact socioculturel et politico-Economique de l'arrivee des refugies dans le district de Nzinigrozou (Macenta)" (Mémoire de maitrise, Universite de Conakry, 1996).

Guyer, Jane. "Wealth in people and self-realization in Equatorial Africa." *Man* 28 (1993): 243–265.

Hamilton, Virginia. "Human rights in Uganda: the reasons for refugees." *United States Committee for Refugees Issue Paper* (August 1985): 1–24.

Hansen, Art. "Once the running stops: assimilation of Angolan refugees in to Zambian border villages." *Disasters* 3 (1979): 369–374.

Hansen, Art. "Managing refugees: Zambia's response to Angolan refugees 1966–1977." *Disasters* 3 (1979): 375–380.

Hansen, Art. "Refugee dynamics: Angolans in Zambia 1966 to 1972." *International Migration Review* 15 (1981): 175–194.

Harrell-Bond, Barbara. *Imposing aid: emergency assistance to refugees*. New York: Oxford University Press, 1986.

Henry, Doug. "Thought and commentary: the legacy of the tank: The violence of peace." *Anthropological Quarterly* 78 (2005): 443–456.

Herbst, Jeffrey. *States and power in Africa: comparative lessons in authority and control*. Princeton: Princeton University Press, 2000.

Hoffman, Danny. "West-African warscapes: violent events as narrative blocs: the disarmament at Bo, Sierra Leone." *Anthropological Quarterly* 78 (2005): 328–353.

Hoffman, Piotr. *Doubt, time, violence*. Chicago: The University of Chicago Press, 1986.

Homer-Dixon, Thomas. *Environment, scarcity and violence*. Princeton: Princeton University Press, 1999.

Holborn, Louise. *Refugees: a problem of our time*. Metuchen, NJ: The Scarecrow Press, 1975.

Hovil, Lucy. "Hoping for peace, afraid of war: the dilemmas of repatriation and belonging on the borders of Uganda and South Sudan." *New Issues in Refugee Research* 196 (November 2010): 1–31.

Hoyweghen, Saskia. "Mobility, territoriality and sovereignty in postcolonial Tanzania." *New Issues in Refugee Research* 49 (October 2001): 1–27.

Hull, Richard. *African cities and towns before the European conquest*. New York: W.W. Norton & Company, 1976.

Human Rights Watch. *Seeking protection: addressing sexual and domestic violence in Tanzania's refugee camps*. New York: Human Rights Watch, 2000.

Human Rights Watch. "Refugee women in Guinea raped." *Human Rights Watch*, September 13, 2000. Accessed August 11, 2012. http://www.hrw.org/en/news/2000/09/13/refugee-women-guinea-raped#_Fuller_Testimonies_from.

Human Rights Watch, "The refugee crisis in Guinea: another Macedonia?" *Human Rights Watch*, October 3, 2000. Accessed October 10, 2012. http://www.hrw.org/news/2000/10/03/refugee-crisis-guinea-another-macedonia.

Human Rights Watch, "Liberian refugees in Guinea: refoulement, militarization of camps, and other protection concerns." *Human Rights Watch Report* 14 (November 2002): 1–25.

Human Rights Watch. "Youth, poverty and blood: the lethal legacy of West Africa's regional warriors." *Human Rights Watch Report* 17 (April 2005): 1–67.

Huth, Paul and Bruce Russett. "Deterrence Failure and Crisis Escalation." *International Studies Quarterly* 32 (1988): 29–45.

Hyden, Goran. *Beyond Ujamaa in Tanzania*. London: Heinemann, 1980.

Hynes, Trycia. "The issue of 'trust' or 'mistrust' in research with refugees: choices, caveats and considerations for researchers." *New Issues in Refugee Research* 98 (November 2003): 1–25.

Inhetveen, Katharina. "'Because we are refugees': utilizing a label." *New Issues in Refugee Research* 130 (October 2006): 1–25.

International Crisis Group, "Liberia and Sierra Leone: rebuilding failed states." *ICG Africa Report* 87 (2004): 1–39.

International Crisis Group. "Stopping Guinea's slide." *ICG Africa Report* 94 (June 2005): 1–32.

Jackson, Robert. *Quasi states: sovereignty international relations and the Third World*. New York: Cambridge University Press, 1990.

Jackson, Stephen. "Sons of which soil? Language and politics of autochthony in eastern DR Congo." *African Studies Review* 49 (2006): 95–123.

Jacobson, Karen. "Refugees' environmental impact: the effect of patterns of settlement." *Journal of Refugee Studies* 10 (1997): 19–36.

Jacobsen, Karen. "The forgotten solution: local integration for refugees in developing countries." *New Issues in Refugee research*, 45 (July 2001): 1–42.

Jacobson, Karen and Loren Landau. "Researching refugees: some methodological and ethical considerations in social science and forced migration." *New Issues in Refugee Research* 90 (June 2003): 1–27.

Jacobson, Karen. *The economic life of refugees*. Bloomfield, CT: Kumarian Press, 2005.

Jeffery, Roger and Patricia Jeffery. "The Bijnor Riots, October 1990: Collapse of a mythical special relationship?" *Economic and Political Weekly* 29 (1994): 551–558.

Jeyifo, Biodun. "Whose theatre, whose Africa? Wole Soyinka's *The Road* on the road." *Modern Drama* 45 (Fall 2002): 449–465.

Kalyvas, Stathis. *The logic of violence in civil war*. New York: Cambridge University Press, 2006.

Kalyvas, Stathis, Ian Shapiro, and Tarek Masoud. "Introduction: integrating the study of order, conflict and violence." In *Order, conflict and violence*, edited by Stathis Kalyvas, Ian Shapiro and Tarek Masoud. New York: Cambridge University Press, 2008.

Kankunda, Marian. "Land tenure and changing pastoral practices in Kashari County 1962–1993." M.A. diss., Makerere University, 1996.

Keen, David. "Incentives and disincentives for violence." In *Greed and grievance: economic agendas in civil wars*, edited by Mats Berdal and David Malone. Boulder: Lynne Rienner Publishers, 2000.

Karugire, Samwiri. *A history of the Kingdom of Nkore in western Uganda to 1896*. Oxford: Clarendon Press, 1971.

Khiddu-Makubuya, Edward. "Voluntary repatriation by force: the case of Rwandan refugees in Uganda." In *African refugees: development aid and repatriation*, edited by Howard Adelman and John Sorenson. Boulder: Westview Press, 1994.

Kisamba-Mugerwa, W. "Rangeland tenure and resource management: an overview of pastoralism in Uganda." *Access to Land and other Natural Resources in Uganda: Research and Policy Development Project Research Paper* 1 (January 1992): 1–37.

Kisangani, Emizet and F. Scott Bob. *Historical Dictionary of the Democratic Republic of Congo 3rd Edition*. Lanham, MD: Scarecrow Press, 2010.

Kok, Walter. "Self-settled refugees and the socio-eocnomic impact of their presence on Kassala, Eastern Sudan." *Journal of Refugee Studies* 2 (1989): 419–440.

Knight, Jack. *Institutions and social conflict*. New York: Cambridge University Press, 1992.

Kuhlman, Tom. *Burden or boon: a study of Eritrean refugees in the Sudan*. Amsterdam: VU University Press, 1990.

Kuhlman, Tom. "Organized versus spontaneous settlement of refugees in Africa." In *African refugees: development aid and repatriation*, edited by Howard Adelman and John Sorenson. Boulder: Westview Press, 1994.

Kibreab, Gaim. "Local settlements in Africa: a misconceived option." *Journal of Refugee Studies* 2 (1989): 465–490.

Kibreab, Gaim. "The myth of dependency among camp refugees in Somalia 1979–1989." *Journal of Refugee Studies* 6 (1993): 321–349.

Kibreab, Gaim. *Ready and willing... but still waiting*. Upsalla: Life and Peace Institute, 1996.

Kibreab, Gaim. "Pulling the wool over the eyes of the strangers: refugee deceit and trickery in institutionalized settings." *Journal of Refugee Studies* 17 (2004): 1–26.

Kohli, Atul. *State-directed development: political power and industrialization in the global periphery*. New York: Cambridge University Press, 2004.

La Fontaine, J.S. *City politics: a study of Leopoldville, 1962–63*. Cambridge: Cambridge University Press, 1970.

Lambert, Richard. *Hindu–Muslim riots in India* (PhD diss., University of Pennsylvania, 1951).

Leeds, Brett Ashley. "Alliances and the Expansion and Escalation of Militarized Interstate Disputes." In *New Directions in International Relations*, edited by Alex Mintz and Bruce Russett. Lanham, MD: Lexington Books, 2005.

Legum, Margaret. "Problems of asylum for Southern African refugees." In *Refugee problems in Africa*, edited by Sven Hamrell. Uppsala: The Scandinavian Institute of African Studies, 1967.

Lemarchand, Rene. *Rwanda and Burundi*. New York: Praeger Publishers, 1970.

Lemarchand, Rene. "Historical setting." In *Zaire: a country study*. Edited by Sandra Meditz and Tim Merrill. Washington, DC: Library of Congress, 1993.

Lischer, Sarah Kenyon. "Refugee involvement in political violence: quantitative evidence from 1987–1998." *New Issues in Refugee Research* 26 (July 2000): 1–24.

Lischer, Sarah. *Dangerous sanctuaries: refugee camps, civil war and the dilemmas of humanitarian aid*. Ithaca: Cornell University Press, 2005.

Locatelli, Francesca and Paul Nugent. *African cities: competing claims on urban spaces*. Lieden: Brill, 2009.

Maconachie, Roy. "New agricultural frontiers in post-conflict Sierra Leone? Exploring institutional challenges for wetland management in Eastern Province." *BWPI Working Paper* 24 (January 2008): 1–27.

Mafeje, Archie and Audrey Richards. "The commercial farmer and his labor supply." In *Subsistence to commercial farming in present-day Buganda*, edited by Audrey Richards, Ford Sturrock and Jean Fortt. Cambridge: Cambridge University Press, 1973.

Malkki, Liisa. *Purity in exile: violence, memory, and national cosmology among Hutu refugees in Tanzania*. Chicago: University of Chicago Press, 1995.

Mama, Amina. "Challenging subjects: gender and power in African contexts." *Identity and beyond: rethinking Africanity, Nordic Africa Institute Discussion Paper* 12 (2001): 9–18.

Mamdani, Mahmood. *Citizen and subject: contemporary Africa and the legacy of late colonialism*. Princeton, NJ: Princeton University Press, 1996.

Mahmood Mamdani, "Understanding the crisis in Kivu: Report of the CODESRIA Mission to the Democratic Republic of Congo September, 1997" (Text report to be submitted to the General Assembly of the Council for the development of Social research in Africa [CODESRIA] in Dakar, Senegal, December 14–18, 1998).

Mamdani, Mahmood, "Uganda and background of the RPF invasion." In *Conflict and ethnicity in Central Africa*, edited by Didier Goyvaerts. Tokyo: Insitute for the Study of the Languages and Culture of Asia and Africa, 2000.

Mamdani, Mahmood. *When victims become killers*. Princeton: Princeton University Press, 2001.

Mamdani, Mahmood. "Political identity, citizenship and ethnicity in post-colonial Africa." Keynote address presented at New Frontiers of Social Policy Conference, Arusha, Tanzania, December 12–15, 2005.

Mararo, Bucyalimwe. "Land conflicts in Masisi, eastern Zaire: the impact and aftermath of Belgian colonial policy [1920–1989]." PhD Diss., Indiana University, 1990.

Mann, Michael. "The autonomous power of the state: its origins, mechanisms and results." *European Journal of Sociology* 25 (1984): 185–213.

Massing, Andreas. "The Mane, the decline of Mali, and the Mandinka expansion towards the South Windward Coast." *Cahiers d'Etudes Africaines* 25 (1985): 21–55.

Mathews, Robert. "Refugees and stability in Africa." *International Organization* 26 (1972): 62–83.

Mbembe, Achille. "African modes of self-writing." *Public Culture* 14 (2002): 239–273.

Mbembe, Achille. "On the power of the false." *Public Culture* 14 (2002): 629–641.

Mbembe, Achille. "Ways of seeing: beyond the new nativism. Introduction." *African Studies Review* 44 (2004): 1–14.

McGovern, Michael. "Negotiation of displacement in southeastern Guinea, West Africa." *Africa Today* 45 (1998): 307–321.

McGovern, Mike. "Conflit régional et rhétorique de la contre-insurrection: Guinéens et réfugiés en septembre 2000." *Politique Africaine* 88 (2002): 84–102.

McGovern, Michael. "Unmasking the state: developing modern subjectivities in 20th century Guinea." PhD diss., Emory University, 2004.

Merkx, Jozef. "Refugee identities and relief in an African borderland: a study of northern Uganda and southern Sudan." *New Issues in Refugee Research* 19 (June 2000): 1–33.

Metcalfe, George. "Effects of refugees on the national state." In *Refugees south of the Sahara: an African dilemma*, edited by Hugh Brooks and Yassin El-Ayouty. Westport, CT: Negro Universities Press, 1970.

Meyer, Birgit and Peter Geschiere. "Globalization and identity: dialectics of flow and closure. Introduction." In *Globalizagion and Identity: Dialects of flow and closure*, edited by Birgit Meyer and Peter Geschiere. Oxford: Blackwell Publishers, 1999.

Meynell, Charles. "Uganda and Sudan." *Minority Rights Group Report*. 66 (December 1984): 1–28.

Migdal, Joel. *Strong societies and weak state: state–society relations and state capabilities in the Third World*. Princeton: Princeton University Press, 1988.

Milner, James and Astrid Christoffersen-Deb. "The militarization and demilitarization of refugee camps and settlements in Guinea, 1999–2004." In *No refuge: the crisis of refugee militarization in Africa*, edited by Robert Muggah. London: Zed Books, 2006.

Mkandawire, Thandika. "Crisis management and 'choiceless democracies'." In *State, conflict and democracy in Africa*, edited by Richard Joseph. Boulder: Lynne Rienner Publishers, 1999.

Moe, Terry. "Power and political institutions." *Perspectives on Politics* 3 (2005): 215–233.

Mogire, Edward. "Preventing or abetting: refugee militarization in Tanzania." In *No refuge: the crisis of refugee militarization in Africa*, edited by Robert Muggah. London: Zed Books, 2006.

Morris, H.F. *A history of Ankole*. Kampala: East African Literature Bureau, 1962.

Morrow, James. "Alliances, credibility and peacetime costs." *Journal of Conflict Resolution* 38 (1994): 270–297.

Muggah, Robert ed. *No refuge: the crisis of refugee militarization in Africa*. London: Zed Books, 2006.

Muggah Robert and Edward Mogire. "Arms availability and refugee militarization in Africa-conceptualizing the issues." In *No refuge: the crisis of refugee militarization in Africa*, edited by Robert Muggah. London: Zed Books, 2006.

Murphy, William. "Secret knowledge as property and power in Kpelle society: elders versus youth." *Africa: Journal of the International African Institute* 50 (1980): 193–207.

Murphy, William and Caroline Bledsoe. "Kinship and territory in the history of a Kpelle Chiefdom (Liberia)." In *The African frontier: the reproduction of traditional African societies*, edited by Igor Kopytoff. Bloomington: Indiana University Press, 1987.

Mushemeza, Elijah. "Politics and the refugee experience in the Africa Great Lakes Region" Paper prepared for presentation at the MASSPM Seminar, Kampala, Uganda, November 1999.

Mushemeza, Elijah. "Politics and the refugee experience: the case of Banyarwanda refugees in Uganda (1959–1994)." PhD diss., Makerere University, 2002.

Mushemeza, Elijah. *Banyarwanda refugees in Uganda 1959–2001*. Kampala: Fountain Press, 2007.

Murphy, William. "The rhetorical management of dangerous knowledge in Kpelle brokerage." *American Ethnologist* 8 (1981): 667–685.

Namusisi, Robina. "The plight of Rwandese refugees in Uganda." LLB diss., Makerere University, 1988.

Neldner, Brian. "Settlement of rural refugees in Africa." *Disasters* 3 (1979): 393–402.

Newbury, Catherine. *The cohesion of oppression: clientship and ethnicity in Rwanda 1860–1960*. New York: Columbia University Press, 1988.

Nyamnjoh, Francis. "Concluding reflections on beyond identities: rethinking power in Africa." In *Identity and beyond: rethinking Africanity, Nordic Africa Institute Discussion Paper* 12 (2001): 25–33.

Nyamnjoh, Francis. *Insiders and outsiders: citizenship and xenophobia in contemporary Southern Africa*. Dakar: Codesria Books, 2006.

Nyers, Peter. *Rethinking refugees: beyond states of emergency*. New York: Routledge, 2006.

Oberg, K. "The Kingdom of Ankole in Uganda." In *African political systems*, edited by Meyer Fortes and Edward E. Evans-Pritchard. Oxford: Oxford University Press, 1940.

Olukoshi, Adebayo. *The elusive Prince of Denmark: structural adjustment and the crisis of governance in Africa*. Uppsala: Nordiska Afrikaninstitutet, 1998.

Omata, Naohiko. "Repatriation is not for everyone: the life and livelihoods of former refugees in Liberia." *New Issues in Refugee Research* 213 (June 2011): 1–29.

Onoma, Ato. *The politics of property rights institutions in Africa*. New York: Cambridge University Press, 2009.

Operario, Don and Susan Fiske. "Ethnic identity moderates perceptions of prejudice: judgments of personal versus group discrimination and subtle versus blatant bias." *Personality and Social Psychology Bulletin* 27 (2001): 550–561.

Packard, Randall. "Debating in a common idiom: variant traditions of genesis among the Ba Shu of eastern Zaire." In *The African frontier: the reproduction of traditional African societies*, edited by Igor Kopytoff. Bloomington: Indiana University Press, 1987.

Paulme, Denise. *Les gens du riz: Kissi de haute-Guinée Française*. Paris: Librairie Plon, 1954.

Paulme, Denise. "La societe Kissi: son organization politique." *Cahiers d'Etudes Africaines* 1 (1960): 73–85.

Peluso, Nancy Lee and Michael Watts. "Violent environments." In *Violent environments*, edited by Nancy Lee Peluso and Michael Watts. Ithaca: Cornell University Press, 2001.

Person, Yves. "Soixante ans d'evolution en pays Kissi." *Cahiers d'Etudes Africaines* 1 (1960): 86–112.

Person, Yves. "Ethnic movements and acculturation in Upper Guinea since the fifteenth century." *African Historical Studies* 4 (1971): 669–689.

Physicians for Human rights. "War-related sexual violence in Sierra Leone: a population-based assessment." A report by Physicians for Human Rights, 2002. Accessed October 13, 2012. https://s3.amazonaws.com/PHR_Reports/sierra-leone-sexual-violence-2002.pdf.

Polzer, Tara. "Invisible integration: how bureaucratic, academic and social categories obscure integrated refugees." *Journal of Refugee Studies* 21 (2008): 476–497.

Pons, Valdo. *An African urban community under Belgian administration*. London: Oxford University Press, 1969.

Posner, Daniel. "The political salience of cultural difference: why Chewas and Tumbukas are allies in Zambia and adversaries in Malawi." *American Political Science Review* 98 (2004): 529–545.

Posner, Daniel. *Institutions and ethnic politics in Africa*. New York: Cambridge University Press, 2005.

Pottier, Johan. "Modern information warfare versus empirical knowledge: framing 'the crisis' in Eastern Zaire, 1996." In *Negotiating local knowledge: power and identity in development*, edited by Johan Pottier, Alan Bicker and Paul Sillitoe. London: Pluto Press, 2003.

Powesland, P. G. "History of the migration in Uganda." In *Economic development and tribal change: a study of immigrant labour in Buganda*, edited by Audrey Richards. Cambridge: W. Heffer and Sons Ltd., 1952.

Rankin, Micah. "Extending the limits or narrowing the scope: deconstructing the OAU refugee definition thiry years on." *New Issues in Refugee Research* 113 (April 2005): 1–29.

Rayfield, J.R. "Theories of urbanization and the colonial city in West Africa." *Africa: Journal of the International African Institute* 44 (1974): 163–185.

Refugee Studies Center, Oxford University. "Refugee status determination and rights in southern and east Africa." International Workshop Report, Kampala, Uganda, November 16–17, 2010 (December 2010). Accessed October 13, 2012. http://www.rsc.ox.ac.uk/events/refugee-status-determination-and-rights/RSDinAfricaWorkshopReport.pdf.

Reno, William. *Warlord politics and African states*. London: Lynne Reinner, 1998.

Reno, William. "Shadow states and the political economy of civil wars." In *Greed and Grievance: economic agendas in civil wars*, edited by Mats Berdal and David Malone. Boulder: Lynne Rienner Publishers, 2000.

Republic of Uganda. *The report of the Commission of Inquiry into Violations of Human Rights: findings, conclusions and recommendations*. Kampala, Uganda, 1994.

Richards, Audrey. "The travel routes and the travelers." In *Economic development and tribal change: a study of immigrant labour in Buganda*, edited by Audrey I. Richards. Cambridge: W. Heffer and Sons Ltd., 1952.

Richards, Audrey. "The problem for Buganda." In *Economic development and tribal change: a study of immigrant labour in Buganda*, edited by Audrey Richards. Cambridge: W. Heffer and Sons Ltd., 1952.

Richards, Audrey. "The assimilation of the immigrants." In *Economic development and tribal change: a study of immigrant labour in Buganda*, edited by Audrey Richards. Cambridge: W. Heffer and Sons Ltd., 1952.

Richards, Audrey. *East African chiefs: a study of political development in some Uganda and Tanganyika tribes*. London: Faber and Faber Limited, 1960.

Richards, Paul. *Fighting for the rainforest*. Oxford: James Currey, 1996.

Richards, Paul. "West African warscapes: War as smoke and mirrors: Sierra Leone 1991–92, 1994–95, 1995–96." *Anthropological Quarterly* 78 (2005): 337–402.

Richards, R.I. "Methods of settlement in Buganda." In *Economic development and tribal change: a study of immigrant labour in Buganda*, edited by Audrey Richards. Cambridge: W. Heffer and Sons Ltd., 1952.

Riviere, Claude. "La toponymie de Conakry et du Kaloum." *Bulletin de l'IFAN. Notes et Documents. Senie B: Sciences Humaine, Dakar* xxvii. (Juillet–Octobre 1966): 1009–1018.

Riviere, Claude. *Mutations sociales en Guinée*. Paris: Editions Marcel Riviere et Cie, 1971.

Riviere, Claude. *Guinea: the mobilization of a people*. Ithaca: Cornell University Press, 1977.

Roscoe, John. *The Banyankole*. Cambridge: Cambridge University Press, 1923.

Said, Twine. "The Banyarwanda citizenship question in Uganda: a case study of Ntungamo district 1959–2002." M.A. diss., Makerere University, 2008.

Salehyan, Idean. "The externalities of civil strife: refugees as a source of international conflict." *American Journal of Political Science* 52 (2008): 787–801.

Salehyan, Idean and Kristin Gleditsch. "Refugees and the spread of civil war." *International Organization* 60 (2006): 335–366.

Samples, John. *The fallacy of campaign finance reform*. Chicago: University of Chicago Press, 2006.

Sanders, Edith R. "The Hamitic Hypothesis: its origin and functions in time perspective." *The Journal of African History* 10 (1969): 521–532.

Sarro, Ramon. "Map and territory: the politics of place and autochthony among the Baga Sitem (and their neighbours)." In *Integration and conflict along the Upper Guinea Coast*, edited by J. Knorr and Trajano Filho. Leiden: Brill, 2010.

Sawyer, Amos. "Violent conflicts and governance challenges in West Africa: the case of the Mano River Basin area." *Journal of Modern African Studies* 42 (2004): 437–463.

Schafer, Frederic. *Elections for sale: the causes and consequences of vote buying*. Boulder, CO.: Lynne Rienner Publishers, 2007.

Scott, James. *Weapons of the weak.* New Haven: Yale University Press, 1985.

Scott, James. *Domination and the arts of resistance: hidden transcripts.* New Haven: Yale University press, 1990.

Scott, James. *Seeing Like a State.* New Haven: Yale University Press, 1998.

Sexana, Naresh C. "The nature and origins of communal riots in India." In *Communal riots in post-independence India*, edited by Asghar Ali. Hyderabad: Sangam Books India, 1984.

Shack, William. "Introduction." In *Strangers in African societies*, edited by William Shack and Elliott Skinner. Berkeley: University of California Press, 1979.

Sharpe, Marina. "Engaging with refugee protection: the Organization of African Unity and African Union since 1963." *New Issues in Refugee Research* 226 (December 2011): 1–40.

Simone, AbdouMaliq. "On the worldling of African cities." *African Studies Review* 44 (2001): 15–41.

Smith, Alastair. "Alliance Formation and War." *International Studies Quarterly* 39 (1995): 405–425.

Smith, Alastair. "Extended deterrence and alliance formation." *International Interactions* 24 (1998): 315–343.

Smith Jr., Dane. "US-Guinea relations during the rise and fall of Charles Taylor." *Journal of Modern African Studies* 44 (2006): 415–439.

Smith, Rodney. *Money, power and elections: how campaign finance reform subverts American democracy.* Baton Rouge: Louisiana State University Press, 2006.

Sommers, Marc. *Fear in Bongoland: Burundi refugees in urban Tanzania.* New York: Berghahn Books, 2001.

Southall, Aidan. "Ethnic incorporation among the Alur." In *From tribe to nation: studies in incorporation processes*, edited by Ronald Cohen and John Middleton. Scranton, PA.: Chandler Publishing Company, 1970.

Spilerman, Seymour. "The causes of racial disturbances: tests of an explanation." *American Sociological Review* 36 (1971): 427–442.

Stedman, Stephen. "Conflict and conciliation in sub-Saharan Africa." In *The international dimensions of internal conflict*, edited by Michael Brown. London: MIT Press, 1996.

Stedman, Stephen and Fred Tanner. "Refugees as resources in war." In *Refugee manipulation: war, politics, and the abuse of human suffering*, edited by Stephen Stedman and Fred Tanner. Washington, DC: Brookings Institution Press, 2003.

Stein, Barry. "ICARA II: Burden sharing and durable solutions." In *Refugees: a third world dilemma*, edited by J. Rogge. Totowa, NJ: Rowman and Littlefield, 1987.

Steward, Charles. "Syncretism and its synonyms: reflections on cultural mixture." *Diacritics* 9 (1999): 40–62.

Summers, Anne and R. W. Johnson. "World War I conscription and social change in Guinea." *Journal of African History* 19 (1978): 25–38.

Suret-Canale, Jean. "La fin de la chefferie en Guinée." *The Journal of African History* 7 (1966): 459–493.

Suret-Canale, Jean. *French colonialism in tropical Africa 1900–1945*. New York: Pica Press, 1971.

Sweezy, Paul. *The transition from feudalism to capitalism; a symposium*. New York: Science and Society, 1954.

Turner, Thomas. *The Congo wars: conflict, myth and reality*. London: Zed Books, 2007.

Tong, James. *Disorder under heaven: collective violence in the Ming Dynasty*. Stanford: Stanford University Press, 1991.

UNHCR and Save the Children-UK. "Note for Implementing and Operational Partners by UNHCR and Save the Children-UK on Sexual Violence & Exploitation: The Experience of Refugee Children in Guinea, Liberia and Sierra Leone based on Initial Findings and Recommendations from Assessment Mission 22 October – 30 November 2001." Accessed October 13, 2012. http://www.savethechildren.org.uk/sites/default/files/docs/sexual_violence_and_exploitation_1.pdf.

UNHCR. "UNHCR note on refugee integration in Central Europe." *UNHCR*, April 2009. Accessed October 13, 2012. http://unhcr.org.ua/img/uploads/docs/11%20UNHCR-Integration_note-screen.pdf.

Unruh, Jon. "Refugee resettlement on the horn of Africa: the integration of refugee and host land use patters." *Land Use Policy* 10 (1993): 49–66.

Utas, Mats. "West-African Warscapes: Victimcy, Girlfriending, Soldiering: Tactic Agency in a Young Woman's Social Navigation of the Liberian War Zone." *Anthropological Quarterly* 78 (2005): 403–430.

Varshney, Ashutosh, Rizal Panggabean and Mohammad Zulfan Tadjoeddin. "Patterns of Collective Violence in Indonesia (1990–2003)." *United Nations Support Facility for Indonesian Recovery Working Paper* 04/03 (July 2004): 1–45.

Van Damme, Wim. "How Liberian and Sierra Leonean refugees settled in the forest region of Guinea (1990–1996)." *Journal of Refugee Studies* 12 (1999): 36–53.

Van Hear, Nicholas. "From durable solutions to transnational relations: home and exile among refugee diasporas." *New Issues in Refugee Research* 83 (March 2003): 1–18.

Vlassenroot, Koen. "The promise of ethnic conflict: militarization and enclave-formation in South Kivu." In *Conflict and ethnicity in Central Africa*, edited by Didier Goyvaerts. Tokyo: Insitute for the study of the languages and culture of Asia and Africa, 2000.

Vlassenroot, Koen. "Identity formation and conflict in South Kivu: the case of the Banyamulenge." *Review of African Political Economy* 29 (2002): 499–516.

Vlassenroot, Koen. "Reading the Congolese crisis." In *Conflict and social transformation in Easter DR Congo*, edited by Koen Vlassenroot and Timothy Raeymaekers. Gent: Academia Press, 2004.

Vlassenroot, Koen and Timothy Raeymaekers. "Conflict and artisan mining in Kamituga (South Kivu)." In *Conflict and social transformation in Easter DR Congo*, edited by Koen Vlassenroot and Timothy Raeymaekers. Gent: Academia Press, 2004.

Watson, Catherine. "Exile from Rwanda: Background to an invasion." *United States Committee for Refugees Issue Paper* (February 1991): 1–20.

Westin, Charles. "Regional analysis of refugees movements: origins and response." In *Refugees: perspectives on the experience of forced migrants*, edited by Alistair Ager. London: Pinter, 1999.

Whitaker, Beth. "Refugees in Western Tanzania: the distribution of burdens and benefits among local hosts." *Journal of Refugee Studies* 15 (2002): 339–358.

Whitaker, Beth Elise. "Refugees and the spread of conflict: contrasting cases in Central Africa." *Journal of Asian and African Studies* 38 (2003): 211–231.

White, Rodney. "The influence of environmental and economic factors on the urban crisis." In *African cities in crisis: managing rapid urban growth*, edited by Richard E. Stren and Rodney R. White. Boulder: Westview Press, 1989.

Wilkinson, Steven. *Votes and violence: electoral competition and ethnic riots in India*. New York: Cambridge University Press, 2004.

Wright, Gwendolyn. *The politics of design in French colonial urbanism*. Chicago: University of Chicago Press, 1991.

Young, Crawford. *Politics in the Congo: decolonization and independence*. Princeton: Princeton University Press, 1965.

Young, Crawford. "Rebellion and the Congo." In *Rebellion in Black Africa*, edited by Robert Rotberg. London: Oxford University Press, 1971.

Young, Crawford and Thomas Turner. *The rise and decline of the Zairian state*. Madison: University of Wisconsin Press, 1985.

Weissman, Stephen. *American foreign policy in Congo 1960–1964*. Ithaca: Cornell University Press, 1974.

Vlassenroot, Koen. "Land and conflict: the case of Masisi." In *Conflict and social transformation in Easter DR Congo*, edited by Koen Vlassenroot and Timothy Raeymaekers. Gent: Academia Press, 2004.

Zackariya, F. and N. Shanmugaratnam. "Moving into the extra household domain: survival struggles of displaced Muslim women in Sri Lanka." In *In the maze of displacement: conflict, migration and change*, edited by N. Shanmugaratnam, Ragnhild Lund and Kristi Anne Stolen, Kristiansand S. Norway: HoyskoleForlaget, 2003.

Zartman, William, I. "Portuguese Guinean refugees in Senegal." In *The internationalization of communal strife*, edited by Manus Midlarsky. London: Routledge, 1992.

Zeleza, Paul Tiyambe. *Rethinking Africa's 'globalization': Volume 1*. Trenton: Africa World Press, 2003.

Zmegac, Jasna Capo. "Ethnically privileged migrants in their new homeland." *Journal of Refugee Studies* 18 (2005): 199–215.

Zolberg, Aristide. *Conflict and the refugee crisis in the developing world*. New York: Oxford University Press, 1989.

Zolberg, Aristide, Astri Suhrke and Sergio Aguayo. *Escape from violence: conflict and the refugee crisis in the developing world*. New York: Oxford University Press, 1989.

Index